MULTICULTURAL JAPAN

Palaeolithic to Postmodern

EDITED BY

DONALD DENOON, MARK HUDSON,

GAVAN McCORMACK, AND TESSA MORRIS-SUZUKI

WITH AN INTRODUCTION BY
GAVAN McCORMACK

CAMBRIDGE
UNIVERSITY PRESS

PUBLISHED BY THE PRESS SYNDICATE OF THE UNIVERSITY OF CAMBRIDGE
The Pitt Building, Trumpington Street, Cambridge, United Kingdom

CAMBRIDGE UNIVERSITY PRESS
The Edinburgh Building, Cambridge CB2 2RU, UK
40 West 20th Street, New York, NY 10011–4211, USA
10 Stamford Road, Oakleigh, VIC 3166, Australia
Ruiz de Alarcón 13, 28014 Madrid, Spain
Dock House, The Waterfront, Cape Town 8001, South Africa

http://www.cambridge.org

First published 1996
First paperback edition 2001

Printed in China through Colorcraft Ltd., Hong Kong

Typeface New Baskerville (*Adobe*) 10/12 pt.   *System* QuarkXPress®   [BC]

A catalogue record for this book is available from the British Library

ISBN 0 521 00362 8 paperback

Contents

Part 3   Contact with the Outside

Part 4   The Japanese Family

Part 5   Culture and Ideology

Figures

Tables

Contributors

AMINO YOSHIHIKO, a specialist in Japanese history and one of Japan's best-known historians, teaches at Kanagawa University, Yokohama.

DONALD DENOON is professor of Pacific Islander History at the Australian National University and specialises in economic and medical history.

CLARE FAWCETT has carried out research into the social context of Japanese archaeology, and now teaches in the Department of Sociology and Anthropology at St Francis Xavier University, Antigonish, Nova Scotia, Canada.

GOTŌ KEN'ICHI, an historian of Indonesia, and especially of the period of Japanese dominance during the Pacific War, teaches at the Institute of Social Sciences, Waseda University, Tokyo.

HANAZAKI KŌHEI is an independent scholar, formerly professor at Tokyo University, specialising in the history of Japan's Ainu and Okinawan minority peoples.

MARK HUDSON is a Foreign Professor of Anthropology at the University of Tsukuba where he specialises in the archaeology and biological anthropology of Japan.

ISHII YONEO, a specialist in Thai history and editor and author of many books on South-east Asia, teaches at the Institute of Asian Cultures, Sophia University, Tokyo.

SIMON KANER is Assistant Director of the Sainsbury Institute for the Study of Japanese Arts and Cultures in the UK and is a specialist in Jomon archaeology.

KATAYAMA KAZUMICHI is a physical anthropologist who has conducted extensive research in the Pacific Islands; he is a professor at the Primate Research Institute of Kyoto University.

GAVAN McCORMACK is professor of Japanese History at the Australian National University and specialises in the twentieth-century history of Japan and her East Asian neighbours.

JOHN C. MAHER is professor of Linguistics in the Department of Communication and Linguisitics at International Christian University, Tokyo where he teaches general linguistics and sociolinguisitics. He specialises in multilingualism in Japan, philosophical linguistics and language and psychoanalysis.

DEREK MASSARELLA, a specialist in early modern relations between Japan and Europe, teaches in the Faculty of Economics, Chuo University, Tokyo.

TESSA MORRIS-SUZUKI is a professor of Japanese History at the Australian National University and specialises in the economic and technological history of Japan.

NISHIKAWA NAGAO, who teaches comparative cultural studies and is a prominent scholar in contemporary European and Japanese history, is an Emeritus Professor of Ritsumeikan University, Kyoto.

NISHIKAWA YŪKO, a social historian specialising in the history of Japanese women, is Professor in the Faculty of Humanities, Kyoto Bunko University.

RICHARD PEARSON is a specialist in East Asian archaeology, residing in Vancouver, British Columbia, Canada.

UENO CHIZUKO, a sociologist specialising in feminist studies and cultural criticism, teaches in the Department of Sociology, Tokyo University.

UTSUMI AIKO, an historian of Japanese colonialism and war, teaches at Keisen Women's College, Tokyo.

Abbreviations

ACA	Agency for Cultural Affairs
ANU	Australian National University
ASEAN	Association of South-East Asian Nations
BG	Bankon-Gudojati
BP	Before Present
DCHE	Deliberative Council on Historical Environments
DCPCP	Deliberative Council on the Protection of Cultural Properties
DNA	deoxyribonucleic acid
EC	European Community
ICU	International Christian University
LDK	Lounge, Dining, Kitchen
LDP	Liberal Democratic Party
MFP	Multifunction Polis
MITI	Ministry of International Trade and Industry
NATO	North Atlantic Treaty Organization
NHK	(Japanese Broadcasting Corporation)
OJ	Old Japanese
POW	Prisoner(s) of War
UN	United Nations

Introduction

GAVAN McCORMACK

Japan is conventionally seen as a monocultural society. Located at the eastern extremity of the Eurasian land-mass and separated from it by a sea that is wider and more dangerous than that which divides the British Isles from the same land-mass at its western extremity, it is apparently distinguished from the countries nearest to it both in its pre-modern institutions (often called 'feudal') and in its modern economic dynamism (sometimes called 'miraculous'). The proposition that Japan is unique and monocultural seems plausible.

Throughout Japanese history, prominent figures have insisted on the distinctness of Japanese identity, from the 'National Learning' (*Kokugakusha*) scholars in the eighteenth century with their stress on a pure and untrammeled (that is, non-Chinese) Japanese essence to late twentieth-century statements by Nakasone Yasuhiro (Prime Minister in the 1980s) that Japan is a homogeneous 'natural community' (as distinct from a Western-style 'nation formed by contract'), and the 'Yamato race' which he insisted had been living 'for at least two thousand years ... hand in hand with no other, different ethnic groups present [in these islands]'.[1] The belief that Japan is a homogeneous, monoracial state is deep-rooted and, as Ivan Hall notes, has long been 'openly sanctioned by the intellectual establishment, public consensus, and government policy'.[2] Unlike other societies which are mixed (*o-majiri*), especially the United States with its 'many Blacks, Puerto Ricans and Mexicans', Japan is thought to be pure and homogeneous, and therefore to have had an easier time becoming an 'intelligent society'.[3]

In the modern (pre-1945) state, the ideology of Japanese homogeneity and superiority was encapsulated in what was described as *kokutai* (national polity), by which the Japanese people were seen as

1

a unique family state united around the emperor. Though discredited by defeat and the collapse of imperial Japan and the Greater East Asia Co-Prosperity Sphere (but not of the imperial line nor of its myths), neither the Occupation nor the post-war Japanese liberal and progressive forces paid much attention to questions of identity. The former concentrated on eradicating militarism while shoring up the imperial institution, and the latter on analysing class while ignoring ethnicity and assuming that a strengthening of individualism and democracy would result from steadily increasing modernisation. The ethnic implications of the aboriginal inhabitants of Japan (the Ainu), or other groups such as the large Korean minority, were reduced to considerations of universal human rights. Deep-rooted assumptions about 'Japaneseness' therefore survived intact.[4]

From the 1980s two phenomena have proceeded on parallel tracks which show no sign of converging: internationalisation and the clarification of Japanese identity. *Kokusaika* – internationalisation – has been a Japanese national goal for over a decade. Trans-border flows of capital, goods, technology and people have reached new heights, and essays and books on *kokusaika* proliferate. For all of this inter-meshing with the outside world, the task of analysing 'Japaneseness', and how notions of it might be reconciled with a *kokusaika* world, remains both complex and sensitive. The stronger the belief in Japanese distinctiveness, the deeper became the concern at the consequences of 'internationalisation' as economic super-power status led to the opening, first of the economy and then of the society, and an influx of migrant workers.

This desire to clarify identity is the local manifestation of the worldwide phenomenon of identity politics. During the 1980s Japan's roots were increasingly traced back to the Jōmon hunting and gathering culture which lasted for about 10 000 years prior to the fourth century BC. Influential statements of the 'true' untrammeled Japanese identity in such terms have been uttered by prominent academics and by political figures such as Ozawa Ichirō, who revealed his romantic inclinations by declaring that Jōmon Japan was not only Japan's own true essence but also the solution to the problems of contemporary civilisation.[5]

In the 1980s the Nakasone government took renewed interest in the task of articulating Japanese 'culture' as an arm of diplomacy. The establishment in Kyoto in 1987 of the International Research Center for Japanese Culture, commonly known by its abbreviated Japanese title of 'Nichibunken', was one expression of this desire to clarify what 'Japaneseness' meant.[6] The founding of Nichibunken was surrounded by controversy, reminding many of the 1930s *kokutai meichō* (Clarifying the National Polity) movement and of the role played by the Kokumin Bunka Seishin Kenkyūjō (National Institute for Culture Spirit).[7] Debate swelled briefly to a climax in exchanges between the head of Nichibunken, Umehara Takeshi, and the Western scholar, Ian Buruma, in the pages of *Chūō Kōron* in 1987.[8] Various academic organisations took critical positions or expressed concern.[9] But that moment soon passed. Post-Nakasone, the work done in Kyoto seemed harmless enough, prominent foreign as well as Japanese scholars cooperated in Nichibunken programs, the budgets were generous, and the opportunities for research were welcome. The case against Nichibunken at its formation seemed stale, as dated as the Cold War. But the issues suddenly resurfaced around the time of the conference which gave rise to this book.

International academic scrutiny of the notion of 'Japaneseness' has been rare. Entitled 'Stirrup, Sail and Plough: continental and maritime influences on Japanese identity', the conference, hosted in Canberra in September 1993 by the Australian National University, was the first devoted to the theme of Japanese 'identity', its origins and trans-formation, through the focus on Japan's relations with neighbouring Asian and Pacific countries. Some fifty scholars, whose expertise ranged from biological anthropology to feminism to Japan's contemporary role in the world, came from Japan, Korea, South-east Asia, Europe and North America, while prominent Japan (and Asia-Pacific) scholars of the ANU and other Australian universities attended.

This book distils the fruits of that conference. It challenges the conventional approach by arguing that Japan has long been 'multicultural', and that what is distinctive is the success with which that diversity has been cloaked by the ideology of 'uniqueness' and 'monoculturalism'. While sympathetic to the Japanese attempt to resist Western cultural hegemonism and the pretence that Western European values are universal, the contributors incline towards post-modern cultural relativism rather than any sort of hegemonism, European or Japanese.

The book has five parts. The first examines the origins of 'the Japanese', with Katayama Kazumichi, John C. Maher and Simon Kaner tackling biological, linguistic and cultural diversity, and Clare Fawcett and Simon Kaner addressing the salience of scholarly work in contemporary debates on identity. The chapters in Part Two explore questions of minorities, especially the Ainu aboriginal peoples in Hokkaido to the north and the Okinawan people of the Ryūkyū Islands to the south. Part Three looks at cultural and political connections with Europe and with East and South-east Asia. It emphasises the early basis of equality and mutual respect that marked these connections and the slide that occurred, reaching a nadir in the war of 1931 to 1945, as Japan entrenched a modern sense of its own identity as superior and distinctive. The fourth part explores the ways in which a peculiar ideology of the family was constructed and came to be thought of as quintessentially Japanese. The final part addresses the tensions between diversity and homogeneity created by industrialisation and colonial expansion, and looks at the changing nature of cultural diversity in Japan in the era of 'internationalisation'.

The archaeological record is controversial. As the past is literally dug up, the political and ideological ramifications of archaeology become acutely sensitive. In no other country does so much public and media attention focus on excavations of ancient settlements. As Richard Pearson notes: 'Archaeology in Japan is high-tech, high profile, big business, and big budget'.[10] The transformation of the landscape by three decades of 'high-growth' development is matched by the transformation of historical understanding consequent upon discoveries unearthed in the process.[11]

As recently as the 1980s there was no real agreement on the population history of the islands. The last few years, however, have seen the emergence of a remarkable consensus, neatly summarised by Katayama's chapter (chapter 1). The comings and goings of peoples to, from, and across the archipelago over the past two millennia can be fairly well understood. It now seems clear that the Japanese population stems from several ancient and distinct waves of immigration. An early (but not necessarily the first) was that of a proto-Mongoloid people from somewhere in the South-east Asian or South China region who (by a route yet unclear) settled in the islands at some point in the Palaeolithic. The civilisation of hunters and gatherers that evolved has been given the name 'Jōmon' after the cord-marked pattern of their earthenware pottery.[12]

Unlike the first wave of immigrants, whose physical characteristics suggest close links with South-east Asia or South China, the second came from North-east Asia, most likely via the Korean peninsula. This migration continued for over a millennium through what are known as the Yayoi and Kofun periods (*ca.* 400 BC to AD 700), and by the latter (Kofun) period there seems to have been considerable mixing of indigenous and immigrant groups as far as southern Tohoku. About a million people left the continent in some 'boat people' saga whose causes are only dimly understood, to settle in the archipelago, until eventually the original Jōmon peoples were outnumbered, perhaps by as much as 10 to 1 (according to Hanihara Kazurō). The archipelago was profoundly transformed as a result. The migrants brought wet rice agriculture and bronze and iron technology.[13] They settled first in northern Kyushu and western Honshu, either merging with and absorbing the aboriginal Jōmon inhabitants or confining them to culturally distinctive formations in the 'peripheral' regions of Hokkaido and Northern Honshu (where they appeared thereafter as Ainu, Emishi, Ebisu) or South Kyushu and the Ryūkyū Islands (where they were known as Kumaso, Hayato, as well as Okinawan). By the seventh century, these North-east Asian immigrants and their descendants constituted between 70 and 90 per cent of the population of the islands (which might by then have amounted to five or six million people), and constructed a distinctive political and cultural order centring on the court which emerged in the Kinai region in the vicinity of present-day Osaka and Kyoto.[14]

As Katayama notes, relatively pure Jōmon characteristics were preserved only in the Ainu communities in the far north. Skeletal, dental and genetic anthropology, and the analysis of the genetic evidence of the different origins of animals closely connected with human habitation, such as dogs and mice, make clear that the modern Japanese are primarily descended from continental immigrants who arrived in the Yayoi and Kofun periods.[15] The idea of a uniquely pure link between the modern Japanese and the ancient civilisation of the Jōmon period cannot be sustained. The Japanese are, like all other modern peoples, a 'mixed race'.

It would be wrong, however, to suggest that this two-stage model of the peopling of Japan has resolved all controversy. At least three problems persist. They concern the very large question of the social relations between Jōmon and Yayoi peoples and the scale of Yayoi immigration; the Pacific relations of the early settlers; and the evolution of their language.

On the first matter, Hanihara, who estimated as many as one million Yayoi-Kofun immigrants, though winning some support from other anthropologists, has been criticised by archaeologists, who believe the rate of immigration was much lower.[16] So far as the second matter is concerned, Katayama notes that skeletal remains of the prehistoric Jōmon and their Ainu decendants closely resemble samples of prehistoric Polynesians and even some Micronesians, which leads him to advance the hypothesis that the Jōmon people may have been ancestral to the Polynesians. That view is supported by the American anthropologist, Loring Brace,[17] but it would seem to contradict much of the linguistic and archaeological evidence for the early Austronesian expansions.[18] An alternative explanation of the physical similarities between Jōmon and Polynesian populations would be a common origin somewhere in South China or South-east Asia.

Two linguistic models seek to account for the historical linguistics of early Japan: one is elaborated in the Maher chapter (chapter 2) and known as the creole model, and the other may be described as a language replacement scenario.[19] Both models view the early agricultural Yayoi period as crucial. Maher supports with linguistic evidence his proposal that extensive trading and other activities in western Japan led to a Yayoi pidgin which eventually stabilised as a creole and became the Japanese language. Hudson's alternative view, based on a comparative cultural perspective, is that the rapid expansion of rice farming through the Japanese islands during the Yayoi is more likely to have led to the replacement of Jōmon languages than to substantial mixing.

Controversy also continues over the relationship between scholarly work on Japan's ancient history and contemporary debates on identity. Pearson comments that, despite its scientific and analytical methods, archaeology has continued to serve as 'an important part of Japanese national historical nativistic discourse', and indeed that the entire discipline in Japan is coloured by pressures 'to elucidate the history of the Japanese rather than to learn about human behavior in general'.[20] Even in the 1990s the long hand of control over the past is exercised in the form of a ban enforced by the Imperial Household Agency over any excavation of 158 major tomb sites thought to contain the remains of imperial ancestors, one purpose of which is to limit the risk of 'embarrassing' archaeological discoveries, particularly any which might throw light on the origins of the imperial family.

In this volume, Fawcett and Kaner explore the politics of archaeology. Fawcett (chapter 4) analyses the role of post-war Japanese governments in using the Asuka region and its history to shape the expression of Japanese identity. While Japanese archaeologists have usually opposed such blatant ideological uses of the past, in a discussion of the Morishōji site in Osaka, Fawcett demonstrates how archaeologists, while in principle opposed to ideological manipulation of their work, are caught in complex webs which may lead them to lend some support, perhaps even unconsciously, to such views, particularly by simplifying the archaeological record in order to make the past more accessible. Fawcett raises issues of history and education that go far beyond the particularities of the Japanese case.

Japan's peripheries, where recognisable Jōmon elements remained longest, and which were last incorporated in the Japanese state, constitute nice studies in the struggle between the ideology of 'Japaneseness' and the reality of difference. The adaptive, historical and evolutionary processes of the development of ancient Ainu and Okinawan societies are slowly coming to light. The relationship of these processes to the formation of a sense of identity in those regions and the complex relationship between that and a broader 'Japanese' identity is still being negotiated.

Tessa Morris-Suzuki (chapter 5) addresses the relations between the Japanese state and the people of the frontier who, until the late eighteenth century, were generally represented as part of Japan's 'barbarian periphery', foreign countries which paid tribute to Japan. Only as Japan became incorporated into the modern world order of nation states was the relationship reconsidered. When Okinawa and Hokkaido were absorbed within the Japanese state in the late nineteenth century their inhabitants, despite being redefined as 'Japanese citizens', nevertheless remained *different* in ways which disturbed official constructions of national uniformity. Ultimately they were redefined as different in terms of time rather than space: as 'backward' rather than foreign. But this process was not without risk, for it might imply that they represented a 'purer' or more 'pristine' expression of 'essential' 'Japaneseness'. Japanese debates about terms such as 'race' (*jinshu*) and '*Volk*' (*minzoku*) therefore focus on these peoples.

Pearson (chapter 6) outlines the development of Okinawan culture as revealed by archaeological research. The Ryūkyū Islands occupy a unique position in the cultural history of East Asia through their spatial location, human adaptation to their environment, processes of interaction with the surrounding regions, and internal social evolution. An exchange network linked the Ryūkyūs and the North Kyushu plain in the early to mid Yayoi period, but the region remained beyond the fringes of the Yamato state of the fifth to eighth centuries, and from 1429 to 1609 constituted a flourishing city state, influenced much more by trade with China than by any contact with Japan, and also trading widely throughout East Asia.

The desire to flesh out the record of the Ryūkyūan past, and to forge from archaeological and literary records a distinctive Okinawan or Ryūkyūan identity has strengthened since the islands were returned from American administration to Japanese rule in 1972. From such a perspective, Japanese 'identity politics' looks quite different from how it appears in Tokyo. Not surprisingly, the Ryūkyūan perspective is sceptical about the pretensions of any monolithic 'Japaneseness'. Increasingly, the Ryūkyūan orientation turns again to the south and the west as well as north, and the independent and cosmopolitan experience of the fifteenth- to seventeenth-century Chūzan kingdom, when Okinawa served as 'a culturally distinct, and peaceful, bridge to the world',[21] gives some insight into what a decentralised, internationally-oriented Japan might aspire to create in the late twentieth century.

Turning to Japan's northern periphery, Hanazaki Kōhei (chapter 7) recounts the attempts to assimilate the Ainu peoples of Hokkaido following their defeat in an uprising in 1788, and the deculturing policies designed to assimilate them into the lower ranks of Japanese society. Cultural revival began, tentatively in 1912 and more vigorously from 1945, leading to a series of Ainu language schools and cultural events, and cultural reassertion began to fuel a sustained effort to achieve cultural (and implicitly political) recognition.

Perceptions of Japan and 'Japaneseness' in the early modern world from European and South-east Asian perspectives are discussed by Derek Massarella (chapter 8) and Ishii Yoneo (chapter 9). The Europeans who came to Japan in the sixteenth and seventeenth centuries were very different from those who followed in the nineteenth century, when European hegemony came to be taken for granted. The notion of European superiority, or 'orientalism', formed no part of the baggage of Europeans in the early modern period. There were no stock images of the 'Orient' nor expectations of stagnation or backwardness to prejudice their judgment, and they were deeply impressed by the civilisation that they encountered. Respect for Japan remained relatively unscathed even in the 1850s. While they respected and were fascinated by Japan, however, European observers did not see it as unique: nor did the Japanese they encountered give voice to any such thought.

A key element of Japan's present identity is the assumption that in the sixteenth century the country was 'open' to foreigners and foreign influence, but thereafter, save for the Dutch and Chinese in Nagasaki and the Japanese presence in the Ryūkyū kingdom and Korea, it was 'closed' under the *sakoku* (closed country) policy and able to enjoy a 'pax Tokugawa'. The long isolation which ensued is supposed to have allowed Japan to achieve so high a level of proto-industrialisation that by the mid-nineteenth century it had achieved the pre-conditions for indigenous industrialisation, with or without the 'opening' by the US navy.

The idea of an open/closed rhythm to Japanese history is too contrived, too conducive to notions of the pure native Japanese tradition as opposed to various defiling, foreign influences, and too much an echo of cyclical models of Asian history to be taken seriously. Even in relation to the late sixteenth century there are fundamental problems. First, it implies that before the later sixteenth century Japan was 'closed'. Secondly, from the 1630s, although the authorities in Edo certainly restricted and sought to control such trade and contacts with the outside world that they permitted, in terms of trade, international relations or cross-cultural control and influence Japan did not cut itself off from the rest of the world. A true *sakoku* policy only emerged after 1793. Thirdly, it is 'Japanocentric', ignoring similar phenomena in China and Korea, and making Japan's 'isolation' appear unique.

While the early modern East Asian world preserved a facade of hierarchical decorum based on the centrality and superiority of imperial China, it actually practised a vibrant, horizontal, multicultural order in which relationships were founded on mutual respect, commercial sense and intellectual curiosity. The Japan–Korea relationship was one between entities which even in the fifteenth century were not 'discrete',[22] and which, after the tragic violence of the late sixeenth-century invasions of Korea, slowly resumed as between virtual equals.[23]

If Hokkaido and Okinawa constitute internal benchmarks of Japanese identity, Korea, China and South-east Asia all represent facets of the Japanese struggle to achieve an outward-looking, non-Western sense of identity that would combine 'Japaneseness', 'Asian-ness', and universal human values. In this book, the failure of such attempts is analysed through a focus on South-east Asia (Gotō Ken'ichi, chapter 10 and Utsumi Aiko, chapter 11) and Manchukuo (Gavan McCormack, chapter 16).

Japan launched its Asian war beneath slogans of 'co-existence and co-prosperity, respect for autonomy and independence, and the abolition of racial discrimination', but under the veneer of these universal values lay a Japanese belief in the 'low cultural level' of the natives, and in practice, relations between Japan and the worlds it was supposedly liberating fell far short of the ideals. Official constructions of modern Japanese identity were always fraught with tensions, which became increasingly evident in the years leading up to the Pacific War. Government policy since the Meiji Restoration had been founded upon emulation of the western great powers. Its aim was the transformation of Japan into an industrialised, militarily powerful nation with its own colonial empire to rival those of Britain and France. As conflict with the west grew, however, Japan's leaders revised the earlier strategy of 'leaving Asia and joining Europe' (*datsu-A nyū-O*), proposing instead to rejoin Asia on whose behalf it would lead a crusade against 'western imperialism'.

The unresolved contradictions of coloniser–liberator became ever more apparent as the war progressed. Gotō's chapter vividly illustrates the ironies of Japan's position by examining the role of Indonesia in the Greater East Asian Co-Prosperity Sphere. Entangled by long-held views of South-east Asia as a 'barbarian' realm, pragmatic desires to exploit the resources of the region, and a Pan-Asian rhetoric which defined Japan as the 'liberator' of Asia, the Japanese military were unable either to treat Indonesia as an equal or entirely to suppress nationalist demands for independence.

Japan's colonial role raised fundamental questions about the definition of the word 'Japanese'. Japan's self-proclaimed mission as 'liberator of Asia' sat uncomfortably with its role as colonial ruler in Korea. The Japanese government tried to blur this contradiction by defining its status in Korea, not as imperialist, but as 'elder brother' nurturing the development of 'younger brother'. This imagery was supported by assimilationist policies imposed on the Koreans, who were enlisted in the Japanese armed forces and enrolled in the family registration system (*koseki*), albeit in a special category which marked them as 'overseas residents'. But the people who were 'Japanese' when it came to military service suddenly ceased to be 'Japanese' after the post-war peace settlement, and were thus deprived of their entitlement to Japanese war and disability pensions. In a final irony, as Utsumi points out, Korean recruits to the Japanese military were deemed by the Allies to be liable for prosecution for war crimes, on the basis of 'Japanese nationality' of which they had since been stripped. So the paradoxes of war created human tragedies whose consequences continue to colour Japan's relations with the Asian region to the present day.[24]

The more complex, 'multicultural' image of Japan presented in this book involves not only awareness of ethnic diversity, but also consciousness of the diverse and changing nature of social institutions like the family. One of the key institutions in the assumption of an eternal, trans-historical, unique 'Japaneseness' has been the idea that the Japanese household both concentrates that essence and ensures its reproduction. Nakane Chie's classic study *Japanese Society* described the *ie*, or hierarchical stem family, as providing the model on which Japanese social relationships were based.[25] Just as the *ie* was a vertical structure in which relations between parent and child were stronger than relations between siblings, so the corporation, the university and even the state itself were vertical structures where the links between superior and inferior mattered more than links between equals. The loyalty which individuals felt towards their family, Nakane argued, was extended to the corporation and to the state. So a timeless and unchanging *ie* became the cornerstone of the vision of Japan as a homogeneous and unique society.

Ueno Chizuko (chapter 12) and Nishikawa Yūko (chapter 13) address these issues. Ueno shows that the *ie* was an ideal type created and propagated in the Meiji period to serve political ends. Ueno's point, widely accepted by Japanese scholars, remains controversial among diehard upholders of uniqueness. As Ueno observes, the

modern state faces a fundamental dilemma. On the one hand, the
family is an important source of social stability; on the other, 'excessive'
loyalty to the family can limit the power of the state to intervene in
everyday life. Meiji ideology addressed this problem by promoting an
image of the state as the over-arching vertical family within which all
lesser family loyalties were subsumed. Although the vertical structure
of the three-generation *ie* was defined as 'normal' in Meiji official
rhetoric because it fitted neatly into this ideology, Ueno points out that,
even in the early twentieth century, a large percentage of the
population lived in family structures which did not conform to the
official ideal.

Nishikawa Yūko contrasts the ideology of the *ie* with another ideal
type popular in the late nineteenth and early twentieth centuries: the
notion of the *katei* or nuclear family. While the idea of the *ie* dominated
official thinking and the idea of the *katei* played a central role in the
popular media consumed by the emerging middle classes, in practice,
Japanese society contained a wide variety of family forms, including
three generational *ie*-style families in rural areas, nuclear *katei*-style
families in the towns, and the single-person households which were
common among the urban poor. This diversity is embodied in the
shape of Japanese housing, where an increasing range of lodging
houses, apartments and other arrangements have developed to serve
the growing complexity of Japanese family forms.

In the last part, the vexed questions of culture and ideology are
considered by Amino Yoshihiko (chapter 14), Nishikawa Nagao
(chapter 15), and Gavan McCormack (chapter 16). Amino challenges
the view of pre-industrial Japan as a nation of rice farmers, showing
that fisher and craft people constituted a much larger part of the
population than previously recognised, and that their distinctive ways
of life played a vital role in the dynamics of cultural change. Nishikawa,
through his analysis of Japanese culture discourse from the 1930s, issues
a radical challenge to the validity of the very concept of 'culture'.
McCormack attempts to bridge the gulf between the aspiration to
'internationalisation' and the desire to hold fast to some (officially
sanctioned) version of 'Japaneseness' by supporting Nishikawa's call for
the dissolution of 'culture' and arguing that true 'internationalisation'
cannot otherwise be accomplished.

The controversial nature of the problem of Japanese identity was
revealed in some of the exchanges during the Canberra conference
and which flowed over into heated debate thereafter.[26]

This book can only hint at the richness of Japan's multiculturalist
tradition. However, the creation of a multicultural future depends on,

and is fed by, the discovery of the multiculturalism of the past. While the monolithic and homogeneous myths of the past served the interests of elites intent on preserving order and control, helping to legitimise established authority, the common people preserved rich and diverse counter-traditions, which were open, bridged social and class distinctions, and had little time for the pretensions of their rulers. From the mountain and seafaring peoples discussed by Amino, through the mediaeval and early modern-urban, mass religious movements,[27] to the contemporary peoples living on the Japanese periphery – such as the 'Yaponesia' (or 'Okinesia') vision described by Hanazaki – they understood the priority of universal, human, moral qualities over the particularistic, ethnic or racial qualities of 'Japaneseness'.

An ideology rooted in the myths of uniqueness and the 'pure' blood tradition is still proclaimed, often stridently, by representatives of the tradition of centralised authority, but the foundations on which they stand are crumbling. From the 1980s a new wave of foreigners, attracted by Japan's prosperity, began to pour into Japan's cities, while the villages (where 'pure' 'Japaneseness' was supposed to be concentrated), suffering depopulation as a result of urban-oriented growth and desperate to find brides for young farmers, began to import brides from China, Korea, the Philippines, Thailand and Sri Lanka. The number of Japanese citizens living abroad, many of them married to foreigners, also increased dramatically. A new stage of hybridisation of culture was underway, carrying with it positive potential for opening, globalising, and achieving *kokusaika* (even if not of the kind desired by cultural mandarins). To carry the process through will require sloughing off the cocoon of Japanese uniqueness. In the 1300-year history of the 'Japanese' state, centralised political authority has been the exception rather than the rule, surviving less than a hundred years of the *ritsuryō* state of the seventh to eighth century and the 'modern' state from 1868. For most of its history, Japan has been a highly decentralised state and society. The consciousness that there was any coherent 'Japan' (a 'Nihonkoku') at all was born, not of the *diktat* of central authorities, but rather of the pilgrimages of monks, the journeying of merchants, and the wanderings of travelling artists.[28] The diverse traditions of the archipelago may flourish again as the current phase of centralised authority is also transcended.

The 1993 Canberra conference may therefore be seen as a pebble cast into a long-undisturbed pond, and the issues of Japanese identity, uniqueness, and relations with neighbouring countries which were touched upon there to be surface phenomena covering deep and unsettled questions about the 'who-ness' and 'what-ness' of Japan.

Notes

1 Nakasone Yasuhiro, speech of July 1985, quoted in Higuchi Yōichi, 'When society itself is the tyrant', *Japan Quarterly*, vol. 35, no. 4, October–December 1988, pp. 350–6, at p. 351.

2 Ivan P. Hall, 'Samurai legacies, American illusions', *National Interest*, no. 28, Summer 1992, pp. 14–25, at p. 17.

3 Nakasone speeches, quoted in William Wetherall, 'Nakasone promotes pride and prejudice', *Far Eastern Economic Review*, 19 February 1987, pp. 86–7.

4 Hanazaki Kōhei, 'Esunishiti to shite no Nihonjin' ('Japanese as ethnicity'), *Sekai*, September 1993, pp. 168–78, at p. 171.

5 Umehara Takeshi, 'Yomigaeru Jōmon' ('Jōmon resurrected'), *Chūō Kōron*, November 1985, p. 142. And recently, Umehara Takeshi, *Nihon no shinsō: Jōmon, Ezo bunka o saguru* ('Japan's depths: searching for Jōmon and Ezo culture'), Tokyo, Shūeisha, 1994. See also Ozawa Ichiro, *Nihon kaizō keikaku* (*Plan for Reform of Japan*), Tokyo, Kōdansha, 1993, p. 175.

6 Though the Japanese title refers to 'Japanese culture', in English the Center prefers instead to use the term 'Japanese studies'.

7 See Ian Buruma, 'A new Japanese nationalism', *New York Times Magazine*, 12 April 1987; Umehara Takeshi, 'Watakushi wa yamatoisuto de wa nai' ('I am not a Yamatoist'), *Chūō Kōron*, August 1987, pp. 242–57; Ian Buruma, 'Hanron–Umehara Takeshi shi wa yahari Yamatoisuto' ('Response: Umehara Takeshi is a Yamatoist'), *Chūō Kōron*, October 1987, pp. 236–43. See also Peter Dale, 'Tendenzen der Japanischen Kulturpolitik' ('Nichibunken and Japan's international cultural policy'), Conference of German Social Scientists on Japan, 'Die Internationalisierung Japans im Spanungsfeld Zwischen Ökonomischer und Sozialer Dynamik', Loccum, Germany, 7 November 1992.

8 See citation in preceding note.

9 See, for a few samples of the Japanese literature, Nihonshi kenkyūkai iinkai (Committee of the Japan History Research Society), ' "Kokusai Nihon bunka kenkyū sentā" no setsuritsu kōsō ni tsuite – Nihonshi kenkyūkai no kenkai' ('On the matters leading to the establishment of the Nichibunken – the position of the Japan History Research Society'), *Nihonshi kenkyū*, no. 284, April 1986, pp. 76–80; Iwai Tadakuma, 'Iwayuru 'Nihongaku' o megutte' ('On so-called 'Japanology'' '), *Nihonshi kenkyū*, no. 285, May 1986, pp. 78–81; Yamamoto Haruyoshi, 'Nihongaku saikō' ('Reconsideration of Japanology'), in Yamamoto Haruyoshi, *Gendai shisō no shōten*, Keisō shobō, 1987, pp. 98–124.

10 Richard Pearson, 'The nature of Japanese archaeology', *Asian Perspectives*, vol. 31, no. 2, 1992, pp. 115–27, at p. 115.

11 See, for example, Fujimoto Tsuyoshi, *Mō futatsu no Nihon bunka* (*Two other Japanese Cultures*), Tokyo University Press, 1988; Arano Yasunori, Ishii Masatoshi and Murai Shōsuke (eds), *Ajia no naka no Nihonshi*, iv, *chi'iki to minzoku* (*History of Japan within Asia, vol. 4, Region and Nation*), Tokyo University Press, 1992; Mark Hudson, 'Constructing Japan: diversity and unification, 400 BC to AD 1600', Göran Burenhult *et al.* (eds), *The Illustrated History of Humankind*, vol. 4, New World and Pacific Civilizations, New York, Harper Collins, 1994, pp. 122–41.

12 For convenient resumés of recent scholarship on these questions see Hanihara Kazurō, 'Nihonjin no keisei' ('Formation of the Japanese'), and

Hayami Tōru, 'Jinkōshi' ('Demographic History'), in Asaō Naohiro *et al.* (eds), *Nihon tsūshi* (*Complete History of Japan*), 25 volumes, Tokyo, Iwanami shoten, 1993, vol. 1, *Nihon rettō to jinrui shakai* (*The Japanese Archipelago and Its People and Societies*), pp. 83–114 and 115–50. Also Hanihara Kazurō (ed.), *Japanese as a Member of the Asian and Pacific Populations*, Kyoto, International Research Center for Japanese Studies, 1992.

13 However, the recent discovery of carbonised rice dating from the Late Jōmon period (*ca.* 2800 years ago) at the Kazahari site in Aomori prefecture strongly suggests that rice culture, albeit of a different strain, may have begun prior to the Yayoi migrations (A. C. D'Andrea, 'Paleoethnobotany of later Jōmon and early Yayoi culture in Northeastern Japan: Northeastern Aomori and Southwestern Hokkaido', PhD dissertation, University of Toronto, 1992).

14 Hanihara, 'Nihonjin no keisei', pp. 95–8.

15 Ibid., pp. 105–6.

16 See Mark Hudson, 'Ruins of identity: ethnogenesis in the Japanese islands, 400 BC to AD 1400', PhD dissertation, Department of Archaeology and Anthropology, ANU, 1995. (Hudson himself, however, supports a high level of Yayoi immigration.)

17 C. L. Brace, D. P. Tracer and K. D. Hunt, 'Human craniofacial form and the evidence for the peopling of the Pacific', *Bulletin of the Indo-Pacific Prehistory Association*, vol. 11, 1991, pp. 247–69.

18 Peter Bellwood, 'Southeast Asia before history', in Nicholas Tarling (ed.), *The Cambridge History of Southeast Asia*, Cambridge University Press, 1991, vol. l, pp. 55–136.

19 Mark Hudson, 'The linguistic prehistory of Japan: some archaeological speculations', *Anthropological Science*, vol. 102, no. 3, 1994, pp. 231–55.

20 Pearson, 'The nature of Japanese archaeology', pp. 120, 123.

21 Yoshida Kensei, 'A peaceful bridge to the world', *Japan Quarterly*, July–September 1992, pp. 288–9.

22 Kenneth R. Robinson, 'Re-drawing the boundaries of fifteenth-century Korean-Japanese relations', *Korea Foundation Newsletter*, vol. 3, no. 2, 1994, pp. 28–30.

23 Papers were presented at the conference on this theme by Kamigaitō Ken'ichi (Nichibunken) and Ha Woo-bong (Chonbok University).

24 For other texts by Utsumi on related matters, see her two essays in Gavan McCormack and Hank Nelson (eds), *The Burma–Thailand Railway: Memory and History*, Sydney, Allen & Unwin, 1993.

25 Chie Nakane, *Japanese Society*, Harmondsworth, Penguin Books, 1973.

26 For example, Sugimoto Yoshio, 'Henbō suru Nihonzō' ('Changing image of Japan'), *Mainichi Shimbun*, evening edn, 5 October 1994; Haga Tōru, 'Nichibunken', *Bunka kaigi*, November 1993, p. 1; Gavan McCormack, 'Kokusaika, Nichibunken, and the question of Japan-bashing', *Asian Studies Review*, vol. 17, no. 3, April 1994, pp. 166–72; Royall Tyler, 'Nichibunken: the threat is in the eye of the beholder', *Asian Studies Review*, vol. 18, no. 1, 1994, pp. 109–14; and Beatrice Bodart-Bailey, 'The 'stirrup, sail and plough' controversy', *ibid.*, pp. 114–16. Hanazaki Kōhei has published a full record of his experiences and impressions of the conference in 'Tabi nikki, 1993 nen', *Misuzu*, nos 400 and 401, July and August 1994.

27 See Amino Yoshihiko, 'Nihon rettō to sono shūhen' ('The Japanese

archipelago and its environs'), in Asao Naohiro *et al.* (eds), *Nihon tsūshi*, vol. 1, pp. 5–37, at pp. 30–1.

28 Yamauchi Masayuki, in Amino Yoshihiko, Itsuki Hiroyuki and Yamauchi Masayuki, 'Nihon minzoku to iwareru mono no shōtai' ('What makes up the Japanese people'), (joint discussion), *Chūō Kōron*, February 1994, pp. 83–95, at p. 91.

PART ONE

Archaeology and Identity

CHAPTER ONE

The Japanese as an Asia-Pacific Population

KATAYAMA KAZUMICHI

Several models have been proposed to explain the origins of the modern Japanese people. The most plausible are the gradual transformation and the Yayoi immigration theories. According to the first, prehistoric Jōmon people became the protohistoric Kofun people without any substantial admixture, and finally evolved into the modern Japanese of the greater part of the Japanese islands. In the second model, immigrant populations from the Asian continent arrived from the Korean peninsula during the Yayoi, and possibly also in the early Kofun period, and played an important role in the formation of the modern Japanese, especially in the main islands of Honshu, Kyushu and Shikoku.[1] In recent years, the immigration model has become widely accepted among anthropologists and archaeologists. I have also come to support this model. This chapter reviews the population history of the archipelago from the viewpoint of physical anthropology, and discusses the biological relations of Japanese populations to circum-Pacific Mongoloid groups.

The First Inhabitants

Recent newspaper articles report that cultural deposits which yielded several Palaeolithic stone tools at the Takamori site in Miyagi prefecture were dated to about 500 000 years BP on palaeomagnetic, thermo-luminesence and ESR evidence, corresponding in age to the early *Homo erectus* stage at Zhoukoudian in China. Although controversy continues over such early dates, it would not be surprising if such deposits were found in Japan because raised land-bridges formed several times following sea-level changes during the mid to late Pleistocene (figure 1.1). Thus the first human inhabitants of the islands may have been a

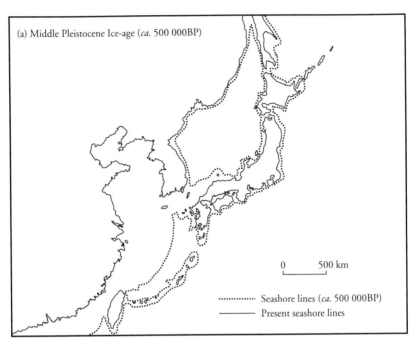

(a) Middle Pleistocene Ice-age (*ca.* 500 000BP)

0   500 km

.... Seashore lines (*ca.* 500 000BP)
———— Present seashore lines

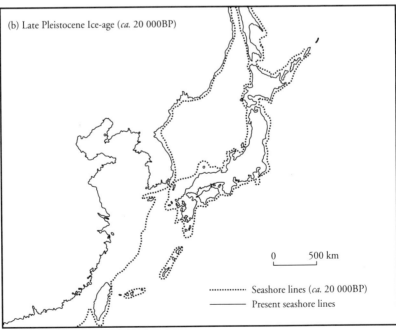

(b) Late Pleistocene Ice-age (*ca.* 20 000BP)

0   500 km

.... Seashore lines (*ca.* 20 000BP)
———— Present seashore lines

group of *Homo erectus* from China. At present, however, we have no idea of their physique, or whether they were ancestral to later Japanese populations.

The 'Minatogawa fossil humans', discovered at the Minatogawa fissure site on Okinawa Island, provide the first good evidence for Palaeolithic people in Japan. These specimens date back to only about 17 000 years ago, but provide the oldest and the best material for detailed examination of Palaeolithic Japanese people. The Minatogawa I male skeleton (the best preserved of the four individuals unearthed there) provides an excellent example. He shows characteristic 'archaic' features common in Palaeolithic human skeletons in East Asia. He was quite small (less than 155 cm tall) and somewhat similar in proportions to modern hunter-gatherer people. However, the skeleton is robust at many points, especially in the lower extremities. According to Suzuki Hisashi's morphological study, the Minatogawa crania seem closer to the Liujiang cranium from Guangxi Province, south China (*ca.* 30 000 BP) than to the Upper Cave crania of north China (*ca.* 10 000 BP). The Minatogawa crania also resemble those of the later Jōmon people.[2] Very few Palaeolithic skeletal remains have been found from the main islands of Japan. Almost all are fragmentary, and all date to the last stage of the late Pleistocene. Their physical characteristics are poorly known, but some circumstantial evidence suggests that Palaeolithic people in the main islands were probably quite similar to the Minatogawa population.

Jōmon People and the Emergence of the Japanese Physique

As a food-gathering culture, the Jōmon lasted for nearly 10 000 years from *ca.* 13 000–2300 BP. A high density of Jōmon archaeological sites has been found all over the islands of Japan, and human skeletal remains have been unearthed from a number of them. Discoveries of skeletal remains are limited mainly to shell middens in coastal areas

Figure 1.1   Pleistocene seashore lines in the Japanese archipelago and the surrounding area
(a) Middle Pleistocene (*ca.* 500 000 BP), in the period of the Takamori *Homo erectus*
(b) Late Pleistocene (*ca.* 20 000 BP), in the period of the Minatogawa modern *Homo sapiens*

Source: Adapted from T. Oba, 'Seishu-hyōki ikō no Nihon-Rettō-Shūhen no kairyu-hensen' ('Current changes around Japan Archipelago in the last glacial period'), *Japanese Scientific Monthly*, vol. 46, no. 10, 1993, pp. 934–8.

and cave sites in the mountains. Especially for the first half of the Jōmon period, the quantity is very small.

Ogata Tamotsu has discussed the people of the first half of the Jōmon period.[3] They were generally short (the estimated average height of adult males is 157.5 cm), and had thick limb bones, short faces, seemingly horizontal supra-orbital margins, and strikingly heavy tooth wear. Concerning the last point, it is quite common to see some saddle-shaped attrition, probably due to the use of teeth for special purposes. On the basis of skeletal features generally, we can presume that the physical qualities of Pleistocene inhabitants were inherited by the Initial and Early Jōmon people.

In the latter half of the Jōmon, large shell mounds were left in many parts of the islands, and many more human skeletal remains have survived. The people seem to have become taller (average stature of an adult male is estimated at 159.6 cm), with more robust limb bones, and more moderate tooth wear. Evidence for intentional evulsion of the front teeth has often been found, suggesting that the habit was common among Jōmon people. A remarkable osteological anomaly, auditory exostosis, is quite common. Its development is believed to have resulted from aquatic activities such as diving for marine or fresh water resources. Among some Jōmon skeletal populations in the latter half of the period, auditory exostosis is frequently present, suggesting that the people dived often as part of fishing activities.

Compared to modern Japanese, the Jōmon people had longer and wider heads, lower and wider faces, strikingly raised glabellas and nasal bones, highly developed masticatory-muscle attachments, much more common edge-to-edge bite occlusals, relatively long forearms and lower legs, and well-developed muscle attachments of the limb bones.[4]

Comparison of cranial measurements reveals that the Jōmon people were closer to the Minatogawa and Liujiang humans from the Upper Palaeolithic, than to the Neolithic people of mainland China who were contemporary with the Jōmon people. The Jōmon appear most similar to the present-day Ainu.[5] Thus it appears that the Jōmon people, who continued a foraging lifestyle for a long time in isolation, maintained the physical characteristics of the first Palaeolithic inhabitants of the islands. Their genetic contribution to the modern Japanese is most clearly seen in the present-day Ainu of Hokkaido.

It is difficult to study properly the human populations of the Yayoi period (300 BC–AD 300) because very few skeletal remains have been found. In general, their dead were buried not in shell middens but in the earth, so the skeletons are usually completely decomposed. Yayoi skeletal remains have only been excavated in any quantity from jar burials in Kyushu and stone coffins in Yamaguchi prefecture.

Compared with the previous Jōmon people, the Yayoi people from northern Kyushu and Yamaguchi were taller (an average stature estimated for adult males is about 163 cm), they had longer faces, and had much flattened orbital and nasal parts. On the basis of this evidence, it seems hard to support Suzuki Hisashi's hypothesis that Yayoi skeletons represent a gracilisation that occurred in a continuous transition from Jōmon hunter-gathering to Yayoi rice cultivation. It is more likely that there was a considerable genetic influence from migrants who arrived from the continent with rice cultivation and metallurgy. There is considerable controversy, however, over the number of migrants and the degree of their influence on the Jōmon inhabitants. Kanaseki Takeo suggested that the migration from the Korean peninsula took place within a limited time and that the migrants were not numerous, whereas Hanihara Kazurō insists that the migrants were extremely numerous (some ten times more than the native inhabitants), and therefore had a great impact.[6] Considering the quite drastic change of physical characteristics, the migrants must have been considerable in number, but Hanihara's estimate of between one and three million people seems exaggerated.

Human skeletal remains excavated from Yayoi period sites in north-western and southern Kyushu, Shikoku Island, and the Kanto coastal areas show a strong similarity to late Jōmon skeletons, with short stature, low faces, developed glabellar eminences, and so on. It is quite likely that in these areas, the Jōmon people survived through the Yayoi period and were increasingly adapted to the recently arrived cultures. They are called the 'native' Yayoi people.

Most Yayoi skeletal remains have been excavated from western Japan, so for the whole of Japan it is difficult to study how the 'native' and 'migrant' Yayoi people mixed to form Kofun-period populations. Except in Hokkaido, the protohistoric Kofun people doubtless arose through intermixture of 'native' and 'immigrant' populations. The degree of intermixture probably varied from one place to another. For example, in Kyushu, Nagai Masafumi concludes that a clear distinction can be made between areas where migrant influence overrode the native and areas where native characteristics persisted even in the Kofun period.[7] According to Terakado Yukitaka, the recent migrants possessed short and broad skulls, high faces and tall stature, and were already dominant in the Kofun period in the Kinki and Chugoku regions.[8] In the Kanto area, immigrant characteristics seem to have become gradually more common through the Kofun period, only becoming dominant in the seventh to eighth centuries.[9]

From the Kofun to the Present

After the Yayoi period it is likely that, except for the Ainu, all Japanese populations, including the southernmost Okinawan islanders, became more or less affected by the north Asian phenotype by at least the tenth century. The physical characteristics of most modern Japanese are quite similar to those of north-east Asians. Only the Ainu inherited Jōmon characteristics without mixing with the Yayoi immigrants.[10] Among the skeletal series from the Kofun period to the present, there is a striking homogeneity among the non-metric cranial traits that have proved useful for studying population structures.[11] So it appears that modern Japanese skeletal morphology had already developed by about the Kofun period. Since then, there has probably been no substantial change in the genetic constitution of the Japanese.

The Yayoi to early Kofun age was thus critical in the formation of the modern Japanese physique and in the ethnic differentiation of the Ainu, Honshu Japanese, and Okinawans. In Hokkaido, the Jōmon people were probably transformed into the modern Ainu by micro-evolutionary processes and admixture with neighbours. In other peripheral parts of the islands, such as the southernmost Ryūkyū Islands, the genetic influence of the Yayoi immigrants was less than in the main islands. That influence was nevertheless substantial with respect to non-metric cranial traits. This view supports the immigration model of Kanaseki and its modified form, the 'dual structure model' proposed by Hanihara.[12]

During the historic age, there has been some secular change in the Japanese people in many physical characteristics. Examples are changes in head form, tooth size and stature, probably caused by isolation, micro-evolution and changes in lifestyle. The most rapid change has been within the last one or two generations. The average height has increased by about 7 cm in the last forty years. In conclusion, therefore, the ethnic Japanese should be considered biologically a mixture of Jōmon people and Yayoi immigrants, whereas the Ainu are very probably the direct descendants of Jōmon people. Jōmon physical characteristics must have developed through isolation and the ultimate origins of the Jōmon people might have been in southern China. Considering their biological features, the homeland of the Yayoi immigrants should very possibly be traced to North-east Asia.

Japanese among circum-Pacific Mongoloids

Should Japan be considered an outpost of the Asian continent or one of the island groups of the Pacific world? The former may be true for the biological origins of the Japanese, and for the ethnic identity of the

majority of people. We learn so much about the histories of China and
Europe that modern Japanese are generally very conscious of the
continental world but very ignorant of the Pacific. As an Oceanist, I am
quite ashamed that most students at Japanese universities have very
limited interest in the countries of Oceania. Bearing in mind some
recent findings in physical anthropology (see below) we should
broaden our view of the relationships of Japanese populations with
circum-Pacific people, and view the Japanese more widely in the
context of circum-Pacific Mongoloid groups.

The first example comes from an anthropometric study of modern
populations in Asia and Oceania. Figure 1.2 is the result of a multivariate analysis based on a total of seven measurements of stature and
facial and head characteristics. Populations are arranged according to
their affinities, following the first principal components of body size
(horizontal axis) and body proportion (vertical axis).[13] The Oceanic

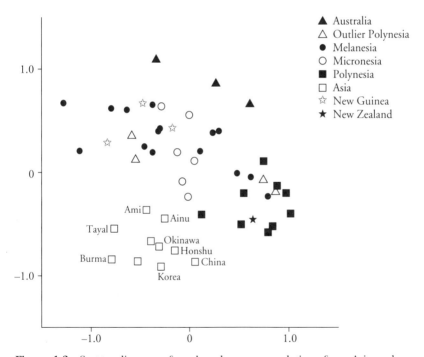

Figure 1.2 Scatter diagram of modern human populations from Asia and
Oceania on the basis of multivariable analyses of body measurements

Source: Adapted from Tagaya Akira, 'Shintai-keisitsu no Tayōsei', in Ōtsuka
Ryūtarō, Katayama Kazumichi and Intō Michiko (eds), *Oseania I: Tōsho ni
Ikuru*, (*Oceania I: Living in the Island World*), Tokyo, University of Tokyo Press,
1993.

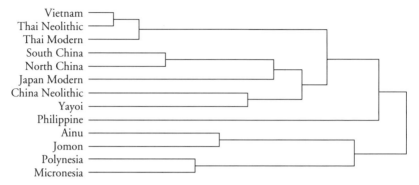

Figure 1.3 Dendogram showing the Euclidean distance relationships of nine Asian and three Oceanic samples based on craniofacial variables

Source: C. L. Brace, M. L. Brace, Y. Dodo, W. R. Leonard, Y. Li, X-Q. Shao, S. Sangvichien and Z. Zhang, 'Micronesians, Asians, Thais and relations: a craniofacial and odontometric perspective', in R. L. Hunter-Anderson (ed.), *Recent Advances in Micronesian Archaeology*, Micronesia supplement 2, University of Guam, 1990, pp. 323–48.

samples are very scattered, whereas all the East Asian samples from Japan, China, Taiwan, Burma and other nearby locations are clustered in a small range, suggesting that East Asian groups are very similar to each other in body form. The Ainu and the Taiwanese aborigines are quite close to some populations from Polynesia and Micronesia, especially in body proportions. Japanese populations, including the Ainu, are close to one another and to other Asiatic samples. This implies that there was originally no great difference between the Jōmon and the Yayoi immigrants.

The second example suggests affinities among human skeletal series from Asia and Oceania. Figure 1.3 is the result of a multivariate cluster analysis using seventeen craniofacial measurements.[14] The prehistoric Jōmon and their Ainu descendants form a series that lies very close to the samples of prehistoric Polynesians and some Micronesians. The modern Japanese skeletons are closely clustered with the modern Chinese series, and the Yayoi skeletons are closely clustered with the Neolithic Chinese series which is contemporary with the Jōmon. The implication is that the Yayoi immigrants were a type of people who, in Neolithic China, were genetically affected more or less by some 'cold-adaptive' north-east Asiatic groups. Alternatively, there may have been some kind of Neolithic transformation of body form within China. The Jōmon people may have been part of a lineage that was spread throughout East Asia in the late Upper Palaeolithic period, and have remained unchanged in isolated areas of Japan, Taiwan, the Philippines, and some parts of coastal China.

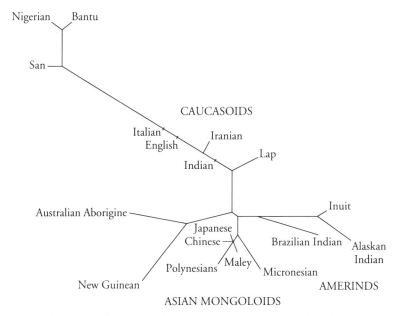

Figure 1.4 Genetic affinity diagram among eighteen modern human populations in the world based on the affinity network analysis of twenty-three polymorphic alleles

Source: Adapted from N. Saitou, K. Tokunaga and K. Omoto, 'Genetic affinities of human populations', in D. L. Roberts, N. Jujita and K. Torizuka (eds), *Isolation and Migration*, Cambridge University Press, 1992, pp. 20–30.

Another genetic study relates the modern Japanese population to human populations world-wide. In figure 1.4, the allele frequencies for twenty-three blood polymorphic loci are compared in a survey of about twenty populations.[15] Here there is a strikingly close relationship between the Japanese and the Asiatic populations from China and Malaysia. Variation in the Asiatic samples is not substantial on a world-wide scale. From the viewpoint of population genetics, East Asians are quite homogeneous. The samples of Polynesians and Micronesians are also clustered with the Asiatic samples. This suggests that although Polynesians and some Micronesians look quite different phenotypically from Asiatic people, they are much more closely related genetically to the Japanese than are the American Mongoloid groups. Their body form may have changed considerably by adaptation to Oceanic environments and because of genetic drift among more or less isolated populations. At least in a genetic sense, it is reasonable to regard many Pacific islanders as 'Asians in the South Pacific'.[16]

The Japanese and the Oceanic Connection

From the biological evidence discussed here, several points can be made about Japanese populations. First, the variability of modern Japanese people seems rather insubstantial in the range of Mongoloid variation. Even the difference between the main island Japanese and the Ainu seems trivial, at least in a biological sense. It is therefore probable that even if there was much influence due to immigration in the Yayoi period, the native Jōmon people and the Yayoi immigrants were not as different from each other as suggested by Hanihara, who argued that they were very heterogeneous in lineage because the former were originally from somewhere in South-east Asia and the latter were from North Asia.[17]

My opinion is that the Jōmon people derived from various Palaeolithic predecessors in Japan, and these predecessors were mainly from somewhere in southern China. The Yayoi immigrants were also from China, but their body form was affected by Neolithic adaptations and/or intermixture with North Asiatic groups. The biological differences between Jōmon and Yayoi people may have been small even if their cultural differences were large. The Jōmon might have been a kind of relict population from the late Upper Palaeolithic, equivalent in age to the Chinese Neolithic, but physically and culturally isolated in the Japanese islands. Perhaps similar populations were present in other peripheral areas of East Asia, such as Taiwan, the Philippines, and probably coastal China. These peripheral East Asian populations, including the Jōmon, may have spoken languages ancestral to languages in the modern Austronesian family. If so, we can form a hypothesis to explain the biological similarity of both the Jōmon people and their probable descendants, the Ainu, to Polynesians and some Micronesians. The biological properties seen in the late Upper Palaeolithic people of Liujiang in China and Minatogawa in Okinawa continued in the Jōmon and have survived in the Ainu. Such properties have also survived more or less in the Polynesians and some Micronesians, via the Lapita people who moved from the Bismarck Islands to West Polynesia some 3600–2500 years ago. The schematic expression of this scenario is given by Brace et al. and Katayama Kazumichi.[18]

In conclusion, Japanese people have their origins in mainland China, and have relatives in Remote Oceania. Therefore, in both the geographical and biological senses, Japan is an outpost of the Asian continent and, at the same time, an island group in the Oceanic world.

Notes

1 For the transformation theory, see Suzuki Hisashi, 'Micro-evolutional changes in the Japanese population from the prehistoric age to the present-day', *Journal of the Faculty of Science, University of Tokyo*, s. 5, vol. 3, part 4, 1969, pp. 279–308. On the immigration theory, see Kanaseki Takeo, 'Yayoi jidai jin' (People of the Yayoi period), in Wajima Seiichi (ed.), *Nihon no Kōkogaku* (Archaeology of Japan), Kawade shobō, 1966, vol. 3, pp. 460–71.

2 Suzuki Hisashi, 'Skulls of the Minatogawa man', in H. Suzuki and K. Hanihara (eds), *The Minatogawa Man–The Upper Pleistocene Man from the Island of Okinawa*, University of Tokyo Museum, Bulletin 19, 1982, pp. 7–49.

3 Oyata Tamotsu, 'Jōmon jidai jinkotsu' (Human skeletal remains of the Jōmon period), *Jinruigaku-Kōza* (A course in anthropology), vol. 5, Tokyo, Yūzankaku, 1981, pp. 27–55.

4 Yamaguchi Bin, 'A review of the osteological characteristics of the Jōmon population in prehistoric Japan', *Journal of the Anthropological Society of Nippon*, no. 90 (supplement), 1982, pp. 77–90.

5 Ibid.

6 Kanaseki Takeo, *Nihon Minzoku no Kigen* (The Origins of the Japanese People), Tokyo, Hosei University Press, 1976; Hanihara Kazuro, 'Dual structure model for the population history of the Japanese', *Japan Review*, no. 2, 1991, pp. 1–33.

7 Nagai Masafumi, 'Hokubu Kyushu, Yamaguchi chihō' (Northern Kyushu and Yamaguchi districts), a paper for the symposium, 'Japanese around the period of state formation', *Kikan Jinruigaku*, vol. 16, no. 3, 1985, pp. 47–57.

8 Terakado Yukitaka, 'Kinki Chūgoku chihō' (Kinki and Chugoku districts), ibid., pp. 57–70.

9 Yamaguchi Bin, 'Higashi Nihon – toku ni Kantō Tōhoku nanbu chihō' (Eastern Japan; with special reference to Kantō and Tōhoku districts), ibid., pp. 70–82.

10 Dodo Yukio, Ishida Hajime and Saitō Naruya, 'Population history of Japan: a cranial non-metric approach', in T. Akazawa, K. Aoki and T. Kimura (eds), *The Evolution and Dispersal of Modern Humans in Asia*, Tokyo, Hokuen-Sha, 1992, pp. 479–92.

11 Dodo Yukio and Ishida Hajime, 'Consistency of non-metric cranial trait expression during the last 2,000 years in the habitants of the central islands of Japan', *Journal of the Anthropological Society of Nippon*, no. 100, 1992, pp. 417–23.

12 Kanaseki, 'Yayoi jidai jin'; Hanihara, 'Dual structure model'.

13 Tagaya Akira, 'Physical characteristic variation among the Oceanic people' in Ōtsuka Ryūtarō, Katayama Kazumichi and Intō Michiko (eds), *Oseania I: Tosho ni Ikiru* (*Oceania I: Living in the Island World*), Tokyo, University of Tokyo Press, 1993, pp. 19–33.

14 C. L. Brace, M. L. Brace, Y. Dodo, W. R. Leonard, Y. Li, X-Q. Shao and Z. Zhang, 'Micronesians, Asians, Thais and relations: a craniofacial and odontometric perspective', in R. L. Hunter-Anderson (ed.), *Recent Advances in Micronesian Archaeology*, Micronesia, suppl. 2, University of Guam, 1990, pp. 323–48.

15 Saitō Naruya, 'Genetic affinity networks of the present Mongoloid populations', paper presented at the First World Conference on Prehistoric Mongoloid Dispersals, 16–21 November 1992, Tokyo.

16 Katayama Kazumichi, 'Were the Polynesians hypermorphic Asiatics? – a scenario on prehistoric Mongoloid dispersals into Oceania', paper presented at ibid.

17 See Hanihara, 'Dual structure model'.

18 Brace *et al.*, 'Micronesians, Asians, Thais and relations'; Katayama Kazumichi, 'A scenario on prehistoric Mongoloid dispersals into the South Pacific, with special reference to hypothetic proto-Oceanic connection', *Man and Culture in Oceania*, no. 6, 1990, pp. 151–9.

CHAPTER TWO

North Kyushu Creole: A Language-Contact Model for the Origins of Japanese

JOHN C. MAHER

Japanese as a Contact Language

The sociolinguistic model proposed in this chapter outlines a language-contact scenario for the origins of Japanese, in contrast to the lineal descent model which has dominated discussions of the topic. In contrast to most previous theories, I suggest that archaic Japan displayed multilingual heterogeneity involving several language communities out of whose mixture and contact evolved a pidgin-creole.

In all societies and at every time, language contact and multi-lingualism have been the norm. Likewise, Japan's linguistic history cannot be characterised by a linear progression nor by a single event but by successive episodes of language mixing. The view proposed here is that the Japanese language developed as a lingua franca in a multilingual environment. Thus, there is no indexable substrate language for Japanese since there was no single substrate; instead, Japanese developed from several speech communities possessing more than one language variety. In recasting Japanese as the product of heterogeneous sociolinguistic pressures, I suggest that the most suitable characterisation of Japanese is that of a pidgin-creole. The linguistic polymorphism of the Japanese is mirrored in their genetic and cultural polymorphism. The population history of Japan (see chapter 1) provides further support for the linguistic model proposed here.

Almost all studies of the origins of the Japanese language have concentrated on reconstructing an original proto-Japanese, typologically related to a single language derivative, say Tungusic or Korean or an ancestral Austronesian. But what might a *sociolinguistic* reconstruction of early Japan look like? Immigrants from the Korean peninsula transformed the economy and culture of the islands, bringing

31

techniques of rice farming, bronze and iron production and new ways of thinking. They also brought new languages.

North Kyushu seems to have been an important transmission point for the migrant peoples. The Fukuoka area in particular, relatively flat with a large bay area, is well known for its contacts with the Korean peninsula and may also have served as a major point of contact between languages. Archaeological and anthropological evidence suggests that this whole area was a frontier or gathering point for Neo-Mongoloid immigrants from North-east Asia. The migrants' language consisted of varieties of peninsular languages. These dialects were relatively homogeneous and the immigrants themselves sufficiently powerful in their (agricultural) economic organisation, community size and military capability (iron and bronze weapons) to dominate the existing language communities. As contact increased between the Jōmon languages (many of which were Austronesian-based) and the new cluster of immigrant language, a lingua franca or 'pidgin' evolved. This Yayoi-Kofun creolised standard, the result of language mixing, I term 'North Kyushu creole'.

Frameworks for a Contact-Induced Japanese

The 'hybrid' hypothesis of the Polivanov-Murayama approach and subsequent interpretations describing an early stage of language mixing are a major development in this topic since a sociolinguistic dimension now comes into play. Perhaps one of the problems in pinning down the origins of Japanese is the researchers' expectations. Have we been 'monolingual-minded', looking for a single source? Perhaps we have been searching for a Rosetta Stone instead of a heap of pebbles. The problem is not that we cannot find the progenitor language of Japanese, but that the very composition of Japanese is a multiplicity. The idea that Japanese is a mixture of languages can be located in the work of Polivanov, Murayama, Chew, Yasumoto and Kawamoto.[1]

Mischsprache ('mixed language') is a well-known concept. It is also difficult and not fully understood. Carlton T. Hodge even warns: 'We must leave open the question whether there really are mixed languages'.[2] The notion of a multilingual formation of Japanese is not new. In several papers between 1918 and 1938 the Soviet linguist, E. D. Polivanov, developed the idea that Japanese was a kind of 'mixed language' combining Austronesian and Altaic elements. This was elaborated by Murayama Shichirō who rejected the emerging hypothesis that Japanese consisted of a 'Malayo-Polynesian' (Austronesian) substratum on which an Altaic superstratum was added. The supposed Altaic features seemed to Murayama to be restricted to 'a few special features of syntax and to a portion of the morphology' whereas important morphological and phonological phenomena, notably intervocalic consonant voicing (*rendaku*) and other structural similarities, could be identified between certain types of Japanese verbs and the Austronesian verb.[3]

Murayama also rejected the notion of a 'proto' or 'primitive' Japanese (*genshi Nihongo*) or *Urjapanisch*. He comments:

> We have lacked any clear-cut concept of to what precisely such term might be understood as having reference ... For my own part I would like to propose that by *genshi Nihongo* we agree to mean that early stage in the development of Japanese at which a more or less unified linguistic system (*tōitsu-teki taikei*) had already evolved, in the course of the mingling and mixing of the various constituent elements that went into the make-up of Japanese – but Japanese as a mixed language.[4]

This notion matches, of course, the possibility that sociolinguistic conditions permitted a mixed language to emerge from two or more languages (Murayama favours a two-language mixture).

It is sensible to deduce that the Japanese archipelago in the land-bridge period was populated by speakers of many diverse languages over different periods. The plural language history which I propose involves the following phases:

1 Palaeolithic Japan, connected to the continent by a land bridge, was subject to continual migration from Asia, and involved languages flowing across three migration routes –
   a Palaeo-Siberian languages from Sakhalin and Siberia in the north;
   b Proto-Altaic languages from West Asia;
   c Austronesian (Malayo-Polynesian) languages from the Ryūkyū Islands in the south.

   These early languages continued to diverge in the isolated hunting communities scattered across this mountainous and heavily forested continental outpost. With the separation of the islands from the continent about 18 000 BC, the languages can be said to have become 'island' languages. They were not 'primitive' in that they were radically deprived of grammar and lexis. Like many languages of indigenous peoples today in Australia or the Amazon, they were sufficiently rich to enable expression related to daily domestic interaction, community ritual, magic and religion, hunting, identification of animal and plant habitats, geographical and seasonal description, and crafts and artistic production.

2 Jōmon period (10 000–300 BC). Languages developed separately in various regions of Japan, along with cultural production (pottery, the bow and arrow, etc.). The Jōmon archipelago was heterogeneous.

Language groups expanded in various regions but in relative isolation.

3 The impact of languages in the Yayoi-Kofun periods is outlined below. In these periods there were many relatively autonomous states in Japan, as recorded by the Chinese in the third century AD. The concepts 'Japan' and 'Korea' are historically meaningless until the end of the Kofun period. Before then, the region known as Wa (or Wo) consisted of a series of tiny states in the west and south of Japan and possibly at the tip of the Korean peninsula.

We can infer from the Chinese history, the *Wei zhi*, that before the rise of a more centralised state in the Kinai, the maritime polities of western Japan were more or less under the control of Queen Pimiha (Pimiko). The ethnic composition of these states may have overlapped with the Kimhae region of the peninsula. There is no evidence of language uniformity throughout the 'Japan' of that period. Separated by distance and tribal affinity for some hundreds of years, it is inevitable that these states possessed their own languages, although some languages would have been shared.

Historical evidence indicates that the community-states of the third century AD remained fairly stable and that Japanese spread as a lingua franca or trade language throughout these communities.[5] This trade language – Japanese – had imposed upon it the speech patterns and linguistic habits of the communities who came to use it. Population infusion does not entail massive language death and decline. Continuity is also likely and it is this which provides a basis for language contact. Successive migration and population flow in continental peripheral regions need not conflict with regional continuity.[6] Further elements of the sociolinguistic scenario are outlined by J. J. Chew:

Each community would have received a different degree of exposure to Japanese before its use began to spread within the community, so that the solutions to problems of communication in Japanese would have received different solutions. For example, the lexicon might have been expanded by the compounding of Japanese elements, or by falling back on the previous lexicon of the community. The degree to which each community indulged in these two procedures would have varied. At first Japanese was propagated by both Chinese and Koreans, neither of whom would have spoken in identical fashion. Soon Japanese themselves would have joined these groups, bringing their own speech habits to the lingua franca. The point here is that the language being propagated was not being spoken uniformly from the start, and different communities would have been exposed to different forms of the lingua franca. The result of which would have been the multiplicity of Japanese dialects, each of which appeared in the moment that Japanese was adopted by one of the numerous political entities which made up Japan at that time.[7]

Together with the distinct languages of peripheral Japan, again one observes that dialects are most diverse and distinct in the peripheral areas of mainland Japan, particularly Kyushu and northern Honshu. Dialects are the result of traces of speech patterns and historical divergence from the creole and pre-proto creole era.

Features of Creolisation

Although they differ on the role of 'Malayo-Polynesian' (Austronesian) languages, John Chew and Kawamoto Takao both proposed pidginisation for the origins of Japanese:[8]

1 The ancestors of the Altaic languages, Korean and Japanese, were in direct contact with each other, possibly as part of a single dialect continuum, and subsequently split on the North-east Asian mainland.
2 By 300 BC, a group associated with Altaic and speaking so-called J-1 invaded the western side of the Korean peninsula, Kyushu and western Honshu.
3 These J-1 speaking invaders subjugated the Jōmon population and their interaction produced the Yayoi culture. This also produced a pidginised J-1:

> the conquerors are probably not all that numerous, but the increased political unity brought about by the conquest leads to the popularity of pidginized J-1. A parallel might be the rapid spread of Pidgin English in Papua New Guinea in our time. As time goes by, the pidginized J-1 is creolized with native vocabulary and became the language of conqueror and native alike – a language which I label J-2.[9]

What I term 'Chew's Principle' (with apologies to Chew) is as follows: each pair of languages (Japanese and Austronesian, Japanese and Uralic, Japanese and Korean) are not genetically related in the sense that they represent the same language adopted by different communities but constitute different languages employed in various parts of an entity which viewed itself as constituting more or less the same community. In a similar fashion, Kawamoto has suggested two linguistic revolutions, the first involving a language of the Oceanic type and the second a language of the Indonesian type. In the first occurrence, some time between several and a few thousand years BC when speakers of the substratum language were living a simple life of hunting, fishing and gathering: 'the speakers of an O-V language accepted the totally different type of language, and first a pidgin and then a creole developed'. The second occurrence, Austronesianisation, 'must have taken place in the century preceding the Yayoi period (*ca.* 300 BC–AD 300) which is characterised by the rice-paddy'.[10]

Combined levels of mixing are proposed here, rather than positing one or other as a (sub- or super-) stratum. That two languages can contribute to the same lexico-grammar or phonological structure is reflected in most of the sources cited above. I emphasise that I refer to a successive mixing of features formed under pressure from various language groups, typically Altaic and Austronesian:

1 Macro-level features from Altaic are a small portion of the morphology, a limited selection of the vocabulary, and certain features of the syntax.
2 Specific examples in Japanese which derive from Altaic might include personal pronouns, interrogatives, causative forms of verbs, and exoactive and endoactive forms of verbs.
3 Macro-level features from Austronesian languages are a 'large portion of the basic vocabulary' (Murayama), tense and aspect, and morphological features.
4 Specific examples in Japanese which derive from Austronesian might include many words of two syllables, no comparison of adjectives, lack of noun gender, verbs not affected by nominative, no verb-tense classification (past, present, future), reduplication (particularly to show plural), frequent phoneme change, no singular/plural in nouns, and few words beginning with [e].

Features which suggest some form of deep convergence such as creolisation are:

• a characteristic Austronesian consonant-vowel-consonant-vowel syllable structure in addition to Altaic grammatical structure;
• evidence in Old Japanese of 'deep' morphological change from Austronesian, specifically prefixing. Altaic morphology is entirely suffixal;
• prenasalisation of certain consonants in Old Japanese, a typical feature of Austronesian.

The fact that two languages (at least) were in contact does not lead us to conclude that pidginisation occurred. Further processes are necessary, for example, simplification of the grammatical system of one of the languages. Katsue Akiba-Reynolds has presented grammatical data to indicate that pre-Japanese does, in fact, resemble a pidgin-creolised language in several respects.[11]

A characteristic and conspicuous feature of creolisation is

reduplication,[12] and this is certainly much in evidence in OJ. Reduplication (*hanpuku*) involves a type of compound in which both elements are the same or only slightly different. Typically, reduplication emerges in order to perform efficiently a variety of functions: for example, to reduce the number of homophonous forms, to extend the meaning of the simple form, to substitute for intensives as in the adjective/verb class. OJ reduplication was a most important grammatical mechanism. It played a role in word formation, intensification and the formation of plurals. In OJ, as in the modern language, nouns were reduplicated for pluralisation:

kazu-kazu (number + number) = many
toki-doki (time + time) = sometimes
yama-yama (mountain + mountain) = mountains
kuni-guni (country + country) = countries
ki-gi (tree + tree) = trees

The Question of Dialects

Dialects are central to a language-contact theory of Japanese. W. A. Grootaers concludes that Japanese dialects 'evolved from a common ancient language into separate localized speech forms because geographical or social distance allowed linguistic changes to develop independently'.[13] Language is constantly on the move. Grootaers is of the opinion that 'Proto-Japanese was probably *only one* [my emphasis] of the Japanese dialects spoken contemporaneously in most of Japan, including Kansai and area east of it'.[14] Antonio Tovar adds: 'Extinct languages live on through their influence as substratum. The passage of the conserved characteristics into the new language is realized during a bilingual stage'.[15]

It is precisely when power, in the form of institutions and administrative authority, is transferred from one place to another (such as Kyushu to Kinai) that the language phenomena resulting from bilingual contact quickly become cemented into the speech of a new structure seeking to establish its authority and influence. This is achieved by means of a new language which, in turn, radiates from a new centre.

We notice the presence of indigenous languages in a supposedly unified Latin, and it is precisely because the clear dialectal difference evident in Vulgar Latin did not match perfectly with later Romance dialects that the enterprise of a Latin dialectology has failed.[16] When we consider that Western Latin voicing at the beginning of the Principate is, in fact, Celtic aspiration (that is, the Latin spoken by the Celts)[17] or that inflection in Romance languages coincides with Celtic inflection, we are led to adopt a more radical position than that of mere substratum. We are indeed dealing with the existence of Celto-Latin and Germanic-Celtic bilingualism of populations in Western Europe. Moreover, as, societal bilingualism continued throughout Western Europe in the free movement of populations, voicing in Western Romance stabilised in the tenth to eleventh century Latin of Leonese notaries to become an established part of Iberian peninsular dialects.[18]

Mixed Languages as an Explanatory Option

Rick Goulden has shown that when English was placed in a Melanesian context and converted to Tok Pisin and Bislama the features of English were not changed into Tok Pisin and Bislama but these languages assimilated the typological features of that area.[19] Among the theories which have been proposed for the origins of Japanese, language mixture, especially pidgin-creolisation, remains the least explored and one for which no comprehensive sociolinguistic framework exists. The fact that these events occurred a thousand or more years ago, and that model interpretations are limited to much later written accounts, regional dialects and indigenous languages (Ainu, Ryūkyūan) adds to the indeterminacy.

Historical linguists are aware that for the genetic classification of languages, the role of mixed languages is considerable. Laszlo Cseresnyesi doubts 'whether the traditional "arboreal" classification is an adequate account of the historical descent of languages, in particular, of Indo-European, Germanic and English' and proposes a revision of the basic assumptions of comparative linguistics 'in the light of alternative ideas derived from typology and the study of areal complexes, i.e. clusters of languages in contact'.[20] Likewise, Bernard Comrie urges 'just because the idea "mixed language" has been misused in the past does not mean that it does not have a proper place in our discussion of the genetic classification of languages'.[21]

In the comparative analysis of Japanese and other languages there is recurrent confusion. Japanese is sometimes close to Austronesian and sometimes not. The same is true of Japanese and Altaic languages. It appears, in other words, to have a mixed or *konketsu-teki* character. Creolisation explains this. Though far from exhaustive, the following speculations suggest that creolisation was at least a factor in the synthesis of languages in early Japan. There is no direct way to test this hypothesis. Needless to say, in the matter of language origins we always see through a glass darkly.

The difficulty of classifying Japanese precisely into one or other typological category accords with what I term 'typological masking', in which a language does not make a 'good fit' on account of its complex (that is, mixed) origins. Todd summarises thus: 'What is clear is that pidgins, by shedding linguistic redundancies, by adopting greater syntactic regularity, by jettisoning linguistic inessentials, have very successfully eradicated the very features which would allow linguists to link them, unequivocally, with a particular language or family of languages'.[22]

I am not looking specifically at Japanese composed of two levels – the superstructure being Altaic and the substructure Malayo-Polynesian. I try rather to view the formation of Japanese from a macro-level, examining the possibility of Japanese as a hybrid language but arising from specific circumstances. We can best view early Japan as a fundamentally multilingual environment in which the whole of the archipelago consisted of multiple language minorities. The linguistic structures of each of these languages reflected their multiple origins: Palaeosiberian such as Ainu, Altaic such as varieties of Korean, and varieties of Austronesian languages which were carried by immigrants from the south. However, throughout the process of fusion the community languages were still sufficiently separate. We know, for instance, that interpreters were needed for communication with parts of eastern Japan during the Nara period. The lingua franca was then gradually adopted as an important working language of intra-national communication, particularly as political power was consolidated during the Heian period.

What Conclusions Can We Draw?

1 Japan's population history cannot be characterised by a single migratory event but by successive episodes.
2 Jōmon, unadmixed Ainu and Okinawans, are biologically closely related to Micronesians, Polynesians and South-east Asians. Although a direct link between the Japanese and Polynesian-Micronesians is as yet unclear, the latter populations derive from South-east Asia.
3 After the end of the glacial period and the Neolithic revolution, a population explosion in North-east Asia caused some so-called Neo-Mongoloid populations to migrate to Japan. Beginning about 400 BC an immigrant population from continental Asia entered the Japanese archipelago via the Korean peninsula into North Kyushu. This population expanded eastward and northward, assimilating the northern populations.
4 Jōmon and Yayoi populations were ethnically and culturally different.

The Jōmon were hunters, gatherers and fishers; the Yayoi people were full-scale farmers.

5 Relations between indigenous and immigrant groups were complex and we do not know how those relations evolved. However, we know that the later arrivals came with advanced technology and were of a different genetic stock than the indigenous peoples.

6 Population and therefore language movement occurred in a well-circumscribed manner. If we can extrapolate when populations are likely to have moved from one place to another, we can assume that language has also been transferred and undergone change.

'North Kyushu Creole': a metaphor for contact-induced change

Hudson has argued convincingly that the spread of a form of Japanese from Kyushu proceeded in tandem with agricultural colonisation in the Yayoi period.[23] Scholars of early Japanese demography have estimated that while the immigrant fraction might have been small, it had a disproportionate influence on the genetic composition of the population due to the growth rate of the dominant population.[24] The immigrants, however, would have to have been in sufficient numbers for a linguistic effect to have taken place. Koyama maintains that the population of Japan increased rapidly from about 0.2 or 0.3 million in the Jōmon period to over 5 million in the eighth century.[25] The anthropologist, Hanihara Kazurō, has attempted to calculate figures for the migrant peoples. His estimate is between 350 and 3000 people per year.[26]

The Yayoi was, therefore, the period of language contact between the Jōmon tribes and the Yayoi migrants. How was communication effected? I suggest that in northern Kyushu a creole emerged. As we know, a pidgin grows up among people who do not share a common language. This pidgin would have been a makeshift, mixed language composed of elements of Jōmon people's speech and that of the Yayoi immigrants. I must stress again, however, that as with the Jōmon people, we have no reason to believe that there was a single Yayoi language. On the contrary, as people were disembarking in Japan over a period of some hundreds of years it is more likely that they displayed considerable speech variation. This may explain the Burmese and even Tamil connections that have been proposed.[27]

As the pidgin stabilises, it quickly becomes the first language of the children of the intermixing peoples. It becomes, in other words, a creole. This creole spread naturally along with population movements as Yayoi settlement fanned out from Kyushu across Honshu. Northern Kyushu lies on a relatively flat plain, which must have facilitated the free movement of peoples for trade and other purposes, and the rapid spread of a lingua franca. What we might call the North Kyushu creole became increasingly popular and widespread as a means of communication, and existing Jōmon languages continued to be transformed under pressure from the new blended language.

The Post-creole Continuum: consolidation and standardisation

In the Yayoi and early Kofun periods we are led to the view that there were two culturally and politically powerful entities in western Japan: Western Seto (northern Kyushu) and Eastern Seto (Kinai and Kibi).[28] From the fifth century, however, the Kinai polity started to have direct contact with the Korean peninsula and the Kyushu route became increasingly marginalised. It was inevitable, therefore, that Kyushu would be weakened, and power gradually moved inland to the Kinai region comprising the Nara Basin and the Osaka plain.

Prior to this shift, the consolidation of power in North Kyushu assisted the standardisation and ultimate spread of North Kyushu creole to other parts of Japan by Yayoi settlers. The history of the Late Han states that the Emperor Kuang presented a seal and ribbon to the ruler of the Wa state of Na, thought to be located around the present city of Fukuoka. The seal was discovered in Fukuoka in 1784. Mutual exchange between Na and the Chinese bolstered Na's legitimacy and the seal was presented in return for tribute offered the Chinese court. Another indication of concentration of power is the presence of bronze objects such as mirrors, swords and spearheads. At first these items were imported from the continent, but before long the Yayoi people learnt to produce their own versions. Excavations at several Yayoi sites in Kyushu have revealed large numbers of bronzes and other prestige goods, such as glass beads and silk.[29]

According to Chinese histories such as the *Wei zhi*, Yamatai was a major polity which controlled a large area. Scholars continue to debate the location of Yamatai, but recent excavations in northern Kyushu strengthen the view that this area (rather than the Kinai) was the rapidly developing centre of Yayoi political hegemony. It was technically the most advanced region at the time and was the closest point to China and the continent. In addition, the presence of mirrors (symbols of power and authority and used in shamanic rites) in so many sites in northern Kyushu – sometimes thirty mirrors in a single burial jar, as in the Kyushu sites of Mikumo and Sugu Okamoto – indicate that Yamatai may have been in the area of Fukuoka.

In sum, North Kyushu fulfilled all the conditions for a major political base from which a rapidly standardising Yayoi creole could have spread:

geographical proximity to the continent, a rich agricultural base, port facilities, evidence of international trade such as the Kōrokan diplomatic guest house, a tradition of large-scale migrations over a long period, and North Kyushu's continuing influence as a centre of trade and commerce in the Kofun and early historic eras despite the growing power of the Kinai-based Yamato state.

Language development in the Nara Basin In the post-creole continuum, the North Kyushu creole began to stabilise further in Honshu. How might this have been effected?

1 Increasing regional prestige of language: large display tombs were built in the Kinai region, particularly on the Kawachi plain.
2 The influence of a major language entity from the continent: horse trappings from the peninsula are found in substantial quantity indicating that new and powerful political forces appeared in Japan. This matches the so-called 'horse-rider' theory in which 'invasions' from the continent helped establish an emergent state in the region.
3 The weakening of regional/tribal languages: a new economic and administrative system promoting hegemonic control of regional lands, people and production (*miyake, tomo-no-miyatsuko, be*) weakened the power of local chieftains. This led to the weakening of the prestige of many local languages and a shift to the lingua franca.
4 The social stratification of language: the increased complexity and rigidity of social interactions may have corresponded to an increasingly well-defined usage of language according to social differentiation.
5 The standardisation of language for the purpose of internal and external relations: from the fifth century, the Kinai polity had direct contact with the Korean peninsula through the inland sea.
6 The cultural diversification of language: archaeological evidence shows an increasing specialisation of life in religion, military activity, arts and crafts. Language became more specialised.

It may not be entirely appropriate to term the emergent Yayoi language a 'creole'. We know, of course, that pidgin and creole languages are formed when varieties are mixed with each other. Pidginisation may be considered a special kind of speech accommodation which occurs when speakers of different codes come into contact with each other.

A protolanguage emerges in the development of pidgins which display all the characteristics of a primary representational system or protolanguage.[30] Once a community has adopted an amalgam of new linguistic waves as input then language expands rapidly: grammar develops, recursion appears, complex structures and marking devices emerge.[31] We may usefully posit the emergence of a proto-creole prior to Japanese. The languages of the Yayoi migrants may have been sufficiently homogeneous to form a kind of standard which successive waves of migrants would have learned as they arrived in North Kyushu. There was a strong admixture from the Kyushu Jōmon languages and this gave the Yayoi Standard its Austronesian elements. The original Yayoi migrant language remained the basic 'standard' form for all purposes of communication, and other more distinctly separate forms (admixtures from Austronesian Jōmon) were positioned at various points on this continuum – which we can now call the North Kyushu creole.

Acknowledgements My sincere thanks to Dr Edward Kidder for his advice and generosity with time and archaeological materials. My appreciation also to the Fukuoka City Museum for its display of Palaeolithic, Jōmon and Yayoi artefacts and the ICU library for patiently procuring arcane material. Finally, I wish to acknowledge John Skahill and Mark Hudson for their erudite reading and comments on an earlier draft of this paper. None of these scholars are necessarily in agreement with its contents. An early version of this paper was presented in the ICU Library Open Lecture Series, 1991.

Notes

1 E. D. Polivanov, 'Predvaritel'noe soobscenie ob etimologiceskom slovare japonskogo jazyka', *Problemy Vostokoved'enija*, no. 3, 1960; Murayama Shichirō, *Nihongo no Gogen*, Tokyo, Kobundo, 1974; J. J. Chew, 'The prehistory of the Japanese language in the light of evidence from the structures of Japanese and Korean', *Asian Perspectives*, no. 19, 1976, pp. 190–200; Yasumoto Biten, 'Nihongo wa dono yō ni tsukurareta ka', in Mabuchi Kazuo (ed.), *Nihongo no Kigen*, Tokyo, 1985, pp. 123–32; Kawamoto Takao, *Jōmon no kotoba, Yayoi no kotoba*, Tokyo, Nupuri Shobō, 1987.
2 Carlton T. Hodge, 'Egyptian and mischsprachen', *Linguistics and Literary Studies in Honor of Archibald A. Hill*, vol. 4, Mohammed Ali Jazàyery *et al.* (eds), The Hague, Mouton, 1979, nos 265–75, p. 26.
3 Murayama Shichirō and Ōbayashi Taryō, *Nihongo no Kigen* (The Origins of Japanese), Tokyo, Kobundo, 1973.
4 Murayama Shichirō, 'The Malayo-Polynesian component in the Japanese language', *Journal of Japanese Studies*, vol. 2, no. 2, 1976, pp. 413–36, at p. 427.
5 H. Okada, 'From Chinese to Japanese: an insight into the ethnic environment of the founding of the kingdom of Japan in 668', *Bulletin of the International Institute for Linguistic Sciences*, vol. 2, no. 4, Kyoto Sangyo University, 1981.

6 Peter Bellwood, 'Cultural and biological differentiation in Peninsular Malaysia: the last 10,000 years', *Asian Perspectives*, vol. 32, no. 1, 1993, pp. 37–60.

7 John J. Chew, 'The significance of geography in understanding the relationship of Japanese to other languages', *Bochumer Jahrbuch zur Ostasienforschung*, vol. 12, no. 1, 1989, pp. 13–49.

8 John J. Chew, 'The prehistory of the Japanese language'; Kawamoto, *Jōmon no kotoba*.

9 Chew, 'The prehistory of the Japanese language', p. 198.

10 Kawamoto Takao, 'Toward a comparative Japanese-Austronesian IV', *Bulletin of Joetsu University of Education*, no. 1, 1982, pp. 1–233. See also Kawamoto, *Jōmon no kotoba*.

11 Katsue Akiba-Reynolds, 'The reconstruction of pre-Japanese syntax', *Trends in Linguistics, Studies and Monographs 23, Historical Syntax*, Mouton, Linguistica Historica, 1984, vol. XII, nos 1–2, pp. 107–25.

12 D. Bickerton, *Dynamics of a Creole System*, Cambridge University Press, 1975; '[R]eduplicated forms occur in all the English-based pidgins and creoles', Loreto Todd (ed.), *Pidgins and Creoles*, Routledge & Kegan Paul, 1974, p. 55.

13 W. A. Grootaers, 'Dialects', *The Kodansha Encyclopedia of Japan*, vol. 2, Tokyo, Kodansha, 1983, p. 156.

14 Ibid.

15 Antonio Tovar, 'Linguistics and prehistory', *Word*, no. 10, 1954, pp. 333–50, at p. 341.

16 A. Martinet, 'Celtic lenition and western Romance consonants', *Language*, no. 28, 1940, pp. 192–217; Tovar (1981) quoted in Laszlo Cseresnyesi, 'Language Contact and Historical Reconstruction: Creolization in English and Indo-European', unpublished ms, Graduate School of Education, International Christian University, 1993.

17 Martinet, 'Celtic lenition'.

18 J. Menendez-Pidal, *Origenes del Español*, Madrid, 1953, at p. 240.

19 Rick J. Goulden (1987), quoted in Chew, 'The significance of geography'.

20 Cseresnyesi, 'Language Contact and Historical Reconstruction'.

21 B. Comrie, 'Genetic classification, contact and variation', *GURT*, 1988: 1989, pp. 81–93, at p. 91.

22 Todd, *Pidgins and Creoles*, p. 39.

23 Mark Hudson, 'The linguistic prehistory of Japan: some archaeological speculations', *Anthropological Science*, vol. 102, no. 3, 1994, pp. 231–55.

24 Koyama Shūzō, *Jōmon Tanken* (Investigation of Jōmon), Tokyo: Kumon Shuppan, 1990.

25 Ibid.

26 Kazuro Hanihara, 'Estimation of the number of early migrants to Japan: a simulative study', *Journal of the Anthropological Society of Nippon*, no. 95, 1987, pp. 391–403.

27 For a critical perspective on Ono Susumu's theory of a Yayoi-period Tamil migration, see Mark Hudson, 'Tamil and Japanese: Ono's Yayoi theory', *Asian and Pacific Quarterly of Cultural and Social Affairs*, vol. 24, no. 1, 1992, pp. 48–64.

28 Gina L. Barnes, *Protohistoric Yamato: Archaeology of the First Japanese State*, University of Michigan Center for Japanese Studies and the Museum of Anthropology, University of Michigan, 1988.

29 On one such site, Yoshinogari, see Mark Hudson and Gina Barnes,

'Yoshinogari: a Yayoi settlement in northern Kyushu', *Monumenta Nipponica*, vol. 46, 1991, pp. 211–35.

30 D. Bickerton, *Language and Species*, Chicago University Press, 1991.

31 G. D. Prideaux, 'Review of Bickerton 1990', *Word*, vol. 42, no. 3, 1991, pp. 303–8, at p. 307.

CHAPTER THREE

Beyond Ethnicity and Emergence in Japanese Archaeology

SIMON KANER

Introduction

Archaeologists have worked for over a century to document the diversity in the material remains of past human activity in the Japanese archipelago. First and foremost has been the classification of archaeological material into a series of 'types', recurrent associations which comprise archaeological 'cultures'. It is now accepted that there were many Palaeolithic, Jōmon, Yayoi and Kofun period cultures. What is less widely agreed is how to interpret this multiplicity. One way has been to regard them as ethnic groups with a shared sense of identity, but this approach is extremely problematic. Incorporating this diversity into general accounts of Japanese archaeology has also caused problems, as archaeologists search for ways to make their esoteric subject matter more comprehensible to the public. As Clare Fawcett suggests in chapter 4, archaeologists often fall back on simplification, stereotypes and familiar images in dealing with the public, leaving their presentations open to political manipulation.

The Wa, Kumaso, Hayato and Emishi are all ethnic groups mentioned in historical sources on early Japan. Unfortunately, these accounts are sparse and mostly written by outsiders. Many scholars have attempted to relate these groups to contemporary Japanese populations. Physical anthropologists and historical linguists have grouped past populations into physical types and language groups. Archaeology has produced accounts of the material remains in terms of repeated sets of associated material culture. The interface between the study of ancient material culture and the study of ethnic groups and 'ethnogenesis', however, remains problematic.

Early Japanese archaeologists were concerned to establish the ethnic or racial identity of the early inhabitants of Japan in order to see how far back a distinctly Japanese identity could be traced. By the 1930s this question receded, and archaeologists concentrated on classifying material types, partly because it was safer in the prevailing political atmosphere. In recent years, however, interest has revived in the identity of the archaeological inhabitants of Japan. Were the Palaeolithic occupants of the archipelago Japanese? Were the Jōmon people more closely related to the Ainu or to the 'Yamato' Japanese? Was there a migration into Japan at the start of the Yayoi period? Was there an invasion in the fourth century AD by horse-riding Tungusic tribes from North-east Asia?

Archaeology is ill-equipped to answer such questions of ethnic identity. Archaeologists detect diversity in a number of aspects of the past. One is diversity in the form, function and style of artefacts and structural remains. Another is diversity in everyday practices, such as the consumption of different foods. It is beyond the bounds of this chapter to rewrite Japanese prehistory placing diversity at its centre, but it is possible to outline the main aspects of such an account. Japanese prehistory and protohistory are divided into four main periods: Palaeolithic, Jōmon, Yayoi and Kofun, and it is possible to see how patterns of diversity changed. The search for diversity throughout the half-million-year human occupation of the island chain requires great flexibility of approach, not least because of changes in material culture and technologies. In the Palaeolithic, most discussion centres around the stone tools that comprise almost all the archaeological record. In the Holocene Jōmon period, the range of material culture that has been preserved increases, with most attention focused on pottery and ceramic styles. In the Yayoi period, metal-working was added to the technological repertoire, while the Kofun period was marked by new ceramic technologies and major construction projects, including massive burial mounds for the elite.

The main aim of this chapter is to show that different ways of life existed in the prehistoric archipelago, and that understanding the processes behind the generation of this variety can replace what has become the dominant discourse in Japanese archaeology, namely the emergence of the Japanese people and of a definable ethnicity. Such diversity tends to be overshadowed in generalising accounts which take these dominant discourses as their theme. Archaeologists, while compiling detailed and complex local developmental schemes, have then tried to simplify these schemes in order to render them more palatable to their audience and major sponsor, the public. In the course of this simplification, archaeologists leave themselves open to charges of conniving in the creation of a homogeneous and unified past.

A number of questions leap to mind when one considers diversity. How can we measure diversity in material culture? Is diversity expressed in different ways and does it express different things in different periods? How do the constraints on diversity change from period to period, for example, by the development of the state? Diversity in prehistoric material culture has been studied in depth, but description is only the first step in recognising diversity in the development of early Japan. How can this diversity be related to underlying social processes? To understand this, we need to understand the social and cultural contexts within which material culture was produced and consumed. The material objects themselves shaped the social relationships of which they were a part. They are not a direct *reflection* of any ethnic group. If material culture was used in signalling identity and ethnicity, then we must be explicit about how this was done. As we will see below, certain sets of material culture cross-cut ethnic boundaries, while others exhibit tremendous diversity within communities, symbolising social status and rank, marking individual position rather than group identity.

Archaeology, Identity, Diversity

Japanese archaeology has been accused of producing an account that ignores diversity as it attempts to construct a specifically Japanese prehistory to account for the emergence of the homogeneous modern nation state.[1] One does not have to look far to discover diversity in modern or historical Japan. The showcase of Japanese history and archaeology, strategically placed near Japan's *genkan* (entrance hall) at Narita Airport, is the National Museum of Japanese History. In the presentation of Japanese folk culture, four lifestyles are depicted: urban, agricultural village, mountain village and fishing village. These lifestyles are supplemented by an exhibit of life in the southern islands. At the twin institution, the National Museum of Ethnology in Osaka, a popular exhibit replicates regional dialects, supporting the common conception of the mutual unintelligibility of Satsuma and Tsugaru speech. Thus, two axes of diversity are already defined: between regions and between types of settlement.

The rich diversity of local traditions has been the object of intense study since Yanagita Kunio's pioneering studies. A critical enquirer, however, may wonder to what extent the traditions of folk culture have real roots stretching back into a timeless antiquity, and to what extent they are products of a capitalist nation state seeking to justify its existence and to maintain its hegemony in part through the manipulation of heritage.[2] It is this scepticism that informs the charges levelled against Japanese archaeology.

With abundant evidence for contemporary and traditional diversity, we can ask to what extent this indicates the existence of different cultures in Japan. Compared with other nations facing problems over a heterogeneous present, Japan does appear remarkably homogeneous. Most of the consumers of Japanese archaeology, the Japanese people, are quite happy with the reconstructions of the past they are offered by archaeologists. Direct links are often drawn between archaeology and the images of traditional life that are actively propounded by a government ideology of *furusato*: stimulating feelings for one's native place in an increasingly displaced, rootless society. These images render the discoveries of archaeology comprehensible to the public who are encouraged to view the people of the past as their ancestors: there is a direct connection between the contemporary 'salary-man' and his stone-age forebear. Peel off the layers of the Japanese cultural onion and the irreducible core of the Japanese spirit is revealed living in a Garden-of-Eden setting next to the primeval Tama River.

The problem revolves around the term 'origin'. If the role of archaeology is to provide an account of origins, then Japanese archaeology has fulfilled its role admirably. The story of the early settlement and development of Japan has been told many times, and the fruits of many years' research have been used in creating an objectivist narrative that amply fills the void left by the rejection of the imperialist narrative that was based on unquestioning acceptance of the early chronicles. The relevance of local sequences to the greater tableau needs to be asserted. Without them it could be said that one origin myth has replaced another. Part of this lies in the way in which Japanese archaeology is perceived as the study of the earliest (pre-)history of the Japanese people, rather than the study of ancient material culture. The process that has received most attention has been the emergence of one race/people and their 'Japaneseness'.

Archaeological Concepts

Archaeologists use a number of concepts to discuss social groupings. The notion of the archaeological culture has a long history, and despite many problems it remains popular in East Asian archaeology.[3] The archaeological culture is a classificatory device, based on detailed observation and description of archaeological material. Closely related to the notion of culture is that of style, so that style zones, geographical regions over which shared styles of material culture appear, have in some cases replaced the culture concept. The archaeological culture is the mainstay of the interpretative framework in Japanese archaeology, its popularity reflected in the continuing attention paid to the greatest proponent of the concept outside Japan, Gordon Childe.

Mortimer Wheeler considered the study of archaeological remains without worrying about the people who left them behind as exciting as examining the 'driest dust that blows'. In trying to get at the 'Indian behind the artefact' however, archaeologists are often lured into the trap of equating their archaeological classifications to groups of people. The device most often employed is ethnicity, and the result is an unhealthy pre-occupation with the ethnic group. The relationship between these ethnic groups then becomes a field of study in its own right, as archaeologists attempt to reconstruct the history of relations between such groups, often attempting to link these hypothetical groups to what they perceive as modern ethnic groups. A large part of the archaeological endeavour becomes oriented towards the search for ethnic origins, a dubious pursuit that often has been – and continues to be – hi-jacked and manipulated for contemporary political expediency, not least in Japan.

Two general problems can be recognised in existing archaeological studies of ethnicity, in Japan and elsewhere. The first is the extent to which historic or contemporary societies can be subdivided into discrete entities such as tribes or ethnic groups. In this book, Nishikawa Nagao makes one of the strongest arguments for this position with respect to Japan. Some will find this position extreme, but at the very least it is likely that different types of social entities were present at different times in the past. Following from this, the second problem is how to relate the archaeological record with past social units when there is no agreement on the types of units we should be looking for, nor is the relationship between archaeological remains and such social units understood. Ian Hodder has worked extensively on the ways in which different groups use material culture to symbolise their identity. He stresses that not all classes of material culture are used in the same way: 'Whether a particular artefact type does or does not express the boundary of an ethnic group depends on the ideas people in that society have about different artefacts and what is an appropriate artefact for ethnic group marking'.[4]

Ethnicity concerns the classification of human groups and implies a concern with what their members have in common, and what sets them apart from other comparable groups. Ethnicity has often been used to indicate a hierarchy of dominance: there is an inherent tendency for ethnic minorities to be assimilated into mainstream nationalities, or to risk alienation and marginalisation from dominant centres. Ethnicity is a way of demarcating the Other. In this way, many of the concerns of much recent archaeology, namely the importance of individual agents and the nature of different ways of doing and seeing things within rather than between particular cultural contexts, are overlooked. The study of ethnicity has led us away from the classification of artefacts, straight past the people themselves, and the way they expressed themselves and their relationships with each other and the worlds they inhabited through these artefacts, to the equally sterile but potentially disastrous classification of human groups. Unless it is possible to demonstrate that ethnicity and identity have a major role to play in the past, they can be considered to be largely irrelevant to archaeology.

An archaeology that tries to reconstruct ethnic groups uses a language of migration and/or indigenous development, with the powerful evocative messages such images carry in the late twentieth century, of invasion, domination and resistance. Is it just coincidence that as soon as supposedly historically documented 'ethnic groups', such as the Kumaso and Emishi, appear on the scene in Japanese archaeology it is in a context of just such narratives? Suddenly, archaeology as the study of the ways in which material culture is used within particular cultural contexts becomes subordinated to the study of the material manifestation of competing human groups.

Backwards Through a Regionalised and Diverse Japanese Past

Contemporary Japanese archaeology operates on at least three different scales: local history, national history, and in an international setting. Considerable attention has been focused on the national scale, particularly on the relationship between archaeology and nationalism.[5] At what scale does ethnicity operate? Perhaps the strongest contrast in modern Japanese identity is with what is not Japanese, that is, not part of the Japanese nation. However, I wish to consider how regionalism and diversity can be used to reorientate discussions about the pre-Yamato origins of Japanese identity.

In the following account of regionalism and diversity in the four main periods of Japanese pre- and protohistory, I differ from most such summaries by going backwards in time. There are a number of reasons why my narrative is structured in this way. The first is that it follows both the archaeological logic of stratigraphy and the logic followed by the archaeologists of Tama New Town, who attempt to relate the modern inhabitants of a place to their prehistoric forebears. This logic works well as an alternative to accounts that start in remote antiquity and move forward. It also allows us to reorient the relationship between the contemporary occupants of a locale and its prehistoric inhabitants as relations of place and residence rather than by ethnicity. Next, such an approach consciously avoids the problem of the discourse of emergence, since we can locate the inhabitants of a particular locale to their forebears without referring to the emergence of the Japanese people in an apparently preordained narrative structure. We can then show the diversity of lifestyles without having to worry about a diversity of ethnic groups. Within this structure it is easier to look at diversity within social groups rather than between them, bringing us closer to the aims of archaeology set out above.

The Kofun Period

The first states in the archipelago appeared in the fourth and fifth centuries AD: they were greatly circumscribed. They appeared along with a particular form of burial structure – the mounded tomb and in particular the keyhole-shaped mounded tomb – from which the period takes its name. Regionalism in this period is often set in terms of political relations within and between clusters of mounded tombs. The centres of political development were the Kinai, Kibi (Okayama), Izumo (Shimane), North Kyushu, Keno (Gumma) and Bōsō (Chiba).

There were considerable regional variations in styles of Kofun-period material culture, not least in the tombs themselves; variations include burial orientation and the type of coffin.[6] Such differences, however, are used in the analysis of developing status differentiation between rulers within the context of alliance formation, rather than suggesting different ethnic groups. The reasons for these differences are not explored; for example, to see whether orientation played a significant role in other aspects of the lives of these groups.

Other regional developments included painted tomb chambers, which flourished in the sixth century in northern Kyushu and the Kanto but were very unusual in the Kinai region.[7] Domestic Haji-ware pottery showed a strong uniformity of style and form in the Kinai, but considerable diversity in assemblage composition in other regions. Similar regional variation can be seen in the stoneware Sue pottery and the cylindrical *haniwa* terracotta tomb sculptures. Regional variation in the forms of iron arrowheads was also very marked.[8]

Such regional variations are interpreted in terms of competition between the elite classes ruling regional polities and their relationships with Yamato. In this way, diversity and regionalism in the Kofun period can be seen to be closer to political processes rather than driven by ethnicity. Some of the defining features of the period were the social and political developments in the midst of which the Yamato state appeared in the Kinai district. These developments led to increasing demarcation of classes of people and the appearance of elite ruling classes and commoners, various ranks of officials and specialist occupational groups including farmers, soldiers, and craft specialists such as potters and blacksmiths. While at the end of the Yayoi period rulers and the ruled were apparently being buried separately but living in the same settlements, by the end of the Kofun period they lived in separate compounds. This increasing diversity is represented by new settlement styles. In addition, though there was more or less parity between the polities that made up the Yayoi social landscape, in the Kofun period a centre developed in the Kinai region that would achieve hegemony over other parts of the archipelago. Thus there appeared qualitative differences between the Yamato state and the other parts of Japan.

A further way in which diversification in material culture was linked to social developments is seen in:

> changes in the social organisation of elite groupings and their control over coffin production between the Middle and Late Kofun periods. The explication of these changes was based on archaeologically documentable trends away from a centralised or homogeneous choice of coffin style and utilisation of raw material toward decentralisation or diversification of productive control, concomitant with the rise of regional social groupings and styles within the Kinai region.[9]

Changes in diversity also played an important part in the developments leading to social stratification between the Early Kofun period and the Late Yayoi period that preceded it:

> [there is] contrast between regional variability among Late Yayoi mound burials and the incredible degree of homogeneity among keyhole-tomb burials in the Early Kofun period. This contrast surely marks the intensification and magnification of interaction between local groupings. Whereas intraregional interaction and subscription to local cultural-stylistic values characterise the chiefly groupings in Late Yayoi, the Early Kofun witnesses the establishment of an interregional network of interaction and elite subscription to a single material culture. This is related to the process of increasing status differentiation within the mature Yayoi-based agricultural society and possibly to the development of stratified marriage classes.[10]

The Yayoi Period

These Kofun period alliances had their origins in social changes in the Late Yayoi period, when there was marked regional differentiation in the degree of political integration and hierarchy in the archipelago. The Yayoi period is divided into four main phases, each of which exhibited regional diversity in pottery styles, burial forms and other categories of material culture. There was great regional variation in burial forms, with over six regional burial zones being recognised archaeologically.[11]

After the tremendous regional diversity of the Jōmon, Yayoi cultures seem much more uniform. This is partly because of the focus on a narrower range of foodstuffs, but also because of a more uniform set of material culture than the Jōmon, many aspects of which appear to have been direct imports from the Asian continent. While the roots of much Jōmon diversity are to be found in local, relatively autonomous sequences of regional development, with local centres of innovation, that of the Yayoi appear to result partly from population movements through the archipelago, particularly with the spread of Early Yayoi Ongagawa pottery:

> As the Yayoi complex spread, first throughout south-western Japan and later through central and northern Honshu, minor regional variations appeared in the pottery. These are believed to reflect divisions previously existing among Jōmon societies that took up the new pattern of life, and it was only after the Yayoi culture became well established that the boundaries of ceramic style zones departed significantly from those drawn in Jōmon times.[12]

This different basis for diversity leads to a different image of regionalism in the Yayoi period than in the Jōmon. The Yayoi period is usually divided into four stages (Initial, Early, Middle, Late), but for most of the period the archipelago can be divided into three zones: pioneer Yayoi in Kyushu and western Honshu, Jōmon-influenced Yayoi in most of eastern Honshu, and Epi-Jōmon in the northernmost tip of Honshu and in Hokkaido.

Hudson argues for 'what seems likely to have been a highly diverse ethnic mix in the western archipelago' in the Yayoi period.[13] Gina Barnes also considers that the differences in the archaeological records of north-eastern and south-western Japan in the Yayoi period, as well as differences between the eastern and western Seto regions 'might even argue for different organisational identities: ethnic groups, tribes or polities'.[14] Historical documents support the notion of several different groups, such as the many countries (*kuni*) of Wa mentioned in the Chinese history, *Wei zhi*. It is not possible, however, to relate these to specific archaeological cultures. Indeed, it is not clear if we should be treating these *kuni* as distinct ethnic groups.

The Jōmon Period

Prior to the appearance of wet-rice agriculture in north-western Kyushu around the middle of the first millennium BC, the Japanese archipelago was occupied by a series of groups of fisher-gatherer-hunters who, at times since the end of the Ice Age, had experimented with the cultivation of some plants. These groups left behind a legacy of rich material culture including a large amount of pottery. The classification of this pottery into some seventy types has traditionally formed the basis for studies of regional developments at this time.

Regional diversity has long been recognised as a defining aspect of the Jōmon period. Compared with the preceding and succeeding periods, a great diversity of subsistence resources was used and a vast array of regional subcultures developed, each defined by distinctive pottery styles.[15] These included the Middle Jōmon mountain cultures and the coastal shell midden cultures. In the Jōmon case, then, regional diversity was stimulated by rich natural environments rather than just the availability of raw materials determining technology, as was the case in the Palaeolithic.

Unlike the Yayoi periods, none of the names of these Jōmon groups are known. This has meant, in part, that archaeologists have been able to focus on diversity within and between these groups and in lifestyles rather than trying to reconstruct ethnic groups. Fruitful approaches are exemplified by Akazawa and Maekawa who study differences in the composition of assemblages of stone tools from sites in different parts of the archipelago or Peter Bleed (1992) who has reconstructed some of the ecological diversity that surrounded the site of Yagi in Hokkaido, or Habu Junko (1993) who has looked at differences in material culture from different sites within one pottery style zone to suggest the existence of different types of site within one settlement system.[16]

Thus, although the Jōmon has been depicted as the basal layer of Japanese culture in popular books, more serious archaeological studies have been advancing our knowledge of the many Jōmon cultures. These Jōmon communities are often considered to have had a high degree of autonomy but there was also a great degree of communication between them.

The Palaeolithic Period

Prior to the appearance of pottery in the archipelago more than 12 000 years ago, the islands were inhabited by small groups of people, and knowledge of their lifestyles and culture depends mostly on the analysis of stone tools. Recent evidence from sites such as Takamori in Miyagi prefecture suggest human occupation occurred at least half a million years ago. Evidence from this early phase is still scant, but this has not stopped certain archaeologists from looking for 'Japaneseness' even at this early stage:

> from around the time when archaic and anatomically modern *Homo sapiens* were moving around in the Japanese islands, a distinctively Japanese culture sprouted . . . In other words the distinctiveness of Japan stems from around the beginning of the Late Paleolithic and the regionalism has continued until today from around 20,000 BP, when the Japanese people can be said to have formed, after which they absorbed culture and the immigration of people from the north or south or directly across the Sea of Japan.[17]

These styles represent distinct regional archaeological cultures, interpreted as the material expressions of tribal groups with common lithic manufacturing techniques, linked to each other through exchange networks. The significance of variation in lithic assemblages and the relations between human groups are still matters for considerable debate.

Before 30 000 BP there is little diversity in stone tool assemblages. The amorphous flakes and occasional choppers were remarkably homogeneous, suggesting opportunistic and flexible subsistence strategies and a possible lack of specialisation in resource utilisation. However, after 20 000 BP, the time from which most Palaeolithic sites are known, there is a

> sudden increase in the number and kinds of functionally specific tools, which exhibit a remarkable diversity both in time and space. Part of this diversity, such as the differences among the named types of 'knives', points and burins, is stylistic and probably reflects the boundary-maintaining mechanisms of human groups that were filling up the available environmental niches. This diversity is also attributable to the intensification of human efforts to procure and process various resources effectively by manufacturing specialised tools.[18]

In this scenario, diversity in the Palaeolithic is explained as a combination of territorial behaviour and technological adaptation to particular environments.

Beyond Ethnicity: Archaeology and Japanese Identity

The cultivation of a sense of ethnicity is one mechanism by which people classify themselves in relation to other individuals and groups. Ethnicity is used in the creation of identity. A sense of a shared past is one way in which this is done, along with a sense of shared descent, language, beliefs and material culture.

Using the past to forge a sense of identity is not, however, the same as attempting to re-create the ethnic groups of the past by analysing archaeological material and historical records. While there is no doubt that the former occurs, it is open to a critique of contemporary political practice and ideological abuse. The latter remains problematic for archaeologists in the absence of direct evidence for ethnic self-awareness in the distant past.

Archaeology is based on inference, whose limits need to be recognised. Inferring the existence of ethnic groups in the past is one thing: to reconstruct them on the basis of archaeological material is another. Prevailing concepts of Japanese identity are grounded in the notion of a homogeneous race and an autochthonous culture. The Canberra conference and the chapters in this book set out to criticise such unified conceptions of identity by encouraging a diversity of approaches and methods. Archaeology is one such method, and while it can be and has been used in the discourse of ethnicity, the archaeological material is better suited to other lines of enquiry, rather than in supporting monolithic images of a single 'Japanese' past. While the archaeological record is extremely diverse, this does not mean that we can necessarily talk of reconstructing a multicultural, or multi-ethnic Japanese prehistory. Rather, archaeological method and theory can be used to appreciate the significance of this diversity in the (pre)historical processes that produced modern Japan. One part of this is to realise that the past was not homogeneous. The actions of Hayato women are just as much part of the Japanese heritage as is the tomb of Nintoku, as are the oral traditions of the Ainu. Archaeology can contribute to the understanding of some of the strands that comprise contemporary Japanese identity without resorting to the language of ethnicity.

Conclusions

A number of issues carry very important conclusions. First, the myth of the unchanging homogeneous past reflecting the homogeneous present has been laid to rest. Second, diversity in material culture must be interpreted in the light of social constraints and contexts which changed through time. The causes of diversity in the Jōmon period are very different to the causes of diversity in the Kofun period. Third, this suggests that the interpretation of diversity calls for a much greater sophistication than just the reconstruction of ethnic groups within the archipelago.

Can diversity and multiculturalism replace the emphasis on writing the history of the origins of Japan? Probably not, unless there is a more radical rethink than is often considered acceptable in Japanese archaeology. Maybe we now need to return to the material culture that is becoming more and more documented. The significance of the great diversity within the material cultural repertoires of the early inhabitants of the archipelago is that it is evidence of the creativity and considerable innovation displayed in so many different ways by those populations. Generalising approaches whose goal is the reconstruction of ethnic groups deny the importance of this creativity and innovation.

Notes

1 Ikawa-Smith Fumiko, 'L'idéologie de l'homogénéité culturelle dans l'archéologie préhistorique japonaise', *Anthropologie et Sociétés*, vol. 14, no. 3, 1990, pp. 50–76. To some extent archaeology has also played a role in breaking down stereotyped views of Japanese history and identity. See, for example, Fujimoto Tsuyoshi, *Mō Futatsu no Nihon Bunka*, Tokyo University Press, 1988.

2 See E. J. Hobsbawm and T. O. Ranger (eds), *The Invention of Tradition*, Cambridge University Press, 1983; Ernest Gellner, *Nations and Nationalism*, Oxford, Basil Blackwell, 1983.

3 On the culture concept, see S. J. Shennan, 'Introduction: archaeological approaches to cultural identity' *Archaeological Approaches to Cultural Identity*, S. J. Shennan (ed.), London, Unwin Hyman, 1989, pp. 1–32.

4 Ian Hodder, *Reading the Past: Current Approaches to Interpretation in Archaeology*, Cambridge University Press, 1986, p. 3.

5 Clare Fawcett, chapter 4 of this volume; Tanaka Migaku, 'Kōkogaku to nashionarizumu' (Archaeology and nationalism), in Tanaka Migaku (ed.), *Iwanami Kōza Nihon Kōkogaku 7: Gendai to Kōkogaku*, Tokyo, Iwanami, 1986, pp. 133–67.

6 Tsude Hiroshi, 'The Kofun period and state formation', *Acta Asiatica*, vol. 63, 1992, pp. 64–86 at pp. 71–2; Wada Seigo, 'Political interpetations of stone coffin production in protohistoric Japan', in R. Pearson (ed.), *Windows on the Japanese Past*, Ann Arbor, Center for Japanese Studies, University of Michigan, 1986, pp. 349–74.

7 Ono *et al.*, 1992, p. 163.

8 Ibid., p. 174.

9 Gina L. Barnes, 1986, p. 314.

10 Ibid., p. 313.

11 Gina L. Barnes, *China, Korea and Japan: The Rise of Civilization in East Asia*, London, Thames & Hudson, 1993, p. 190; Mark Hudson, 'Rice, bronze, and chieftains: an archaeology of Yayoi ritual', *Japanese Journal of Religious Studies*, no. 19, 1992, pp. 139–89 at pp. 156–68; Ono *et al.*, 1992, p. 136.

12 C. Melvin Aikens and Takayasu Higuchi, *Prehistory of Japan*, New York, Academic Press, 1982, p. 244.

13 Mark Hudson, 'Ethnicity in East Asian archaeology: approaches to the Wa', *Archaeological Review from Cambridge*, vol. 8, no. 1, 1989, pp. 51–63 at p. 59.

14 Barnes, *China, Korea and Japan*, p. 18.

15 Kobayashi Tatsuo, 'Regional organization in the Jōmon period', *Arctic*

Anthropology, vol. 29, no. 1, 1992, pp. 82–95; Peter Bleed, 'Ready for anything: technological adaptation to ecological diversity at Yagi, an Early Jōmon community in southwestern Hokkaido, Japan', in C. M. Aikens and S. N. Rhee (eds), *Pacific Northeast Asia in Prehistory: Hunters-Fishers-Gatherers, Farmers, and Sociopolitical Elites*, Pullman, Washington State University Press, 1992, pp. 47–52.

16 Akazawa Takeru and Maeyama Kiyoaki, 'Discriminant function analysis of later Jōmon settlements', in Pearson (ed.), *Windows on the Japanese Past*, pp. 279–92.

17 Okamura Michio, 'The achievements of research into the Japanese Palaeolithic', *Acta Asiatica*, vol. 63, 1992, pp. 21–39.

18 Fumiko Ikawa-Smith, 'Late Pleistonce and early Holocene technologies', in Pearson (ed.), *Windows*, pp. 279–92.

CHAPTER FOUR

Archaeology and Japanese Identity

CLARE FAWCETT

Archaeologists and historians have long realised that their disciplines provide as much of a window on the present as they do on the past. The past is frequently re-created and reinterpreted to invent traditions which justify contemporary social and political conditions. Over the past decade, archaeologists have dug into the history and practices of their discipline to find evidence of the social, political, cultural and economic influences on archaeological practices, interpretation and presentation.[1] They discover that archaeological research often reflects the dominant ideologies of the societies in which it is carried out.

In this chapter I discuss the relationship between Japanese archaeology, society and identity and demonstrate how archaeological information allows individuals and communities in Japan to learn about their local and national cultural origins and identity. To begin, I describe how sites, artefacts and information are presented to the public. I then analyse several examples of archaeological popularisation, and ask whether archaeological presentations are related to the ideologies of homogeneity and cultural uniqueness or whether archaeology provides a means of questioning these notions.

Presentation of Archaeology to the Public

Since the Early Meiji period, archaeology has been an important way for the Japanese people to learn about the prehistory and early history of the archipelago. Only since the end of the war in 1945 and public acknowledgment of the fictional character of the origin myths found in the histories *Kojiki* and *Nihon Shoki*, however, has archaeology been considered the sole reliable source of information about prehistoric Japan. Information about archaeology is available through newspapers, magazines and television. People also read books about archaeology, are introduced to the discipline through school textbooks and teachers, visit sites and museums, attend public lectures, and hear about archaeology from friends.

The amount of information produced by the mass media has certainly increased over recent decades. Journalistic interest began with the excavations of the Yayoi-period Toro site in the late 1940s when, during the post-war confusion, people were eager to read recent studies of the ancient history of Japan.[2] Through the 1950s and 1960s articles about archaeology continued to appear in the press. Many of these newspaper stories discussed the problems faced by archaeologists trying to preserve sites in the face of development. Journalists were instrumental in saving a number of sites and raising public consciousness of the problem of site preservation.

In the early 1970s with the excavation of Takamatsuzuka, a late seventh- or early eighth-century tomb in the Asuka area, however, journalistic coverage expanded dramatically. During the 1970s and into the 1980s there was a noticeable increase in the amount of archaeological news available through newspapers. Some interest was spurred by the unusual nature of the Takamatsuzuka tomb, but even when the initial excitement ended, articles about archaeology continued to appear. This reflected an increasing awareness resulting from the dramatic expansion of archaeological rescue work during the 1970s and 1980s.[3]

School textbooks, which outline Japanese and world prehistory,[4] and school visits to sites and museums are the first introduction most people have to the subject. These early encounters influence most people's understanding for the rest of their lives. Site explanation meetings or open days are easily accessible and increasingly popular. One reason for this is the enormous number of sites. Many are in suburban areas and the neighbouring people are generally curious. Many people find these visits more informative and more fun than visiting a museum, since they see work in progress – often in their own neighbourhood. Children usually visit a site on a school outing at least once during their primary school years.

Archaeology is a popular topic in the press and on television. Short reports discussing local and national excavations and discoveries appear almost daily in Japan's largest newspapers: the *Mainichi*, *Asahi* and *Yomiuri*. During the mid-1980s, in one year and excluding redundant stories, 2000 articles were published in regional and national newspapers.[5] Since site reports are too technical for the general reader, newspapers extract information. Popular magazines, such as the *Asahi Graph*, also report on archaeology. These reports are illustrated with photographs of artefacts and sites. The Asahi Newspaper Company also produces booklets such as 'Ancient History Excavations 1978–1982' which summarise finds throughout Japan. Other published sources are popular books and journals. Popular journals on history, such as the *Rekishi Dokuhon* series, offer summaries of work in a format that is easy to understand, using less technical vocabulary than would be found in an academic journal. The editors and authors are often university professors or specialists from research centres and museums, although some articles are also written by non-specialists. The focus of the papers tends to be questions which would interest the public.

On television, the NHK (Japan Broadcasting Corporation) often reports important discoveries on the national news and discusses local excavations in regional news broadcasts. For example, in March 1985 there were twenty-one items dealing with archaeology in the Kinki area NHK morning news. Programs on archaeological themes also appear quite often on television and are very popular. In many cases, the theme is not an excavation but a broader one, such as 'Where did the Japanese people come from?', 'A voyage through Chiba prefecture' or 'The temples of Ancient Asuka'.

In these forms, information is readily available to the citizen. For school children, archaeology is taught as Japanese history. Mass media reporting is the most popular way of continuing to learn about the past after graduation. Many non-archaeologists associate learning about archaeology with visits to famous sites or museums when travelling, or visits to neighbourhood excavations on open days. Since a vast and ever-increasing amount of excavation is done, one of the concerns of archaeologists is maintaining control of the interpretation and presentation of the past. In the next section, two case studies illustrate the varying degree of their influence over interpretation.

Control of Archaeological Presentation: Asuka and Morishōji

Asuka Mura

In the late 1960s and early 1970s the LDP-dominated national government began to use archaeological and historical remains as symbols of a new Japanese identity. This trend coincided with a growth of post-war nationalism which continued throughout the 1970s and 1980s. One example is the development of a national park and special preservation area in Asuka Mura, Nara prefecture. The national government defined the goal of preservation as the creation of a monument to the Japanese national heritage.

The name 'Asuka' denotes both a locale and a village at the southern end of the Nara Basin. The locale encompasses an area about three kilometres wide from east to west and about four kilometres from north to south. Today, most of Asuka falls within the village of Asuka Mura. Other parts of ancient Asuka are administered by the local governments of Kashiwara City, Sakurai City, and the town of Takatori, among others.[6]

Asuka was important from the time of the introduction of Buddhism into Japan, in either the year 538 or 552, until 710, when the Imperial Palace was moved to Heijō-kyō in the northern part of the Nara Basin. This period is often called the Asuka period. The leaders of Japan (both the imperial family and other important families or clans) lived in the Asuka area, which was the administrative centre of the Japanese state.[7] Since the Japanese remained in contact with the people and rulers of the various nations of China and the Korean kingdoms of Silla, Paekche and Koguryo, many aspects of Chinese culture, including the writing system, the Buddhist religion, administrative procedures, urban planning and medicine, were introduced during the period.

The Asuka area contains a variety of important sites, incuding seventeen palace sites built and used between 592 and 710; the Asuka stones, a series of 'unusually shaped granite stones and stone carved figures'[8] scattered around southern Asuka; the remains of many temples sponsored by the most powerful clans during the sixth and seventh centuries; and tombs, often called the Asuka Kofun (*kofun* describes mounded tombs), built during the sixth and seventh centuries. The most famous is Takamatsuzuka, which became known throughout Japan in 1972 when spectacular painted frescos were discovered on the interior walls of its burial chamber. Various features of the tomb suggest close associations between the leading families of Asuka Japan and the continental kingdoms.

A final artefact of historic Asuka is a series of early poems in the *Man'yō-shū*, Japan's first compilation of poetry, dating from the eighth century. The poems were composed by renowned poets, the emperors who ruled from Asuka, members of noble or imperial families, and anonymous poets, some of whom may have been commoners. They describe many landmarks familiar to visitors to contemporary Asuka. Asuka can be reached easily by train on the Kintetsu line. The town itself is small. Most of the buildings have been repaired or reconstructed in the style of traditional farm buildings. Subsidies to villagers through special legislation have been largely responsible for these expensive renovations. Hints that this is a preserved area are manifest: signposts direct visitors to the four national park sites of Iwaido (a district containing a training and accommodation centre), Amakashi no Oka (a hill from which visitors can look out over the area), and the Ishibutai and Takamatsuzuka tombs. A tourist centre has been set up opposite the train station, and not far from the centre of town is the Asuka National Historical Museum.

A visitor is struck by the tranquillity of the countryside in an area which is rapidly becoming urban. The area immediately surrounding Asuka Mura is less touched by urban sprawl than other nearby towns due to the creation of several national parks and natural and historical preservation areas during the 1970s and 1980s. In 1980, furthermore, special legislation was enacted to ensure the preservation of Asuka as an area of historical importance and scenic beauty while guaranteeing a relatively undisturbed work and home environment to the several thousand inhabitants of the village.

As an area replete with sites described in the literary classics, Asuka has been of historical and spiritual interest to some Japanese for centuries. The first 'Asuka Boom' occurred in the Meiji period when scholars reassessed the *Man'yō-shū*. At this time the idea of Asuka as 'the home-town of the Japanese heart' (*Nihon no kokoro no furusato*) was first used. During the Second World War Asuka was often discussed in terms of the 'Japanese spirit'. Some authors wrote positively about the ideal which could be found at the home of the ancient Japanese nation. Others were more cynical, asking why the imperial power that was identified with Asuka was leading hundreds of thousands of Japanese to their deaths.[9]

During the Occupation (1945–51), the tone used by authors continued to differ. Some still focused on Asuka's natural and historical environment, suggesting that in Asuka the spirit of the ancient Japanese people could be found. Others saw it in a more negative light. For them, it was a place where struggles for authority between the ancient clans had resulted in the creation of the imperial line and thus the imperial myth. Whether seen in a positive or a negative light, however, many people thought of Asuka as a repository of the history and spirituality of the Japanese people.

During the 1950s 'The theory of Asuka as the Japanese hometown' (*Asuka Furusato Ron*) was revived. In 1953 Hoda Yōjurō wrote:

Visiting Asuka is a trip in which you can visit older Japanese sites than by visiting the Tempyō period temples or the *Man'yō-shū* sites. It is a trip to understand the ancient people's creativity by seeing the traditional lifestyle of the people living there today. In Asuka you can find the *Nihon no honyū* (the real Japan) and *genshi* (beginnings [of Japan]).[10]

The significance for later debates is Hoda's emphasis that it is not only the historical, archaeological, or even scenic sites which are of interest. Rather, in the lifestyles of the village people the visitor can find an

ideal form of traditional Japan as it was at the beginning of history. As
Brian Moeran points out, in the increasingly industrial and urban
society of contemporary Japan, 'the countryside, together with all its
values of "tradition", "harmony", "cooperation" and "groupness", is
exoticised by those living in urban surroundings that are hardly
conducive to small group cooperation'.[11]

On 1 January 1966 the Special Action Law for the Preservation of
Historic Environments in Ancient Capitals (*Koto ni okeru Rekishiteki Fūdo
Hozon no tame no Tokubetsu Sochi Hō*) was proclaimed by the national
government. This law called for city planning to include both
preservation areas and special preservation areas. The latter would be
subject to severe restrictions regarding rebuilding, paint and roofing
changes, and the posting of signs or advertisements. The original law
included Kamakura and Kyoto as protected ancient cities, and it was
soon decided that Asuka Mura and Kashiwara City should be added.[12]
This decision began a long debate at the executive, legislative and
administrative levels of the national, prefectural and municipal
governments. The national government, led by the Prime Minister's
Office and the Ministry of Construction, wanted to preserve the area
as a designated historical environment. It saw Asuka as an important
national monument and encouraged a thriving tourist industry with
much input and sponsorship from the private sector. Archaeologists,
represented by the Agency for Cultural Affairs (ACA) and its parent
organisation, the Ministry of Education, were also interested in assuring
the preservation of the area because of its historical value for the
people and for scholarly research. They were not interested in using
Asuka as a symbol, nor did they encourage large-scale tourism.

The people of Asuka Mura generally opposed a special preservation
status. Several village council members owned construction companies
with a stake in development rather than preservation. Furthermore,
villagers not directly involved in the construction industry feared
government restrictions on the use of modern farm equipment and
construction materials to renovate homes. They believed that if Asuka
Mura were given special preservation status, these restrictions would
inevitably be placed on them since the legislation would be aimed not
only at archaeological sites, but at the village itself. Since the national
government wanted to remake the entire area into an image of
traditional rural Japan, villagers were also worried about 'tourist
pollution'. This problem became apparent by 1970 when as many as
3000 people visited the Ishibutai site during a single day during the 26
October weekend. Lines of tourists wound for three kilometres through
the narrow roads.[13]

Vocal debates began in the early 1970s. Two committees, the

Deliberative Council on Historical Environments (*Rekishiteki Fūdo Shingi Kai* or DCHE) which represented the Prime Minister's Office, and the Ministry of Education's Deliberative Council on the Protection of Cultural Properties (*Bunkazai Hogo Shingi Kai* or DCPCP), evaluated the situation during the summer of 1970. The people in the Asuka area made their opinions known through the press and through mediation talks between the Governor of Nara prefecture and the Prime Minister. In December 1970 the cabinet decided, on the basis of the DCHE and DCPCP reports, to implement the 'Measures concerning the conservation of historical landscapes and cultural heritages in the Asuka area' (*Asuka Chihō ni okeru Rekishiteki Fūdo oyobi Bunkazai no Hozon nado ni kansuru Hōsaku ni tsuite* or the 1970 Asuka Area Plan).[14] The cabinet provided 6.9 billion yen to begin the Asuka Preservation Project, which would be overseen by the Ministry of Construction over a three-year period. The project was based on the Law for the Preservation of Cultural Properties, the Ancient Cities Preservation Law, and the City Planning Law, and the government decided not to make a special law for Asuka preservation. The plan called for the expansion of preservation areas, special preservation areas and scenic areas, and for the designation of more historic sites. It also suggested that important sites should be bought and cleaned up if necessary. In addition, the government suggested that improvements should be made in local roads and that a history museum and buildings for research and accommodation should be built and national parks created at Ishibutai, Amakashi no Oka and Iwaido.[15] Finally, the cabinet's plan called for the creation of a preservation corporation (*zaidan*) to organise financial assistance from private companies.[16]

The 1970 Asuka Area Plan tended to follow the suggestions of the DCHE rather than those of the DCPCP. It became clear that control over the administration of cultural properties in the area had shifted from the ACA, which favoured a plan based on preservation, to the Ministry of Construction backed by the Prime Minister's Office, both of which favoured a plan based on tourism. Although many villagers continued to protest against the enlargement of preservation areas, they tended to prefer control by the Ministry of Construction because they realised that this arrangement would provide better subsidies and fewer restrictions. Nara prefecture, which mediated between the villagers and the ministries, agencies and offices of the national government, also preferred management through the Ministry of Construction. The prefecture assumed that these powerful and wealthy bureaucratic arms could provide better subsidies than the ACA, which wielded less power in the national bureaucracy.

The decision by the cabinet to adopt the 1970 Asuka Area Plan was a major turning point, since it established the interests of the Prime Minister's Office and the Ministry of Construction. The government began implementing its plans early in 1971. In March the DCHE decided to increase the size of the Asuka preservation areas. The ACA could not but be pleased with this decision since it meant that valuable sites would be preserved. Nevertheless, it feared that these increases were being made primarily for the sake of the tourist industry. For the time being, the plan satisfied the villagers since they began to receive better funding.[17]

In April 1971 the Kansai economic circles (*zaikai*), specifically the Kansai Economic Federation (*Kansai Keizai Rengōkai* or *Kankeiren*), an organisation of businesses in the Kansai area, and the Federation of Economic Organisations (*Keizai Dantai Rengō Kai* or *Keidanren*), a Japan-wide organisation of businesses that tends to be weighted towards the Kanto area, started the Asuka Preservation Foundation (*Asuka Hozon Zaidan* or 'the Foundation') as a juridical person. The Foundation, which was to be directed by Matsushita Kōnosuke who was a driving force in the business community, was created with 500 million yen provided by the two business groups and a government grant of 59 million yen. The Foundation's purposes were: first, to help conduct projects related to the development of the area's historical, scenic and environmental properties; second, to help build a residence and research centre capable of housing a hundred people, and an information centre opposite the railway station; and third, to help finance land improvement projects and subsidise people who had been obliged to make sacrifices for the sake of scenic preservation.[18] The Foundation was established on 1 April 1971.

During the 1970s visitors flocked to Asuka. The discovery of wall frescos at the Takamatsuzuka tomb in March 1972 and the coverage of the site on the front pages of the major newspapers attracted even more visitors. As Asuka became popular with tourists, the Ministry of Construction continued to develop the area as a tourist site. In March 1973 a tourist office was opened in the town. This was followed by the opening of the Iwaido National Park in July 1974, the Asuka National Historical Museum (*Kokuritsu Asuka Rekishi Shiryōkan*) in March 1975, and the Ishibutai National Park in September 1976. In October of the same year cabinet decided to expand the preservation area of Takamatsuzuka by adding 9.3 hectares of land surrounding the tomb.[19] In 1977 cabinet revised its policy to allow the creation of four national parks within Asuka. The last two parks, Amakashi no Oka and Takamatsuzuka, were opened in April 1980 and October 1985. By 1989, 8 billion yen had been spent on these four parks, which covered a total area of 47.1 hectares. The goal of these parks was to create preservation and recreation facilities for visitors, while preserving the living environment of residents. The funds were used to administer and maintain the parks, to buy land, and to pay compensation money for lack of business to the construction industry.[20]

The problem of Asuka Mura had still not been resolved by the end of the 1970s. Development continued in non-preservation areas near the town. This frustrated many residents, who felt that they had been inadequately compensated for revenue lost due to prohibitions on the development of land. In addition, with the opening of two national parks and a historical museum, not to mention the publicity from Takamatsuzuka, Asuka received more tourists than ever. Villagers felt even more strongly that special legislation was needed to provide funds to compensate them for financial loss and inconvenience. This pressure resulted in the village head of Asuka and the governor of Nara prefecture asking the Prime Minister to reconsider the possibility of special legislation. They argued that Asuka Mura should be a national responsibility since the site was of national importance.[21] The result of this request was a decision by the national government that special legislation was indeed necessary.[22] Consequently, the budget guidelines for 1980 included in the budget of the Prime Minister's Office plans for 3 billion yen to be earmarked for the Asuka Preparatory Fund.[23] The Asuka funding was assured by the passage of the Special Action Law regarding the Preservation of the Historical Environment and the Lifestyle Environment of Asuka Mura (*Asuka Mura ni okeru Rekishiteki Fūdo no Hozon oyobi Seikatsu Kankyō no Junbi nado ni kansuru Tokubetsu Sochi Hō*) on 26 May 1980.[24]

Since the passage of this law, the national government has paid 2.4 billion yen, the prefectural government 600 million yen and the village government 100 million yen into the Asuka Preparatory Fund. In the 1989 fiscal year the annual interest from this fund amounted to 240 million yen. This money will be used to help the village people and residents understand the purpose of the Asuka project, to keep the village clean, to conduct site surveys, to fund the decoration of buildings, to construct building foundations, to support agriculture and forestry, and to develop agricultural roads and irrigation systems. Throughout the 1970s the creation of a national historical park and historical and scenic preservation areas created conflict at various levels of government. Today, Asuka is a well-known tourist spot and people are encouraged to visit the area as a way of learning about the origins of their country and to enjoy the traditional landscape.

Asuka is an example of the use of history by the government. The preservation of the area was negotiated when Japan was once again beginning to search for the country's 'original' cultural identity. As the area where, according to semi-historical but largely legendary accounts (that is, in the *Kojiki* and *Nihon Shoki*) the Japanese state began, Asuka seemed an excellent place to create a 'hometown of the Japanese heart'. Despite opposition from local people, the Japanese government and business elites who formed the Asuka Preservation Foundation had little difficulty in moulding Asuka into a national monument.

Asuka's symbolic value is illustrated in this passage in a pamphlet published by the Asuka Preservation Foundation:

> In various nations there are various histories and traditions rooted in the nation's heart, the people's spirit and the people's character. Asuka is a land which must be called the home of the Japanese people's heart (*Nihon kokumin no kokoro no furusato*). It was here, in the area often housing the capital city during the century between the reigns of Emperor Suiko and Emperor Temmu, that a great reformation took place. It was here that the foundations of the ancient nation of Japan were gradually solidified. And it was here that, with the introduction of Buddhism and other aspects of culture from the Asian continent, the ancient culture of Japan blossomed. In Asuka, where one can touch the ancient palaces and burial mounds, we can truly feel ancient Japanese history. And here, the contemporary environment evokes the historical environment described by the songs of the *Man'yō-shū*. In Asuka we can recall ancient Japan.[25]

Thus, the people are once again linked to the imperial past, despite the efforts of post-war archaeologists to rid ancient history of nationalist ideology. More importantly, ancient history was created outside the discipline of archaeology. The focus of preservation has been based on the need to reconcile the tourist industry with the residents. Archaeologists continue to work in Asuka and valuable research is being carried on through institutes such as the Nara National Cultural Properties Research Institute's Asuka Historical Museum and the Asuka and Fujiwara Palace Site Research Department, as well as the Kashiwara Archaeological Institute. Nevertheless, the image that visitors receive from the tourist industry is largely based on creative fantasy, as an ambience of ancient rural tranquillity is laid over the reality of contemporary Japanese life.

Morishōji Site, Osaka

In contrast to Asuka, the public presentation of the Yayoi-period Morishōji site in Osaka City was carried out almost entirely by archaeologists. In June 1992 the Osaka City Cultural Properties Association (*Osaka Shi Bunkazai Kyōkai*) employed approximately thirty full-time archaeologists who worked in two sections – the Naniwa branch office in central Osaka, and the Nagahara branch office in the southern part of the city. The mandate of the Association is to excavate prehistoric and historic sites threatened by destruction due to construction projects initiated by either public or private developers. Association members consider public education about Osaka's past to be an important part of their job.

Soon after my arrival in Osaka in June 1992 I was told that one of the Association's archaeologists would give a talk entitled 'Osaka during the Yayoi period and the Morishōji site'. This talk was for elementary school children and members of the local historical society but was open to the general public. On Friday afternoon therefore, I set off to attend the presentation. Emerging from the subway I found myself in the dense urban environment characteristic of most of Osaka. Cars, buses and trucks barrelled past on a four-lane thoroughfare. To my left stood a soba shop and, to my right, a 7-Eleven convenience store. I was reminded of a comment made a professor of archaeology at Osaka University – that people are interested in local sites because all neighbourhoods have similar houses, stations, restaurants and people. There are no local characteristics, so a site can give an area a local flavour.[26] I walked through side-streets and alleys toward the Asahi ward (town) hall. The spacious second-floor auditorium was filled with about 350 chattering sixth-graders and perhaps fifty elderly men and women. The aim of the talk was to introduce the audience to the archaeology of their neighbourhood during the Yayoi period (300 BC–AD 300). To do this, the archaeologist described results from the Association's excavation of the local Morishōji site, a village of about 2000 people which had been inhabited during the Yayoi period.

First the archaeologist discussed excavation, stressing the idea that 'Japanese history is in the earth'. He described site stratigraphy using slides to demonstrate how the colour and texture of the soil changes throughout the site. He pointed out that artefacts in the lower levels are usually older than those above. He also showed slides of features and artefacts found through excavation, such as the large, dark circles of earth which represent refilled pit houses, or small middens that contain deer and boar bones. Secondly, he introduced the idea that one goal of archaeology is to understand the lifestyle of the people who once inhabited Japan. He showed photographs of Yayoi pit houses reconstructed by archaeologists. He mentioned that domesticated pigs have recently been identified in Yayoi Japan and that the boar bones found at Morishōji may also be pig. While showing a slide of a house floor with excavated pits, he pointed out that 'during the Yayoi period people dumped their garbage on the site, but they were clean. They only threw their raw garbage into certain pits. They had a clean lifestyle (*kirei na seikatsu*)'. This comment is interesting in light of the importance given by modern Japanese to cleanliness in their homes and neighbourhoods.

The third theme was connections between Morishōji and Yamatai – the 'country' ruled by a Queen Himiko reported by Chinese historians in the *Wei Zhi*, or Record of Wei, completed in AD 297. This document records a visit by Chinese travellers to a land which they named 'Wa'. Chinese accounts discuss the political organisation of Wa as comprising 'more than one hundred communities'. One community named 'Yamatai' was said to be ruled over by a female leader named 'Himiko', who had 'one thousand women as attendants but only one man. He served her food and drink and acted as a medium of communication. She resided in a palace surrounded by towers and stockades, with armed guards in a state of constant vigilance'. In addition to these tantalising details, we are told that Himiko sent tribute to the emperor of China and, in return, received many gifts including 'two swords five feet long, one hundred bronze mirrors, and fifty catties each of jade and of red beads'. When she died Himiko was buried in 'a great mound ... more than a hundred paces in diameter'.[27]

Japanese scholars have spent decades debating the location and significance of Yamatai. Himiko was probably a real person who lived during the Yayoi period. We know from excavations that the political organisation of Japan at this time must have been that of chiefdoms – a situation which could well have resembled that described in the *Wei Zhi* as numerous small countries. Yayoi sites do yield bronze mirrors from China and, by the end of the period, leaders were buried in large burial mounds.

In recent years the debate has taken hold of the public imagination. In 1989 the excavation of the Yoshinogari site in Kyushu opened up new speculation. The spectacular Yayoi village site of Yoshinogari was surrounded by a moat and seems to have had multi-storey buildings which resemble those seen in Yamatai by the third-century Chinese visitors. The way this discovery has been handled by the media and archaeologists is another story. The Association's archaeologist linked the Morishōji site with Yoshinogari and Yamatai as a way of generating audience interest. Archaeologists often criticise the media for making such naive connections, but the more I saw of the public presentation by archaeologists themselves, the more I became convinced that they have a part in publicising archaeology in this way. Furthermore, through this third theme, the archaeologist moved the audience from the local level and linked the Morishōji site with questions of Japanese national identity.

Before leaving, students were reminded by a vivacious public servant that they and their families should visit the exhibition of Yayoi pottery-making, house-building and cooking, to be mounted in a local park by Association archaeologists over the weekend. At this exhibition they might touch the pit houses with their hands. The young woman's final comment – 'go to the library, go to the site, take care of the flowers and your neighbourhood' – shows the degree to which archaeological work is tied to pride in local community identity. Encouraged by these comments, I visited the park the following Sunday afternoon.

Iris Festival

Yayoi exhibit

The festival at which the Yayoi exhibition was featured was in honour of the blooming irises. These festivals draw together people from neighbourhoods to celebrate the passing seasons and give them a sense of community. While the primary goal of the festival was to view the irises, Asahi ward officials wanted to use the festival to commemorate the ward's sixtieth anniversary. To do this they planned an event to help residents learn about the history of the ward – an archaeological exhibition featuring the Yayoi-period Morishōji site. As a North American, I noted this 'natural' connection between archaeology and history. In Canada and the United States where archaeology is firmly embedded in the discipline of anthropology, this connection is rarely made.

The park was large, perhaps a kilometre long. In the middle was a pond with a super-highway running over one end. Under the highway, vendors were selling *yakitori* and other festival foods. I walked beneath the super-highway and part of the way around the pond to the Yayoi exhibition. Association archaeologists had set up a small booth. On the back wall were photographs of local Yayoi-period site excavations and artefacts. Lying on a table were a stone axe and adze both hafted with wooden handles; two young boys were examining them. In front of the booth was a large wooden mortar which contained a few grains of rice which children and adults were invited to pound with a long, stone pestle. Children and their parents crowded around the booth looking at the photographs, pounding on the rice and watching an older man – an Association employee – demonstrate a wooden implement which made fire. Near the booth was a table where female volunteers and one of the part-time female excavators (*hojoin*) had set out small sheets of tinfoil on which lay tiny piles of pink-coloured, unpolished rice. Apparently this rice was cooked 'in the traditional Yayoi style'. Visitors were reminded that, according to the third-century Chinese accounts, the Yayoi people did not have chopsticks but ate with their fingers; visitors were asked to also use their fingers.

The Association's archaeologist was standing in the reconstructed frame of a Yayoi-period pit house. He was tending a small but very smoky fire in which stood two medium-sized, earthenware pots, replicas of Yayoi pottery, filled with cooked rice and potatoes. He explained to the visitors (several middle-aged women and two boys), that Yayoi people used to cook their food this way. Over the hill and near the river a professional potter, who makes replicas of Yayoi pottery in his spare time, was supervising a huge bonfire. I noticed pottery buried among the ashes and burnt stumps of wood. The potter told me that these replicas were made by school children to whom he teaches pottery-making. He had been making Yayoi-style pottery for about thirty years. He enjoys experimenting with various methods and working out for himself how to replicate prehistoric materials, forms and decoration, although he has little formal knowledge of archaeological methods or results.

Gradually the rain began; a little at first and then a downpour. We stood under a tarpaulin looking at the bonfire. It was big enough and wouldn't go out within the next hour. The Yayoi pottery replicas would be sufficiently fired by then. I headed back to the reconstructed pit house. Before leaving the park I visited a small pond filled with hundreds of blooming irises – the *raison d'être* for the festival. Japanese visitors walked slowly around the pond under umbrellas, taking photos of the blooms.

The themes of the public lecture and the Morishōji exhibition are worth considering in detail. Perhaps the theme most common to public archaeological exhibits is the replication of the lifestyle of the prehistoric Japanese. The Association's exhibition was no exception. Archaeologists were trying to present local residents in 1992 with an image of the kinds of tools used by the Yayoi people who had lived in this area over 2000 years ago, the kinds of houses they had lived in, and the sorts of food they ate. Although the archaeologists themselves know that they are offering speculations, this does not come across in the exhibition. Volunteers are rarely conscious of the leap of faith they make when attributing a 'reality' to their replication of Yayoi life. The presentation of the Morishōji site to the public illustrates the degree to which archaeologists help municipal officials create a local identity for urban Japanese. Over the past two decades Japanese municipal planners and developers have been trying to draw residents to their neighbourhoods. One device is to use archaeological parks, museums and exhibitions to create a sense of local identity. They no longer emphasise their communities' industrial development as they would have thirty years ago. Rather, local governments and businesses stress the historical sites and cultural properties.

Archaeology does, therefore, provide a concrete symbol of the history of the local area. Archaeologists, interested in promoting their work, are willing to introduce the public to the basic principles of archaeology. They do so, however, within the constraints of unconscious assumptions. First, they assume direct historical continuity between the culture of the Yayoi people and the present-day Japanese. Secondly, they assume that they understand something of the past 'lifestyles' of the Yayoi people. In some cases, present cultural patterns which are considered distinctively or even uniquely Japanese are 'discovered' in the past, verifying that these prehistoric people must indeed have been Japanese. An example of this is the cleanliness of the Yayoi pit houses which was assumed to represent a notion of cleanliness which is inherently Japanese. Finally, they assume that they can generate public interest by tying local sites to more famous national sites. In the case of Morishōji, the Association's archaeologist made his site more interesting in the eyes of the general public by encouraging speculation about the relationship between Morishōji, Yoshinogari and Yamatai.

Conclusion

In contemporary Japan archaeological sites and artefacts help create a sense of identity. Archaeology provides a means of understanding the past. Professional archaeologists and members of the general public often assume that the exercise of discerning evidence for specific cultural traits currently considered distinctively or even uniquely Japanese will help the people understand who they are – that is, will help them form a cultural identity.

This creation of identity can occur at the local or the national level. In the example of the Morishōji site, the public lecture and Yayoi-lifestyle reconstruction were both organised by local authorities who wanted to make people in the Asahi ward aware of the history of their neighbourhood. Archaeologists describing the site to the public, however, tended to emphasise the qualities which made it a source of knowledge about the ancestors of the Japanese people in general, rather than the residents of Osaka in particular. The presentation of the Morishōji site can be seen as strengthening notions of homogeneity and the unbroken line of descent of the people and their culture from prehistoric times.

Asuka Mura creates a sense of national identity in a quite different way. The site was moved into the spotlight of national attention by the national government at a time when there was an efflorescence of interest in things Japanese. This phenomenon has been called *Nihonjinron*.[28] Harumi Befu defines *Nihonjinron* (which he calls *Nihonron*) as a literature that 'purports to demonstrate the uniqueness of Japanese culture, society and national character'.[29] It defines Japan's uniqueness in terms of qualities such as harmony, cooperation, vertical social structure, and an emphasis on intuition and non-verbal communication; all characteristics which, supposedly, are found only in Japan.

Ross Mouer and Sugimoto Yoshio use *Nihonjinron* to refer to an extensive literature describing and propagating 'popular stereotyped images of Japanese society' which has mushroomed in Japan and abroad over the past few years.[30] They argue that the increased discussion of, and belief in, these stereotyped images, particularly in the notion that Japanese society is organised exclusively in terms of a consensus or group model, are a response to Japan's increased interaction with Western nations. They point out, furthermore, that this view of Japanese society as an integrated whole tends to serve the interests of elites rather than those of the ordinary people, because it bolsters the notion that the people should cooperate with established authorities (be they business or government) for their own good, as well as the good of Japan.

The *Nihonjinron* phenomenon is related to the international context of Japan; it is an ideology that seeks to define a distinctive Japanese identity in response to a century-long influx of Western ideas and material culture. This identity binds the people in a cohesive and consensus society led by business and political elites. *Nihonjinron* has nothing to do with the reality of past or present Japanese society. It is an ideal, an ideology, and a new form of nationalism. Japanese nationalism of the late twentieth century has symbolic content quite different from that of the pre-war period. Nevertheless, as in pre-war Japan, this new nationalism works to create a sense of solidarity and what it means to be Japanese. Ancient history has been used to create a sense of identity.

It was during the late 1960s and early 1970s that the national government, joined by the Nara prefectural government and the Japanese business elite, began to use the Asuka site as an explicit symbol of Japan. It is interesting that they chose Asuka since, in many ways, the period of history it represents demonstrates the enormous amount of cultural borrowing over the past two millennia. The Takamatsuzuka tomb, for example, suggests that Japan was in close contact with continental nations and was heavily influenced by continental ideas (if not continental immigrants). Nevertheless, the reading of the past which visitors absorb at Asuka focuses on the depth and continuity of the unique Japanese culture which was created there.

Knowledge of the archaeological record has increased rapidly. Archaeologists, furthermore, have become more and more involved in presenting their findings to the public. Today, sites are presented in the mass media, at open days and in museums as examples of local and national heritage. The stress which archaeologists place on reconstructing lifestyles of the 'Yayoi people' or the 'Jōmon people' tends to result in the assumption that, during prehistoric times, the people were more similar than different and that they were quite distinctive from other people around the world. In this way archaeology tends to strengthen notions of cultural uniqueness and homogeneity.

Notes

1 P. Gathercole and D. Lowenthal (eds), *The Politics of the Past*, London, Unwin Hyman, 1990; B. G. Trigger, *A History of Archaeological Thought*, Cambridge University Press, 1989; H. Tsude, 'Nihon kōkogaku to shakai' (Japanese archaeology and society), in Tanaku Migaku (ed), *Iwanami Kōza Nihon Kōkogaku 7: Gendai to Kōkogaku*, Tokyo, Iwanami, 1986, pp. 31–70.

2 Niiro Izumi, 'Jānarizumu to kōkogaku' (Journalism and archaeology), in Tanaku Migaku (ed), *Iwanami Kōza Nihon Kōkogaku 7*, pp. 109–232.

3 H. Yamaguchi, '*Shimbun no Kōkogaku Hōdō ni Kansuru Naiyō Bunseki*' (A content analysis of archaeological reports in newspapers), BA thesis, Department of Archaeology and Ethnology, Faculty of Letters, Keio University, January 1985.

4 C. Fawcett and J. Habu, 'Education and archaeology in Japan', in P. Stone and R. MacKenzie (eds), *The Excluded Past: Archaeology in Education*, London, Unwin Hyman, 1990, pp. 217–30 at pp. 217–27.

5 Niiro, 'Jānarizumu to kōkogaku', p. 220.

6 Asuka Historical Museum, *Guide to the Asuka Historical Museum*, W. Carter (trans.), Nara National Properties Research Institute, Nara, Japan, Asuka Historical Museum, Nara prefecture, 1978, p. 4; J. E. Kidder, 'Asuka and the Takamatsuzuka tomb', *Archaeology*, vol. 26, no. 1, 1973, pp. 24–31.

7 G. L. Barnes, 'Protohistoric Yamato: archaeology of the first Japanese state', *Michigan Papers in Japanese Studies*, University of Michigan Center for Japanese Studies, Ann Arbor, no. 17, 1988, pp. 24–5.

8 Asuka Historical Museum, *Guide*, p. 20.

9 Kadowaki Teiji, 'Asuka kan no hensen' (Changing views of Asuka), *Asuka Kodai to Gendai*, Nara Bunkazai Hozon Renraku Kai and the Kansai Bunkazai Hozon Kyōgikai (ed. and pub.), 1971, pp. 44–52.

10 Ibid.

11 B. Moeran, *Language and Popular Culture in Japan*, Manchester University Press, 1989, p. 181.

12 Asuka Kokudo Kōen Shutchōjo, *Kokudo Asuka Rekishi Kōen Jigyō Gaiyō* (National Asuka Historical Park Work Synopsis), Kinki Chihō Kensetsu Kyoku Asuka Kokudo Kōen Shutchōjo, Nara prefecture, 1989, p. 1.

13 *Asahi Shimbun*, 1 November 1970.

14 Asuka Kokudo Kōen Shutchōjo, *Kokudo Asuka Rekishi Kōen Jigyō Gaiyō*, p. 1; Parks and Recreation Foundation, Japan, *Outline of Parks and Recreation Foundation and Five National Government Parks*, Parks and Recreation Foundation of Japan, Tokyo, n.d., p. 17.

15 M. Iseki, 'Asuka hozon mondai no haikei to mondaiten' (Background and problems of the Asuka preservation problem), in Bunkazai Hozon Zenkoku Kyōgikai (ed.), *Bunkaisan no Kiki to Hozon Undō*, Tokyo, Aoki Shoten, 1971, pp. 147–55 at p. 155.

16 *Asahi Shimbun*, 19 September 1970; Nara prefecture, 'Asuka Mura Tokubetsu Sochi Hō Gaiyō' (Synopsis of the Special Action Law of Asuka Mura), *Asuka Mura ni okeru Rekishiteki Fūdo no Hozon ni kansuru Tokubetsu Sochi Hō Kankei Hōrei Shū*, Nara prefecture (ed. and pub.), Nara, 1981, p. 5.

17 *Asahi Shimbun*, 12 and 22 March 1971.

18 *Asahi Shimbun*, 2 April 1971; T. Kubo, 'Dai 2 bunkakai: gendai no ideorogi – Jōkyō to bunkazai hozon' (The second section: contemporary ideology – the current situation of cultural properties preservation), *Bunkazai o Mamoru Tameni 8*, Bunkazai Hozon Zenkoku Kyōgikai (ed. and pub.), Tokyo, 1973, pp. 9–13; R. Okuda, 'Asuka Kokyō no hozon' (The preservation of the Asuka ancient capital), *Asuka: Tokubetsu Rippō no Ayumi*, Nara Prefectural Government (ed. and pub.), Nara, 1981, pp. 4–8.

19 Nara Ken, *Asuka: Tokubetsu Rippō e no Ayumi* (Asuka: The Path to Special Legislation), Nara prefecture, 1981, p. 19.

20 Okuda, 'Asuka Kokyō no hozon'.

21 Asuka Shutchōjo, *Kokudo Asuka Rekishi Kōen Jigyō Gaiyō*, p. 2.

22 Ibid., p. 8.

23 Okuda, 'Asuka Kokyō no hozon'.

24 Nara prefecture, 'Asuka Mura tokubetsu sochi hō gaiyō', pp. 65–70.

25 Asuka Hozon Zaidan, 'Tobu tori no Asuka' (Asuka of the flying bird), *Asuka: Hozon 10 Nen no Ayumi* (Pamphlet of the Asuka Hozon Zaidan), nos. 1–2, Nara prefecture, 1981, p. 1.

26 Tsude Hiroshi, personal communication, 6 June 1992.

27 R. Tsunoda and L. C. Goodrich, *Japan in the Chinese Dynastic Histories*, South Pasadena, California, PD and Ione Perkins, 1951.

28 R. Mouer and Sugimoto Y., *Images of Japanese Society: A Study in the Structure of Social Reality*, London, Kegan Paul International, 1986, p. xx.

29 H. Befu, 'Civilization and culture: Japan in search of identity', in T. Umesao, H. Befu and J. Kreiner (eds), *Japanese Civilization in the Modern World: Life and Society*, Senri Ethnological Series 16, National Museum of Ethnology, Osaka, 1984, pp. 59–75 at p. 66.

30 Mouer and Sugimoto, *Images of Japanese Society*.

PART TWO

Centre and Periphery

CHAPTER FIVE

A Descent into the Past: The Frontier in the Construction of Japanese Identity

TESSA MORRIS-SUZUKI

'TimeSpace' and Japanese History

In an article published a few years ago, Immanuel Wallerstein wrote of the need to reconsider our notions of 'TimeSpace' in history. 'TimeSpace' is, I feel, a rather uncomfortable word: the language of a social scientist trying to borrow physicist's clothes. But the point which Wallerstein's article made was an important one. His argument was that the way in which we carve up time for the purposes of study is inseparably connected to the way in which we carve up space. Our conventional divisions of time and space, Wallerstein suggested, can no longer be regarded as given and absolute, but need to be opened up to critical examination. It is necessary to 'start down a very difficult, very unsettling road of questioning one of the bedrocks of our intelligence, our certainties about space and time. At the end of the road lies not simplicity but complexity. But our geohistorical social systems are complex; indeed, they are the most complex structures in the universe. ... '[1]

Wallerstein's comments fly in the face of our commonsense perception of things. In the humanities and social sciences (unlike the abstruse world of advanced physics) time and space seem at first glance to be clearly distinct dimensions of reality. Time, to put it crudely, is the realm of the historian; space the realm of the geographer. But a little reflection shows that matters are not as simple as this. In the everyday language of modern society we are forever projecting contemporary spatial divisions back upon time – perceiving 'our' past in terms of national or cultural entities which had no reality before the nineteenth or twentieth century. On the other hand, we also constantly and unconsciously impose temporal notions upon present geography, describing exotic societies as 'ancient', 'primitive', 'mediaeval', 'stone-age'. This blurring of the notions of time and space is particularly evident in the language of ethnic or national identity. When we confront the unfamiliar, we may deal with it in either of two ways: by defining it as spatially different – 'foreign'; or by defining it as temporally different – 'backward', 'undeveloped', 'primitive', a projection of the past into the present. Our decision whether to consign difference to the dimension of space or the dimension of time has profound implications for the way in which we see the whole world.

This chapter is an exploration of some notions of Japanese identity in terms of concepts of space and time. Its starting point is the question of Japan's frontiers. The modern Japanese nation state, quite clearly, is an artificial construct whose boundaries were drawn in the second half of the nineteenth century. These boundaries enclosed within the nation state a wide range of groups with different dialects, lifestyles and beliefs. A particularly problematic relationship existed between the state and the frontier communities ('frontier', that is, from the metropolitan Japanese perspective), who had traditionally had only tenuous connections with the centres of Japanese power. Of these communities, the most important were the Okinawan inhabitants of the Ryūkyū archipelago to the south and the Ainu inhabitants of Hokkaido, Southern Sakhalin and the Kurile Islands to the north. The story which this chapter tells is one of a gradual shift in the images which Japanese officials and intellectuals mobilised in their efforts to define and tame the frontier: a shift, above all, from images of spatial difference to images of temporal difference. By looking at this shift we can, I think, explore quite important changes in the categories which have been used to represent 'Japaneseness' and to locate Japan's place in the world order. At the same time, we can also raise some wider questions about the way in which the relationship between large, state-organised societies and small, non-state societies is conceived in other parts of the world.

The Changing Shape of the World

At the beginning of the eighteenth century the world, seen from the vantage point of Japan, was still infinite. For most ordinary people, the known world stretched as far as the nearest range of mountains or the nearest castle-town, and then blurred into the realms of hearsay and travellers' tales. As far as they were concerned, the concept 'Japan' would have had little meaning or importance. The term *kuni* (country) referred primarily to the local domain or region, and people from distant parts of Japan were strangers whose curious customs were liable to provoke laughter.[2] But among the substantial stratum of literati (mostly urban, but also including some well-to-do farmers), Japan's contacts with the outside world in the sixteenth and early seventeenth centuries had stimulated an intense interest in Japan's place in the wider world – an interest which survived the tight restrictions on foreign contact imposed from the 1630s onwards.

The prevailing image of the world from this perspective was a mental map borrowed from China, according to which the known, settled, orderly centre (*ka*) was surrounded by boundless circles of increasing strangeness, disorder and barbarism (*i*). This *ka-i* vision of the world is nicely illustrated by the widely-sold *Japanese–Chinese Illustrated Encyclopaedia* (*Wakan sansai zue*) of 1712, which combined information from the Ming Dynasty Chinese *Illustrated Encyclopaedia* with information gathered by Japanese scholars from various sources. In the *Japanese–Chinese Illustrated Encyclopaedia* the world outside Japan is divided in two. Immediately surrounding Japan are the 'foreign countries' (*ikoku*) – including China, Korea, the Ryūkyū kingdom, Ezo (the Land of the Ainu), Tongking and Cochin – whose inhabitants write with Chinese characters and eat with chopsticks. Beyond that lie the realms of the 'outer barbarians' (*gai-i*), who write horizontally and eat with their hands.[3] The *gai-i* include a number of readily recognisable societies such as Siam, Luzon, Java, Bengal and Holland, as well as other less familiar places like the Land of Bird People and the Land of Creatures with Six Legs and Four Wings.

In this order of things, it is interesting that both the Ainu and the Ryūkyūans, who were later to be enfolded into the Japanese state, are clearly defined as foreign. Indeed, in the official rhetoric of Tokugawa Japan up to the end of the eighteenth century we can observe a deliberate effort to maintain the boundaries which separated the frontier societies from 'Japan proper'. These policies were part of an important reordering of the *ka-i* system in the official thinking of the period: a conscious effort to define Japan itself, rather than China, as *ka* – the centre of the world.[4] To claim a place at the centre of things it was necessary for Japan, like China before it, to receive tribute from the 'barbarians' on its periphery. The invasion of the Ryūkyū kingdom by the southern Japanese domain of Satsuma in 1609 had established a tributary relationship between the Ryūkyūs on the one hand and both Satsuma and the Japanese shogunate on the other. In the north, meanwhile, the domain of Matsumae had been granted a monopoly of trade with the Ainu, and the ritual exchange of goods between prominent Ainu and the lord of Matsumae was interpreted from the Japanese side as the payment of tribute (although it was interpreted in a quite different light by the Ainu themselves). The whole symbolic significance of these tribute payments rested on the fact that they could be seen as representing the submission of foreign peoples to Japanese power.[5] So every opportunity was taken to ensure that the ritual of the tribute mission emphasised the exotic appearance of the Ryūkyūan and Ainu emissaries – the Ryūkyūans with their brocade robes, strange headgear and Chinese weaponry; the Ainu with their fur robes, earrings and flowing beards.

It was characteristic of the *ka-i* system that this difference was symbolised, above all, in appearance and etiquette: hairstyles and clothing, footwear and tattoos, diet and housing, festivals and ceremonies were the parameters which defined the foreign, and which were repeatedly described in the wonderful travellers' tales brought back by venturous Japanese from the Ryūkyūs and the Land of the Ainu.[6] The maintenance of difference, therefore, was primarily a matter of controlling dress and manners. So Matsumae prohibited Ainu from wearing straw raincoats and straw sandals (the common dress of Japanese farmers) as well as from learning the Japanese language, while the Ryūkyūan emissaries to Japan in 1709 were instructed to carry equipment 'of the sort used in a foreign court, so that they cannot be mistaken for Japanese'.[7]

In the course of the eighteenth century, however, the foundations of the *ka-i* order began to be challenged by a profoundly different vision: a vision conveyed through the new iconography of western maps of the world. The first world maps had been brought to Japan by Spanish and Portuguese missionaries in the decades immediately before the establishment of the Tokugawa shogunate. Initially, however, they seem to have been admired for their decorative rather than for their scientific qualities. Western maps were lovingly copied on to ornamental screens, just as an artist might paint a map of the stars on to a ceiling, not to convey a lesson in astronomy but to impart a particular ambience to the decoration of a room.[8] It was only in the early eighteenth century that geographical texts, like those of the scholar and official, Arai Hakuseki, began to draw on western sources, and not until the end of the century that Japan's place in the world began to be interpreted in terms of the new western-inspired cosmology.

The shift in perspective which this required can be appreciated if we look at a volume like the *Illustrated Overview of the Countries of the World* (*Bankoku ichiran zūsetsu*), published in 1810. Here the world has become finite – a charted, measured globe depicted on the final pages enclosed within a geometric network of latitude and longitude. This world, the author explains, contains five Great Regions (*taishū*) called Asia, Europe, Africa, North America and South America[9] and each

Great Region again is divided into clearly bounded states whose place can be defined in a universal mathematics of degrees, minutes and compass directions. It is true that the identity of some of these states remains mysterious: the description of Japan (*Dai-Nihon*) is followed by speculation about the possible existence of a country named Fusaokoku, somewhere to the east in the Pacific, which in turn is followed by a rather detailed description of another neighbouring country, Hachijōjima.[10] (This would probably come as a surprise to most modern Japanese, for whom Hachijōjima, best known as a holiday resort island, is very much part of Japan.) Nevertheless, it is clear that, with the help of European ideas imported through the Dutch, the Japanese sense of space was undergoing a Copernican revolution. The clearest representation of the newly emerging vision was the adoption of the western cartographic convention in which the terrestrial surface of the globe is parcelled out between nation states, each of which is defined by an unequivocal boundary, and coloured with its own uniform colour.

Significantly, although the *Illustrated Overview*'s list of Asian countries includes the Ryūkyū kingdom, as well as China, Korea, Taiwan, and other countries, Ezo (the Land of the Ainu) has now disappeared from the map, for the encounter with the modern European sense of nationhood was a matter of practical politics as well as scholarship. To the north, the Russian empire had extended its boundaries into Kamchatka by the beginning of the eighteenth century, and by the 1730s was reaching even into the northern Kurile Islands, everywhere imposing a policy of Russification which involved converting the indigenous populations to Orthodox Christianity, endowing them with Russian names and dressing them in Russian dress.[11] In response, the Japanese shogunate felt obliged to assert its claim to control over the Ainu by a policy of Japanisation. About the turn of the nineteenth century, the economic and political rights of Matsumae Domain over Ainu territory were transferred to the shogunate, and a series of measures were introduced to 'turn the Ainu into Japanese'.[12]

The phrase itself (which recurs in the official writings of the period) is significant. 'Japaneseness', clearly, was not a matter of race or inheritance, but something which could be acquired by the adoption of the 'right' customs. Just as difference had been symbolised mainly by outer appearance and etiquette, so now Japanisation was enforced by requiring Ainu to shave their beards, cut their hair in the style of Japanese farmers, wear straw sandals and raincoats, eat rice and (more occasionally) learn the Japanese language. These measures were enforced by a combination of metaphorical carrots and literal sticks: compliant Ainu were treated to feasts and sometimes awarded medals to celebrate their 'change of customs' (*kaizoku*);[13] the obstinate were reduced to submission by physical force. In practice, however, resistance was widespread and the shogunate lacked the means to achieve anything more than a very patchy and superficial destruction of Ainu tradition.

Civilisation, Race and the Frontier

A thorough-going political acceptance of the new, western-inspired view of the world came only after the middle of the nineteenth century. In response to growing foreign pressure, the Japanese government redefined the nation's boundaries, in 1869 incorporating the Land of the Ainu under the new name of Hokkaido, and ten years later unilaterally declaring its control over the old Ryūkyū kingdom (which was now to be designated Okinawa prefecture). Having drawn a line around the limits of the nation, the new Meiji government then embarked on the task of turning the people of the frontier into Japanese citizens.

The ideas which inspired this new phase of assimilation, however, were very different from those which had inspired the Japanisation policies of the shogunate. The concept of civilisation behind this new *mission civilatrice* was no longer the concept of *ka*, with its emphasis on order, stability and etiquette, but rather a concept strongly influenced by nineteenth-century European thinkers like the French historian François Guizot, whose work inspired the great Meiji westerniser, Fukuzawa Yukichi. According to Guizot, civilisation meant 'the fact of progress and of development; it at once evokes the idea of a people on the move, not in order to change place, but in order to change their way of life: a people whose condition expands and improves'.[14] This modern version of civilisation – translated into Japanese by the neologism *bunmei* – was dynamic, where the concept of *ka* had been static, and was defined less in terms of correct behaviour than in terms of material wealth and power.

The logic of *bunmei* therefore required that the Japanisation policies imposed upon Ainu and Okinawans from the late nineteenth century should dig deep into the structures of everyday life. Now it was not only dress, hairstyles and language that were required to change, but the whole material basis of life. In Hokkaido, the Ainu were deprived of the land which they had hunted and fished and the river banks where they had grown small crops of millet and vegetables. These were replaced by plots of infertile farm land where they were supposed to conform to the Meiji image of the Japanese commoner by becoming peasant farmers. In Okinawa the traditional communal system of land ownership was abolished in 1899, and repeated efforts were made to inculcate the progressive, industrious spirit which was seen as a hallmark of the modern Japan.[15]

The western idea of 'civilisation', however, was deeply entangled with another, and more problematic idea: the concept of race. Nineteenth-century European nationalism, by and large, envisaged the nation state as founded upon the blood bonds of common ancestry (the very word 'nation' is, after all, derived from the Latin word for 'birth'). It also, in many cases, attempted to explain power relations between nations in terms of the evolutionary struggle between races. *Jinshu* – the modern Japanese word for race – begins to appear in the last decades of the Tokugawa period, although at that stage it was often used in a rather haphazard way. For example, the 1853 *Account of the Countries and Ocean Routes of the World* (*Bankoku kairō no ki*) tells the reader that New Holland (that is, Australia) is so called because it has recently been developed by 'the Dutch race' (*oranda jinshu*).[16] (At this time, of course, Japan was still obtaining most of its knowledge of the outside world from the Dutch.) But once again it was the great westeriser, Fukuzawa Yukichi, who helped to introduce the systematic notion of racial classification into Japanese thought. His *Account of the Countries of the World* (*Sekai kunizukushi*), published in 1869 and intended as a geography textbook, introduces the reader to a neatly colour-coded vision of the world. The population of the globe is divided into five races (Fukuzawa uses both the words *jinshu* and *hitotane*, the second being an alternative reading of the same Japanese characters): Europeans are white, Asians 'slightly yellow', Africans black, the people of the Pacific Islands brown and the inhabitants of 'the mountains of America' red.[17] Fukuzawa's account of Asia, incidentally, is accompanied by an illustration of 'a Chinese servant of the Asian race' which is a perfect replica of nineteenth-century western orientalist iconography.

Japan, of course, embarked on its policy of westernisation at a time when rather crude theories of racial evolution were at their most influential. It was not surprising, then, that questions of race became part of the polemics of modern nation-building. Early Japanese archaeologists and anthropologists argued passionately over the racial origins of the Japanese and their relationship to Okinawans, Ainu, Koreans, Chinese, South-east Asians and even sometimes to Sumerians, Greeks and Jews.[18] The Ainu–Japanese relationship was particularly fiercely debated, with some (like the pioneering ethnographer, Tsuboi Shōgorō, 1863–1913) arguing for separate racial origins; others, including Tsuboi's former student, Torii Ryūzō (1870–1953), argued that the Ainu were the indigenous inhabitants of Japan, while the majority Japanese (*wajin*) were descendants both of Ainu and of more recent migrants to the archipelago.[19] All of this, of course, was accompanied by the same rituals of skull-measuring and bone-collecting which characterised European and American ethnography of the same period.[20]

For many Japanese intellectuals, though, nineteenth-century western racial theories were profoundly disturbing – understandably so, since these theories were, by and large, constructed in such as way as to justify notions of European superiority. The nationalistic philosopher and journalist, Miyake Setsurei (1860–1945), in a popular work published in 1891, observed that the widely accepted theory which identified large skulls and domed foreheads as marks of the more intelligent races would imply that the Ainu were more intelligent than the Japanese, a proposition which he clearly considered too absurd to deserve further discussion.[21] Racial theorising presented other problems. In Europe, where colonial empires were mostly imposed upon distant peoples with visibly different physical characteristics, ideas about racial evolution resonated comfortably with political expediency. But it was a very different matter in Japan, whose emerging empire was imposed upon neighbouring countries with whom the Japanese had obvious physical affinities.

This probably helps to explain why, from the Late Meiji period onward, rhetoric about *jinshu* (race) tends to be overshadowed by rhetoric about *minzoku*. *Minzoku* is a word whose most apt translation is the German word *Volk*. Like *Volk*, *minzoku* has powerful overtones of communal solidarity, but is equivocal about the basis of that solidarity. While race is clearly based on inherited physical characteristics, a *minzoku* may be held together by blood bonds, nationality, culture or some combination of these things. Probably the earliest use of the word *minzoku* appears in the works of certain members of the Meiji-period Popular Rights movement, who used the word in a quite different sense, as a translation of the French *Nationale* in the expression *Assemblée Nationale*.[22] By the beginning of the 1890s it was being more widely used by writers such as Miyake Setsurei and the nationalist and geographer, Shiga Shigetaka, but its meaning remained ill-defined and it was not clearly distinguishable from other parallel terms such as *jinshu* and *kokumin* (citizens).[23] By the following decade, however, the word was acquiring a clearer focus. Haga Yaichi's *Ten Theses on National Character* (*Kokuminsei jūron*) of 1908, for example, begins by explaining that each *minzoku* is distinguished not only by the colour of hair and skin, but also by its 'ethnic qualities' (*minzokuteki seishitsu*), which emerge from language, customs, history, political structure, interaction with other peoples, etc.[24] Haga then goes on to describe the 'ethnic qualities' or national characteristics of the Japanese, among which he includes traits such as patriotism, practicality and an appreciation of nature.

Eleven years later the historian, Kita Sadakichi (1871–1939), launching his new journal *Minzoku to rekishi* (*Minzoku and history*) observed a recent upsurge of interest in the nature and origins of the *Yamato minzoku* ('Yamato' being a poetic term for Japan which, in the early twentieth century, had strong nationalist overtones). Kita's journal itself, together with the journal *Minzoku*, published from 1925 under the auspices of the famous ethnographer, Yanagita Kunio (1875–1962), indicates a growing urge to pin down the character and substance of the ethnic community. The rising tide of debate on *minzoku* can be related in part to two key events which occurred in the shadow of the First World War: the signing of the Treaty of Versailles, with its emphasis on the notion of national self-determination, and the 1919 Mansei Rebellion against the nine years of Japanese colonial oppression in Korea. But the articles in *Minzoku to rekishi* also illustrate the deep complexities and ambiguities of the *minzoku* debate.

Kita's historical studies emphasised, not racial purity, but rather the diversity of Japan's origins. Over the course of time, Ainu, Koreans, Chinese and others had been assimilated and blended into the community of the Japanese people.[25] The diversity of origins, however, was used to deny rather than to affirm contemporary social diversity. The hallmark of 'Japaneseness', in Kita's view, was the ability to consume difference and transform it into the body of the organically united *Volk*, so that now 'we, the Japanese *minzoku*, almost without distinction possess the same myths and legends, speak the same language, cherish the same ideas and beliefs, and, as the strongest bond of all, are united from above by the rule of a single unchanging imperial dynasty'.[26] *Minzoku*, then, was not a matter of biology but of culture and above all of ideology: the acceptance of a set of beliefs and institutions which made one 'truly Japanese'. The interpretation achieved two things. It took hold of certain features of the modern Japanese nation state – the striving for linguistic uniformity, the exaltation of the role of the emperor, etc. – and essentialised them, projecting them back upon history as the eternal features of the Japanese people. At the same time, it offered to the people of Japan's expanding empire, among them the people of the frontier regions, the possibility of acceptance as 'Japanese', but only at the cost of their total submission to a prescribed set of cultural, linguistic and ideological norms. This vision of the Japanese *minzoku* came eventually to provide support for the Japanese government's assimilationist policies towards its colonies: policies which included forcing Koreans to adopt

'Japanese' names and encouraging intermarriage between Japanese and Koreans.[27]

Pasts and Foreign Countries

But the notion of the Japanese *minzoku* as a transcendental melting-pot failed to make sense of the very real differences and discrimination which existed, both within the bounds of the Japanese nation state and between Japan and its colonies. Scholars like Kita Sadakichi were obviously aware of this problem: Kita himself was a pioneering researcher of the history of the oppressed and socially isolated *burakumin* community, and his research helped to trace the roots of anti-*burakumin* prejudice to the social hierarchies of mediaeval and early modern Japan.[28] At least as far as the societies of the frontier were concerned, one way out of this dilemma was offered by the evolutionary ideas embodied in western-inspired notions of *bunmei* (civilisation). The sense of 'civilisation' as something achieved through different stages of development allowed difference to be reinterpreted in *temporal* rather than *spatial* terms: as 'backwardness' rather than 'foreign-ness'. Thus, it became possible to conceive of a single national community in which the differences between centre and periphery represented not the products of separate histories, but different positions along the timeline of a single historical trajectory.

The basis for such an interpretation had already been laid by the pioneers of Japanese archaeology, whose work emphasised the links between the material culture of the Ainu and of the earliest inhabitants of Japan. In Kita Sadakichi's writings, the contemporary Ainu community becomes a living image of the past: a society still undergoing the transformation to fully fledged 'Japaneseness' achieved by their predecessors in other parts of the Japanese archipelago many centuries ago. The Russian, Nikolai Nevsky, and other linguists had traced links between Okinawan and early forms of the Japanese language,[29] and the ethnographer, Yanagita Kunio, had helped to track down connections between the myths and folk practices of Okinawa and the lost traditions of various parts of Japan. It is, indeed, in Yanagita's writings that this sense of the frontier as past achieves perhaps its most eloquent expression. As one recent reappraisal of Yanagita's work points out, his ethnographic writings began by emphasising the diversity of social forms within the Japanese archipelago, seeing different areas and different social structures as having their own particular histories. As time went on, however, his approach shifted to one which defined difference increasingly as a product of time rather than space. The central areas of Japan now came to be seen as representing the most modern forms of Japanese society, and the periphery as containing survivals of more ancient linguistic and social structures.[30] This approach is particularly evident in Yanagita's work on Okinawa, which became (in Alan Christy's telling phrase) an 'antique shop of ethnography'.[31] As Christy points out, Yanagita's description of his journey to Okinawa in 1921 imposes:

> a reverse time line on the geographical terrain of his trip. Beginning his journey on the east coast of Kyushu (in Oita prefecture), Yanagita travels south along the coast, through Amami Oshima, Okinawa, Miyako and Yaeyama [the southernmost island of the Ryūkyūs] . . . As the trip continues south, . . . he records fewer descriptions of the present, longer meditations on the past, and imaginings of past common lives and gruesome deaths. In particular Yanagita's tale of his trip is littered with the narrative bodies of the dead, as if to highlight the potential danger in the trip, as well as to suggest a descent into the past (the land of the dead). By the time he has reached the southern end of his journey, he has not only covered a great distance but also a great time.[32]

By the 1930s, therefore, the transformation was almost complete. The societies of the frontier had shifted, in the framework of Japanese scholarship, from being 'foreign countries' (*ikoku*) to being communities that not only were Japanese, but *always had been Japanese*, only Japanese stranded in an earlier phase of historical evolution. Perhaps the most striking example of this incorporation of the Ainu into the Japanese past has been the reconstruction of Ainu as 'hunter-gatherers'. A large volume of archaeological and documentary evidence shows that Ainu communities in the sixteenth and seventeenth centuries lived mainly on hunted and gathered foods, but also grew small crops of millet and vegetables, while Sakhalin Ainu farmed dogs, which they used for food and fur, and as hunting and draft animals. There are also clear records indicating that trade with the Japanese in the eighteenth and early nineteenth centuries discouraged Ainu crop-growing, partly for simple reasons of comparative advantage, and partly because Japanese traders deliberately tried to prevent the Ainu from farming, so forcing them to spend more time on the fishing and hunting activities which provided the basis of the northern border trade.[33]

Yet most standard texts on the Ainu are strangely silent about this evidence, preferring instead to follow an approach typified by the 1992 edition of the *Encyclopaedia Britannica*, which tells us that Ainu were 'hunters, fishers and trappers, until the Japanese moved into Hokkaido and attempted to settle them in farming'.[34] One of the best-known contemporary Japanese examples of this approach is the work of the philosopher, Umehara Takeshi, who argues that the culture of Japan's pre-agrarian Jōmon period (which existed before the gradual spread of the rice-growing Yayoi culture from about 300 BC) continues to exist in Ainu society 'in its purest form'.[35] Umehara himself suggests that the notion of Ainu as the 'original Japanese' contributes to the contemporary cause of Ainu liberation by emphasising the common ethnic and cultural origins of Ainu and majority Japanese, and so helping to overcome prejudice.[36] But this obscures the claim of the Ainu (and other minorities) to be treated as equal in their own right, and not just because they are related to somebody else. Equally importantly, the search for common prehistoric origins has tended to dehistoricise the experience of the frontier communities: by presenting them as fossilised remnants of the Japanese past it denies their internal dynamism and their continuing contribution to the shaping of the region's history. The curious blind spot in the historiography of the Ainu can, I think, only be explained by a deep-seated urge, on the one hand, to identify the Ainu as part of the Japanese past, and on the other to accept a stage theory of development in which 'hunter-gatherer' is always a stage prior to 'agricultural'. It thus becomes impossible to conceive of Ainu culture as a culture which has become increasingly de-agrarianised by contact with an evolving Japanese economy.

The view of the frontier embodied in the writings of scholars like Umehara is not wrong in any simple factual sense. Both Okinawans and Ainu clearly have historical, linguistic and cultural links to other parts of Japan, just as Okinawans also have links to Taiwan and Southeast Asia, and Ainu to the peoples of eastern Siberia and the Aleutian Islands. But the attempt to define the societies of the frontier as 'ancient' fragments of Japan is problematic because it presumes the existence of some eternal and absolute 'Japaneseness' in which people can be included or from which they can be excluded. The aim of this chapter has been, on the contrary, to show how much the conceptual frontier between 'Japan' and its neighbours is created and re-created out of a ceaseless and still continuing interplay between similarity and difference, outside and inside, space and time. The rediscovery of this interplay requires not only, as Wallerstein suggests, the 'unthinking' of our accepted categories of social science, but also the 'unthinking' of a fixed and unchanging category called 'Japan'.

Notes

1 Immanuel Wallerstein, 'The invention of TimeSpace realities', in I. Wallerstein (ed.), *Unthinking Social Science: The Limits of Nineteenth-Century Paradigms*, London, Polity Press, 1991, p. 148.

2 At least one early nineteenth-century guide for travellers within Japan found it necessary to warn its readers not to laugh at the strange manners and customs of those from different regions; see Constantine N. Vaporis, 'Caveat viator: advice to travellers in the Edo period', *Monumenta Nipponica*, vol. 44, no. 4, 1989, esp. p. 478.

3 Terajima Ryōan, *Wakan sansai zue*, vol. 1, Tokyo, Nihon Zuihitsu Taisei Kankōkai, 1929, esp. p. 217; see also Torii Ryūzō, *Kyokutō minzoku*, vol. 1, Tokyo, Bunka Seikatsu Kenkyūkai, 1926, p. 130.

4 See, for example, Ronald P. Toby, *State and Diplomacy in Early Modern Japan*, Princeton, Princeton University Press, 1984, pp. 217–19.

5 David Howell, 'Ainu ethnicity and the boundaries of the early Japanese state', *Past and Present*, no. 142, 1994.

6 See Sakakura Genjirō, 'Ezo zuihitsu' (1739), in *Hoppō mikōkai kobunsho shūsei*, vol. 1, Tokyo, Sōbunsha, 1979, p. 73; for other descriptions of Ainu and Ryūkyū society see Arai Hakuseki, 'Ezo shi' (1720), in ibid; Morishima Chuyo, 'Ryūkyū dan' (1790), and anon., 'Ryūkyū kaigo' (1850), both reproduced in *Edoki Ryūkyū mono shiryō shūran*, vol. 4, Tokyo, Honpō Shoseki KK, 1981.

7 Quoted in Kamiya Nobuyuki, *Bakuhansei kokka no Ryūkyū shihai*, Tokyo, Kokura Shobō, p. 255; for an important discussion of this logic of difference, see also Kikiuchi Isao, 'Kyokai to minzoku', in Arano Teiji *et al.*, *Ajia no naka no Nihonshi*, vol. 4, Tokyo, Tokyo Daigaku Shuppankai, 1992; I have discussed this point in greater detail in 'The frontiers of Japanese identity', in H. Antlöv and S. Tonnesson (eds), *The Politics of Identity in Asia*, Copenhagen, NIAS Books (forthcoming).

8 On early maps of the world, see Muroga Nobuo, 'Atarashii sekai no ninshiki: Namban sekaizu byōbu', in *Daikōkai jidai no Nihon 5: Nihon kara mita ikoku*, Tokyo, Shōgakukan, 1978.

9 *Bankoku ichiran zūsetsu*, 1810; original held in Tōyō Bunko, Tokyo, catalogue no. XI-I-II, vol. 1, p. 8.

10 Ibid., pp. 9–11.

11 See, for example, S. P. Krasheninnikov, *The History of Kamchatka*, (1764), facsimile edn, K. L. Holmes (ed.), Richmond, Richmond Publishing Company, 1973, pp. 239–80.

12 Takakura Shinichirō, *Shinpan Ainu seisakushi*, Tokyo, San-Ichi shobō, 1972, p. 139.

13 Ibid., p. 187; see also Kikuchi Isao, *Hoppōshi no naka no kinsei Nihon*, Tokyo, Kokura shobō, 1991, pp. 11–13.

14 François Guizot, *Histoire de la Civilization en Europe depuis la Chute de l'Empire Romain*, 6th edn, Paris, Victor Masson, 1951, p. 14.

15 See Alan S. Christy, 'The making of imperial subjects in Okinawa', *Positions: East Asia Cultures Critique*, vol. 1, no. 3, 1993.

16 *Bankoku kairō no ki*, vol. 2, March 1853; original held in Tōyō Bunko, Tokyo.

17 Fukuzawa Yukichi, *Sekai kunizukushi*, reproduced in *Fukuzawa Yukichi zenshū*, vol. 2, Tokyo, Koumin Tosho, 1926, p. 689.

18 See Yamaoka Michio, *Nihon minzoku no yūrai*, vol. 1, Tokyo, Yoshifusa

Yugensha, 1993; at p. 30 Yamaoka noted that the more exotic early theories of the racial origins of the Japanese included Kimura Takatarō's theory that the Japanese were descendants of ancient Greeks, Ishikawa Sanshirō's theory of Sumer origins and Koyabu Zenichirō's notion that the Japanese were a lost tribe of Israel.

19 Ibid., pp. 25–33.

20 See Richard Siddle, 'Academic exploitation and indigenous resistance: the case of the Ainu', in Noel Loos and Takeshi Osanai (eds), *Indigenous Minorities and Education: Australian and Japanese Perspectives on their Indigenous Peoples, the Ainu, Aborigines and Torres Strait Islanders*, Tokyo, Sanyusha Publishing Co., 1993, pp. 40–51.

21 Miyake Setsurei, *Shin zen bi Nihonjin* (1891), reproduced in Ikimatsu Keizo, *Nihonjinron*, Tokyo, Toyamabō, 1977, p. 19.

22 Yun Kōn Cha, 'Minzoku gensō no satetsu', *Shisō*, no. 834, December 1993, p. 13.

23 See, for example, Miyake, *Shin zen bi Nihonjin*, in Ikimatsu, *Nihonjinron*, p. 11.

24 See Haga Yaichi, *Kokuminsei jūron*, (1908) reprinted in Ikimatsu, *Nihonjinron*, p. 127.

25 See, for example, Kita Sadakichi, 'Nihon minzoku to wa nani zō', *Minzoku to rekishi*, vol. 1, no. 1, 1919.

26 Kita Sadakichi, '*Minzoku to rekishi hakkō shuisho*', *Minzoku to rekishi*, vol. 1, no. 1, 1919, p. 1.

27 For a poignant account of this policy and its tragic social consequences, see Utsumi Aiko, 'Kokuseki ni honrō sareta hitobito', in Doi Takako (ed.), *Kokuseki o kangaeru*, Tokyo, Jiji Tsūshinsha, 1984.

28 See Kita Sadakichi, 'Tokushu buraku no seiritsu enkaku o ryakujo shite sono kaihō no oyobu', *Minzoku to rekishi*, vol. 2, no. 1, 1919; see also Ueda Masaaki, *Nihon minzoku bunka taikei 5: Kita Sadakichi*, Tokyo, Kōdansha, 1988, pp. 34–6.

29 See Okinawa Ken, *Okinawa Ken shi*, vol. 1, Naha, Okinawa Ken, 1977, pp. 694–5.

30 Fukuta Ajio, 'Shoki Yanagita Kunio no kenkyū to gendai minzokugaku', in Amino Yoshihiko (ed.), *Rekishigaku to Minzokugaku*, Tokyo, Furukawa Shobunkan, 1992, pp. 135–56; for this concept of centre and periphery, see particularly Yanagita Kunio, 'Katatsumuri kō', in *Teihon Yanagita Kunio shu*, vol. 18, Tokyo, Chikuma Shobō, 1964, and Yanagita Kunio, 'Kyōdo seikatsu no kenkyūhō', in *Teihon Yanagita Kunio shū*, vol. 25, Tokyo, Chikuma shobō, 1964.

31 Christy, 'The making of imperial subjects in Okinawa', *Positions*, vol. 1, no. 3, p. 623.

32 Ibid., p. 626.

33 See, for example, Hanazaki Kōhei, *Shizuka na taichi*, Tokyo, Iwanami Shoten, 1993, pp. 79 and 132; I have discussed this point in more detail in 'Creating the frontier: border, identity and history in Japan's far north', *East Asian History*, no. 7, June 1994, pp. 1–24.

34 *New Encyclopaedia Britannica*, vol. 1, Micropaedia, 15th edn, Chicago, Encyclopaedia Britannica Inc., 1992.

35 Umehara Takeshi and Fujimura Hisakazu (eds), *Ainugaku no yoake*, Tokyo, Shōgakukan, 1990, p. 13.

36 Ibid., p. 54.

CHAPTER SIX

The Place of Okinawa in Japanese Historical Identity

RICHARD PEARSON

Introduction

Ninety years have passed since the first discoveries of prehistoric pottery by Torii Ryūzō in the Yaeyama Islands, at the Kabira shell-mound. Later, pioneering research by Tokunaga Shigeru led to the discovery of ancient deer fossils on Iejima. Excavations by Ōyama Kashiwa of the Iha shell-mound confirmed that Okinawa had been populated by ancient people. Tawada Shinjun summarised the prehistory of the Ryūkyūs as a few dedicated scholars pieced it together in the aftermath of the Pacific War.[1] The establishment of the Okinawan Archaeological Association, and the outstanding accomplishments of a new generation of scholars who emerged in the 1960s, brought Okinawan archaeology to a new level. Economic development in the past two decades has provided opportunities for many extensive excavations, leading to a deeper understanding of ancient culture and, unfortunately, complete excavation and destruction of countless sites.

Humans arrived in Okinawa more than 30 000 years ago. While sites on the main islands of Japan have yielded artefacts possibly as old as 200 000 years or more, human fossils are rare and fragmentary; Okinawa still yields the most complete fossil record of the archipelago. A gap of 10 000 years separates the Okinawan Pleistocene human fossils from the oldest sites of the Shell-mound period.[2] Whether Palaeolithic populations died out, to be replaced by post-Pleistocene populations is debated. Suzuki Hisashi argues that the present-day Okinawans are 'direct descendants of the Minatogawa man' (see below), while Takamiya Hiroto leaves open the question of direct ancestry.[3]

At first, the living patterns of post-Pleistocene cultures can be said to follow the basic Jōmon tradition of southern Kyushu. In the islands as far south as Okinawa, the basic Jōmon tradition of hand-built, low-fired ceramics continued for almost 5000 years, but the distinctive accessories and secondary tools found in Jōmon sites are absent. Peoples of the Early Shell-mound period did not make clay figurines or the polished stone ornaments of central and north-eastern Japan, but made distinctive bone pendants (usually of dugong) of butterfly (sometimes called dragon) form. They are found with pottery of Early Shell-mound periods IV and V, dating to around 3000 to 2500 BP.

Subsistence and burial patterns were completely different from those of the prehistoric peoples of coastal China, where rice culti-vation began as early as 5000 BC. There appears to be no close sim-ilarity with Taiwan, where early agriculture was also practised and cultivated rice has been dated to about 1500 BC. Some authors believe that rice cultivation in Okinawa may have started by about AD 200, while others think that both dry field and rice cultivation could have occurred at this time, but these beliefs have not been confirmed.[4] Charred rice remains date to the Heian period.

A series of depressions and ridges, thought to be part of a dry field system, associated with a well-like feature and postulated water channel, have been found at Nūribaru, Uehara, Ginowan, Central Okinawa, in a layer which has yielded pottery sherds from the Middle Shell-mound period (roughly 2400 years ago). Stone tools which look like reaping knives, a whetstone and a scraper have also been recovered. This may be a horticultural site, dating slightly earlier than comparable sites in Kyushu.[5]

In the Late Shell-mound period the ceramics of Okinawa show general but weak correspondences with those of the Japanese islands in the presence of plain pottery and grey *Sue* stoneware, but the paths of cultural development diverge sharply. Okinawan sites remain relatively small, displaying no evidence of social stratification or craft specialisation until the tenth or eleventh centuries with the production of *Sue* pottery on Tokunoshima.[6] There is evidence of sporadic contacts with China and continued contacts with Japan. There is no evidence of the concentration of wealth seen in the Kofun burial mounds of Japan or the advent of state centralisation which occurred in the Yamato Basin in the seventh century. The processes which led to secondary state formation in the Yamato Basin did not affect the Ryūkyū Islands at that time.

From the twelfth to sixteenth centuries secondary state formation took place under stimulation from China and Japan. In some aspects, this process was similar to what occurred in the Yamato Basin centuries earlier. Through contact with the China coast, new technology, values and social concepts entered the Ryūkyūs. Fortifications were constructed with coral limestone walls, and overseas trade assumed great importance. While castles are common in Japan, the configuration of Okinawan castles is distinctive. The advent of state organisation in the Ryūkyūs contrasts with cultural development in Taiwan and the Philippines, where society remained at the chiefdom level. Judging from the absence of large burial facilities and palatial residences in Okinawa for all but the Chūzan kings, it seems that there was an emphasis on communal living and a strong *kyōdōtai* (communal group) without the deep social cleavages which distinguished Chinese imperial society. Social cohesiveness may prove to be a distinctive characteristic of Okinawa.

The island groups of Miyako and Yaeyama (both of which comprise the Sakishima archipelago to the south of Okinawa), were first occupied in the second millennium BC. Excavations at the Soedo site, Tarama Island, the Otabaru site on Ishigaki, and new dates from the third excavation of the Shimotabaru site on Hateruma, confirm that the oldest populations made low-fired earthenware, while sites from around the first millennium BC are non-ceramic. While earlier archaeologists expected that the earliest cultures of the Sakishima Islands must have been direct importations from the Philippines or the east coast of Taiwan, recent opinion is that so-called southern traits, such as *Tridacna* shell adzes and perforated shell pendants, are shared with cultures of the Philippines and Micronesia, but the basic subsistence pattern and artefact inventory share many features with the islands to the north. Opinions vary as to whether the non-ceramic sites represent a new, intrusive population into the Sakishima Islands.[7]

Reddish-brown earthenware in association with Chinese celadon has been recovered by archaeologists from the University of Kumamoto on Batanes, northern Philippines. Their report shows no vessels with external lugs, typical of Yaeyama, and there is no discussion of cultural relationships with Yaeyama.[8] The external lug pottery of later sites, from about the tenth century, appears to resemble the shape of soapstone bowls imported to Okinawa from southern Kyushu. Sites yielding Chinese white wares dating to the late eleventh century have been found in Yaeyama as well as Okinawa. Yaeyama and Miyako have fortified sites of the same time span as the Gusuku period of Okinawa (AD 1200 to 1609). In the sixteenth century the southern islands came under the control of the Chūzan kingdom.

The Ryūkyū Islands occupy a unique position in the culture history of East Asia through their spatial location, human adaptation to their island environment, processes of interaction with surrounding regions, and internal social evolution.

Figure 6.1 Okinawa and surrounding region

The Spatial Location of the Ryūkyūs

While it is usual to consider the Ryūkyūs as marginal to East Asia, they lie in the centre of the East China Sea, almost equidistant from Japan, China and the islands of Micronesia, and occupy the northern edge of South-east Asia (figure 6.1). For the location of major Okinawan sites mentioned in this chapter, see figure 6.2. While Okinawa can be said to be central, its protection by sea from the centres of East Asian power permitted cultural independence. The islands form a long, continuous arc: voyagers through the islands from Kyushu to Okinawa were always within sight of land. The fact that the largest land-mass lies in the middle of the arc, at the point of greatest distance from neighbouring land-masses, was doubtless significant in the independent evolution of early Okinawan culture. A gap of almost 300 km separates Okinawa from Miyako. Contacts across this gap were later and less intense than those which occurred among the islands to the north.

Environment and Adaptive Processes

From several points of view, the Ryūkyū Islands constitute a transitional zone within East Asia. While the climatic index falls completely within the subtropical range, the dominant species in the forests are *Castanopsis seiboldii* (*shii*), which has a northerly distribution within the genus *Castanopsis*.[9] Hotta Mitsuru characterised the Okinawan forests as warm temperate relics in island isolation. Thus the mountain forests, even of the Yaeyama group, can be seen as extensions of the laurel-leaved forests of southern Japan. The ancient Okinawan people harvested the *shii* nuts and mountain yams, as did the people of Kyushu. At the same time, Pacific island vegetation, including species of mangrove, pandanus, and other shore plants, extends north into the Ryūkyūs from South-east Asia, providing a wide range of plant materials which are important in daily life.

A marine transition zone also occurs, caused by the northerly flow of the Black Current. As far north as Amami Ōshima, extensive coral reefs create wide lagoons. Water temperatures do not fall below 20 degrees Celsius in winter. The reefs provide extensive fish and mollusc resources. The molluscs also provided important raw materials for tools and ornaments. Shell midden analysis shows an increase in the diversity of shell species used for food in the Late Shell-mound period.[10] No other region in East and South-east Asia possesses the same combination of natural resources: temperate relic broadleaf evergreen forest, coral reef lagoon, and Indo-Pacific strand vegetation.

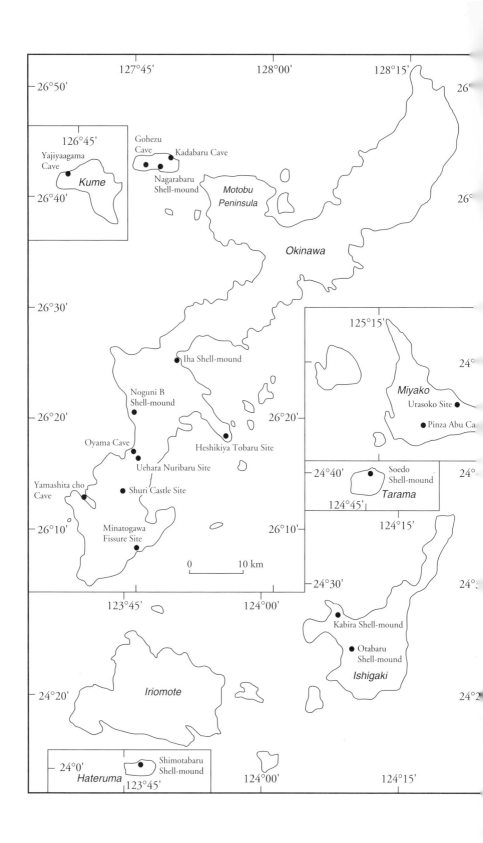

What patterns of human adaptation distinguish Okinawan culture, and how did they arise? We know little or nothing of the living patterns of the most ancient populations of the Ryūkyūs, since we do not have tool assemblages or tool remains. On the basis of skeletal morphology, mitochondrial DNA, and studies of teeth, it is postulated that the oldest populations of Okinawa and Japan came from South-east Asia.[11] Subsequent post-Pleistocene populations, judging from the occurrence of *tsumegatamon* ('thumbnail impressed') pottery, and later Jōmon pottery types, came from Kyushu but were still of the earlier type of generalised Mongoloid population, as postulated by Hanihara Kazurō. In the Early Shell-mound period (roughly 6000 to 300 BC), populations living in the broadleaf evergreen forests of Kyushu migrated into the Ryūkyūs and gradually adjusted. Hunting patterns changed to suit local conditions. Wild boar bones are found but arrowheads are rare. In the middle layer of the Noguni B site, which produced abundant *tsumegatamon* pottery, more than 600 individual wild boar were represented in one concentration 2 metres in diameter. Kishimoto Yoshihiko concluded that hunting methods must have been very effective. The stone tool assemblages of the Initial and Early Jōmon sites resemble those of the main islands of Japan. They include polished adzes, chipped adzes with edge grinding, whetstones, stone mortars, and concave stones. These tools are similar to those found in Kyushu. By the Okinawan Late Jōmon, at the time of the Iha pottery type, dated to about 3500 years ago, and its successor the Ogido type, scrapers, arrowheads, and other hunting tools are rare.[12]

Although stone arrowheads are less common in Okinawa than in Kyushu, several dozen have been recorded in Okinawan Jōmon sites of various periods.[13] Some are made of chert, which came from the Motobu Peninsula of Okinawa. Many are made of obsidian, which has been traced to Koshidake, in Saga prefecture. Small flakes in sites such as Kanegusuku indicate that both chert and obsidian arrowheads were finished on the sites, rather than traded as finished artefacts.

During the Late Shell-mound period (300 BC to AD 1100–1200) adaptation continued (see table 6.1 for two cultural chronologies in current use.) Whereas sites in the Early Shell-mound period are usually at the foot of cliffs or inland, those of the Late Shell-mound period occur in sand dunes next to the sea. Sites are larger and more numerous, suggesting an increase in population, and the subsistence

Figure 6.2 Major Ryūkyū sites mentioned in chapter 6

base was broadened. The shell deposits are well defined, with greater numbers of large, thick shells, suggesting a more extensive use of lagoon resources. Pecked stone tools with depressions for processing nuts and shellfish, may indicate that people were devising new ways to process locally available foods. Stone tools generally show diversification, while adzes decline in frequency, their blades showing heavy use from processing nuts or digging through shells. Abundant net weights made of perforated shells provide evidence of intensive fishing.

Pottery diversified from a single vessel shape in the Early Shell-mound period, a small version of the ubiquitous Jōmon deep jar, to three forms – the *kame* (wide-mouthed), *hachi* (straight-sided), and *tsubo* (narrow-necked). The new pottery shapes may be said to be a distant reflection of Final Jōmon or Yayoi forms. Shell tools and ornaments developed in Okinawa. The list of shell artefacts is impressive: spoons or ladles, scraping tools made from opercula, knives, net weights, arrowheads and ornaments. Large shells may also have been used for boiling water.

The development of a specialised adze industry in the Sakishima Islands, known from discoveries at the Urasoko site, Miyako Island, provides another example of adaptation to local conditions about 1800 to 2500 years ago. In the Gusuku period, beginning about AD 1200, the settlement pattern shows a new trend. The distribution of Gusuku sites follows closely the areas of raised limestone or limestone-sandstone, which were important for dry field cultivation, and possibly for stock-raising.[14]

Cultural Inputs and Interaction

The relationship of people of the Ryūkyūs to their environment is not the only window for understanding the development of their culture. Patterns of interaction with surrounding areas have played a major role.

Although we can confirm the early arrival of Palaeolithic peoples in Okinawa, we do not have a clear idea of their relations with mainland China or the islands of Japan. Vertebrate fossils have been found in at least 104 locations in Okinawa, both from Tertiary and Quaternary contexts, and *Homo sapiens* fossils have been found in at least six localities. The most typical context is a deposit of brownish clay, mixed with angular limestone fragments, either in cave floor deposits or in limestone fissures. Fossil assemblages generally consist of a wide range of species including elephant, deer, wild boar, wild cat, fruit bat, rat, frog, and reptile and bird species. The extinct deer, *Metacervulus*

Table 6.1 Cultural chronology of Okinawa

Dates	Miyagi and Takamiya (1983)	(Okinawa ken 1982)
AD 1609		
	Final Gusuku 1550–1609	
	Late Gusuku 1450–1550	
	Middle Gusuku 1350–1450	
	Early Gusuku 1200–1350	Gusuku 1100–1500 AD
AD 1000		
900		
800		
AD 750	Fensa Lower-layer Pottery	
700		
600		Late Shell-mound
500		100 BC–AD 1100
400	Late IV 250–1200	
300		
AD 250		
200	Late III 150–250	
100		
1	Late II 100 BC–AD 150	
BC	Late I 300–100 BC	
		Middle Shell-mound
	Early V 500 BC–300 BC	500–100 BC
	Early IV 1000–500 BC	
1 000 BC		Early Shell-mound
	Early III 2000–1000 BC	
2 000 BC		
	Early II 4000–2000 BC	
3 000 BC		
4 000 BC		Initial Shell-mound
5 000 BC	Early I 6000–4000 BC	10 000–1500 BC
6 000 BC		
7 000 BC		
8 000 BC		
9 000 BC		
10 000 BC		
10 500 BC		
	Palaeolithic	Palaeolithic

Source: Miyagi and Takamiya, *Okinawa Rekishi Chizu*, p. 14; Okinawa ken Kyōiku Iinkai (Okinawa Prefectural Board of Education), *Horidasareta Okinawa no Rekishi*, Naha, Okinawa ken Kyōiku Chō, Bunka Ka, 1982.

astyolodon, migrated from China during the Early Pleistocene, while *Archidiskodon* (or possibly *Palaeoloxodon*) and *Capreolus* migrated by a land bridge from Taiwan, at the end of the Early Pleistocene. Some scholars postulate a Late Pleistocene land bridge from north-eastern Taiwan to Yaeyama, Miyako, Okinawa and Amami Oshima, existed as late as 20 000 years ago. Evidence is not conclusive, but a submerged Pleistocene land surface, showing signs of rapid subsidence, has been located at a depth of more than 1000 metres, between Okinawa and Miyako.[15]

The most prominent find is a limestone fissure at Minatogawa in southern Okinawa, which is about 15 metres deep and 40 to 150 centimetres wide. From 1968 to 1974 three excavations yielded *Homo sapiens* bones belonging to between five and nine individuals. Radiocarbon dates of 18 250 ± 650 years BP (TK−99) and 16 660 ± 300 years BP (TK−142) were determined.[16] The Minatogawa specimens are similar to the Liujiang skeleton of Guangxi, China, which is dated between 10 000 and 30 000 years.

Christy Turner has proposed that the Minatogawa dentition is Sundadont, which means the population is southern derived, in contrast to the Sinodont teeth of Yayoi and later peoples. One of the Minatogawa specimens shows ritual tooth ablation of the lower central incisors, a custom which was most common in Japan in the Middle Jōmon (*ca.* 2500–1500 BC). The Minatogawa example is by far the oldest in Japan.[17]

From a cave site at Yamashita-chō, in a low limestone ridge near Naha Harbour, Okinawa, fragments of a tibia and femur belonging to a juvenile female *Homo sapiens* were recovered from the upper part of Layer IV. From a pooled sample of charcoal from Layers III and V, a radiocarbon date of 32 100 ± 1000 BP was determined.[18] Four other sites yielding *Homo sapiens* fossils have been reported by Takamiya: Kadabaru Cave, Iejima; Oyama Cave, Okinawa; Shimoji Cave, Kumejima; and Pinza Abu, Miyako. Fossilised bone fragments belonging to a one-year-old infant have also been found in the Yajiyaagama Cave site, Kumejima.[19]

Fragments of cranium and vertebrae, as well as a deciduous tooth, were found in the Pinza Abu cave deposit on Miyako Island after water screening some 10 tonnes of fossil-bearing clay.[20] Associated faunal materials include deer, boar, wild cat and rats, all of which are extinct. Although radiocarbon dates of 25 800 ± 900 BP (TK–535) and 26 800 ± 1300 BP (TK–605) were determined from charcoal in the upper clay layer of the site, the relationships of these dates to the fossils is not entirely clear; the authors of the site report suggest a date of around 20 000 years ago and concluded that the Pinza Abu specimens were 'morphologically slightly older' than those of Minatogawa.[21] Sakura Hajime concludes that the specimens from Pinza Abu and Minatogawa represent a single population which inhabited the Ryūkyūs in the Late Pleistocene. Hasegawa Yoshikazu has classified the palaeontological deposits of the Ryūkyūs into two stratigraphic layers, based on mammalian fauna, especially deer and wild boar; fluorine content of the bones, and radiocarbon dates.[22] The older layer yields deer and is dated to about 30 000 BP. It includes Yamashita-chō and Gohezu Cave. The upper, more recent layers yield only wild boar (Nagara-baru, Iejima, and the Upper Minatogawa deposit). The intermediate of these two layers, in which deer and boar remains occur together, corresponds to the horizon of Minatogawa man (Lower Minatogawa deposit).

The Minatogawa fissure did not yield any artefactual material. The Iejima and the Yamashita-chō sites yielded modified fragments of deer antler, mandible, and leg bones (femur, tibia, and tarsal). Antler fragments consist of the basal portion of the antler with a small portion of surrounding cranium, or antler tips. The long bone fragments are usually notched at one or both ends, and are referred to as double-notched bone artefacts. The Yamashita-chō site yielded three stone specimens thought to be tools.[23] One piece is said to resemble a chopper, while the other two are spherical stone objects 7 to 8 centimetres in diameter. These three objects are made from local Tertiary sandstone. Not all scholars consider these to be artefacts.

Katō Shimpei has concluded that the so-called bone artefacts have been created by the gnawing of deer.[24] In other localities such as Zhoukoudian, China, bone modification was created by the chewing of carnivores; however carnivores were not present on Okinawan sites, judging from the bone assemblages. Takemoto Seishun and Asato Shijun state that since not one stone tool of the Palaeolithic has been found on Okinawa this seriously weakens the assertion that there is a Palaeolithic *culture*.[25] However, there is some indication that stone tools may yet be found. The Tsuchihama Yaya site, Amami Ōshima, has yielded a shale pointed tool associated with a radiocarbon date of 18 000 BP, and flakes, raw material fragments, and three artefacts with traces of grinding, from a layer dated to 21 400 BP. Takamiya Hiroe has surveyed bone assemblages of the late Pleistiocene and Early Holocene from surrounding regions in East and South-east Asia.[26] Some of these may also have been created by the chewing of carnivores or deer, and he concludes that others, with convincing evidence of human modification into well-recognised artefact types, are later in age.

The earliest clear evidence of a relationship with Kyushu lies in *tsumegatamon* pottery and associated large edge-polished adzes. *Tsumegatamon* pottery dates to about 10 000 BP in Kyushu, but to about

6500 BP in Okinawa.[27] Sasaki Kōmei mentions that the thumb-nail impressed pottery of the Ryūkyūs has been found in layers lying above the Akahoya volcanic ash, and therefore should be dated to about 6400 years ago. It has been suggested that the *tsumegatamon* pottery of the Ryūkyūs is typologically distinct from that of the main islands of Japan.[28] It is underlain at the Noguni B site by plain sherds of a form with a pointed base, in the lower layer, dated to 7130 ± 80 BP.

Takamiya Hiroe has documented the movement of Early Jōmon pottery types from Kyushu to Okinawa in the Early Jōmon of Okinawa, and the emergence of the Murokawa Lower-layer type in Okinawa. In the Middle Jōmon of Okinawa local pottery types developed: Gushikawa, Kamino C, and Omonawa Zentei. In the Late Jōmon, six pottery types are believed to be independent of Kyushu. Despite their independence, the presence of sherds of the Izumi and Ichiki types of Kyushu provide evidence of continued interaction in the Middle Jōmon. Kyushu Jōmon sherds can be distinguished from Okinawan sherds through neutron activation analysis.[29]

One of the most exciting episodes of Okinawan prehistory relates to the exchange network between the inhabitants of Okinawa and the high chiefs of the North Kyushu Plain in the Early and Middle Yayoi period. Bracelets of the *gohōra* shell, found in the deep waters of the outer edges of coral reefs from Amami Ōshima to the south, were manufactured in the Ryūkyūs and traded to the north, where they belonged only to the highest chiefs. Yayoi pottery vessels were exchanged from Kyushu to Okinawa, sherds being found on dozens of sites in the Ryūkyūs. Shell plaques appear to have decorated the garments of the elite who may have been engaged in the trade, and a few individuals in the Ryūkyūs were buried in Yayoi-style cist burials constructed of coral. Cone shells (*imogai*) from the Ryūkyūs, and probably other goods, travelled along the Japan Sea coast as far as southern Hokkaido, being found in sites such as Usu 10.[30]

Historical relationships between Okinawa and the main islands of Japan changed dramatically by the end of the Yayoi period, as the exchange system of shell bracelets disappeared. (Bracelets continued to be made in the shapes of shells, but the material was semi-precious stone.) The reorganisation of long-distance exchange appears to be partially the result of a shift in the centre of political power from northern Kyushu to the eastern part of the Inland Sea and the Kinai region.

In the Kofun period (AD 250–600) new distribution systems of continental mirrors, iron weapons, and semi-precious stone beads expanded and contracted within the Japanese main islands but did not enter the Ryūkyūs. After the Iwai rebellion of AD 528, North Kyushu was incorporated into the Yamato state, becoming an important outpost facing not only Korea but also to the south. The region was controlled from the provincial administrative post of Dazaifu, some 15 km inland from the present Fukuoka City. In the seventh and eighth centuries, and probably much earlier, the Yamato state kept the land and sea routes to Dazaifu open, and Yamato ships patrolled the Ariake Bay and Satsuma Peninsula regions of Kyushu.[31]

Wooden slips (*mokkan*) used for administrative documents, dating to the eighth century, have been found in excavations at Dazaifu. A few of these identify the islands of Amami and Okinoerabu. Other historical materials identify Yaku, Tane, Tokara, Sae, 'Nikai', Toku, Kumi, and Sonkaku. Sae and Sonkaku have not been matched to modern place names. The occurrence of Kofun burial mounds on Tane, and two very old Shinto shrines on Yaku, has led Mishima Itaru to conclude that Tane and Yaku were the southern frontier of the Yamato state at the time of Dazaifu.[32] Red dye, made from the *akagi* tree (*Bischofia javanica*) may have been exported from Amami to Yamato, and it is also possible that Okinawa sent banana fibre to Yamato.[33]

From the Kofun to the Heian periods, soapstone cooking cauldrons were quarried in the Hogetto sites near Oseto in modern Saga prefecture, and traded to the Ryūkyūs. Fragments of these cauldrons are relatively abundant on Okinawan sites. Vessels were also traded to the Kinai and Kanto regions in large numbers, and have been found in hundreds of sites in western Japan.[34] *Sue* vessels were also traded to Okinawa, and *Sue* kilns have been found at Kamuiyaki on Tokunoshima.[35] Asato Susumu considers the Ryūkyū-wide distribution of the Ryūkyūan *Sue* ware, termed '*kamuiyaki* related ceramics' after the *kamuiyaki* kilns, to be of great significance in Okinawan prehistory, because it means that all the islands were linked into a locally based social and economic network.[36] A similar pattern probably occurred in the Yayoi in the main islands.[37] The indigenous pottery of the *gusuku* sites mentioned below displays shapes derived from the soapstone and *Sue* vessels which were traded earlier.

The Chūzan Kingdom as a City State

Following two centuries of competition between several polities on Okinawa, the Chūzan kingdom defeated its southern rival (Nanzan) in 1429 and its northern rival (Hokuzan) in 1416, and established the Ryūkyū kingdom, as it was called by the Chinese. It remained an independent trading state until 1609, when it was taken over by the Satsuma domain of Kagoshima, in southern Kyushu. Unlike the territorial states of East Asia which surrounded it, Okinawa developed as a city state.[38] In the fifteenth and sixteenth centuries, it possessed a number of distinguishing features: a well-defined core which was the Shuri castle; economic self-sufficiency; political independence and self-government. Although the Chūzan kingdom was small, its political independence allowed it to control and dispose of its surplus on projects that directly benefited the city and its ruling groups.

City states develop when polities in the surrounding areas are relatively weak. This seems to apply to Okinawa, which was in maritime contact with Japan and China but outside their territorial grasp. Most city states depend on trade and commerce with areas outside their control, their economies fluctuating with similar trends in the larger economic system. The city state comes to an end when the citizens' perception of their independence is forcefully changed, by whatever means.

Okinawa lay beyond the outer edges of the Yamato state which developed from the fifth to eighth centuries. From the eighth to twelfth centuries trade in utilitarian goods, such as soapstone cooking vessels, was carried out, but Okinawa remained beyond the political control of Japan until it was taken over by the Satsuma domain in 1609. Okinawa was brought into the Chinese imperial system as a tributary state but maintained a good deal of political autonomy from China. The particular structure of power of the Ryūkyū Kingdom, in which the sister of the ruler was the chief priestess, is replicated in contemporary island ceremonies involving male councillors and female priestesses.[39]

Historical Relations with China and Japan

Okinawans began to engage in informal private trade with China by at least the beginning of the twelfth century. At about the same time, a period of internal fighting in Japan is said to have led to a flow of political refugees who brought new knowledge and skills into the Ryūkyūs. However, the power to transform Okinawa into a trading kingdom came from China, rather than Japan.[40]

The peculiar characteristics of the China trade were of crucial significance. Three forms of trade occurred, with differing social and political ramifications. They were official tributary trade, private trade, and relaying or trans-shipping trade. These kinds of trade were linked together as goods flowed from one system into another. Official tributary trade, which had developed in China from the Han dynasty, based on the ideology of Chinese economic superiority, required that states surrounding China pay homage to the emperor, in return for which they provided lavish gifts. Tributary states were given privileges to trade at certain ports. Some goods were carried to individual countries in East and South-east Asia, to be sold or distributed to political allies. At the official level of state interaction, tributary trade was the official means of commerce. It legitimised and supported the Okinawan state and provided wealth for public projects and the maintenance of the royal family.

This type of trade was established in 1372 soon after the beginning of the Ming dynasty. Since it was official trade it was described in historical documents, such as the Chinese dynastic annals and various records of the Ryūkyū kingdom. Tribute missions provided an opportunity not only for official trade but also for private trade, since the members of the tribute mission also engaged in buying and selling for personal profit. Okinawans sent tribute missions annually at the beginning of the Ming, and every second year from 1470. Of all of the tributary states, Ryūkyū, the last to be included in the system, sent by far the most missions, a total of 171, while Japan sent only ten.[41] The tribute ships, carrying as many as 200 passengers, represented substantial investments of diverse groups of people. Many reasons for the privileged status of Ryūkyū have been proposed. At the official level, Ryūkyū was to be rewarded for its filial devotion and respectful behaviour, in contrast to Japan, for instance. Cao Yonghe has emphasised that the Hongwu emperor (1368–1398) needed a pretext to import Ryūkyū horses which were used by the military to help consolidate the new regime.[42] The frequent Ryūkyū missions must have provided some kind of relief for the Fujian merchants who suffered from the constriction of trade following the Ming ban (see below).

Imperial missions which carried out the investiture of the king of Ryūkyū as a vassal ruler of China were also part of the tributary system. As Arne Rokkum notes: 'The Chinese ruled by the example of the gift, by the law and etiquette of a transaction at court between an envoy and an emperor'.[43] From the detailed account of the investiture of King Shō Sei in 1534 by the Chinese envoy, Chen Kan, we learn that a special ship (sometimes two ships) carrying 350 passengers who stayed in the Ryūkyūs for almost five months was built for the occasion. In 1392, to facilitate the official tributary trade, the Chinese emperor assigned a group of Fujianese, with their families, to be employed as navigators, interpreters, and advisers. In addition, the Chinese furnished ships for the tribute missions. The use of such technical advisers occurred in South-east Asia as well. The Chinese formed a community near the port of Naha (Kumemura) and their duties went far beyond the transport of tribute, to the transmission of learning, laws, and ritual.[44]

Official Chinese ambivalence to foreign trade at the beginning of the Ming dynasty, because it lost money and made the movements of coastal populations difficult to control, was broadened to outright official prohibition of all kinds of private trade with the Ming ban from 1368 to 1567. This ban, along with the complete prohibition of trade with Japan from 1523, was of fundamental importance in the development of Okinawan society and culture since it provided opportunities for relaying or trans-shipping, and the wide commercial and cultural contacts which the trade involved. The Okinawans relayed goods received from China at the time of tribute missions to Japan, Korea, and South-east Asia, at a handsome profit, and also relayed goods from these regions to China as part of their tribute. They also developed new crafts in Okinawa for the production of tribute goods, such as fine lacquer.

Private trade was extremely important in two contexts. First, it was the sole means of exchange between Okinawan polities and China before the establishment of the tributary relationship at the end of the fourteenth century. P. D. Curtin notes that generally in East and South-east Asia, from Song to Early Ming (about 960 to 1430), private trade was important and was controlled and encouraged by the Chinese government.[45] Fujianese white wares dating to the eleventh and twelfth centuries, along with early types of celadons of similar dates, have been found on many sites both on Okinawa and in Yaeyama, while a few sites such as Heshikiya Tobaru on the Katsuren Peninsula of Okinawa have yielded some sherds of Tang ceramics as well.[46] Judging from the great volume of Chinese ceramics recovered in the Ryūkyūs, private trade remained important throughout the fifteenth and sixteenth centuries. (It may be more appropriate to term it unofficial trade, since it must have been close to smuggling in many instances.) The fact that the coastal regions of Fujian teemed with pirates suggests that there was a great deal of informal interaction throughout the region.

Trade with Japan was carried out by private merchants from Hakata, Sakai, Bonotsu, and Hyōgo. The Japanese state did not have the power to control private trade.[47] With the imposition of the Ming maritime ban, Naha became an international port to which ships from Japan and other South-east Asian countries came to secure Chinese goods. Ryūkyū ships carried goods to Japan as well, and Ryūkyū state envoys travelled to the Kinai region every three or four years, from 1413 to the 1460s. The Japanese tribute ship which sailed from Sakai in 1451 carried a huge amount of sappanwood, used for dyeing, which the Japanese secured from South-east Asia by trans-shipment via Ryūkyū. While official envoys were exchanged between Korea and Ryūkyū in the late fourteenth century, by the middle of the fifteenth century gifts were sent on the ships of the Hakata traders, because of the high risk from pirates.[48]

Through trade, Okinawa entered into the Chinese diaspora, a nation of socially interdependent, spatially linked communities, joined by kinship among overseas Chinese groups and sharing Confucian cultural and political values. The articulating units in the diaspora were three types of cities. The largest, such as Guangzhou or Quanzhou, were cities set in the political framework of a major empire. Next were ports of regionally strong states, such as Cambay or Ayutthaya, and the third were city states such as Malacca, Aden, or Okinawa. Different levels of producers and consumers were linked. There were producers of manufactured goods, trading ports, suppliers of raw materials, and groups on the edge of the system such as pastoral nomads.

The peculiar combination of formalised tribute, in which Okinawa held an established place in the Chinese imperial structure, and the commercial diaspora, in which trans-shipment was the main money-maker, created a special situation for the development of Okinawan society and culture. Okinawa's relationship with the Quannan region of Fujian also had a special effect. This region was isolated from Han culture until the late Tang (AD ninth and tenth centuries). Its economy expanded rapidly through the tenth and eleventh centuries, with the expansion of trade from Guangzhou to Quanzhou. In the early eleventh century unofficial trade in and out of Quanzhou was substantial and there was no revenue collected by the state. Trans-shipment of goods from South-east Asia was a substantial part of this trade.

How did the Okinawan economy link to the Chinese economy? Hugh Clark states that there was a substantial drop in trade passing through the Quanzhou Trade Superintendency in the thirteenth century, caused by piracy, corruption and the enormous costs of supporting the southern branch of the Chinese imperial clan in Quanzhou, and the western branch in Fuzhou.[49] He believes that some of the lost trade may have been diverted to local smuggling, in which case it would disappear from official statistics but not from the local economy. If this were the situation in Quanzhou, could it be that the trade moved offshore, to places like Okinawa? Did Okinawa assume some of the trans-shipment trade of Quanzhou?

Two great peaks of Ming prosperity may also be relevant to political events and periods of intense castle construction activities in Okinawa. The first occurred in the early fifteenth century, the period of consolidation of Shuri power and the construction of Shuri castle, and the second in the late sixteenth and early seventeenth centuries, when

Okinawa was invaded by Satsuma, and its political independence came to an end.

Conclusion

The adaptive, historical and evolutionary processes of the development of ancient Okinawan society are slowly coming to light. The relationship of these processes to the formation of Okinawan identity is complex:

> A common experience as a condition, however, may not outlive its particular epoch with the motivated symbols to which it is conditioned, and why should it? Different times, different fashions: could it not as well be an experience in the passing – of transition, opposition, or interstice, which motivates the shared consciousness?[50]

I have presented an overview of the development of Okinawan culture as it can be determined from archaeological research. The historical identity which Okinawans construct from the narratives created by archaeologists, historians, and other students of culture, is negotiated. Ulf Hannerz proposes that a cultural flow, which is shared by several subgroups, and is reproduced in differing forms, 'consists of the externalization of meaning which individuals produce through arrangements of diverse forms and the interpretations which individuals make of such displays – those of others as well as their own'.[51]

The processes of externalisation of meaning are created by scholars, cultural institutions and government agencies, as well as individual Okinawans. While this chapter does not address the problems of the construction of Okinawan identity, it is important to recognise the significance of archaeological research at the local and national levels.

In the year 1 April 1992 to 31 March 1993, Okinawa prefecture was in the midst of its third development plan. Emphasis has been placed on infrastructure; agricultural development, roads, airports, residential areas, public facilities, golf courses, beach areas, resorts, and new facilities within the military bases. Okinawa enjoys a special status within Japan, by which 80 per cent of all development projects are funded directly by the central government. In many cases, an additional 10 per cent of the cost is borne by the prefectural government. As in other parts of Japan, archaeological research is controlled by the Cultural Section of the Board of Education at all municipal levels.

To organise the mitigation of damage from development and co-ordination of emergency excavations, basic site data are necessary. Of the fifty-three municipal units (that is, *shi, chō, son*), thirty-seven have completed detailed site inventories and surveys, which are published as separate monographs, sometimes with all-colour illustrations. The total cost of these surveys in 1992 was US$404 040. There were thirty-four salvage excavations costing a total of US$4 439 500. In particular, the reconstruction of Shuri Castle is remarkable. The castle was completely destroyed in 1945. Subsequently the US Military Government built the University of the Ryūkyūs on the site. After the Reversion to Japan in 1972, the University was removed and rebuilt in much expanded form at Nishihara. Reconnaissance and restoration of Shuri Castle began as early as 1972. Cost of this work to the end of 1992, contributed by the Prefectural Board of Education, amounted to over US$8 million.[52] The commitment to public archaeology in Okinawa, traditionally the poorest prefecture in Japan, is imposing indeed, even if it is much less than the support given to Osaka, Tokyo, and rapidly developing prefectures such as Chiba.

Notes

1 Takemoto Seishun and Asato Shijun, *Nihon no Kodai Iseki: Okinawa* (*Ancient Sites of Japan: Okinawa*), Tokyo, Hoikusha, 1993, p. 248; Tokunaga Shigeru, 'Fossil land mammals from the Ryūkyū Islands', *Proceedings of the Imperial Academy of Japan*, vol. XII, 1936, pp. 255–7; and 'Bone artifacts used by ancient man in the Loochoo Islands', *Proceedings of the Imperial Academy of Japan*, vol. XII, 1936, pp. 352–4; Ōyama Kashiwa, 'Ryūkyū Iha Kaizuka Kenkyū no Kiso' ('Basic study of the Iha shellmound, Ryūkyū'), *Jinruigaku Zasshi*, no. 36, 1911, pp. 1–29; Tawada Shinjun, 'Ryūkyū rettō no Kaizuka Bunpu to Hennen no Gainen Hōi' ('Contributions to general ideas of the distribution and chronology of shellmounds in the Ryūkyū Islands'), *Bunkazai Yōran*, 1960, pp. 32–67.

2 Oshiro Itsurō, *Ushinawareta Dōbutsu: Okinawa no Kaseki* (*Vanished Life: Fossils of Okinawa*), Naha, Shinsei Tosho Shuppan, 1987, p. 101.

3 Suzuki Hisashi, 'Skulls of the Minatogawa man', in Suzuki Hisashi and Hanihara Kazurō (eds), *The Minatogawa Man: The Upper Pleistocene Man from the Island of Okinawa*, University Museum, University of Tokyo, Bulletin no. 19, 1982, pp. 7–49; Takamiya Hiroto, 'Subsistence and adaptation processes in the prehistory of Okinawa (1)', paper delivered at the 15th Congress of the Indo-Pacific Prehistory Association, Chiangmai, Thailand, January 1994.

4 Richard Pearson, 'Taiwan and its place in East Asian prehistory', in K. C. Chang, K. C. Li, A. Wolf, and A. Yin (eds), *Anthropological Studies of the Taiwan Area: Accomplishments and Prospects*, Taipei, Taiwan National University, 1989, pp. 111–41; Takamiya Hiroe, 'Senshi Kodai no Okinawa' ('Okinawa in prehistory and ancient times'), *Nantō Bunka Sōsho* (*Series in Southern Culture*), no. 12, Tokyo, Daiichi Shobō, 1991, p. 11; Asato Susumu,

Kōkogaku kara Mita Ryūkyū Shi, Jō, Ge (Ryūkyū History as Seen from Archaeology, Volumes 1, 2) Naha, Okinawa Bunko, 1991.

5 Ginowan Shi Kyōiku Iinkai, *Uehara Nūribaru Iseki no Kinkyū Hakkutsu Chōsa no Kekka Gairyaku (Summary of the Results of the Salvage Excavations at the Uehara Nūribaru Site)*, Ginowan Shi Kyōiku Iinkai, 1993.

6 Asato Susumu, 'Okinawa no Hirosoko Doki, Kamuiyakikei Doki no Hennen ni Tsuite' ('Concerning the chronology of flat-bottomed and Kamuiyaki-type pottery of Okinawa'), *Higo Kōkogaku*, no. 8, 1991, pp. 579–93.

7 Takemoto and Asato, *Nihon no Kodai Iseki: Okinawa*, p. 242.

8 Faculty of Letters, University of Kumamoto, *Bataan Island and Northern Luzon*, University of Kumamoto, 1983.

9 Hotta Mitsuru, 'The vegetation of Kume', in Ryūkyū Archaeological Research Team, *Subsistence and Settlement in Okinawan Prehistory: Kume and Iriomote*, Vancouver, Laboratory of Archaeology, University of British Columbia, 1981, pp. 154–68.

10 Richard Pearson, 'Archaeology of the Ryūkyū Islands from the Yayoi to Kofun period', presented at the International Symposium, Japanese Archaeology in the Protohistoric and Early Historic Period; *Yamato and Its Relations to Surrounding Populations*, Universitat Bonn, 1992.

11 Kokuritsu Kagaku Hakubutsukan, *Nihonjin no Kigenten: Nihonjin wa Doko Kara Kita Ka? (Exhibition on the Origins of the Japanese: Where Did the Japanese Come From?)*, Tokyo, Yomiuri Shimbunsha, 1988; Hanihara Kazurō, 'Dual structure model for the population history of the Japanese', *Japan Review*, no. 2, 1991, pp. 1–33; C. Turner, 'Teeth and prehistory in Asia', *Scientific American*, February 1989; and 'Sundadonty and sinodonty in Japan: the dental basis for a dual origin hypothesis for the peopling of the Japanese islands', in Hanihara Kazurō (ed.), *Japanese as a Member of the Asian and Pacific Populations*, Kyoto, International Research Center for Japanese Studies, 1992.

12 Kishimoto Yoshihiko, 'Nantō no Doki Kigen o Megutte: Tsumegatamon Dōki ni Tsuite no Ichi Kōsatsu' ('Concerning the origins of pottery in the southern islands: a consideration of thumbnail-impressed pottery'), *Amami Kōko*, no. 2, 1991, pp. 5–28; Sasaki Kōmei, 'Nihonshi Tanjō' ('The birth of Japanese history'), *Nihon no Rekishi (History of Japan)*, vol. 1, Tokyo, Shūeisha, 1991, p. 349.

13 Chinen Isamu, 'Nansei Shotō no Sekki' ('Stone tools of the south-west islands'), in Miyagi Eishō and Takamiya Hiroe (eds), *Okinawa Rekishi Chizu*, Tokyo, Kashiwa Shobō, 1983, p. 90.

14 Asato Shijun, 'The distribution of Tridacna shell adzes in the southern Ryūkyū Islands', *Bulletin of the Indo-Pacific Prehistory Association*, no. 10, 1991, pp. 282–91; Miyagi Eishō and Takamiya Hiroe (eds), *Okinawa Rekishi Chizu (Historical Atlas of Okinawa)*, Tokyo, Kashiwa Shobō, 1983, p. 21.

15 Kokuritsu Kagaku Hakubutsukan, *Nihonjin no Kigenten: Nihonjin wa Doko Kara Kita Ka?*, p. 40; Oshiro, *Ushinawareta Dōbutsu: Okinawa no Kaseki*, p. 104.

16 Motozaki Kotarō (ed.), *Ryūkyū Ko no Chishitsu Monogatari (The Geological History of the Ryūkyū Arc)*, Naha, Okinawa Taimusu Sha, 1985, p. 227.

17 Baba Hisao and Narasaki Shūichirō, 'Minatogawa man, the oldest type of modern *homo sapiens* in East Asia', *Daiyonki Kenkyū (Quaternary Research)*, vol. 30, no. 2, 1991, pp. 221–30; Turner's work is cited at note 11; Kokuritsu, *Nihonjin no Kigenten: Nihonjin wa Doko Kara Kita Ka?*, p. 45.

18 Takemoto and Asato (eds), *Nihon no Kodai Iseki: Okinawa*, p. 56.
19 Takamiya, 'Senshi Kodai no Okinawa'; Motozaki (ed.), *Ryūkyū Ko no Chishitsu Monogatari*, p. 230.
20 Sakura Hajime, 'Pleistocene human bones found at Pinza Abu (Goat Cave), Miyako Island – a short report', *Bulletin of the National Science Museum*, Tokyo, series D 7, 1981, pp. 1–6.
21 Okinawa Ken Kyōiku Chō Bunka Ka, *Pinza Abu: Pinza Abu Dōketsu Hakkutsu Hōkoku* (*Pinza Abu: Report of the Excavation of Pinza Abu Cave*), Okinawa prefecture, 1985, p. 178.
22 Sakura Hajime, 'Pleistocene human bones found at Pinza Abu (Goat Cave)', p. 5; Hasegawa Yoshikazu, 'Notes on the vertebrate fossils from the Late Pleistocene to Holocene of Ryūkyū Islands, Japan', *Daiyonki Kenkyū* (*Quaternary Research*), no. 18, 1980, pp. 263–7.
23 Takamiya, *Senshi Jidai no Okinawa*, p. 47.
24 Katō Shimpei, 'Okinawa no Iwayuru Sajō Kokki ni Tsuite' ('Concerning the so-called double-notched bone tools from Okinawa'), *Kōkogaku Jānaru*, no. 167, 1979, pp. 72–5. Compare A. J. Sutcliffe, 'Similarity of bones and antlers gnawed by deer to human artifacts', *Nature*, no. 246, 1973, pp. 428–30.
25 Takemoto and Asato, *Nihon no Kodai Iseki: Okinawa*, p. 203.
26 Takamiya, *Senshi Jidai no Okinawa*, p. 112.
27 Takamiya Hiroto, L. A. Pavlish, and R. Hancock, 'Instrumental neutron activation analysis (INAA) of Okinawan pottery: can it be used to identify prehistoric contact?', *Bulletin of the Indo–Pacific Prehistory Association*, no. 10, 1991, pp. 292–306; Takamiya Hiroe, 'Nantō Kōko no Zatsuroku' ('Miscellaneous records of the archaeology of the southern islands'), vol. 1, *Nantō Kōko*, no. 11, 1991, pp. 21–36.
28 Sasaki, 'Nihonshi Tanjō', *Nihon no Rekishi*, vol. 1, p. 349; Kishimoto, 'Nantō no Doki Kigen o Megutte: Tsumegatamon Doki ni Tsuite no Ichi Kōsatsu', pp. 5–28.
29 Takamiya Hiroto, 'Neutron activation analysis of pottery sherds from the Murokawa shell midden, Okinawa, Japan', MA paper, Archaeology Program, University of California, Los Angeles, 1988.
30 Tōkyō Kokuritsu Hakubutsukan, 'Kaijō no Michi' ('Sea routes: history and culture of Okinawa'), *Okinawa no Rekishi to Bunka*, Tokyo, Yomiuri Shimbunsha, 1992, p. 41.
31 Mishima Itaru, 'Dazaifu to Nantō' ('Dazaifu and the southern islands') in Okazaki Tadashi Sensei Taikan Kinen Ronshū Henshū Iinkai (eds), *Higashi Ajai no Kōkogaku to Rekishi-Ge* (*The Archaeology and History of East Asia*), 2, Kyoto, Dōmeisha Shuppan, 1987, pp. 359–60.
32 Ibid.
33 E. Walker, *Important Trees of the Ryūkyū Islands*, Naha, United States Civil Administration of the Ryūkyū Islands, 1954, p. 159; Mishima, 'Dazaifu to Nantō', pp. 359–60.
34 Kamei Meitoku, 'Heian–Edo Jidai' ('Heian to Edo Periods'), in Tsuboi Kiyotari (ed.), *Zusetsu Nihon Shi* (*Japanese History as Told by Archaeological Excavation*), Tokyo, Shin Jimbutsu Ōraisha, no. 6, 1986, pp. 258–98.
35 Okinawa Kenritsu Hakubutsukan, *Tokubetsu Ten, Gusuku: Gusuku ga Kataru Kodai Ryūkyū no Rekishi to Roman* (*Special Exhibition, Gusuku: Ancient Ryūkyū History and Romance Told by the Castles*), Tomigusuku, Okinawa Kenritsu Hakubutsukan, 1985, p. 75; and Isen Chō Kyōiku Iinkai, *Kamuiyaki*

Koyōsekigun (*The Group of Old Kiln Sites of Kamuiyaki*), vol. 1, Isen Chō Maizō Bunkazai Hakkutsu Chōsa Hōkoku Sho no. 3, Isen chō, Isen chō Kyōiku Iinkai, 1985.

36 Asato, *Kōkogaku kara Mita Ryūkyū Shi, Jō, Ge*, p. 579.

37 Richard Pearson, *Ancient Japan*, New York, G. Braziller, 1992, p. 143.

38 Richard Pearson, 'The Chuzan Kingdom, Okinawa, as a city state', in T. Charlton and Dr Nichols, *The Archaeology of City States: Cross Cultural Approaches*, Smithsonian Institution Press (forthcoming).

39 Arne Rokkum, 'Godesses, priestesses, and sisters: vital characters of an eclipsed kingdom', D Phil. dissertation, Department and Museum of Anthropology, University of Oslo, 1992, p. 5.

40 Sakihara Mitsugu, *A Brief History of Early Okinawa Based on the Omoro Soshi*, Tokyo, Honpō Shoseki Press, 1987, pp. 118, 124; Takara Kurayoshi, *Ryūkyū Ōkoku* (*The Ryūkyū Kingdom*), Tokyo, Iwanami Shinsho, 1993, pp. 43–6.

41 Takara, *Ryūkyū Ōkoku*.

42 Cao Yonghe, 'Hin Kabuchō no Chūryū Kankei' ('Relations between China and Ryūkyū in the Hongwu era'), *Urasue Shiritsu Toshokan Kiyō*, no. 4, pp. 13–33.

43 Rokkum, 'Godesses, priestesses, and sisters', p. 29.

44 Gerhard Mueller, *Wohlwollen und Vertrauen: Die Investiturgesandschaft von Chen Kan im Jahr 1534 vor dem Hintergrund der politischen und wirtschaftlichen Beziehungen des Ming-Reiches zu den Ryūkyū Inseln zwischen 1372 und 1535*, Wurzburger Sinologische Schriften, Heidelberg: Ed Forum, 1991, pp. 105 and 44.

45 P. D. Curtin, *Cross-Cultural Trade in World History*, Cambridge University Press, 1984, p. 125.

46 Kin Seiki, 'Okinawa ni okeru Jūni, Jūsan Seiki no Chūgoku Tōjiki' ('Chinese ceramics of the 12th, 13th centuries found in Okinawa'), *Okinawa Kenritsu Hakubutsukan Kiyō*, no. 15, 1989, pp. 1–22.

47 Takara, *Ryūkyū Ōkoku*, p. 100.

48 Sakai Shi Hakubutsukan, *Hakata to Sakai* (*Hakata and Sakai*), Sakai Shi Hakubutsukan, 1993, p. 106; Takara, *Ryūkyū Ōkoku*, p. 98.

49 Hugh R. Clark, *Community, Trade, and Networks: Southern Fujian Province from the Third to the Thirteenth Century*, Cambridge University Press, 1991, p. 175.

50 Rokkum, 'Godesses, priestesses, and sisters', p. 2.

51 Ulf Hannerz, *Cultural Complexity: Studies in the Social Organization of Meaning*, New York, Columbia University Press, 1992.

52 Okinawa Ken Kyōiku Chō Bunka Ka, *Bunka Gyōsei Yōran*, Okinawa prefecture, 1993, pp. 61–70.

CHAPTER SEVEN

Ainu Moshir and Yaponesia: Ainu and Okinawan Identities in Contemporary Japan

HANAZAKI KŌHEI

(translated by Mark Hudson)

An incident on 15 June 1983 made a deep impression on me. An Aboriginal Australian had come to Hokkaido to visit the Ainu. He had been sent to Europe and Japan as part of a campaign to stop uranium mining on Aboriginal sacred land, and introduced himself as an anti-nuclear ambassador assigned by the Australian Aboriginal Land Council. I took him to the house of an Ainu family in Sapporo and we had a long conversation. He began to talk about the history of his people: 'In 1788 a thousand Britons arrived in our continent on board a single fleet of ships. Most were criminals sent out to build a colony on our land. From that year, the Dreamtime of Aboriginal Australians was shattered and a history of unhappiness and suffering began'. An Ainu woman replied: '1789, the year following the start of your sorrows, saw the Kunashir-Menash Revolt which was the last systematic resistance by us Ainu against Japanese aggression and exploitation. Before that our ancestors had resisted Japanese invaders for more than 300 years, but from that time until this day we have been deprived of our dignity as an indigenous people and, under the control of the Japanese state, forced to assimilate with the Japanese and to suffer discrimination'.

Talking of the suffering and conflict etched in their histories, the Aboriginal man and the Ainu woman embraced and wept. This was an impressive reference to a history I had never encountered.

As is well known, 1789 was the year of the French Revolution. Compared to this, the Kunashir-Menash Revolt – an incident in a corner of North-east Asia – may seem unimportant. It is little known in Japanese history; indeed, most Japanese people know almost nothing about it. Recently, however, there has been a reconsideration of modern world history which had been written and read as a simple account of the world-wide expansion of western European civilisation.

117

In the context of 'other world histories', resulting from the debate over the 500th anniversary in 1992 of Columbus's voyage, because of its place in the wider history of the Asia-Pacific region we can no longer ignore the Kunashir-Menash Revolt.[1]

Ezo and the Ainu as Barbarians

Recently historians have used the concepts of 'Japanese-type *ka-i* system' and *kaikin* to describe early modern Japanese foreign relations.[2] *Ka-i* and *kaikin* were Chinese foreign policies but, compared with the original Chinese view of *ka-i* (a civilised centre surrounded by barbarians) which was based on cultural supremacy, in their Japanese application these systems were centred on military power and the emperor.

The Japanese *ka-i* system was established in the 1630s. After this, the state prohibited Christianity and foreign customs, and strictly enforced assimilation. At the same time, in Ezo (Hokkaido) there was a strict separation between the territory used only by the Wajin (Japanese) and the land where the Ainu lived and traded. The Ainu were considered a separate race; politically they were *kegai no tami* (people whom the emperor's teachings had not reached), and economically they were the objects of trade. To the Tsugaru, Nanbu and other domains, the Ainu who lived in northern Tohoku were, as 'aliens', kept strictly apart from the ordinary people. They were not allowed to own fields for agriculture, and socially they were assigned to the lowest class which also contained beggars, outcasts and lepers.[3] At this stage, however, most of Ezo was still the free land of the Ainu. They maintained their own language and culture, living by gathering, hunting and fishing without outside restraint. Their homeland, the *Ainu moshir* or 'calm land of human beings', was truly an 'alien country' to the Wajin.

In 1669 the Shakushain War afforded the opportunity for ethnic unification and independence. The background to this revolt – the largest in Ainu history – was the forced imposition of unequal trading agreements by the Matsumae domain. This conflict was finally suppressed through deception, and the direct control and plunder of the Ainu people were intensified. The Ainu were debased by their trading partners and forced to produce goods (primarily marine products) for exchange.

From the middle of the eighteenth century, merchants with large amounts of capital divided Ezo (including the southern Kuriles) into several *basho* or trading posts and established the '*basho* contract system' whereby Ainu supplied labour to produce goods for Honshu or for export to China. The Ainu were forced from their villages to the *basho*

where they were exploited day and night like slaves. Their numbers
dropped sharply and they were faced with the crisis of uprooting their
culture and lifestyle.

The Kunashir-Menash Revolt arose through anger over oppression
and exploitation by Wajin rulers and merchants. The Ainu of Kunashir
Island (at present Russian territory) and the Okhotsk Sea coast
(Menash district) of eastern Hokkaido attacked the armed Wajin and
killed about seventy of them. When the Matsumae domain army came
to suppress the revolt, the Ainu accepted the advice of their elders and
put down their weapons, hoping to negotiate. With its overwhelming
military power, however, the Matsumae army beheaded thirty-seven
leaders and forced pledges of submission from the rest. After this, the
Ainu of these regions were suppressed even more fiercely; as a people
they were almost eradicated.

Comparisons with Ryūkyū History

A unified kingdom was established in the Ryūkyūs in 1429. Ships were
despatched to China, Japan, Korea and South-east Asia, and this transit
trade produced a zenith of prosperity from the end of the fifteenth to
the early sixteenth centuries.[4] At the beginning of the seventeenth
century both Ezo and the Ryūkyūs were brought into the *bakuhan*
system, but recent historians have noted that both were basically 'alien
countries within the *bakuhan* system'.[5]

In Ainu history there was no unified polity corresponding to a
state. In 1669 more than 2000 Ainu from all regions gathered at
the request of Shakushain and surrounded the Matsumae domain.
The Shakushain War can be seen as a movement towards the political
confederation and unification of Ainu regional groups, but the war
ended in defeat and there was no unification or declaration of
sovereignty.

Unlike the Shimazu clan's conquest of the Ryūkyūs, the invasion
of Hokkaido was not accomplished in one episode. After their defeat
in the Shakushain War, each Ainu leader had to offer a seven-article
personal contract to the lord of Matsumae. The first article declared
that 'Whatever I am ordered by the [domain] lord, I, my descendants,
my relatives by blood, and my fellow countrymen and women will,
without exception, not disobey'. This was very similar to the
'Regulation Clause 15' which the Shimazu clan made the Ryūkyū King,
Shō Nei, sign after his capture in 1611. The gist of that clause was
that 'Although the Ryūkyūs have long been a dependant of the
Shimazu clan, I have committed the great crime of neglecting my
bounden duties. In spite of this, I am permitted to return home and

am allotted the [Ryūkyū] archipelago [from the Shimazu clan]. I give thanks for this great favour and my future descendants will not break this written vow'.

The Meiji State and Forced Assimilation

For the Ainu people the Meiji state system was the beginning of still more suffering. The Japanese state changed the name 'Ezo' to 'Hokkaido', incorporated southern Sakhalin and the Kurile Islands into its territory, and sold off these 'internal colonies' to Wajin colonists. The *Ainu Moshir* (the mountains, plains, rivers and oceans where they lived a peaceful life under nature's blessing) was declared *terra nullius* and taken from them. Their hunting and fishing lifestyle was prohibited and they were driven into deep poverty. With the proclamation of the Family Registration Law in 1871, the Ainu were incorporated as 'commoners' (*heimin*) with the added entry of 'former aborigine' (*kyū dojin*). Strict prohibitions regarding Ainu customs were issued and violators were subject to severe punishments. The Ainu were also forced to adopt Japanese-style names. They were regarded as a primitive race who had not yet developed the benefits of civilisation. Under the rule of the survival of the fittest they were doomed to extinction, and as such they were taught that the only path left was to abandon their customs and culture, to assimilate with the Japanese and to become members of that supreme race. In order to become Japanese, the ideology and policy of the Meiji government was for the Ainu to become farmers.

In 1899 the government enacted the Hokkaido Former Aborigines Protection Act. As a relief measure for the poverty-stricken Ainu, this law was based on the free grant of up to 15 000 *tsubo* (4.95 hectares) of land to each household, and included fixed social security measures for the poor, sick, aged, and disabled, as well as the creation of primary schools for Ainu children. This Act, however, only provided land to Ainu engaged in agriculture. Those involved in other pursuits such as fishing received no assistance.

The primary schools for 'former aborigines' had the effect of increasing the attendance rate among Ainu children, but the contents and principles of schooling were not only discriminatory, but the objectives also included the abandonment of Ainu ethnic culture and thorough indoctrination to make the children loyal subjects of the imperial state. These policies are well illustrated by the 'devoted' primary school teachers who aspired to the complete eradication of the Ainu language in education.

The 'Punishment' of the Ryūkyūs

The situation in the Ryūkyūs was rather different. Although the country had a king, it was made into a retainer of the Satsuma domain. It also received investiture (*cefeng*) from the Qing court and became a retainer of both China and Japan. For this reason the Japanese government was more cautious in the Ryūkyūs than in Ezo.

First, in 1872 the government changed the Ryūkyū 'kingdom' to a 'domain' (*han*). The king was invested as a 'domain king', instead of the usual title of domain lord or *daimyō*. In 1875 the despatch of tributary envoys to China was prohibited, and decrees ordered the use of the Meiji calendar, reform of the domain government, the establishment of army outposts, and a visit to Tokyo by King Shō Tai. As these demands deprived the Ryūkyūs of their sovereignty and autonomy, over a period of five years they tried various forms of resistance including petitions, filibusters, and appeals to the Qing court. Reaching the end of its patience, in 1879 the Japanese government forcibly turned the islands from a domain into a prefecture with the help of some 500 police and soldiers. The king was made to leave his castle in Shuri. These actions were described as 'punishment' for failure to obey Japanese orders of 1875 and 1876. After this punishment, the administration of Okinawa was marked by the 'preservation of old customs' policy, pacifying public opinion by preserving various customs with the aim of bringing about gradual change. Land tax reforms, for example, which had been carried out on mainland Japan in 1873, were introduced by Okinawa prefecture together with land consolidation measures only in 1903.

The differences in the treatment of the north and the south by the Japanese fostered a feeling of superiority by Okinawans, who regarded it as an insult to be placed on a par with the 'Taiwan aborigines and the Ainu of the north'.[6]

The Assertion of the Ainu People in the Modern Era (1912 to 1945)

In the Taishō era (1912–1926) the voice of the Ainu people gradually began to be heard in Japanese society. Worries over the future of the Ainu, improvements in education, and protests against discrimination dominated debates. Excellent poets and writers on Ainu language and literature appeared among the people. The value of *yukar* (mythic epic poems) and other works of the oral tradition came to be appreciated as part of Ainu culture. Many gems of verse were composed by Ainu poets using the *tanka* form, and their anger and sadness over their stigma as a 'doomed race' slowly became famous.

To take one example, Iboshi Hokuto (1902–1929) was a poet who died very young. While working in Tokyo, Iboshi learnt about the *Suiheisha Sengen* (the '"Levellers" Declaration'), a declaration for the human rights of *burakumin* outcasts. He also met the 'father of Okinawan studies', Iha Fuyū (1876–1947). Iboshi wrote: 'Being instigated by strong desires that research on the Ainu should be conducted by their own hands and that the Ainu revival must come from themselves, I left a pleasant Tokyo and once again became a person of the *kotan* (village)'. In 'A profile of the Ainu' he asserted:

> The virtue of water is that it is water, the virtue of fire is that it is fire. The significance of being is in itself. Koreans have virtue as Koreans. The Ainu have consciousness as Ainu. The *Shamo* should also awake as *Shamo*.[7] Once all people respect each other and develop their respective ethnic identities as their uniqueness, the universe of human beings will flourish. Ah! How far must we go before we reach our ideal universe?
>
> I am Ainu! I never hesitate to say this. Lurking at the bottom of that cry is the pride of an indigenous people. We must reject the absurd contempt of social conventions and realise our pure essence as a people.[8]

This self-assertion which flowed from the bottom of Iboshi's soul included a universality based on a declaration of ethnic consciousness and the pride of an indigenous people. This cry can be said to reach across time to the other indigenous peoples of the world today.

A *tanka* poem that is representative of Iboshi's work is:

> *Ainu to iu atarashiku yoi gainen o naichi no hito ni ataetaku omou*
> (I aspire to give the new, worthy concept of Ainu to the people of the mainland.)

In this *tanka* we can hear an echo of the ideas of the '"Levellers" Declaration' (*Suiheisha Sengen*): 'Now is the time, we honour our name *Eta*'.

In the early Shōwa era, at the same time as the demands of pioneers like Iboshi, there was a movement from within the Ainu people to improve their lives. Following these developments, in 1930 the Hokkaido Ainu Association was established on the initiative of the Hokkaido prefectural government. Although it was influenced by the assimilationist policies of government officials, the newspaper of this organisation, the *Ezo no Hikari* (The Light of Ezo), served as a forum for the exchange of information and views between the Ainu of each district and pressed for the Hokkaido Ainu Youth Congress held in Sapporo in 1931.

Also at this time, a resistance movement was organised among the Asahikawa Ainu when there was a move to use land granted to the Ainu to make Asahikawa City into the northern base of the Japanese Imperial Army. In 1932 a meeting of representatives from all over Hokkaido was held at the request of the Asahikawa Ainu. The Pan-Hokkaido Former Native Representatives' Congress Declaration demanded the 'thorough reorganisation' of the Law for the Protection of Former Natives and the 'reappropriation without limits of the land of the Chikabumi Ainu village'. This declaration reflected the gradually increasing consciousness of the people in their move from discrimination to emancipation, but with the plunge into fifteen years of war, these developments were crushed.

From 1945 to 1972

For the Ainu who hoped for a revival of their people, as well as for the Korean minority in Japan, the unconditional surrender of Japanese imperialism in 1945 meant the possibility of emancipation. The hope was born that they would not again have to suffer pity and contempt as a 'doomed race' and the injustice of being made to become completely Wajin Japanese. A 1946 congress in Shizunai on the central Pacific coast saw the unprecedented participation of 2000 Ainu from all over Hokkaido, who decided to incorporate a Hokkaido Ainu Association. It would be twenty more years, however, before a level of political activity was reached whereby Ainu identity was clearly Ainu, when their ethnic self-assertiveness was strongly emphasised, and when they could regain their rights.

In 1968 celebrations took place for the centenary of the Japanese settlement and development of Hokkaido. These celebrations became an opportunity for the revival of the Ainu because, in the one-sided praise for the history of Japanese settlement and colonisation, the sacrifice and continued suffering of the Ainu was ignored. Totsuka Miwako (b. 1948), who expresses the feelings and thoughts of the people through her poetry, was just twenty years old. Having experienced discrimination herself, Totsuka wrote to the readers' column of the *Hokkaidō Shimbun* newspaper:

> This year the Hokkaido centenary celebrations seem to have become a matter of considerable concern for the people of Hokkaido, but I have little interest in these events. The reason why is because I am an Ainu. From long before the Meiji era our ancestors were subjected to oppression of various sorts. Even in the advanced society we live in today, if an Ainu wants to marry a Wajin Japanese it is not unusual for them to be faced with difficulties. It is also a fact that some people living together with us on this same island of Hokkaido look down upon the Ainu people.
>
> Naturally I respect the efforts of those people who came to Hokkaido with

its difficult climate and who overcame many difficulties to lay the foundations of the current prosperity of the island. But I also hope that the blood shed by us Ainu which has soaked through the base of the Hokkaido Centenary Memorial Tower [in Sapporo] will not be forgotten.[9]

This modest appeal announced an ethnic revival movement. In her outstanding poems Totsuka denounced the Japanese over the history and current state of the Ainu.

The sculptor, Sunazawa Bikki (1931–1990), protested against the design of a bronze sculpture entitled 'Group in a Snowstorm' which had been planned by Asahikawa City as part of the Centenary. Sunazawa argued that the figure of an Ainu elder kneeling before Wajin settlers and showing them the way represented a master–servant relationship. On the day of the unveiling ceremony in 1970 Sunazawa single-handedly distributed leaflets which he had printed to the people of the city. Later he created many famous sculptures showing his true genius.

Just at this time, meetings and demonstrations against the Vietnam War and student revolts against the political and educational systems were reaching a climax. There were also major revolts against the pollution and destruction of the countryside caused by development. These anti-development movements aroused interest in local identity and regional histories, and in both Hokkaido and Okinawa ethnic consciousness was strengthened. Yuki Shōji (1938–1983), an Ainu from the Kushiro region of eastern Hokkaido, argued for the necessity of an autonomous, organised ethnic movement in his 1970 article 'An appeal to my fellow men: the way of Ainu as naturalists':

In order to carry through our genuine claims, we must be aware of the importance of organised action as an ethnic group. From many scholars the Ainu have amassed a vast amount of material necessary for the ethnic emancipation movement. Together with the historical evidence, we can know the true meaning of hypocrisy. The people of Ainu descent must profit from this knowledge, strengthen their morale, and prepare for an economic struggle. We must begin a steady struggle.

When we turn our attention to all social problems, do not excuse hypocrites, co-operate with other organisations, participate in the problem of the many ethnic minorities around the world, utilise the many lessons of the historical past, and work towards the promotion of world peace and human rights, then the new path of Ainu history will begin. Is it just a dream that many people of Ainu descent have the strong conviction that that time will come in the not-too-distant future?[10]

This declaration marked the start of Yuki's activism. In 1972 he organised the Ainu Emancipation League, and in that same year its members and supporters occupied the rostrum of the joint conference of the Anthropological and Ethnological Societies being held at Sapporo Medical College and publicly questioned the assembled scholars: 'Is the debate on the Ainu at this conference being held from the viewpoint that the Ainu people are already extinct? Or is it based on the realisation that the Ainu are still living at the present, that they will not become extinct, that they are confronting the conquering Japanese state?' This request for a public debate was rejected. In this period, however, there was a clear step towards a new Ainu history.

The Development of the Ainu People's Movement and Ethnic Assertion

From the 1970s the movement for the recovery of the dignity and rights of the Ainu people made great advances. One reason for this was the wave of large-scale development projects that reached Hokkaido. Secret plans for Hokkaido to become an energy source for national industrial development resulted in the announcement in 1970 of the construction of a large oil-generated power station to be built on the south-western Pacific coast of the island. Opposition by local fishermen and farmers began at once. In particular, the Ainu fishermen of the Usu area, where there had long been Ainu *kotan*, repeatedly resisted by non-violent direct means, pleading for their Ainu compatriots to protect the ocean and the earth. Some concerned young Ainu gave passionate support to this cause and in 1973 they published the first issue of a monthly newspaper called *Anutar Ainu* (We Human Beings). This newspaper played a pioneering role with articles dealing with discrimination, Ainu cultural inheritance, and the words of Ainu elders, but came to an end in 1976 with issue 20.

Activities relating to ethnic cultural inheritance also increased. In 1972 Kayano Shigeru (b. 1926), an Ainu living in Nibutani, a village in Biratori-chō with a large Ainu population, opened the Nibutani Ainu Culture Museum to display the ethnographic collection he had collected. Putting his rich knowledge of the Ainu language to practical use, Kayano was also diligent in writing about Ainu *yukar*, folk tales, daily life and folk artefacts, and worked towards the spread of a wider acquaintance of Ainu culture. Later, he particularly put his efforts into the revival of the language and in 1983 began the Nibutani Ainu Language School. This school continues today under the auspices of the Hokkaido Utari Association (see below). In 1987 an Ainu language school was also opened in Asahikawa. These were the first Ainu language schools in Japan. As public money was obtained, this was also the first time the Ainu people secured the official opportunity to study their language and, as such, the schools represented a major development. In 1993 there were eleven Ainu language schools in Hokkaido, each with a small amount of public funding. An Ainu dictionary produced by the Ainu people is also being compiled by Kayano.[11]

In addition to these developments, the study of traditional Ainu lifeways, memorial services for ancestors who fought against the Wajin invaders, the revival of welcoming ceremonies for salmon moving upstream to spawn, and other activities were eagerly carried out throughout Hokkaido.

The Movement for New Legislation

At present the most comprehensive Ainu organisation is the Hokkaido Utari Association. *Utari* means 'fellow countrypeople' in the Ainu language. The Association has fifty-eight branches across Hokkaido and in 1991 there were 15 711 members. Since 1961, when a budget was obtained from the Ministry of Welfare, this organisation has measured progress in the lifestyle and welfare of the Ainu in Hokkaido. The motive behind this budget, however, was not compensation for historic wrongs committed by the Japanese state, but simply part of a social welfare policy for the poor and needy.

Entering the 1980s, interest in the restoration of ethnic rights became stronger among the members of the Association and it incorporated the functions of an ethnic corporation. At the 1984 general meeting it was decided to abolish the Former Aborigines Protection Act. A draft law regarding the Ainu people was adopted and a resolution made to enact it. The preamble to the draft of this 'new law' stated that:

> This law aims for the recognition that the Ainu people exist within Japan with their own unique culture, and for the respect of ethnic dignity and the guarantee of ethnic rights under the Japanese Constitution. It also noted that the reason for the law was that:
> The Ainu problem is the shameful historical outcome of the Ainu people having been thrust aside in the formation of the modern Japanese state. The law also relates to the important question of the guarantee of basic human rights under the Japanese Constitution. The resolution of this sort of problem is the responsibility of the government and, with the recognition that this question affects all citizens [of Japan], we hereby abolish the humiliating, discriminatory law, the 'Hokkaido Former Aborigines Protection Act', and enact a new law relating to the Ainu people.

The Association concentrated on organising the enactment of this new law and worked on the Japanese government to this end. While attaching a reservation to the demand for special seats for Ainu representatives in the National Diet and in local parliaments, the governor and parliament of Hokkaido supported the demand and requested the government to enact the law.

In 1991 the Japanese government finally recognised the Ainu as an ethnic minority, but it has not yet accepted that they are an indigenous people. The reason why aboriginality is not recognised is said to be that there is still no agreed international definition of the term and therefore the government is not sure if the Ainu are indigenous. Because of this attitude, the Japanese government has not enacted the new law, but public support for its enactment has been increasing. If the movement to enact the law is successful, it will be an important first step towards a multi-ethnic and multicultural Japanese state and society.

Exchanges and Solidarity with the World Indigenous People's Movement

International exchanges between Ainu and indigenous peoples from all over the world began gradually from the late 1970s. The Ainu, who previously had had little chance to learn about the situation of such peoples, began to take a more international role. The rights of indigenous peoples were widely taken up as part of the problem of human rights, and a trend towards solidarity with other peoples in a similar situation arose.

In 1986 the Hokkaido Utari Association sent a request for an investigation of the Ainu ethnic question to the United Nations Human Rights Committee, and since 1987 the director of the Association has been sent to the Working Group on Indigenous Populations of the UN Human Rights sub-committee, reporting on the history and current state of the Ainu. In response to this activity, the Japanese government gradually changed its previous emphasis that 'the Ainu have already assimilated with the Japanese and do not exist as a people', and in 1989 finally announced that 'we will deal with the Ainu question as an ethnic problem'. In 1989 indigenous people, mainly from the Asia-Pacific region, were invited to Hokkaido and an international congress discussed common problems. In 1993 an International Forum for Indigenous Peoples was also held in Nibutani.

Parallel with the movement for the assertion of Ainu identity and the restoration of ethnic rights, there was a movement which directly confronted discrimination. In 1981 an advertisement placed in the *Japan Times* by Japan's largest travel company was designed to encourage foreign tourists to visit Hokkaido, but it used discriminatory language. On a trip to Hokkaido, it said, you could see an 'old real

Ainu village' and the 'famed hairy Ainu'. In negotiations during the six-month period of impeachment, at first the management of the travel company could not understand why this was discriminatory, but later came to recognise the historical structure of discrimination against the Ainu and apologised for the advertisement.

In 1986 Prime Minister Nakasone Yasuhiro declared that the educational level of the USA was low because of the presence of many blacks and other non-white ethnic groups; in contrast, as an ethnically homogeneous nation, Japan enjoyed a high level of education. Nakasone was severely criticised both inside and outside Japan. The Ainu rose up at once in indignation and organised an 'Ainu people speak up for their own existence' meeting in Tokyo. The following year there was an 'Ainu from all over Japan bear witness' meeting in Sapporo where Ainu identity and solidarity with other discriminated minorities were discussed, taking the first steps towards multi-ethnic coexistence.

The 'Northern Territories' Question

Under the terms of the 1875 Russo–Japanese Treaty of Exchange of Sakhalin for the Kurile Islands, the southern Kuriles became Japanese territory. However, the rights of the indigenous Ainu inhabitants were ignored. After Japan's defeat in the Second World War these islands came under Soviet control. The Japanese have stressed that they are an 'intrinsic part of Japan' and have pressed for their return. The 1982 general meeting of the Hokkaido Utari Association criticised the fact that the movement for the return of the 'northern territories' completely ignored the rights of the indigenous Ainu and resolved to 'reserve the Ainu's rights as the indigenous people of the Kurile Islands'.

One intellectual who reacted sensitively was Arasaki Moriteru (b. 1936), a former Chancellor of Okinawa University and an active promoter of the Okinawan people's movement. Arasaki argued that the 'return' of Okinawa in 1972 (after American occupation following the war) was 'in reality a part of the policy of strengthening the US–Japan military alliance, and was neither a first step towards an autonomous development of the region nor sufficient to appease the islanders' feelings of pride and desire for emancipation'. He warned against repeating the same mistake in the resolution of the 'northern territories' question.[12] Arasaki also supported the idea of Ainu artist, Toyo'oka Masanori (b. 1945), that a solution to the problem could be devised by building a 'philosophy of ethnic coexistence' with the indigenous Ainu, the former Japanese inhabitants and the present

Russian ones all respecting each other's positions. If the 'northern territories' question could be resolved in such a way, that 'would mean a big transition for the Japanese nation', a transition 'from a homogeneous, standardised, rigid state to a gentle state comprising cultural and regional diversity'.[13]

Yaponesia

In 1945 the Japanese and American armies clashed on Okinawa Island. After the war, the island was placed under the rule of the US High Commissioner until 1972. Even after its 'return' to Japan, the occupation of the central part of the island by a US military base for a long time forced distorted economic development through reliance on income from the base.

In the 1970s both Okinawa and Hokkaido were designated as energy sources for the rest of Japan. The construction of the Kin Bay Petroleum Storage Depot on Okinawa, begun at almost the same time as the return of the island, was met by strong local opposition. Construction went ahead, but the concept that the ocean was the basis of survival for the local people was born from this protest movement. In 1980 when the Japanese government's plan to dispose of nuclear waste in the Pacific became known, the Okinawans forged links with the anti-nuclear people of the Palau Republic and their consciousness of themselves as a Pacific Island people was strengthened.

Recently the Okinawan economy has turned into the 'tourism-dependent type' and, with the national rush for resort development from 1988, beaches and land for golf courses have been bought up using capital from 'Yamato' (as the Okinawans call mainland Japan). This resort development has caused various strains within the islands. Despite this enforced marginalisation, the Okinawan people have not assimilated with Yamato but, based on region and ethnicity, are trying to establish their own identity with regard to thought, culture and government. Among Okinawan intellectuals, the word 'Yaponesia', coined in 1960 by the novelist, Shimao Toshio (1917–1986), struck a sympathetic response and has become entrenched. Shimao saw the Japanese archipelago as a group of islands like Polynesia, Micronesia, Melanesia and Indonesia, and derived the name from the concept that these island peoples seem to share certain characteristics. While this idea was widely accepted, the writer on Okinawan people's history, Miki Takeshi (b. 1940), noted that it was difficult to see present-day Yamato as a '-nesia' and that only the Ryūkyū arc had maintained such characteristics. He therefore proposed the concept of 'Okinesia' and argued that this should be separated from 'Yaponesia'. In turning the

Ryūkyūs into an 'Okinawan cultural sphere', an 'international concept, developed on the ocean and unconnected with narrow-minded nationalism and the belief in the sanctity of the imperial system', could be constructed.[14]

Arasaki Moriteru has concluded that the desire for 'self-reliance' can be found among many Okinawan people in the 1990s. He sees 'self-reliance' as sharing in the recovery of cooperativeness in Okinawan society and calls for the creation of a 'peaceful and carefree Okinawan society'. Arasaki has also drawn attention to a draft Constitution of the Republic of Taiwan, drawn up by a sect aiming at national independence within the opposition Democratic Progress Party. This Constitution advocates equal relations between four cultural groups and Arasaki comments that 'this cultural pluralism contrasts sharply with the mono-ethnic ideology of a Japanese state that can reject a proposal (in the Ainu "new law") for a parliamentary seat for the Ainu people'.[15]

Conclusions

An understanding of Ainu and Okinawan history means acknowledging that the majority ethnic group occupying central Japan invaded those other regions of the archipelago which were once 'alien countries', turned them into colonies, conquered and controlled the independent ethnic groups who lived there and forced them to assimilate.

Ainu and Okinawan experience also suggests the need for a new look, not just at Japanese history but also at world history from the viewpoint of ethnic groups who were conquered and controlled, and makes us reflect on the discrimination inherent in the ideology of assimilation born from the processes of civilisation and modernisation.

Recent efforts to restore Ainu ethnic identity and the self-reliance of Okinawa, while recovering the consciousness of ethnic and regional cooperation, are also movements aimed at autonomy and self-government. These efforts include the demand that the state ideology and political system of the Japanese state take the coexistence of many ethnic groups and cultures as a prerequisite, and press for a change in that view of identity which sees the Japanese state as the exclusive possession of the homogeneous majority of Japanese, and urge the development of social and political movements which would enable the expansion of democratic spaces within the Japanese archipelago where different individuals and different groups of people can live together in harmony.

Notes

1 On the Ainu uprisings see Heinz Hugo Alber, 'Die Aufstände der Ainu und deren geschichtlicher Hintergrund', *Beiträge zur Japanologie*, Bd. 14, Vienna, 1977 (eds).

2 Arano Yasunori, 'Nihongata ka-i no keisei' ('The formation of the Japanese-type *ka-i* system'), and Emori Susumu, 'Ezo-chi no rekishi to Nihon shakai' ('The history of 'Ezo' and Japanese society), *Nihon no Shakaishi (The Social History of Japan)*, vol. 1, Tokyo, Iwanami, 1987, pp. 183–226 and 311–51. (In the Japanese context *kaikin* means the closing of ports to international shipping. A more detailed English discussion of these terms, and of Arano and Emori's ideas, can be found in Katō Eiichi, 'The age of the great voyages and Japan's "national seclusion"', *Historical Studies in Japan (VII), 1983–1987*, National Committee of Japanese Historians (ed.), Tokyo, Yamakawa, 1990, pp. 21–58. Eds)

3 Emori, 'Ezo-chi no rekishi to Nihon shakai'.

4 Takara Kurayoshi, *Ryūkyū Ōkoku (The Ryūkyū Kingdom)*, Tokyo, Iwanami Shinsho, 1993. See also Richard Pearson's comments in chapter 6 of this volume.

5 Takara, *Ryūkyū Ōkoku*.

6 See the *Ryūkyū Shinpō* editorial in the section on the 1903 Jinruikan Affair in Ōta Masahide, *Okinawa no Minshū Ishiki (The Public Consciousness of Okinawa)*, Tokyo, Shinsensha, 1976.

7 *Shamo* is an Ainu word for the Wajin. It was originally pronounced *Shisam* and meant 'neighbour', but became corrupted. The corrupted form often conveys censure.

8 Iboshi Hokuto, 'Ainu no sugata' ('A profile of the Ainu', *Iboshi Hokuto Ikō: Kotan (Posthumous Works of Iboshi Hokuto: Kotan)*, Tokyo, Sofukan, 1984.

9 Totsuka Miwako in *Hokkaidō Shimbun*, 13 May 1968.

10 Yuki Shoji, 'In favour of the Utari: naturalists – the Ainu way', *Kotan no konseki – Ainu Jinkenshi no Ichidanmen (Traces of the Kotan: A Cross-section through the History of Ainu Human Rights)*, Asahigawa, Asahigawa Jinken Yōgo Iinrengōkai, 1970.

11 On Nibutani and the Ainu ethnic revival, see Katarina Sjöberg, *The Return of the Ainu: Cultural Mobilization and Practice of Ethnicity in Japan*, Chur, Switzerland, Harwood Academic, 1993 (eds).

12 Arasaki Moriteru, *Yawarakai shakai o motomete: Okinawa dōjidaishi (In Search of a Gentle Society: A History of Contemporary Okinawa)*, vol. 4, 1988–1990, Tokyo, Gaifūsha, 1992.

13 Arasaki, *Yawarakai shakai o motomete*.

14 Miki Takeshi, *Okinesia Bunkaron: Seishin no Kyōwakoku o motomete (A Theory on Okinesia Culture: In Search of a Spiritual Republic)*, Tokyo, Kaifūsha, 1988.

15 Arasaki, *Yawarakai shakai o motomete*.

PART THREE

Contact with the Outside

CHAPTER EIGHT

Some Reflections on Identity Formation in East Asia in the Sixteenth and Seventeenth Centuries

DEREK MASSARELLA

A key element of Japan's present identity is embedded in the assumption that in the early modern (more precisely the Azuchi-Momoyama) period, the country was 'open' to foreigners and foreign influence; then, save for the Dutch and Chinese in Nagasaki and the Japanese presence in the nominally independent Ryūkyū kingdom and in Korea, the country was 'closed' by government diktat enabling Japan to enjoy the benefits of a 'pax Tokugawa'. The quality of that supposedly blissful era is captured in an anti-Christian tract dating from the end of the 1630s, in words that reflect what was becoming an official Tokugawa ideology: 'The Empire is at peace, the land in tranquillity, the reign of longevity. The people partake of the virtue of the ruler and his subject princes. Verily, our age can be called another sainted reign of Engi, a golden age indeed'.[1] According to some scholars, the fruits of the 'pax Tokugawa' were inestimable, for Japan then achieved a significant level of proto-industrialisation, and by the mid-nineteenth century Japan had achieved the necessary pre-conditions for indigenous industrialisation, whether or not Perry's black ships had turned up in 1853.[2]

The idea of an open/closed rhythm to Japanese history has its appeal. The receptiveness to foreign cultural influence during the Azuchi-Momoyama period resembles Japan's earlier flirtation with Chinese culture during the Heian period. Things Chinese were then very much in vogue before they were rejected – after the Japanese had absorbed whole chunks of Chinese culture. A similar phenomenon would be repeated during the Meiji period with Europe and the United States the focus of Japan's attention. Such a pattern of openness and withdrawal is too neat, too schematic, too contrived, and too much an echo of earlier cyclical models of Asian history to be taken seriously.

Even in relation to the Azuchi-Momoyama period there are several fundamental problems. First, it implies that before the later sixteenth century Japan was closed. This was not the case. Secondly, from the 1630s, although the bakufu certainly restricted and sought to control such trade and contacts with the outside world that it permitted, in terms of trade, international relations or cross-cultural contact and influence Japan did not cut itself off from the rest of the world. A true *sakoku* policy only emerges after 1793.[3] Thirdly, it is 'Japanocentric', ignoring similar phenomena in China and Korea, and making Japan's 'isolation' appear unique.

Nevertheless, on the face of it Japan does appear to be open and outward-looking in the late sixteenth and early seventeenth centuries, symbolised by the short-lived craze for *namban* or southern barbarian clothes, accessories and cuisine among the upper classes, before (from the reign of the third shogun) the bakufu decided to restrict the country's foreign relations. This apparent shift from an open to a closed country is often taken as synonymous with the evolution of Japan's relationship with the Europeans who came to its shores from the 1540s.

The ninety years between 1549 (when Francis Xavier reached Japan) and 1639 (when the Portuguese were expelled in the aftermath of the Shimabara Christian millennarian uprising), used to be described, at least in the non-Japanese literature, as Japan's 'Christian century'. Historians like to give labels to eras, but unlike other labels, such as the Thirty Years' War or the *sengoku jidai*, this label was no mere description. It implied that Christianity was quite central to the formation of the early modern Japanese polity. But seen from the perspective of endogenous developments which pre-date the arrival of the Portuguese – the ambitions, efforts and policies of the three hegemons (Oda Nobunaga, Toyotomi Hideyoshi and Tokugawa Ieyasu) to assert their authority, dominate and reduce their rivals, and legitimise their power – the pernicious doctrine of Christianity was just one potential focus of opposition that these warlords had to confront, challenge and, if need be, destroy as Japan made its transition from war to peace.

In reality, the role of Europeans in early modern Japanese state-building is secondary, quite different from the primary role which Leonard Andaya ascribes to Europeans in the process of state formation in Maluku (the Moluccas). In Maluku those sultans who dealt directly with Europeans enhanced their dignity, prestige and authority over rivals, augmenting their own power.[4] The emergence of a strong, central authority in early modern Japan made such a development impossible. The centre was able to stamp its authority more firmly over the periphery. Again, the label 'Christian century' implied that Christianity was emblematic of the 'West' and that the Jesuit and mendicant attempts to convert Japan reflected a general European project of conquest, empire, and dominion through conversion, what Stephen Greenblatt calls 'Christian imperialism' and Vassilis Lambropoulous 'the enterprise of salvation [that] colonized the world' under the aegis of the early modern European sovereign states.[5]

One of the most distinguished scholars of early modern Japan, Professor Jurgis Elisonas (George Elison), says that the Christian century 'would be a mere interlude were it not for its causal relation to the Sakoku policy. The total rejection of Christianity helps to define an era'. He even speaks of the Jesuit mission as part of 'a heroic effort to westernise' Japan.[6] But Elisonas's remarks are open to doubt. First, they are teleological. He writes in the manner of a Greek tragedy with the actors cast in roles which propel them towards an inevitable outcome. This is highly effective as a literary device, less convincing as history. Secondly, the remarks do not apply to the English or Dutch, nor even to the majority of Portuguese who came to Japan to trade, not to harvest souls. The Protestants did not deny that they were Christians and the shogunate accepted their claims to be of a different Christian hue from the Iberians, even if periodically Japanese officials entertained doubts.[7] Thirdly, recent scholarship on the Christian impact on Meso-america reminds us of the important debate in the New World about strategies to convert the indigenous people, and about how much accommodation there should be with native traditions. In practice, until the mid-sixteenth century Christianity in Mexico was preached and indigenised in such a way as to preserve, rather than obliterate, native traditions. By the early seventeenth century the Church had became both an agent of colonial policy and an institution of the colonial regime and forceful conversion was deemed the most suitable way to proceed.[8] Fourthly, it is true that the affair of the *San Felipe*, the Manila galleon wrecked off the Kyushu coast in 1596, provided the Church in Japan with its first martyrs, because of some defiant, offhand remarks supposedly uttered by the ship's pilot that the Spanish king (since 1580 king of Portugal as well, a development the Japanese knew about) had used the friars as his vanguard in the conquest of the New World. But by the time that the conquistadors had reached the eastern shores of the Pacific, their capacity to translate the confident rhetoric of conquest and conversion into action beyond Europe and the New World was spent. When Hideyoshi (1586–1598) sneezed, by threatening invasion, the Spanish in Manila caught a cold.[9] Fifthly, the term 'westernise' implies a clash of cultural values: those of a robust, confident, intolerant Europe with an arrogant sense of superiority, versus those of Japan. For Elisonas, the cultural values of Japan are symbolised by the temples and shrines that the Jesuits and their supporters razed and are reflected in the principles of social organisation implicit in the doctrine of neo-Confucianism, which he sees as central to the Tokugawa efforts to establish ascendancy. The Western values are those of Christianity, or more precisely, of Roman Catholic Christianity. In suggesting a clash of cultures, Elisonas anticipates Edward Said's notion that European expansion was premised on the presumption of cultural hegemony, 'the idea of a European identity superior in comparison with all the major non-European peoples and cultures' articulated in his highly influential book, *Orientalism*.[10]

Did Japan's encounter with Europe represent such a clash of cultures? The answer is important, not least because of the use which has been made since then of the supposed open/closed character of Azuchi-Momoyama Japan, and the degree to which the image of a Japan threatened by a predatory West before shrewdly deciding to limit contact with foreigners and pursue its own course permeates modern Japanese consciousness. First some words about terminology.

I have suggested that some labels for events are neutral and unproblematic. Others are not. Prime examples are the terms 'East' and 'West', and 'Europe' and 'Asia'. The terms East and West originated during the Enlightenment. They were adapted most suggestively in the nineteenth century to distinguish what was perceived as a vigorous, progressive and modernising Europe from a stagnant and largely despotic and increasingly undifferentiated Orient, stretching from the Levant to the China Seas. They have continued to find employment in the twentieth century, although with diminishing precision. After the Second World War they were used to define the Cold War division of the world, ironically placing Japan firmly in the West alongside the liberal democracies of Europe and the United States, the self-proclaimed heirs of the Enlightenment's civilising mission, countries that stood tall and proud against a new oriental despotism: Soviet-style communism.[11] Even after the Cold War, the terms find service as labels to contrast the dynamic East and South-east Asian economies with the supposedly welfare-saturated, sclerotic European ones. In this latest guise, the polarities have acquired a nasty cultural subtext in which unregulated, un-unionised Asian sweat shops are alleged to threaten the civilised values embodied in the concept of the welfare state – the yellow peril of the late twentieth century. This caricature is mirrored in the uninformed attacks on the values and aspirations of the 'Western' liberal democratic state by the leaders of Singapore and Malaysia, an occidentalism as ludicrous as the orientalism from which it is hatched.[12] Once more Japan confounds the schema. It does not fit neatly into the slot where the polarities suggest it should. 'East' and 'West' confuse rather than enlighten.

'Asia' and 'Europe' are easy to deconstruct but difficult to replace. Strictly speaking, 'Asia' should not be used when referring to the early modern period; it is a later invention. Ideally it should not be used at all. K. N. Chaudhuri has deconstructed the concept, arguing that Asia is a derogatory, Western concept, which only has meaning as the antithesis of Europe: an area comprising peoples and cultures that are clearly not European in terms of religious belief, colour, customs or the arts (nor, one might add, in their social, economic and political relations). Chaudhuri points out that no similar term exists in any Asian language and even questions the validity of Asia and Europe as geographical expressions. This is wholly consistent with logic, but to outlaw the term Asia would create insuperable problems, for, as Chaudhuri remarks, alternatives defy 'our intuitive notions of plausibility' (and accepted notions and categories of historical explanation). Chaudhuri contemplates 'Indian Ocean' as an alternative to Asia. It would stretch plausibility too far to include the Central Asian steppes and deserts (or, for that matter, China, Korea and Japan), although his model suggests that they constitute part of a continuum that links diverse geographical and settlement patterns and gives them a shared history. Rather than substituting 'Indian Ocean', which as he notes is not entirely absent from Arabic or some Indian languages (nor even from Chinese or Japanese), or devising some other term, Chaudhuri pauses and reinstates 'Asia', emphasising that Asia and Asian in his usage 'do not refer to something that needs the prior concept of Europe and people with history to make sense'.[13]

Equally large problems arise with the terms 'Africa' and 'African'. Chaudhuri does not suggest that Europeans invented Asia in order to dominate it, even if the myth of a stagnant Orient provided a convenient justification for European imperialism there. But Kwame Anthony Appiah notes that the pan-Africanism of the nineteenth century

> was founded not on any genuine cultural commonality, but . . . on the very European concept of the Negro . . . [T]he 'whites' invented the Negroes in order to dominate them. Simply put, the course of cultural nationalism in Africa has been to make real the imaginary identities to which Europe has subjected us.[14]

This discussion is by no means irrelevant to Japan, for the Japanese have their own problems with terminology. The terms *seiyō* and *tōyō*

have the specificity lacking in 'East' and 'West', and were used from
the eighteenth century. The former was associated with Western
learning brought by the Dutch, knowledge quite distinct in Japanese
minds from the Christian doctrines brought by the southern barbarians
in the sixteenth century. In the later eighteenth century, but not
before, *seiyō* began to resonate with connotations of cultural clash.
Initially, Western learning posed a threat to the professional status of
Japanese intellectuals and medical practitioners versed in Chinese
classics and applied learning. In the course of the nineteenth century,
however, it became associated with a perceived military threat from
Europe and the United States. Moreover, Japan had problems with the
word 'China'. 'Chūgoku' and 'Chūka' implied Middle Kingdom
civilisation, and hence a superiority, which was obnoxious to *Kokugaku*
(National Learning) scholars who preferred less-loaded terms such as
'Kara' and 'Shina'.[15] In the late nineteenth century Japanese
intellectuals became adept at employing imaginary identities, and
particularly those current at the time in Europe regarding Asia and
the Orient (the construction of Asia that Chaudhuri refers to) and
giving them an unexpected twist – the reverse Orientalism which Said
alludes to.[16]

In brief, Elisonas errs in painting Japan's encounter with Europe in
the Azuchi-Momoyama period as a clash of cultures, East versus West,
Europe versus Asia, not least because these terms are products of a
later and totally different sort of encounter. Perhaps this will be clearer
if we try to be more precise about the Europeans who reached Japan
and how they saw the non-European world that they had arrived in.

One thing stands out: the idea of Europe barely existed, except as a
geographical expression. There was no overarching sense of European
identity among the denizens of Portugal, Spain, the United Provinces,
England and other places who came to Japan in the sixteenth and
seventeenth centuries. Allegiance was primarily local, hardly surprising
at a time when, for example, 'county' and 'country' were used
interchangeably by Englishmen. This is not to suggest that the mental
universe of early modern Europeans was parochial. Religion was one
force capable of firing the imagination and transcending local
preoccupations. But Europe was split along confessional lines in a
struggle of monumental consequence. It involved intellectual and
political choices, profound issues of principle that men and women
were willing to die for. It was as contentious and divisive an ideological
struggle as the Cold War in our own century, and it was not fought by
proxies. The stakes were high: the seventeenth century was a time of
Protestant retreat, from 50 per cent of the continental land-mass to just
20 per cent.[17] The Reformation had also shattered the imagined

community of Christendom, the adoptive heir of the Roman Empire. In the Middle Ages, Christendom had provided a focus of identity that transcended allegiances to family and locality. After the Reformation, 'Christendom' became partisan in meaning (or more partisan, for the claims of the Church of Rome had long been rejected by the Orthodox churches). As a result of the schism between Catholic and Protestant, Christendom no longer provided a pan-European focus as it had during the Crusades. The broken pieces left a legacy of division. In post-Reformation Europe, global pretensions carried a negative association and on various occasions the Spanish and Dutch were charged with aspiring towards Universal Monarchy.[18]

Identity was more developed at the micro-level in some of the sovereign states, notably among the English. Oliver Cromwell could speak of God's Englishmen and use it as a rallying cry against the enemies of the English republic. But the Levellers could talk as fluently and confidently of the rights of the free-born English smarting under a Norman yoke. Identity was not just one of religious bond. The Dutch revolt from Spain was fuelled by Calvinist zeal, but Calvinists were not a monolithic entity and constituted, at most, 55 per cent of the Dutch population. Dutch patriotism was a result, not a cause, of the war. Out of the triumph of battle, a people without the reassuring certainties of common language, settled borders, or monarchy were left with the challenge of forging a common identity that would cement the tenuous foundations of their young republic. They were successful. In 1706 Roemeyn de Hooghe described his native Dutch Republic as 'most singular', peopled by thrifty, solvent burghers who preferred commerce over aristocracy and basked in the rays of 'good governance'. He was reproducing values to which his contemporaries subscribed, even if these values were crumbling when he wrote.[19]

If there was no overarching concept of Europe, there was no corresponding vacuum in East Asia. The Sino-centric Confucian world view stressed the Middle Kingdom's moral and cultural superiority over the surrounding barbarians, who acknowledged their inferiority by sending tribute missions to Beijing and kowtowing before the Son of Heaven. At the micro-level in Asia, the Japanese, who at various times coveted the idea of the Middle Kingdom for themselves, did not lack a sense of identity. The Europeans who came to Japan were not confronted by a people without a history, such as the Caribs and Arawaks appeared to be when Columbus encountered them. The Japanese polity had a far longer history than the early modern sovereign states of Europe, and Hideyoshi was not shy about reminding the Europeans about this pedigree. His decree of 24 July 1587 outlawing Christianity begins: 'Japan is the land of the Gods'.[20] The point was elaborated in letters to Portuguese and Spanish representatives in Goa and Manila. Hideyoshi articulates a somewhat muddled philosophy: 'To know Shinto is to know Buddhism and Confucianism'.[21] A nonsense maybe, but the words of this assertion and other comments in the letters were well-chosen, full of calculation. They can be read as a statement of his ambition for hegemony in Asia, of which the disastrous invasions of Korea in the 1590s were meant to be the opening shot.[22] If so, the ambition assumes that under Hideyoshi's rule Japan could upstage the Europeans in a common Asian cultural space, which, following mediaeval Japanese Buddhist notions of the Three Kingdoms, he defines as running from India, through China, to Japan, and on to which he posits a common cultural identity. More certain is that Hideyoshi's words were intended to assert a Japanese identity quite distinct from those of the southern barbarians and Japan's immediate neighbours.[23] By asserting that Japan was not at the margin of the Three Kingdoms, as the orthodoxy suggested, Hideyoshi uncannily anticipated *Kokugaku* thought. The early Tokugawa, as in much else, built upon Hideyoshi's legacy and the refrain that Japan was the land of the Gods became a *leitmotif* of official anti-Christian propaganda.[24] However, it was only in the late eighteenth and early nineteenth centuries, with the teachings of the Mito School, that the concept of Japan rather than China as the Middle Kingdom comes into its own as a potent ideology.[25]

What can one say about the attitudes to non-Europeans that the Europeans brought with them to Asia? The alleged remarks of the wretched pilot of the *San Felipe* about the friars acting as Philip II's vanguard provided Hideyoshi with the pretext to teach the missionaries a bitter lesson. But the remarks reflect the reality of Spanish might in the first half of the sixteenth century, not the situation at the dawn of the seventeenth. Moreover, they trivialise the European intellectual response to the encounter with new worlds and ancient civilisations. The encounter with the New World was highly problematic for Europeans; that with Asia less so. Asia and its commodities had been familiar since the days of the Roman Empire and before, and it was, of course, the quest for the Indies that resulted in the 'discovery' of the New World. A completely New World had not been anticipated by Europeans and the reality of the Americas took a long time to fix itself in their mental map of the world; until well into the sixteenth century, central and north America were represented by a number of European cartographers as promontories of Asia.[26] The Europeans had intruded physically into the New World and, equally unexpectedly but with none of the disruption and destruction that accompanied the European move across the Atlantic, the native Americans had intruded into the European intellectual universe. They had to be accommodated. Asians already had been, in a manner. For the mediaeval mind the lands around the Indian Ocean and beyond were places of riches, esoteric goods, inhabited by all kinds of strange people and beasts. But the shift from the Indies as an 'oneiric horizon' for Europeans to a horizon of commercial opportunity,[27] peopled by kings, courtiers, city dwellers, farmers, merchants and traders rather than Cyclops and assorted other monsters and freaks happened swiftly after the da Gama voyages.

The Columbian encounter neither shattered nor reshaped the basic tenets of the European mental world, certainly not as profoundly as the Copernican and Galilean revolutions.[28] Even so, in order to govern and convert the native Americans it was necessary for the Iberians to understand them, their society, language, culture and environment. For these reasons, a number of what can accurately be called early ethnological studies were undertaken. Most remained unpublished.[29] An important exception was the work of the Spanish Jesuit, Jose de Acosta, *Historia natural y moral de las Indias*. This appeared in Spanish in 1590 and was soon translated into Italian, French, Dutch, English, German and Latin.[30]

De Acosta had lived in Peru from 1572 to 1586 and in Mexico from 1586 to 1587. In Peru he had undertaken three journeys into the interior and was not lacking in first-hand experience of Indian culture. He emphasised, and this is one of his claims to originality, the superiority of empirical knowledge over untested, accepted opinion which, even had it originated from the hallowed pens of the Ancients, should be overthrown when experience and observation found it to be wrong.[31] De Acosta was aware that lessons could be drawn from his knowledge and experience in the New World and that these lessons could be applied elsewhere in the missionary field, in the East Indies and in parts of Europe.

In an earlier work, *De procuranda indorum salute* (1588),[32] intended as a primer for novices, de Acosta classified the 'barbarian' inhabitants of the worlds in which the Europeans now found themselves. He defined three categories of barbarian: those who lived in stable, settled societies, who knew of and used letters; those who were unlettered but nevertheless lived in organised, governed societies; and those who lived unsettled and ungoverned who were almost, but not in fact, bestial.[33] The first is directly relevant to the East Indies, including Japan. In de Acosta's assessment, these people did not depart much 'from right reason and the common usage of humanity'. They have a stable form of government [respublica], public laws, fortified cities, respected magistrates, secure and prosperous commerce, and that which is most important, use and knowledge of letters, for wherever there are books and written monuments, the people are more humane and politic. To this class belong in the first rank the Chinese who have written characters which appear to be like the Syriac, and which I have seen. The Chinese are reported to flourish greatly, with an abundance of books, splendid academies, the authority of magistrates and laws and a magnificence of buildings and public monuments. Following them are the Japanese and many other provinces of East India.[34]

The Aztecs and Incas and some lesser kingdoms and principalities belonged in de Acosta's second category, and because they entertained 'such a monstrosity of rights, customs and laws' and violence they needed to be subjected to a 'superior power' (that is, Spain), although there should be some accommodation with their existing social and religious practices.[35]

De Acosta's third category was to go through several metamorphoses, eventually becoming the noble savages of the Enlightenment. Here belonged most of the people of the New World, although examples could be found in Asia in the Moluccas. They were savage, almost like wild beasts 'who scarcely have human feeling; without law, king, pacts, magistrates or government', living rough and raw with no fixed abode, sometimes man-eaters. They had to be forced into civilisation and coerced to adopt the true religion.[36] Interestingly, in his anti-Christian polemic *Ha Daiusu* (Deus Destroyed), Fabian Fucan, the Japanese apostate, declared that 'Because of their arrogance 'the Southern Barbarians' do not even consider the Japanese to be human'.[37] In the immediate aftermath of the Columbian encounter there had indeed been some speculation as to whether the Amerindians were human or bestial. It was quickly concluded that they were human. Had they been considered beasts they would not have been judged to possess a soul and could not have been converted.[38] Fabian was probably recycling and distorting information about the New World which he had acquired during his Jesuit training, but his assertion concerning Jesuit perceptions of the Japanese is wrong.

De Acosta incorporates and reshapes notions and categories already well-established in European intellectual discourse. The opposition between civilised and uncivilised (or barbarian) peoples can be traced to the Ancients from whom, among others, mediaeval authors, including Marco Polo, took it up.[39] As with earlier writers on this subject, Europe remains the point of departure for de Acosta, his reference from which to locate other people. *Prima facie* this appears Eurocentric, even hegemonic, for Chinese, Japanese and others' adherence to non-Christian values relegates them to an insuperably inferior status *vis-à-vis* Europeans. This conceptualisation recalls mediaeval notions of hierarchy. Roger Bacon, for example, held that a people's position on the ladder of civilisation was determined by how close they approached Christianity in their religious beliefs.[40] Similarly, de Acosta assumes that Europeans enjoy a special place in God's plan because their forebears had followed reason and accepted his revelation thereby assuring Europe, or more precisely Christendom, its privileged status. Such special pleading was not unique to Christian writers. According to the Islamic conceptualisation, the civilised world was the House of Islam, and the uncivilised and inferior was the House of War, usually identified with the Christian world.[41] Nor is such pleading as hegemonic as it appears at first sight.

If there is a hierarchy of civilisation, it follows that no single strategy for conversion could be applied to all barbarians. The Chinese and Japanese, de Acosta notes, differ from 'right reason and the usage of mankind', but he is imprecise about how far they differ. If government, law and commerce are taken as indicators, the degree of departure is not much. If the written script, and by implication for de Acosta the language, is taken as the criterion, then the degree is greater. Despite de Acosta's vagueness and inconsistency on this matter, he is adamant that neither the Chinese nor the Japanese should be coerced into accepting Christianity because they have, and exercise, reason. They should be guided by that faculty towards accepting the Christian revelation, much as the Greeks and the Romans and the pagan peoples of Europe had accepted God's message before them.[42]

De Acosta's emphasis on reason is important. According to his distinguished predecessors, revelation in itself did not provide a sufficient basis to prove to non-Christians the fundamental truth of the New Testament and Decalogue, the superiority of Christian values and, in the case of the New World, the appropriateness of European forms of government, codes of law and social relations. These could only be demonstrated with reference to the law of nature. Natural law provided the very first principles of human relations and the foundation of social organisation. It enabled one to assume a world community, a common humanity. It was held to be obvious to all rational minds, to all humans.[43] However, de Acosta did not believe that the norms of natural law were identical with European values, structures or institutions. To assume that they were would justify a policy of forced conversion, and would add substance to the view that Europeans sought to impose cultural hegemony as they went overseas. But de Acosta firmly opposed forced conversion in the case of China and Japan. He judged it suitable only for those unfortunates in his third category. His purpose in writing stemmed from his conviction that it was absolutely necessary to acquire knowledge and understanding of other people, their languages and customs, in order to preach the gospel; otherwise the effort would get nowhere.[44]

The need for knowledge and understanding of others implied that there had to be a measure of accommodation in one's dealings with them. This was, of course, the rule that made the Jesuits' Society so distinctive from its foundation and which eventually got the Jesuits into deep trouble when they applied it in China.[45] For de Acosta, the rightness of the Christian message and the errors of pagans were never in doubt, but by arguing that difference had to be recognised, analysed and understood, not just noted let alone ignored, comparison becomes possible, as do respect, admiration and, indeed, a questioning of self.[46] Michel De Montaigne suggested that the barbarian was not only present on the Celtic or Nordic fringes of Europe, a view common to many Renaissance thinkers, but at the very centre: Europeans, then engaged in bloody wars of religion, may call the cannibals barbarians 'by reference to the laws of reason, but not in comparison with ourselves, who surpass them in every kind of barbarity', he declared.[47] The implication was that the Europeans as much as the cannibals deviated from right reason and the law of nature. The Dominican friar, Domingo Navarrete, who spent twenty-two years in Asia, echoes De Montaigne noting that the 'Chinese and Japanese are not barbarians, for they live ordered and orderly lives, and are governed by rational laws'. To suggest that people who had some customs 'that are against reason' were barbarous would be a *reductio ad absurdum*, for many Europeans regarded bullfighting and duelling as barbarous.[48] Gottfried Wilhelm Leibniz, who was greatly influenced by Jesuit accounts of China and neo-Confucianism in particular, went further. He believed 'that Chinese missionaries should be sent to teach us the aim and practice of natural theology, as we send missionaries to instruct them in revealed theology'. He was advocating reciprocity not hegemony, a point which had already been made, although for different purposes, by Pierre Bayle.[49]

Quite different are the assumptions behind the hierarchies of peoples that emerge in the nineteenth century. Maurice Herder, for one, equated progress with humanity's relentless advance towards Christianity,[50] and it was Ernest Renan's conviction about the superiority of Christianity that led him to assert: 'Everyone who has been in the Orient or in Africa will have been struck by the kind of iron circle in which the believer's head is enclosed, making him absolutely closed to science, and incapable of opening himself to anything new'.[51]

By then, of course, the upheavals associated with the Industrial Revolution and French Revolution had so much transformed the non-confessional domain that European progress and superiority seemed inevitable and self-evident. Herder's and Renan's conceptualisation of the relations between people, their raw advocacy of European hegemony, was alien to the Europeans who came to Japan in the sixteenth and seventeenth centuries. The Europeans were certainly impressed by the civilisation that they encountered, but their reaction was not the wonder or marvel that Stephen Greenblatt makes much of for the New World encounter, where the Europeans' sense of wonder transformed itself into the desire to possess, own, or even destroy the new-found other.[52] In this respect, Charles Taylor's remarks are worth quoting in full. Taylor speaks of the 'intuitions about the equal value of culture' as being 'deep' within the Western tradition:

> the various Jesuits in the sixteenth and seventeenth century [*sic*] who tried to assimilate to Indian or Chinese culture in order to convert these peoples . . . had already separated off the superiority of the Christian faith, about which they had no doubts, from any purported superiority of Western culture, which they were putting in question. True, there arose between them and us lots of progress theories which reduced everyone else to stepping stones to ourselves as the definitive culture. But this other intuition has always been there, and has motivated much of the work in other-cultural studies, to which the west has given itself more than any previous society.[53]

Taylor's essay is general and tentative and almost entirely undocumented, but his own intuition is shrewd. In the early modern period Europeans did not carry notions of superiority in their baggage as they journeyed across the Indian Ocean. The mental furniture in their world view was not what we would now describe as 'orientalist'. There were, as yet, no stock images of the 'Orient' nor standard expectations of stagnation or backwardness indelibly impressed upon the European collective consciousness to prejudice judgment. Proselytising in Japan did not equal 'westernisation', any more than modernisation in the nineteenth and twentieth centuries has equalled westernisation. To get the measure of this assertion let me quote Alexander Crummell's description of the African 'Negroes' written about 1860:

> Africa is wasting away beneath the accretions of moral and civil miseries. Darkness covers the land and gross darkness the people . . . Licentiousness abounds everywhere. Moloch rules and reigns throughout the whole continent, and by the ordeal of Sassywood, Fetiches, human sacrifices and devil-worship, is devouring men, women, and little children.[54]

The words could have come from sixteenth- or seventeenth-century descriptions of Africa or the Americas, but Crummell's is not the voice of the colonial dispossessor. He was a black-American, naturalised Liberian, Episcopalian priest educated at Cambridge. The 'savage' had become 'civilised', the civilising mission had triumphed, so completely that Crummell was externalising the contemporary European conceptualisation of Africa as the dark continent. In the words of Basil Davidson: '[a]lienation . . . became naturalized'.[55] But nothing is quite as simple as it seems. Crummell was not the ventriloquist's dummy of colonialism triumphant, he was also one of the founders of Pan-Africanism. He believed in the African motherland of the black people.[56] He was, therefore, among the first to embark on the now familiar quest for the roots from which Afro-Americans believe they were wantonly severed. Some later travellers along this highway have rejected their 'American' identity, preferring to adopt another, such as Islam. But does this not suggest that their destination is an imagined community furnished with invented traditions? Crummell's journey is quite unlike the Japanese experience in the sixteenth and early seventeenth centuries. Christianity, even had its missionaries wanted to, could not have been forced on Japan. The Japanese had the option to say no and to mean it. In this sense, Japan's encounter with Europe is vastly different from that of Europe's encounter with the New World or Africa. In the 1850s the Japanese were still largely respected, unlike the Chinese (perhaps in both cases we should speak more accurately of the idea of Japan and China).[57]

But the world had passed over that great divide, the 'Industrial Revolution'. Perhaps more than anything else this gave substance to the idea of Europe – the phenomenon that Chaudhuri sketches, Europe before Asia – a place inhabited by people that only have historicity because of Europe and Europeans. The world of de Acosta and Leibniz had long vanished. The flood of information that de Acosta and others had called for had convinced Europeans that they had little beyond antiquarian matters to learn from Asia. In the nineteenth century there were new hierarchies, new criteria for ranking peoples and cultures, and the Japanese were not very happy with the place the Europeans assigned to them. If Europeans and Americans were capable of imagining communities and inventing traditions, the Japanese were to prove equally adept.

There was nothing unique about that, although it is a matter of considerable interest that the fruit of such imaginings and inventions, Japan's modern myths, is still not questioned in today's Japan with the rigour and intensity which scholars elsewhere have used to deconstruct the myths prevailing in their societies.[58]

Notes

1 Anon., *Kirishitan Monogatari*, trans. in George Elison, *Deus Destroyed*, Cambridge, Mass., Harvard University Press, 1973, p. 374.

2 Denis O. Flynn, 'Comparing the Tokugawa shogunate with Hapsburg Spain: two silver-based empires in a global setting', in James D. Tracey (ed.), *The Political Economy of Merchant Empires: State Power and World Trade 1350–1750*, Cambridge University Press, 1991, pp. 332–59, esp. p. 351 and 354; also ibid., p. 356, n. 55.

3 See Bob Tadashi Wakabayashi, *Anti-Foreignism and Western Learning in Early-Modern Japan*, Cambridge, Mass., Harvard University Press, 1986, pp. 59–61.

4 Leonard K. Andaya, 'Cultural state formation in Eastern Indonesia', in Anthony Reid (ed.), *Southeast Asia in the Early Modern Period*, Cornell University Press, 1993, pp. 34–5.

5 Stephen Greenblatt, *Marvellous Possessions*, Chicago University Press, 1991, p. 70; Vassilis Lambropoulous, *The Rise of Eurocentrism: Anatomy of Interpretation*, Princeton University Press, 1993, p. 327.

6 Elison, *Deus Destroyed*, p. 1; George Elison, 'The cross and the sword: patterns of Momoyama history', in George Elison and Bardwell L. Smith (eds), *Warlords, Artists and Commoners: Japan in the Sixteenth Century*, University of Hawaii Press, 1981, p. 82.

7 Shiryo Hensan-jo (ed.), *Diary Kept by the Head of the English Factory in Japan*, vol. 1, Tokyo, Tokyo Daigaku Shuppansha, 1978, pp. 300 and 303; Paul van der Velde and Rudolf Bachofner, (eds), *The Deshima Diaries Marginalia 1700–1740*, Tokyo, Japan–Netherlands Institute, 1992, pp. 104 and 116.

8 Sabine MacCormack, *Religion in the Andes: Vision and Imagination in Early Colonial Peru*, Princeton University Press, 1991; Fernando Cervantes, 'Christianity and the Indians in early modern Mexico: the native response to the Devil', *Historical Research*, vol. LXVI, June 1993, pp. 177–96.

9 J. S. Cummins (ed.), *Suceso de las Islas Filipinas*, Cambridge, Hakluyt Society, 1971, pp. 114 and 158.

10 Elison, *Deus Destroyed*, p. 4; Elison, 'The cross and the sword', p. 80; Edward W. Said, *Orientalism*, New York, Vintage Books, 1979, p. 7. Although dealing mostly with the Middle East, Said's Orient is sometimes stretched further east to include Japan, with unfortunate results. He suggests 'occasional instances of native intransigence' disturbed the peace 'when a group of Japanese Christians threw the Portuguese out of the area', p. 73). Said's thesis is reassessed in Carol A. Breckenridge and Peter van der Veer (eds), *Orientalism and the Postcolonial Predicament: Perspectives on South Asia*, University of Pennsylvania Press, 1993. Said himself develops his argument in *Culture and Imperialism*, London, Chatto and Windus, 1993.

11 Hugh Seton-Watson speaks of the (then) EC and NATO as appropriating 'the mystique of Europe, implying . . . that those beyond the line are sunk in a lower level of civilisation, in fact in barbarism' ('What is Europe, where is Europe', *Encounter*, July–August 1985, p. 14).

12 Samuel P. Huntingdon, 'Clash of civilizations?', *Foreign Affairs*, Summer 1993, pp. 22–49; Michael Vatikiotis, 'The golden mean', *Far Eastern Economic Review*, 14 October 1993, pp. 23–4.

13 K. N. Chaudhuri, *Asia before Europe*, Cambridge University Press, 1991, pp. 22–3 and 27–8. Cf. Michael Pearson's discussion of the same problem (M. N. Pearson, 'Introduction I: the subject', in Ashin Das Gupta and

M. N. Pearson, (eds), *India and the Indian Ocean 1500–1800*, Delhi, Oxford University Press, 1987, pp. 9ff. Pearson reminds us that 'Indian Ocean' is a translation from the Arabic (p. 9). My usage of Asia and Asian, Europe and European is in the conventional geographical sense and with respect to Asia does not imply that the peoples, cultures and societies occupying the diverse regions of that space derive their identity only in relation to Europe.

14 Kwame Anthony Appiah, *In My Father's House: Africa in the Philosophy of Culture*, Oxford University Press, 1992, p. 62. See also Basil Davidson, *The Black Man's Burden*, London, James Currey, 1992.

15 Wakabayashi, *Anti-Foreignism*, pp. 31, 41 and 42.

16 Said, *Orientalism*, p. 322. On the use made of *tōyō* by Japanese intellectuals after the Meiji Restoration, see Stefan Tanaka, *Japan's Orient: Rendering Pasts into History*, Berkeley, University of California Press, 1993.

17 Jonathan Scott, 'Radicalism and restoration: the shape of the Stuart experience', *Historical Journal*, nos. 31–2, 1988, p. 460. A century later Voltaire was confident that the Catholic advance had been checked and that when viewed from a global perspective Roman Catholicism was a minority faith, 'little more than a twenty-sixth part of the inhabitants of the known world' (*Philosophical Dictionary*, Penguin edn, p. 141). Compare this assessment with Maeno Ryotaku's in 1777, the year before Voltaire's death: 'Buddhism has spread over one-fifth of Asia, Confucianism, one-tenth of Asia, Christianity dominates the rest of the world' (quoted in Wakabayashi, *Anti-Foreignism*, p. 50).

18 Steven Pincus, 'Popery, trade and Universal Monarchy: the ideological context of the second Anglo-Dutch War', *English Historical Review*, vol. 107, no. 1, 1992, pp. 1–29.

19 Simon Schama, *The Embarrassment of Riches*, Berkeley, University of California Press, 1988, p. 53.

20 Elison, *Deus Destroyed*, p. 115.

21 Hideyoshi quote in Herman Ooms, *Tokugawa Ideology*, Princeton University Press, 1985, p. 46.

22 This is the interpretation that Ooms gives, ibid.

23 The point made by Ooms, ibid., p. 47.

24 For examples, see Elison, *Deus Destroyed*, pp. 305, 355, and 203.

25 Wakabayashi, *Anti-Foreignism*, pp. 51–7.

26 Folker Reichert, 'Columbus und Marco Polo – Asien in Amerika', *Zeitschrift für Historische Forschung*, vol. 15, 1988, pp. 52 and 56.

27 Jacques Le Goff, 'The Medieval West and the Indian Ocean: an oneiric horizon', in Jacques Goff (ed.), *Time, Work, and Culture in the Middle Ages*, Chicago University Press, 1980, pp. 189–200.

28 J. H. Elliott, *The Old World and the New 1492–1650*, Cambridge University Press, 1992; Anthony Pagden, *The Fall of Natural Man*, Cambridge University Press, 1986; Anthony Grafton, *New Worlds, Ancient Texts: The Power of Tradition and the Shock of Discovery*, Cambridge, Mass., Harvard University Press, 1992.

29 Such ethnological endeavours had been anticipated by mediaeval Arab writers. For a highly illuminating discussion of early Arab ethnology and the function it served (to create a common cultural identity, not to facilitate conversion) see Al-Aziz Azmeh, 'Barbarians in Arab eyes', *Past and Present*, vol. 134, February 1992, pp. 3–18.

30 A modern text, edited by Eduardo O'Gorman, was published in Mexico City

in 1962 and the Hakluyt Society published an English edn, *The Natural and Moral History of the Indies*, Clements Markham (ed.), 2 vols, London, Hakluyt Society, 1880. For an extended discussion, see Pagden, *Fall of Natural Man*, ch. 7, to which I am greatly indebted.

31 Pagden, *Fall of Natural Man*, pp. 152–3.

32 This was published at Salamanca in 1588 together with the first two books of the *Historia* as *De natura novi orbis libri dvo, et De promulqatione evangeli apud barbaros, sive, De procuranda indorvm salute libri sex*. There is a modern Spanish translation of *De procuranda* in *Bibliotteca de autores Espanoles*, vol. 73, Madrid, 1954.

33 Ibid., pp. 392–3.

34 Ibid., p. 392. John H. Rowe, 'Ethnography and ethnology in the sixteeenth century', *The Kroeber Anthropological Society Papers*, vol. 30, 1964, pp. 16–17, contains an English translation. My translation largely follows Rowe. See also Pagden, *Fall of Natural Man*, pp. 162–3.

35 *Bibliotteca de autores Espanoles*, pp. 392–3.

36 Ibid., p. 393; Rowe, 'Ethnography and ethnology', p. 18; Pagden, *Fall of Natural Man*, p. 164.

37 Elison, *Deus Destroyed*, p. 286.

38 Pagden, *Fall of Natural Man*, pp. 67–8.

39 W. R. Jones, 'The image of the barbarian in Medieval Europe', *Comparative Studies in Society and History*, no. 31, 1971, pp. 376–407; Arnaldo Momigliano, *Alien Wisdom: The Limits of Hellenization*, Cambridge University Press, 1975; Pagden, *Fall of Natural Man*, pp. 15–26; John Critchley, *Marco Polo's Book*, Aldershot, Variorum, 1992, pp. 98–114.

40 Critchley, *Marco Polo's Book*, p. 149.

41 Bernard Lewis, *The Muslim Discovery of Europe*, London, Weidenfeld and Nicolson, 1982, pp. 171 and 173.

42 The *Historia* is dismissive of Chinese writing. See Markham (ed.), *Natural and Moral History*, pp. 401–2; Pagden, *Fall of Natural Man*, p. 190. *Bibliotteca de autores Espanoles*, p. 393; Rowe, 'Ethnography and ethnology', p. 17.

43 Pagden, *Fall of Natural Man*, pp. 61–4; Anthony Pagden and Jeremy Lawrence (eds), *Francisco de Vitoria: Political Writings*, Cambridge University Press, 1991, pp. xiv–xv.

44 Pagden, *Fall of Natural Man*, pp. 157–8.

45 On the centrality of accommodation to the Society of Jesus, see John W. O'Malley, *The First Jesuits*, Cambridge, Mass., Harvard University Press, 1993, pp. 81, 111–12, 255–6, 265, 267, 342, 370.

46 Not that comparison had been absent from mediaeval writers. Marco Polo makes many comparisons between Europe and Cathay but in the manner of projecting European assumptions on to, for example, the Great Khan's government of Cathay (the righteous monarch, surrounded by a magnificent court dedicated to the pursuit of the common weal). The intention is to make it seem less different, more familiar. But this is precisely the convention de Acosta attacks and seeks to break free from. In connection with Polo, see Critchley, *Marco Polo's Book*, pp. 114–25.

47 Jones, 'The image of the barbarian', pp. 400–4; Michel De Montaigne, *Essays*, Harmondsworth, Penguin, 1993, p. 212.

48 J. S. Cummins, *A Question of Rites: Friar Domingo Navarrete and the Jesuits in China*, Aldershot, Scolar Press, 1993, p. 212.

49 Leibniz quoted in Donald F. Lach, 'Leibniz and China', *Journal of the History*

of Ideas, no. 6, 1945, repr. in Julia Ching and Willard G. Oxtoby (eds), *Discovering China: European Interpretations in the Enlightenment*, Rochester University Press, 1992, pp. 101–2. See also Lach, 'The sinophilism of Christian Wolff (1679–1754)', *Journal of the History of Ideas*, no. 14, 1953, repr. in Ching and Oxtoby, *Discovering China*, pp. 117–30. Amie Godman Tannenbaum, *Pierre Bayle's Philosophical Commentary: A Modern Translation and Critical Interpretation*, New York, Peter Lang, 1987, pp. 145–6.

50 Maurice Herder, *The Languages of Paradise: Race, Religion, and Philology in the Nineteenth Century*, Cambridge, Mass., Harvard University Press, 1992, p. 49.

51 Renan quote in Albert Hourani, *Islam in European Thought*, Cambridge University Press, 1992, p. 30. On Renan, see also Olender in Herder, *The Languages of Paradise*, ch. 4, *passim*.

52 Greenblatt, *Marvellous Possessions*, *passim*. For a contrary view, see James Lockhart, 'Trunk lines and feeder lines: the Spanish reaction to American resources', in Kenneth J. Andiren and Rolena Adorno (eds), *Transatlantic Encounters: Europeans and Andeans in the Sixteenth Century*, Berkeley, University of California, 1991, pp. 93–4.

53 Charles Taylor, 'Comparison, history, truth', in Frank Reynolds and David Tracy (eds), *Myth and Philosophy*, Albany, NY, State University of New York Press, 1990, p. 47. He does not believe that 'intuitions about the equal value of cultures' applied in the New World (p. 43).

54 Crummell quote in Appiah, *In My Father's House*, pp. 22–3.

55 Davidson, *Black Man's Burden*, p. 27.

56 Appiah, *In My Father's House*, ch. 1, *passim*.

57 Cf. Oscar Wilde's comment: 'the whole of Japan is pure invention. There is no such country; no such people'. Quoted in Appiah, *In My Father's House*, p. 148.

58 On this, see Carol Gluck, *Japan's Modern Myths: Ideology in the Late Meiji Period*, Princeton University Press, 1985.

CHAPTER NINE

Siam and Japan in Pre-Modern Times: A Note on Mutual Images

ISHII YONEO

Siamese contact with Japan might be traced back to the end of the fourteenth century when an Ayutthayan royal envoy to the Korean court reportedly made a one-year stay in an unidentified place in Japan before reaching the Korean capital in 1388.[1] There are a few more references in Korean sources to the visits of Siamese envoys, who might or might not have touched Japanese soil before they reached the Korean capital. These records of sporadic Siamese contact with Japan, however, do not necessarily imply that the Thai ever entertained an idea of opening trade relations with Japan in those early years.

The earliest commercial contact of the Siamese with Japan was made not directly but through the intermediary of the Ryūkyūan merchants, who seem to have started their visits to Ayutthaya in the first decades of the fifteenth century. They exported to Ayutthaya such Japanese products as swords and paper fans in exchange for Siamese sappanwood and pepper, which were eventually brought to China as their tribute, whereas the Japanese swords, as is widely known, were cherished by the Siamese royalty as part of their indispensable regalia. Thus, thanks to the Ryūkyūan traders, Japan had been known to the Siamese, by the fifteenth century at the latest, as a producer of swords as well as refined fans.

Starting in the beginning of the next century, the Iberians began their religious-military expansion toward Asia. The Portuguese, who occupied Malacca in 1511, sent their envoy to the Siamese capital of Ayutthaya in the following year. Obviously the Portuguese wanted to establish friendly relations with Siam which had been a long-time overlord of their new possession. Seeing the advantage of obtaining firearms, the king of Siam hastened to conclude a treaty of friendship and commerce with the Portuguese in 1516 and permitted them the erection of a *padrão* or stone pillar with coat-of-arms surmounted with a wooden cross.[2] A few decades later, Dominicans (1566), Franciscans (1585) and Jesuits (1607) established missions for their subsequent activities in the outskirts of Ayutthaya.[3] Incidentally, the Portuguese, who happened to bring the first muskets to Japan in 1543, came from the port of Ayutthaya.[4] It is widely known that, thanks to the already existing forging technique for Japanese swords, the Portuguese muskets began to be reproduced locally, enabling the eventual unification of decentralised Japan by Oda Nobunaga (1534–1582) who revolutionised traditional warfare by mass employment of musketeers.

In 1549 the Spanish Jesuit, Francis Xavier, commenced his first mission in Kyoto and other provinces in western Japan, gaining more than fifty converts. When the pro-Catholic policy was suddenly changed into a suppressive one by Hideyoshi and his successor Ieyasu, not a small number of these Japanese converts, known as *kirishitan*, tried to find their way to religiously-tolerant South-east Asian countries, including the Siamese kingdom of Ayutthaya. The Siamese kings granted the Japanese immigrants to Ayutthaya a patch of land in the southern suburbs of the capital, where they formed a semi-autonomous community, called in Thai *ban yipun*, under a compatriot chief appointed by the Siamese authorities. The population of the Japanese settlement is estimated variously at between 1000 and 8000 but the most probable number might be 1000 to 1500 at most. Those Christian refugees constituted probably a substantial portion of the Japanese population in Ayutthaya. This is attested by the account of Padre Antonio Francisco Cardim, who is said to have administered the sacrament to 400 Japanese Christians (*a 400 japoes christaos*) on one Sunday in the year 1627 at his church on the outskirts of the Siamese capital.[5]

Besides these Christians, the Japanese settlement must have been populated by ex-samurai of the defeated anti-Tokugawa daimyos, who had become jobless in their homeland and hoped to break fresh ground overseas. Their expertise in martial arts seems to have been welcome by the Siamese kings, who employed them as mercenaries. They were grouped into a 'department' officially known as *Krom Asa Yipun*, or the Department of the Japanese Volunteers. Under the direct supervision of the king, they were conveniently mobilised from time to time to suppress revolts against their masters in different parts of the realm. This position of the Japanese, however, occasionally forced them to be involved in political struggles at the court. A classic example is the case of Okya Senaphimuk or Yamada Nagamasa, chief of the *Krom Asa Yipun*, who, after the demise of his lord king Songtham in 1628, was alienated from power by the usurper Prasatthong and assassinated two years later, after having been sent to the remote province of Ligor as governor.

Living in the port-city of Ayutthaya, the Japanese were understandably engaged in various aspects of commercial transactions, both with Nagasaki and in later years with other ports of Asia such as Batavia, then under Dutch administration. They were great exporters of deer-hide to Japan. Together with sappanwood, this constituted a major export item from Siam in the first three and a half decades of the seventeenth century. The VOC records continue to refer to the Japanese merchants as its arch-enemy. With their superior ability to collect deer-hide from local people thanks to their abundant capital in silver, they always threatened Dutch hegemony in this lucrative trade. After the introduction in 1636 of the seclusion policy of the Tokugawa shogunate, which made further Japanese involvement in Ayutthayan trade impossible, the Japanese who were left behind in Siam had to survive by participating in the intra-regional trade of Siamese rice and tin with the rest of South-east Asia.

The latter half of the sixteenth century saw a boom (which continued in subsequent centuries) in the export to European markets of Japanese handicrafts. Japanese lacquerware, known as 'Japan-ware', was greatly admired in many parts of Europe. These elaborate products of Japanese craftsmanship seem to have also been sold in Siam. An inventory of export items from Nagasaki to Ayutthaya in the late seventeenth century enumerates a variety of elaborate handicrafts from Japan including not only lacquerware (boxes, letter-boxes, pillow stands, etc.), but also copperware (lamps, kettles, frying pans, and others), large and small wooden boxes, high-quality paper, gold wire, silverware, etc.[6] These items of high artistic value must have been cherished by Siamese royal families and nobility, as was the case in Europe. In this connection, it is interesting that the fame of Japanese craftsmanship is still retained in an early nineteenth-century Thai poem which refers to the Japanese being *chang di* or skilful craftsmen.[7]

Pax Tokugawa might have erased the previous image of Japan as 'land of the warriors'. In the late sixteenth century, however, when 'Japanese pirates' or *wakō* were still rampant in Asian seas, the Siamese kings had enough reason to worry about the fate of their trading vessels which might suffer from the plunder of these pirates. To these justifiable fears was added another piece of worrying news, most probably brought from Japan by Catholic priests then stationed there, namely the aggressive and expansionist policy of Hideyoshi Toyotomi. Hideyoshi (1586–1598) invaded Korea (1592–1598) and threatened the Spanish colonial government of the Philippines (1591). The well-known episode of King Naresuen (1590–1605) offering (in vain) military help to China when the *pax sinica* was disturbed by the militant master of the newly unified island state of Japan, indicates that Japan was then viewed by the Thai as a military threat.[8]

Thus, the Ayutthayan images of pre-modern Japan must have been multifaceted. Due to the prominence of religious refugees in Ayutthaya, the Japanese might have appeared in Thai eyes as Christians. Then too, the Japanese were welcomed as warriors who were employed by the Siamese kings as their mercenaries. As well, the Japanese were famed for their skill in handicrafts, as is referred to in the Siamese poem which praised Japanese craftsmanship. And Japan was feared for some time as a military threat which could possibly disturb the peace of Asia.

What, then, was the corresponding image of the kingdom of Siam and the Siamese people entertained by the Japanese in the pre-modern period? One of the oldest terms referring to Siam in Japan was *shamu* or *shamuro*, which might have come into the Japanese vocabulary through the Portuguese in which Siam was called *Syao*. This became *shamo* when it was used to refer to a fighting cock – fighting cocks were imported to Nagasaki for popular entertainment in the early Tokugawa period. Through the Chinese writings the Japanese came to be acquainted with Siam which is pronounced as *suenro* in Chinese. This term is found in an early eighteenth-century Japanese encyclopaedia, called *Wakan-Sansai Zue*. In the entry under *suenro*, or in its Japanese reading *shamuro*, Siam is described as a kingdom in South *Tenjiku* or 'India', whose kings used to send three vessels to Japan annually for trade. The entry also mentioned that descendants of earlier immigrants from Japan still lived there. Import items from Siam mentioned in the encyclopaedia include such local products as sappanwood, pepper, deer-hide, sugar and natural drugs, as well as such foreign goods as cotton fabrics from India and frankincense from Yemen or Somalia.[9] Ships from Siam, which is 2400 *li* distant from Japan, were considered to be larger than ordinary Chinese junks. *Wakan Sen-yōshū* or *An Illustrated Book of Japanese and Chinese Vessels* (1761) gives a detailed description of the *Senra-sen* or Siamese ships as measuring 15 to 20 *ken* (27 to 36 metres) in length, able to carry as much as 1 020 000 to 1 030 000 *kin* for a small vessel and 2 million *kin* of cargo for a vessel of larger make.[10]

In 1606 Shogun Tokugawa Ieyasu sent an official letter to the king of Siam, thereby heralding the opening of diplomatic ties with this Buddhist kingdom. Earlier in 1604, however, the first vermilion-sealed travel passes, known in Japanese as *Goshuin-jō*, had already been issued to four Siam-bound Japanese trading ships. Thereafter, until 1635, fifty-·five *Goshuin-jō* were granted to the investors of the Goshuin-sen for the

Nagasaki–Ayutthaya trade. Then the adoption of the complete seclusion policy by the Tokugawa shogunate made further voyages impossible. During the three decades of flourishing trade between the two countries, Edo, then the capital of Japan, was visited by at least six or perhaps seven missions despatched by the Ayutthayan court. But when another Siamese junk tried to enter the port of Nagasaki in 1656 with an official letter from the king of Siam, its entry was prohibited and the ship had to leave port without having made any official contact with the Japanese authorities.

After 1636 the Japanese were neither able to proceed to Siam from Japan, nor allowed to repatriate from Ayutthaya where they had settled. Thus, the Japanese were completely deprived of ways and means of updating their knowledge about Siam, which was to be fossilised in the memory of subsequent generations. To this trend, the writings of former residents of Ayutthaya made an immeasurable contribution. Among them is a popular account of early seventeenth-century Ayutthaya, said to be written by a Japanese named Chihara Gorohachi.[11] This book is, however, generally thought to be a colourful narrative based on a story probably told by a one-time resident of Ayutthaya rather than Chihara's original work. But it makes a good summary of the Japanese knowledge of Siam during the *sakoku* period.

> Siam is a large and prosperous country, conveniently located in the South Seas so as to attract many merchants ships from abroad. From Japan too, Japanese merchants used to frequent Siam for business for many years. From the years of Gen'na (1615–1624) through the later years of Kan'ei (1624–1644), the *rōnin* or warriors who lost their lords after the defeats of the battle of Osaka (1614–15) or the earlier battle of Sekigahara (1600), as well as the defeated [Christian] rebels of the Shimabara Uprising, went to settle in Siam in great numbers. Thanks to their military prowess in expelling pirates at sea and bandits on land, many of them were favored by the Siamese kings who granted them a plot of land which is named the Japanese Town. These Japanese immigrants built their houses along the sea [*sic*]. Those who lived in Siam for a long time got married and had children. It is said that more than eight thousand Japanese once lived there.[12]

Among the Japanese migrants to Siam, probably the best-known is Yamada Nagamasa, whose dramatised life story greatly contributed to the formation of a stereotyped image of ordinary Japanese on pre-modern Siam, even to this day. About 1612 Yamada, one-time palanquin bearer of the lord of Numazu, is believed to have travelled to Siam. Within a little over fifteen years of his service in the Siamese court, he was promoted from the lowest nobility rank of *khun* to the senior rank of *Okya*, as the chief of the Department of Japanese Volunteers. His feat was later exaggerated to such an extent that in some popular accounts, he was quoted as 'a king of Siam'. This inappropriate image was left uncorrected in the absence of further contact with Siam during the *sakoku* period.

Even in those days, however, effort was not spared by the Tokugawa shogunate to collect information about the outer world to update existing knowledge. For example, since 1644 the governor of Nagasaki had been charged with the task of collecting foreign intelligence through the news brought by the Dutch vessels as well as the Chinese junks of various provenance, including Siam. In the mid-nineteenth century, when Japan began to be visited by ships from the west, the Tokugawa government had all existing documents concerning foreign countries compiled in over 300 volumes.[13] But the knowledge about foreign lands obtained from these sources remained the monopoly of senior officials of the shogunate for a long time and was seldom shared by the populace, who were left ignorant about developments outside Japan.

Notes

1 Vol. 46 of the Korean dynastic history, the *Koryo-Si*, refers to the arrival of a Siamese royal mission which is said to have been despatched by the Siamese king in the year AD 1388 to the court of Korea and which had spent one year in Japan on the way.

2 Rong Syamananda, *A History of Thailand*, Bangkok, Thai Watana Panich, 1973, p. 41.

3 For the early Christian missions in Siam, see Manuel Teixeira, *Portugal na Tailandia*, Macao, Direccio dos Services de Tourismo, Imprensa Nacional de Macao, 1983, pp. 273–409.

4 John Villiers, 'The Portuguese and the trading world of Asia in the sixteenth century', in Peter Milward (ed.), *Portuguese Voyages to Asia and Japan in the Renaissance Period*, Tokyo, The Renaissance Institute, Sophia University, 1994, p. 3.

5 Antonio Francisco Cardim, *Batalhas da Companhia de Jesus na sua Gloriosa Provincia do Japão*, Lisboa, Imprensa Nacional, 1894, p. 287.

6 See, for example, the inventory of export items of 1682 found in *Toban-Kamotsuchō*, Naikaku Bunko, Tokyo, 1970.

7 The Royal Academy of Siam, *Prachum Charuk Wat Phrachetuphon (Collected Inscriptions of Wat Phrachetuphon)*, vol. 2, Bangkok, B.E. 2472 (1929), pp. 483–4.

8 O. W. Wolters, 'Ayudhā and the rearward part of the world', *Journal of the Royal Asiatic Society*, 1968, pp. 166–78.

9 Terajima Ryōan, *Wakan-Sansai Zue*, Tōkyō, Tokyo Bijutsu, 1984, p. 219. This implies the importance of Ayutthaya as a port of trade which linked West Asia and East Asia.

10 Kanazawa Kanemitsu, 'Wakan Sen-yōshū' in *Nihon Kagaku Koten Zenshū*, vol.
  12 Tokyo, Asahi Shinbunsha, 1943, p. 200. One *kin* is equivalent to 600 g.
11 The seven-volume account is entitled *Senrakoku Fudo-gunki*.
12 Quoted by Uchida Ginzō in *Nihon to Taikoku to no Kankei*, Osaka, Sogensha,
  1941, pp. 16–17.
13 The compilation is known as *Tsūkō ichiran*.

CHAPTER TEN

Indonesia under the 'Greater East Asia Co-Prosperity Sphere'

GOTŌ KEN'ICHI
(translated by Minako Sakai and Tessa Morris-Suzuki)

Introduction

In autumn 1991 Emperor Akihito made the first visit by a Japanese emperor to three countries in South-east Asia: Thailand, Malaysia and Indonesia. Although the visit occurred in an atmosphere of tight security precautions, all three countries officially welcomed this epoch-making event as a reflection of their friendly relations with Japan. However, the major Indonesian newspaper *Suara Pembaruan* marked the occasion with an editorial entitled 'Wound healed, but scar remains' – an apt reminder of the three and a half years of the 'Greater East Asia Co-Prosperity Sphere', whose memory lingers in the hearts of the peoples of South-east Asia.

This chapter aims to elucidate the modern history of Japan in the Asia-Pacific region by analysing Japanese wartime relations with South-east Asia, and particularly with Indonesia. As an introduction, it may be helpful to survey the process of Japanese identity formation in the context of modern Asian history, and the characteristics of bilateral relations between Japan and Indonesia before the war.

Japan in Asia: the Formation of Japan's Self-Image

The world view of the Japanese before the Meiji era may be represented by the phrase *ka-iteki chitsujokan* (a world view based on the Chinese model of civilisation and barbarism). In *Ka-i tsūshōkō*, Nikshikawa Joken, a leading intellectual in the early eighteenth century, divided Asia into two categories; 'foreign countries' and 'outer barbarians'. The former included Korea, the Ryūkyū Islands, Taiwan, Tonkin, Cochin China, which were under the influence of

160

Chinese culture, while the latter included most of South-east Asia except Vietnam. Nishikawa presented an interesting account of characteristics of economy and culture in each country.[1] Morris-Suzuki (chapter 5) and Nishikawa (chapter 15) have usefully analysed these perceptions in this book.

However, when the prestige of China plummeted after the Opium War, Japanese intellectuals redefined China as a sort of barbarian realm. A popular song of the early Meiji era demonstrates this change: 'among the five continents, it is shameful that Asia is half-civilised'. Japan no longer paid homage to its former teacher, nor took any pride in the tradition of belonging to the civilised Chinese world. This change is characteristic of Japanese modernisation with its *datsu-a nyū-ō* spirit, which strove to sever ties with Asia and assimilate with the West, and it suggests Japan's inferiority complex towards the West. The ideology of the 'Greater Asia Co-prosperity Sphere' came into existence as a sort of deformed amalgam of those two sentiments.

It goes without saying that in the hierarchical world view of the modern Japanese, South-east Asia – previously described as 'barbarian' – held a low rank. The following is a story about Singapore by a famous writer which appeared in an elementary school textbook (*Jinjo Shogaku Kokugo Dokuhon, Dai Sanki – National Language Reader for Ordinary Elementary Schools, Third Period*, p. 22) published in 1908:

> Upon my arrival, a number of black natives dashed to me to pick up my luggage and to take it to the horse-drawn carriage. The noise was such that I thought they were quarrelling. Natives in strange attire had smiles on their wild black faces. They looked like demons, or monks in training.

This attitude to 'the natives' reflects the fact that the Japanese, who were treated as 'honorary whites' within South-east Asia, had obtained at least *de jure* equality with the West by the end of the nineteenth century, while South-east Asian countries were still under Western control. Even today, the Japanese have not entirely cast off this misconception of South-east Asian culture as inferior. What deserves attention in this connection, however, is that the Japanese had detached themselves from Asia, but yet had not been admitted into the Western community. They suffered from an unease and dissatisfaction that might even be described as a sense of victimisation. These complicated feelings became evident among politicians and military leaders after Japan's withdrawal from the League of Nations in 1933.

While the sense of cultural superiority to South-east Asia was taking root in Japanese minds, another view of South-east Asia also emerged. Once Japan's economic and political status rose after the Russo–

Japanese War and the First World War, Japanese people came to share the view that South-east Asia held great economic value for Japan. It was thirteen times as large and three times as populous as Japan and could provide raw materials as well as a large market for Japanese industry. However, until the mid-1930s Japan's *Nanshin seisaku* (Southward Advance Policy) emphasised peaceful means of gaining access to these resources. Nevertheless, Japan's increasing interest in South-east Asia alarmed the Western colonial powers. Above all, the Netherlands suspected that the ultimate target of the Southward Advance Policy was the Dutch East Indies. The Netherlands was on guard against Japanese military invasion although it did not publicise these suspicions.[2]

In these circumstances Japan, which had emphasised cooperation with the West in foreign policy, withdrew from the League of Nations after the Manchurian incident. This was the first step towards a 'de-westernisation' and eventually an 'anti-western' policy. In the following years various ideologies emerged, including the concept of the *Tōa shin chitsujo* (New Order in East Asia) and the Greater East Asia Co-prosperity Sphere, which emphasised Japanese leadership in Asia. Underlying these slogans was a belief that the world order had been created by the Western powers for their own advantage at the expense of Asians, and that the Japanese New Order would redress this inequity. At that time, the Japanese were unaware of the irony that their claim to leadership in Asia was based solely on a self-image of Japan as the only country in Asia to achieve the very 'Western-style modernisation' which Japan criticised and rejected.

To summarise, Japanese perceptions of South-east Asia and its relations with the region prior to the Second World War were: in economic terms, South-east Asia was 'enormously rich in unexploited resources'; it was also politically 'subordinate to Western rule' and 'culturally inferior'. To overthrow the colonial system in South-east Asia, Japan, as a superior Asian fellow-nation, should acquire the resources of the region and use them to create a new order in Asia. It was this logical construction which was presented to South-east Asia during the war.

The perceptions of pre-war Indonesian nationalist intellectuals under Dutch military rule can be simplified by stating that two contrasting perceptions of Japan co-existed. One was shared by Mohammad Hatta and Sutan Sjahrir, who had studied in Holland and espoused Western democracy. Hatta had spent a month in Japan immediately after Japan's withdrawal from the League of Nations and this experience convinced him that the slogan 'Asia for Asian Nations' was just a ploy by the military fascists who dreamed of making Japan the leader of Asia. After the outbreak of war in 1941 Hatta, in exile on Bandanaira Island, wrote an article entitled 'Pacific war and Indonesian people'. He argued that the war had broken out because of Japanese expansionism, and that Indonesians could not but fight on the side of Western democracy, against Japanese imperialism.[3]

Hatta's militant advocacy of democracy, however, was not popularly supported (a fact which Sjahrir deplored). In Indonesia, and particularly in Java, friendly feelings towards Japan had been widespread since the beginning of the century. The good impression created by *Toko Jepang*, Japanese shops, was reinforced by the inflow of Japanese industrial products, especially cotton textiles, in the 1930s. This helped to pave the way for 'Japan's return to Asia'. Parindra, the biggest political party in the 1930s, represented this pro-Japanese perspective, arguing that cooperation with Japan would help Indonesians to cast off Dutch colonialism. This is what Subardjo, another leading nationalist, meant when he stated that 'Indonesian nationalism and the Japanese Asiatic movement share a common cause'.[4] Before Parindra's dream could materialise, however, the war broke out.

Indonesia under the 'Greater East Asia Co-Prosperity Sphere'

Strategies for the Occupation Policy

In the 1930s Japan was dependent on important resources, including oil, from abroad; 60 per cent of oil imports came from the United States. Japan's decision to fight against the Allies presupposed that oil could be obtained from Indonesia. Therefore, the Japanese course of action that led to the occupation of South-east Asia, starting from the allusion to military southward advance in the 'Outline plan for dealing with the circumstances accompanying the transition in world affairs' of 27 July 1940, was ill-prepared and reckless. As the British historian, Christopher Thorne, puts it, the Japanese occupation policy was an 'ad hoc plan' and there were no common principles regarding the 'basic character of governments to be established in the countries under Japanese rule'.[5]

It was only three weeks before the onset of war that the blueprint for the occupation policy was finalised in the decision of the Liaison Council of the Military Command and Government entitled *Nampō senryōchi gyōsei jisshi yōryō* ('Guidelines for implementing the administration of the southern occupied areas'). Its focus was on the 'restoration of security, urgent acquisition of important resources for self-defence, and the establishment of self-sufficiency of the military forces in operation'. These principles, generally referred to as the three principles of military rule, played an important role in occupation policy. Another point made by this document was that 'independence movements should not be encouraged too soon'. Despite pre-war rhetoric about the liberation of Asia, this statement makes explicit the final target of the southward advance.

By the first half of 1942 the whole of South-east Asia had come under Japanese rule. For strategic reasons, Burma and the Philippines were acknowledged as independent in the *Daitō-a seiryaku shidō taikō* ('Outlines for the guidance of political strategy in Greater East Asia') of 30 May 1943. At the same time, it was decided that Indonesia and Malaya should be under permanent control as sources of important resources, and that this decision should not be announced for the time being. The main reason for avoiding the term 'independence' or any equivalent was that the Japanese regarded Indonesia as 'a place rich in human and natural resources'. To disguise this fact, natives were deemed to have a low cultural standard: '[The Indonesians] are of a low cultural standard and their economy is weak. Therefore there is no possibility of a successful future if we grant independence to them. If independence is given to an unqualified country, Japan will inevitably become involved in its internal affairs'.[6] These words from a military officer represent the general view among the Japanese. Such a view was shared by Colonel Nakayama Yasuto, a high-ranking officer in Java, who wrote before the war: 'the natives live an idle life and the level of politics and of culture is indeed low'.[7]

The Japanese superiority complex and self-appointed leadership are well exemplified in the 'cosmic order' in which Japan and adjacent Asian nations were ranked. Japan was the sun (the central organising force), regulating the orbits of each nation (this was generally interpreted to mean the recognition of self-government and independence), and providing light and energy for the prosperity of the nations. Asian countries 'received light and warmth' and 'revolved around Japan'. During the 'Greater East Asia War', numerous analogies of this type emerged to justify Japan's hegemony.[8]

The Greater East Asia Conference

In autumn 1943, as the war situation worsened, Japan hammered out the concept of an Absolute Defence Sphere (*zettai kokubō ken*) in which Indonesia was defined as a base providing food, other natural resources and an enormous amount of human resources (*rōmusha*). On 5 and 6 November in Tokyo, 'capital' city of the 'Greater East Asia Co-Prosperity Sphere', the Greater East Asia Conference assembled. Representatives from six 'independent' countries attended: Japan, Manchukuo, Thailand, China, the Philippines, Burma and Premier Chandra Bose of the Free India Provisional Government (as an observer). In closing the conference, they issued a Greater East Asia communique. This avoided the term 'Greater East Asia Co-Prosperity Sphere', which would indicate Japanese leadership, and emphasised 'the construction of an order of co-existence and co-prosperity, mutual support for autonomy and independence, and the abolition of racial discrimination'.

The mainstream interpretation of the Greater East Asia Conference has been negative, suggesting that it merely presented a display of 'Greater East Asia co-prosperity' after a series of hasty preparations.[9] 'The Greater East Asia Conference must have appeared to the eyes of Asian peoples, who longed for complete independence based on racial self-determination, as a farce played by traitors who had succumbed to Japanese imperialism.'[10] In recent years, however, after the publication of the diary of Shigemitsu Mamoru, the Minister of Foreign Affairs who actually staged the conference, some historians have re-evaluated the communique as an attempt to present a lasting ideological statement on the war and an image of an ideal post-war society, at a time when Japan's defeat was anticipated. For example, Miwa Kimitada compares the declaration with the Atlantic Charter, which was unable to make a clear statement renouncing colonial rule. He sees the document as a far-sighted one in which 'we can recognise the ideals of the international society, which is yet to be established even in present days'.[11] Satō Kenryo, who served in the army, writes in his memoirs: 'this ideal marked an epoch in world history, and particularly in the rise of East Asia. The advocacy of the abolition of racial discrimination produced pro-Japanese feelings among the Greater East Asian countries'.[12]

Let us see how the Greater East Asia declaration, which seemingly upheld universal values such as autonomy and independence for all nations, was related to the national aspirations of the Indonesians for independence. Indonesia was considered a 'southern life-line' for Japan, and yet Indonesia, which made up 60 per cent of the population of South-east Asia, was excluded from the conference, as were Malaya, Indochina, and of course, Korea and Taiwan. Because of this fundamental defect, the Greater East Asia declaration was no different from the Atlantic Charter, which also evaded the issue of autonomy for South-east Asian peoples. The exclusion of Hatta and Sukarno (whose strategy had been independence through cooperation with Japan) made them even more distrustful of Japan. (Sukarno was, of course, later to become leader of Indonesia.)

How did the leaders of 'independent' countries regard the conference? The Burmese Prime Minister, Ba Maw, criticised the Japanese military administration in his post-war memoirs, but evaluated the conference as the first embodiment of an emerging spirit in Asia, and a forerunner of the Bandung Conference twelve years later. Ba Maw seems to have shared the Pan-Asianist view. He may have felt that to deny the significance of the conference (at which he was a representative) would negate his own role in history, and that his attendance was legitimate in terms of the wider purposes of the war. In this connection he praised the speech of the Filipino president, J. Laurel, describing it as 'coming straight from his heart and brimming with the Asian anger and defiance of all those who had enchained its people for centuries'.[13]

Laurel alone emphasised solidarity with Indonesia, which was not invited (though he did not refer to Malaya): 'When we cooperate with peoples of Java, Borneo and Sumatra which share the identical interests with Burma, Manchukuo, Thailand, China and other nations in the area, and become linked to Japan in a firm union, we will make a very strong organisation ... '.[14] Since Japan did not approve the independence of Indonesia, this issue received no further attention and Laurel's speech had minimal influence. However, a year later, in April 1945 at the Greater East Asia Ambassadors' Conference in Tokyo, Philippines Ambassador Vargas presented a proposal supporting the independence of the East Indies. The approval of this proposal is one example of the seeds of solidarity among South-east Asian people which germinated during the war.

Although Japanese commitment to South-east Asia, which peaked at the Greater East Asia Conference in 1943, was basically self-serving, this year marked the emergence of a powerful Japanese consciousness of being part of Asia, albeit in a distorted form. From this year onwards, Japan began to act positively in relation to other Asian countries. Tōjō Hideki, who was the first Prime Minister to pay an official visit to South-east Asia, pursued the following itinerary:

13 March Visit to Wang Ching-Wei at Nanking
23 March Meeting with Ba Maw, head of the Burmese government to advise on Japanese policy for Burmese independence
1 April Visit to Manchukuo
5 May Visit to Manila, to advise on Japanese policy on the independence of the Philippines
3–7 July Meeting with Phibunsoughram, on the recovery of the lost territory
Meeting with Chandra Bose in Singapore
Meeting with Ba Maw in Singapore to finalise the independence issue
Meeting with Sukarno and Hatta in Jakarta

Visits of Indonesian Leaders to Japan

While Japan was vigorously liaising with South-east Asia in late November 1943, Sukarno, Hatta and Ki Bagus Hadikusumo visited Japan. Their purpose was reported as follows: 'The Javanese have finally been liberated from Dutch oppression and have been granted the honour of participating in Greater East Asia. This visit is to pay homage and to observe Japan at war'.[15] In other words, Japanese authorities showed them Japan's battles on the 'home front' in order to win their trust and to inspire them to further cooperation. After meeting the emperor, Sukarno stated: 'Upon my return to Indonesia, I will make every effort to lead 40 million Javanese in order to pursue this war. It is my responsibility to reciprocate what I have received from the Emperor'.[16]

It goes without saying that Sukarno's intention was not to strengthen cooperation with Japan. He and the two other leaders were aware of the independence of Burma and the Philippines, and his visit occurred while memories of the Greater East Asia Conference, attended by leaders of the 'independent countries', were still fresh in the minds of both sides. Indonesian and Japanese leaders had quite different aspirations. Despite Sukarno's 'heart-felt appeal for a positive indication' on the independence issues, the Japanese authorities responded with a vague statement that 'after the victory, your wish will be surely fulfilled at an appropriate time', and repeated their requests for cooperation.[17] However, the Japanese authorities felt obliged to appeal to the Indonesian people by lifting the ban on a national anthem, 'Indonesia Raya', and the red–white national flag, which had been prohibited immediately as soon as the military administration was formed in Java.

But when, on return to Jakarta, the Indonesian leaders paid a courtesy call on the military authorities, Military Administrator Kokubu told them that it would be difficult to permit the use of the national flag. Miyoshi Shunkichirō, an official interpreter for their visit, wrote: 'You received lavish hospitality and were too generously treated in Japan. You should think of the Japanese central government as your grandfather, whereas the military administration here is your father. A grandfather usually spoils his grandchild, but a father educates him with discipline for his future'.[18] In this statement we can see a rationale totally at odds with that of the Greater East Asia Declaration and its references to 'mutual respect based on autonomy and independence'. Indonesian leaders had hoped that their country would become the third 'independent' country in the 'Southern Co-prosperity Sphere', but their hopes were dashed. Nor could they meet any of the 'Co-prosperity Sphere' leaders during their visit. This experience of being ignored must have left some resentment in Sukarno's mind.

Twelve years later, in April 1955, as the first Indonesian President, Sukarno convened the 'Afro-Asia Conference' at Bandung. In his inaugural speech he described it as 'the first international conference held among the coloured races'. He referred to the 'Anti-Imperialist, Anti-Colonialist League' Conference held in Brussels in 1927 as its precedent, but he did not mention 'the first conference exclusively of Asians'. There is, of course, a decisive difference between Japanese leadership during the war and the claim by Indonesian leaders to be standard bearers for the peoples of Asia and Africa. But it is reasonable to think that Sukarno had the Greater East Asia Conference in mind when he emphasised Bandung's role as an 'international conference of the coloured races', and stressed Indonesia's leadership as a major power. Incidentally, Shigemitsu Mamoru, Minister of Foreign Affairs in the Tōjō Cabinet which convened the Greater East Asia Conference, held the same post in the Hatoyama Cabinet at the time of the Bandung Conference. Speaking in the Japanese Diet, he stated that the Bandung Conference had 'great significance since the purpose is to enhance mutual understanding and amicable relations in the area'. Shigemitsu must surely have recalled the Greater East Asia Conference of yesteryear.[19]

Rationale for Cooperation with Japan

The 'Koiso Statement' (7 September 1944) greatly changed the policy of the *Daitō-a seiryaku shidō taikō*, which had aimed to incorporate Indonesia as a Japanese territory. The Koiso Statement promised 'the independence of East Indies in the near future'. The origins of this change can be traced to an official document by the Ministry of Foreign Affairs, dated 17 July 1945, which dealt with the final stage of the Indonesian independence issue. This stated that:

1 The independence movement in the 'East Indies' had been 'active since before the war' and had 'fully cooperated with Japan', and hoped to achieve independence 'in accordance with Japanese plans'.
2 The 'Greater East Asia Declaration' and the independence of Burma and the Philippines had enhanced Indonesian desire to achieve independence, and therefore 'in order to pursue the purpose of Greater East Asia Declaration and to compensate them for their cooperation and desire, it was appropriate to make some kind of declaration of intent'.[20]

This document suggests that Japan, having committed itself to the Greater East Asia Joint Declaration and other statements of war aims, now found itself obliged to apply them to Indonesia.

In this connection the statements of Hatta require examination. As mentioned above, immediately after the outbreak of war Hatta had argued that 'in order to fight against Japanese imperialism, we must join the western democracy camp'. He added that 'he would prefer death for ideals rather than shameful life'. However, during the military administration, Hatta was forced to become a realist, pursuing his ideals through 'cooperation with Japan', and was in a position which obliged him to convey Japanese policies and opinions to the Indonesian people. However, although Hatta's speeches seemed to be passing on opinions 'from above', he was no mere spokesman for the Japanese government. Within the bounds permitted by the authorities, he sought to express alternative views and emphasise his own nationalist sentiments.[21] For instance, at a major rally to commemorate the first anniversary of the start of the war (8 December: *Kō-A bi* or 'Raising Asia Day') he stated that 'Indonesia was liberated from the Dutch imperialism by Japan. *We never want to be ruled by any foreign country again*. This feeling is shared by all of us, irrespective of age. *All Indonesian youth would rather be drowned in the sea than succumb to colonisation*' (emphasis added). On the first anniversary of the military administration, he said: 'The Japanese military authorities have reiterated that they landed in Indonesia not to exploit, but to help liberate Indonesia from Dutch imperialism, so as to establish an order for co-prosperity in Greater East Asia'.

Hatta's speech at the 'Thanksgiving Meeting' in Tokyo in June 1943, after the military authorities had permitted the Indonesians to participate in 'administration', is also of great interest:

> [this decision by the Japanese government] did not surprise us because we have been long expecting it. After the fall of Singapore and the landing of the Japanese Army in Indonesia, we believed the Japanese statement that 'Japanese will not take over British, American and Dutch colonial policies. Our purpose is to liberate South-east Asian countries from colonialism and to establish the Greater East Asia Co-prosperity Sphere'.

Hatta also observed that in 'the Greater East Asia Co-Prosperity Sphere' 'the cause' will be only achieved when each race has 'political participation', and continued: 'we have no reason to feel concern that our treatment will be any different from that received by Burma and the Philippines'. In Hatta's understanding, the Greater East Asia Conference was 'the venue where Indonesian independence was confirmed' and the Koiso statement was a much delayed fulfilment of Japan's obligations. He stressed that independence is not a gift from outside: 'a fine, powerful nation state can be completed only by our own sacrifice and devotion'. All his speeches reflected his strong belief in national self-determination. Sukarno also used the tactic of thanking Japan publicly for its promise to grant independence, while appealing to his countrymen for self-sacrifice:

> No matter if independence is promised ten times, a hundred or even a thousand times, if we don't fight, or if we don't acquire power to achieve independence, we can never obtain it. If a people possesses an ardent spirit and will, no one can stop them from achieving independence.[22]

As these statements indicate, Hatta and Sukarno did not instruct their countrymen to support Japan, nor did they express gratitude. They used the platform provided to them to talk directly to the people and express their views on national self-determination, something which was banned during Dutch colonisation. At the same time, they showed Japan that Indonesians were watching to see how sincerely Japan would carry out its promise, and demonstrated a determination to keep pressing the issue.

Politically-aware Indonesian listeners must have understood the 'real intention' of Sukarno and Hatta when they appealed to their countrymen in their new national language, Bahasa Indonesia. This was perhaps the main reason why they were not regarded as opportunistic traitors after the war, despite their collaboration with Japan.

The 'Cultural Level of the Indonesians' and the Independence Issue

Japan's willingness to offer a possibility of Indonesian independence when the war situation deteriorated raises important questions. Did Japan cease to look down on the Indonesians and admit that their cultural level had been elevated? Was Japan ready to grant independence unconditionally?

Saitō Shizuo played an important role as an elite bureaucrat in the Military Government Planning Division in Java (and was later posted as ambassador to Indonesia and Australia). According to Saitō, absolute allegiance of children to parents, and of subjects to the emperor, was the essential basis of all social order. He stated that Japan was 'the centre of Greater East Asia, whereas other states rotate around it, thus forming one body'. Within this patron–client relationship, Saitō argued that 'the Indonesian cultural level was still very low' and the fact that 'independence was granted to them' was 'a remarkable event in world history'. It attested, he claimed, to the moral nature of the cause of the Japanese Empire and to the 'holiness of the objective of the Greater East Asian War'.

Concerning Indonesian independence, he stated first that independence could only be achieved by establishing the Greater East Asia Sphere – 'to overcome independence will be eventually to bring it about' – and secondly, that the cultural level of the Indonesians was low, and that discipline was necessary if they were to achieve independence. Whether they could achieve it or not was 'dependent upon the efforts of Japanese leaders'. Thus it was necessary for the Japanese to 'lead the Indonesians with great affection'.[23] This view was not unique. The Japanese Army's highest echelons advised the emperor that 'the natives – "the Indonesians" – are good for nothing at present, but they will be educated gradually'.[24] This represents the general Japanese perceptions of South-east Asia at that time.

Conclusions

'An order of co-existence and co-prosperity, respect for autonomy and independence, and the abolition of racial discrimination' – these were the universal values which Japan stated as war objectives. In practice, however, relations between Japan and Indonesia fell far short of these ideals. It is not possible to erase the *ex-post facto* meaning of these concepts, but from the standpoint of wartime events the more magnificent the concepts of the conqueror, the more self-righteous and fictitious they appeared. Moreover, beneath these pronouncements of universal ideals lay a Japanese belief in the 'low cultural level' of the natives: a belief which Japan attempted to substantiate through scientific research.[25]

In 1992, fifty years after the commencement of Japanese military rule, the issue of 'comfort women', the darkest side of the 'Greater East Asia Co-Prosperity Sphere', emerged as a topic of debate. This was not just a domestic issue, but caused a great sensation in neighbouring countries and the wider world community. The government officially admitted for the first time that women were recruited not only from Korea and Taiwan, but also in large numbers from occupied South-east Asian countries such as Indonesia and the Philippines, and that Dutch nationals were also among the 'comfort women'. In 1991 Indonesians who were drafted as auxiliaries by the Japanese military organised a movement to claim unpaid salaries from the Japanese government after half a century. Those who had been forced to support the 'Greater East Asia Co-Prosperity Sphere' were finally raising their voices.

On the other hand, as the emperor's visit symbolically indicated, economic and political ties between Japan and South-east Asia are stronger than ever, even in comparison with the time of 'Greater East Asia Co-Prosperity Sphere'. However, there is still a great gulf between

Japan and South-east Asia, especially in terms of the mutual human understanding which underpins political and economic relations, and also in terms of their perceptions of the war period. Today, half a century after the dissolution of the 'Greater East Asia Co-Prosperity Sphere', Japanese consciousness of South-east Asia, of the whole Asia-Pacific region, and of modern history, needs to be severely re-examined.

Notes

1 Ishii Yoneo, 'Tōnan Ajia chiiki ninshiki no ayumi' ('Changing perceptions of South East Asia') *Jōchi Ajiagaku*, vol. 7, 1989, pp. 2–3.

2 Elsbeth Locher-Scholter, 'Changing perceptions of Japan in the Netherlands and Netherlands East Indies before 1942', *Journal of the Japan–Netherlands Institute*, 1990, *passim.*

3 Mohammad Hatta, *Kumpulan Karangan* (*Collected Works*), Jakarta, Penerbitan Balai Buku Indonesia, 1952, p. 145.

4 Ahmad Subardjo, preface to the Japanese edn of his *Lahirnya Republik Indonesia* (*The Birth of the Republic of Indonesia*), Jakarta, P. T. Kinta, 1972.

5 Christopher Thorne, *The Issue of War: States, Societies and the Far Eastern Conflict of 1941–45*, London, Hamish Hamilton, 1985, p. 116.

6 Satō Kenryō, *Daitō-a sensō kaikoroku* (*Memoires of the Greater East Asia War*), Tokyo, Tokuma shoten, 1966, p. 317.

7 Nakayama Yasuto, 'Ran'in no genjō to sono dōkō' ('The current situation and trends in the Dutch East Indies'), *Gendai*, September 1941, pp. 113–18.

8 Otaka Shojirō (ed.), *Daitōa no rekishi to kensetsu* (*The History and Construction of Greater East Asia*), Tokyo, Seikōdō, 1943, p. 708.

9 Ozaki Hideki, *Kyū shokuminchi bungaku no kenkyū* (*A Study of Literature in the Ex-Colonies*), Tokyo, Keisō shobō, 1971, p. 63.

10 Kisaka Junichirō, *Shōwa no rekishi, vol.7, Taiheiyō sensō* (*A History of the Shōwa Period, vol. 7, The Pacific War*), Tokyo, Shōgakukan, 1982, p. 205.

11 Miwa Kimitada, *Nihon: 1945 nen no shiten* (*Japan from the Viewpoint of 1945*), Tokyo, Tōykō Daigaku Shuppankai, 1986.

12 Satō, *Daitō-a sensō kaikoroku*, p. 319.

13 Ba Maw, *Breakthrough in Burma: Memoirs of a Revolution, 1936–46*, New Haven, Yale University Press, 1968, p. 341.

14 'Daitō-a sensō kankei ikken: Daitō-a kaigi kankei' ('One issue in the Greater East Asia War: on the Greater East Asia Conference'), document held in the Diplomatic Archives of the Foreign Ministry, Tokyo.

15 *Asahi Shimbun*, 4 November 1943.

16 *Asahi Shimbun*, 16 November 1943.

17 Miyoshi Shunkichirō, 'Jawa senryō gunsei kaikoroku (10)' ('Memoires of the Military Administration of Occupied Java, part 10'), *Nissai mondai*, April 1966, pp. 67–9.

18 Ibid., p. 71.

19 For details, see Gotō Ken'ichi, *Kindai Nihon to Indonesia* (*Modern Japan and Indonesia*), Tokyo, Hokuju shuppan, 1985, ch. 5.

20 'Higashi Indo dokuritsu sochi ni kansuru ken (1945 July 17)' ('On measures for the independence of the East Indies, 17 July 1945'), document held in the Diplomatic Archives of the Foreign Ministry, Tokyo.

21 Speeches referred to here are all quoted from M. Hatta, *Kumpulan Pidato 1942–49* (*Collected Speeches 1942–49*), Jakarta, Yayasan Idayu, 1981.

22 Sukarno, 'Kanmei to chikai' ('Impressions and vows'), *Shin Jawa*, January 1944, p. 321.

23 Saitō Shizuo, 'Higashi Indo dokuritsu shidō no ichi shihyō' ('A guideline for independence in the East Indies'), *Shin Jawa*, ibid., pp. 21–3.

24 'Nampō senryō chiiki no genjō to heiryoku un'yō ni tsuite no sanbō sōchō jōsōan' ('Draft report to the emperor from the chief of staff on the present situation in the southern occupied areas and on the deployment of military forces'), 29 May 1942, document held in the War History Section of the Defence Agency Archives, Tokyo.

25 For instance, in Java under Japanese rule, an intelligence comparison between Japanese and Sundanese pupils was conducted through standard deviation research. The result was used to emphasise that the Japanese were the most competent people: Shinagawa Fujirō, 'Indonesiajin no chinō' ('The intellect of the Indonesians'), *Shin Jawa*, December 1944, pp. 37–45.

CHAPTER ELEVEN

Japanese Army Internment Policies for Enemy Civilians During the Asia-Pacific War

UTSUMI AIKO

(translated by Meredith Patton)

Introduction

Above Semarang in central Java, as the aeroplane prepares for landing and loses altitude, orderly rows of white crosses set in a green lawn come into view. Adjacent to the airport there lies a large cemetery, the resting place of the Dutch people who died in Java during the Pacific War. I visited this cemetery, Kalibanten, in August 1992 and August 1994.

Large and small crosses are arranged in a step formation around a large central cross. The children's crosses are smaller, while those of the women are rounded off at the edges like flower petals. To each of the graves of Jewish people the Star of David is affixed. Into each of the Islamic grave markers is engraved a small circle. There are about three thousand of these graves here, and reading the names and dates engraved on the white markers I find that there are many who died in the years 1944 and 1945; also that many of these were children and elderly people.

In the western corner of the cemetery the statues of two women stand facing each other, against the background of the airport. The statue on the left stands head cast down, as if in great sadness. The face of the other statue is severe, even angry, and she rests her hand on the shoulder of the other woman, seeming to stare into the distance. Between them stand the statues of two children, hands linked. Facing this group is a statue of a young boy, hoisting a hoe on his right shoulder, his thin left hand clasping an axe. His shaven head is abnormally large, his eye-sockets sunken, his cheeks hollow. Barefoot and clad only in a loincloth, his figure is skeleton-like, every bone visible and countable, representing an advanced condition of

174

starvation. 'Youth Camp, 1944–1945, Bankon-Gudojati' reads the inscription on the base of this statue. BG was also the military internment centre run by the Japanese army. In the dusk of evening there is an eeriness about this statue.

Although the conditions of the concentration camp of Auschwitz are well-known in Japan, there are probably few Japanese people who are able to imagine the civilian internment centres run by the Japanese Imperial Army. Indeed, almost no concern has been paid in Japan to the problem of the internment of civilians of the Dutch empire. Perhaps it was rationalised, on the basis of the Dutch being imperialists, or through the argument that a certain amount of brutality is inevitable during wartime. In Holland, and other countries where the victims came from, handwritten notes and diaries are repeatedly published, and large numbers of individual testimony remain in public archives and war museums.[1]

Among the war crimes for which Japan was made to account, the Allied forces placed most emphasis on the internment and mistreatment of internees from their own countries. At the Provisional Dutch-Indies Court Martial opened in Batavia (now Jakarta) after the end of the war, those who had had connections with the internment centres were the very first to be judged. The Japanese personnel responsible at the internment centres, charged with first-degree war crimes and sentenced to death by shooting, were followed by the Korean supervisors, who were judged to be equivalent to the Japanese, on account of having been 'employed by the enemy country, Japan'.

Among the Japanese people charged with war crimes, there is a high degree of discontent with the trials. Along with the feeling that the whole proceedings could not be helped since Japan had been vanquished in the war, lingering complaints remain about cognitive differences regarding what constitutes 'war crimes', differences in the consideration of the accountability of those concerned, inadequate procedure at the trials, insufficient understanding of court procedure, translation problems, etc., as well as claims that the trials were unfairly conducted in a spirit of revenge. Reflected in such complaints is a certain victim mentality: a sense that these people were not being made accountable for war crimes but were sacrifices at an unjust trial. Records and diaries attesting the unfairness of the trials for class B and C war crimes continue to be published in Japan.[2]

Just as former Dutch internees are unable to forget the criminal wartime actions of the Japanese during their internment at the camps, the Japanese and Koreans who worked at the camps continue to attest to the brutality they suffered at the hands of the Dutch army following the end of the war and the unfairness of the military trials. On either side, the experiences of the victims continue to be written. The tales of the victims are comprehensive and carefully detailed, with many concrete examples. In all of them, a world that their assailants are unable to visualise is revealed.

In this chapter, I wish to consider the relationship between 'victim' and 'aggressor' in wartime, through the central topic of the military internment centres for enemy citizens operated by Japan on the island of Java.

Japanese in 'Enemy' Countries/'Enemies' of Japan

Who is the 'Enemy?'

The fate of people who leave their native land to live in another is often swayed by the relationship between those two countries. The declaration of war by Japan – which had a history of colonisation and workers leaving their home country since the Meiji period, in what was termed 'the building' of their country – had a momentous effect on the lives of Japanese citizens living abroad.

On 8 December 1941 Japan declared war on Britain and the United States. Japanese who were living in these countries, as well as those resident in British and American colonies, instantly became enemy citizens. Canada, Australia and Holland subsequently entered the war, and Japanese living in these countries were also then designated enemy citizens. Enemies of Japan in the Pacific War amounted to some twenty-seven countries, with a combined total of 560 000 resident Japanese, or citizens of Japanese descent.[3] It is already well-known in Japan and elsewhere that 126 000 civilians of Japanese descent who were living on the west coast of the US were forcibly incarcerated in internment centres located in the inner continent. Japanese and citizens of Japanese descent were also interned in Canada.[4]

In Asia, the history of Japanese overseas workers was already deeply engraved. At Davao in the Philippines there was an established Japanese community; however, upon the declaration of war General Douglas MacArthur issued an 'Order for the Forcible Internment of Japanese'. The Japanese in Singapore were incarcerated in the Changi gaol. On Java many Japanese had emigrated to run businesses, such as the Toko Jepan (or 'Japanese shops'), and had integrated their lives with those of the other inhabitants. In Malaya, Borneo and Sumatra there were Japanese plantations of rubber, coffee and coconut palm. In addition, there were also immigrant fishermen from Okinawa; and Japanese divers in search of white mother-of-pearl operated from the Arafura Sea off the coast of New Guinea to the

Torres Straits near northern Australia. In the midst of worsening US–Japan relations, a withdrawal of overseas Japanese citizens was carried out. The last evacuation boat from Java, the *Fuji Maru*, carried 1802 civilians, far in excess of its loading capacity. Those Japanese left behind at the start of the war were imprisoned, and later kept in internment camps in Australia.[5]

On the other hand, there were people living in Japan who also became designated 'enemies' due to the outbreak of war. The Ministry for Home Affairs was responsible for dealing with foreigners residing within Japan. Prior to the outbreak of war the Ministry compiled the 'Special Wartime Arrangements Plan' containing directives for the treatment of foreign citizens during 'periods of emergency'. In this 'plan', along with directives for the establishment of internment centres, were instructions for the treatment of aliens should a state of emergency arise. Foreign citizens were first to be separated into those who were to be arrested and investigated, those to be expelled, and others; absolute power to arrest those from either of the two former categories, in the event of any emergency, was stipulated.

More detailed directives were given concerning those among the foreign residents who came from 'enemy' states. According to the directives, those foreign citizens who could reasonably be suspected of spying were subject to arrest. Those subject to internment included enemy military personnel, including airforce and navy personnel, males over eighteen years of age, those with special technical qualifications such as radio and military technicians, and any 'spy suspects' who had not been arrested. Internees were directed to be divided into those from 'enemy' states, those from third countries, and to be further divided into male and female internees, as well as being isolated from outside contact. Considering that, at the time, Japan's 'enemies' amounted to twenty-seven different countries, this cannot have been an easy task. In addition to this, the Japanese army had proclaimed its mission to 'liberate' the colonies of Asia; the treatment of the native people from these colonies was therefore another problem to be considered. The Ministry of Home Affairs decided on the following classification and treatment of Asian peoples:

• residents of Hawaii to be treated as 'Americans', but Filipinos not to be included in this category;
• Canadians and Australians to be treated as 'British', but Indian, Malay or Burmese people not to be included in this category;
• White Russians not to be counted as Soviet citizens;
• Dutch not to be included among Indonesians;

• Vietnamese and Cambodian people not to be included in the category of 'French';
• Americans of Japanese descent to be treated as Japanese, and other persons holding dual nationality to be treated as Japanese.[6]

The Ministry of Home Affairs thus separated citizens of imperial powers and native Asians in countries colonised by those powers, and dealt with them accordingly. Plans for the internment of enemy citizens were drawn up in the second half of 1941, just before the outbreak of the Pacific War. The number of American citizens resident in Japan, particularly those classified as 'white Americans', had decreased by about half since the previous year. Among US citizens resident in Japan, the majority were Americans of Japanese descent, about 85 per cent of whom were students. Even these, who as Japanese Americans were eligible for the same treatment as Japanese citizens, had for the most part returned to the US by exchange ferry before the war started. The internment of American citizens left in Japan – 1044 people – began on 9 December 1941, the day after war broke out. In the regions eventually occupied by Japan about 14 000 US civilians were incarcerated, while the number of American military personnel captured in the battle for the Philippines and other areas amounted to about 17 000. In all, about 30 000 Americans were detained by the Japanese army.

The majority of British citizens living in Japan had also left the country by August 1941, when measures were introduced to freeze their assets. British citizens living in China, 'Manchukuo' (the Japanese puppet state of Manchuria), Shanghai and Hong Kong were also evacuated. British citizens interned in Japan following the outbreak of the war numbered 690. However, in Malaya and Burma, due to the unexpectedly swift advance of the Japanese army, about 14 000 civilians who were unable to escape were detained. British citizens captured and detained following the fall of Singapore numbered 99 000.[7]

In the Dutch East Indies there were roughly 100 000 Dutch settlers, including those who had been born and brought up in Indonesia. Because their home country had by this time been overrun by Nazi Germany, the Dutch settlers had nowhere to evacuate to when the Pacific War broke out. The exiled Dutch government established in London subsequently declared war on Japan. The Japanese army, which had announced the commencement of hostilities with the Dutch East Indies on 12 January 1942, captured and occupied the oil bases at Balikpapan on Borneo (now Kalimantan) and Palembang in Sumatra in quick succession, the Dutch-Indian army finally surrendering at Java on 9 March. In addition to the large number of Allied forces captured, a further 100 000 civilians were rounded up and interned during the Japanese occupation.

How to Treat Internees?

The treatment and management of the internees was divided among three Japanese ministries, those in 'inner Japan' falling under the jurisdiction of the Ministry for Home Affairs, those in the 'external territories' of Taiwan, Korea and Sakhalin under the Ministry of Colonies, and those in the occupied territories under the army and navy. External relations which pertained to internees were dealt with through an 'Office for Affairs concerning Civilians in Enemy Territories', set up by the Foreign Ministry. The aim of this office, in addition to the handling of matters concerning captives and internees, was the investigation and improvement of living conditions for Japanese citizens resident overseas, but this office was not established until December 1942, nearly a year after the start of the war. It can be considered that the seriousness of the problem of how to treat prisoners and internees was not sufficiently acknowledged by the wartime government of Japan.[8] The awareness of the Japanese government regarding the internees can be further questioned in the light of the fact that, at the beginning of the war only a vague policy on the treatment of enemy civilians in occupied areas had been established. This stated that 'Persons failing to cooperate with the policies of the military government or respond to directives issued shall be expelled, and/or other appropriate measures taken as seen necessary'.

Japan went to war with virtually no policy for the treatment of prisoners, especially enemy civilian internees. It could further be said that this problem was not even one of great concern for the Japanese government.[9]

In contrast with the attitude of the Japanese government towards internees, on the day that internment of enemy citizens in Japan commenced the International Red Cross Association requested cooperation from the Japanese government in the collection of information on this matter. Similarly, on 27 December the US expressed its intention to apply the conditions concerning the humane treatment of wartime captives stipulated in the Convention for the Treatment of Prisoners of War (henceforth referred to as the Geneva Treaty), and the Geneva Red Cross Treaty. While it was acknowledged that Japan had not ratified these treaties, the hope for 'mutual application' of the conditions of the treaties to civilian internees as well as prisoners of war was clearly expressed.[10]

Prior to the Second World War there had been no conflict which generated comparable numbers of non-combatant internees, so there had been no treaty concluded that dealt specifically with the treatment of such internees. The US authorities therefore proposed that the Geneva treaties covering the humane treatment of captives in wartime be applied also to non-combatant internees. In Japan, the Minister for Foreign Affairs, Minister Togo, considering the effects that this application would have on the hundreds of thousands of Japanese civilians detained in enemy countries, indicated to the head of the Treaties Bureau, Matsumoto Shun'ichi, that the matter be discussed with the army and navy.[11] At a meeting of the Army High Command Bureau of the Ministry of War, the Military Protection Bureau of the Ministry for Home Affairs, the Ministry for Territorial Affairs and other relevant bureaus and offices, the views of the various bodies were canvassed, and it was accepted that Japan should agree to 'apply' the Geneva Convention 'within the limits of our capability'. The army's response to the Ministry for Foreign Affairs was that Japan should limit its reply to the statement that it had no objection to 'taking measures in accordance with' the Convention.[12]

The Japanese government was being asked to 'apply' the conditions of an international treaty, which it had not ratified, to captives and other internees. Having imposed the caveats 'within our capabilities' and 'taking measures corresponding with the convention's conditions', the government agreed to return the answer of 'corresponding application' of the Convention. In other words, regarding conflict between the application of the treaty and domestic Japanese legislation, in particular the Peace Preservation Law, the Military Criminal Code, the Court-martial Law, etc., this 'corresponding application' was interpreted as including 'the application after suitable amendment of those areas of the Geneva Treaty so as to conform with the reality of our situation, and with the domestic laws and regulations of our own country, Japan'.[13] The reply of the Ministry for Foreign Affairs to Britain and the US added to the Convention the condition that 'internees not be subjected to manual labour against the free will of the individual concerned', and stated that all countries concerned should, within the limits of their capabilities, mutually apply (*mutatis mutandis*) the Convention's conditions to all internees.[14]

The Allied countries interpreted this as equivalent to 'ratification' of the Convention by Japan, therefore binding Japan to the Convention's conditions. Protests registered afterwards by the Allied states about violation of the Convention by Japan concerning the treatment of prisoners and internees reflect their assumption that Japan had actually ratified the Convention through its statement of 'corresponding application'. A discrepancy in the interpretations of articles of the Convention concerning the treatment of prisoners and internees can thus be discerned from the very beginning. At first however, the Ministry for Foreign Affairs, with almost no understanding of the gravity of the problem of internees and captives, seems not to have recognised the importance of this problem of interpretation.[15]

In the Geneva Convention that was to be applied to civilian internees, detailed regulations cover all aspects of the lives of prisoners of war, including the establishment of internment camps, food and clothing, and sanitary requirements for the camps. In all, there are ninety-seven articles detailing the human rights of prisoners, including the obligation of the captors to provide them with food of equivalent quality and amount to that provided to reserve troops, sufficient drinking water, prohibition of the use of food/water rations to inflict group punishment, the obligation of the captors to provide clothes, shoes and underwear to the prisoners, the provision of adequate water to maintain personal sanitation, the obligation not to subject captives to unsuitable physical labour, the right of captives to receive wages for labour performed in captivity, and so on.

Having promised at least 'corresponding application' of this Geneva Convention, why did Japan come to be responsible for the events represented by the statue of the starving boy with the hoe who guards the graves at Kalibanten Cemetery?

Internees in the Occupied Territories

A large number of enemy citizens lived in the areas of South-east Asia that were eventually occupied by Japan. In the early period of the Occupation, because there were no special regulations to deal with these people, many of them were permitted to continue living in their own homes or in the homes of acquaintances. These were managed under district garrisons; however, because this arrangement was undesirable in terms of security, in February 1942 hastily designed measures were conveyed from the Army Ministry to the relevant divisions of the occupying forces. According to these directives, rations for detainees would correspond to those provided to prisoners of war, but the detainees would not be prevented from supplementing these rations in order to maintain themselves. Internment centres would be set up on a centralised basis. Investigation of all internees would be carried out; those deemed no threat to security measures would be released under appropriate surveillance after swearing a pledge. Internees could request employment, and any other problems regarding treatment were to be dealt with according to the 'Essential

Points on the Handling of Foreign Internees' stipulated by regulations issued by the Ministry for Home Affairs on the treatment of internees within Japan.[16]

Internees were permitted to supplement any inadequacies in their food ration at their own expense. Those without the necessary means to do so were allowed to earn wages by requesting to work. Although there must have been difficulties for the internees in adapting to a lifestyle contained and constricted through these conditions, it can be said that up to this point the treatment of the internees by the Japanese authorities was comparatively lenient. Once the military administration was established, the management of detainees was transferred to the administration's command headquarters.

An internment centre was opened at Hong Kong in February 1942, and 2818 people were imprisoned there. At Singapore, renamed 'Shōnantō', or 'Bright Southern Island' by the Japanese Occupation, internment commenced from May of the same year, and by August a military internment centre had been opened by the military administration's command headquarters; 2946 people were interned at this centre. In Borneo the internment of enemy citizens began in July 1942, most of them priests and nuns from the Roman Catholic Church. The garrison there was managing 618 internees, but in March of 1943 consolidation of the internees into one location, an internment centre for prisoners of war, was carried out. In Thailand and Burma the internment of civilians was carried out by individual military divisions. In Sumatra over 10 000 civilians were detained, while in Java the total number of enemy citizens imprisoned was as high as 70 000 (see table 11.1).

At Manila in the Philippines, where military rule was officially established on 3 January 1942, internment of enemy citizens by the Japanese commenced on the same day; 3355 American, British and Dutch citizens were contained at the internment centre for enemy citizens at Saint Thomas University.

According to the account of a British woman and her daughter who were captured and interned at Saint Thomas internment camp in Manila while evacuating to India from Shanghai, morning roll call at the camp was at 6 a.m., night roll call at 9 p.m., and lights out at 10 p.m. There was absolutely no privacy in the camp, and although the climate was so hot as to make showers four times a day a necessity, so little water was provided that this was a hopeless wish. There was a constant and serious struggle against dirt, bedbugs and lice. To the internees, accustomed to the comfortable life of colony settlers, the over-density of the camps must have been almost unbearable.

As indicated in the instructions from the Minister for War

Table 11.1 Organisation of civilian internment camps

According to the 'Regulation for the Treatment of Military Internees', November 1943

Name of camps	No. of internees	Comments	Internee deaths
Java Internment camps First est. April 1942	Dividing into 3 categories		6353
Formalised April 1944	69 779 (June 1945)	23 667 men 31 174 women 14 938 children	
Sumatra Internment camps First est. May 1934 Formalised April 1944	11 865	2296 released while under control of Military Administration	1217
Philippines Internment camps First est. Mar. 1942	3355	Cebu, Bacolog and other camps transferred to control of Manila December 1943	185
Formalised January 1994	5884		
Malaya Internment camps First est. August 1942	2946	1097 released by Military Administration but later re-interned	219
Formalised January 1944	3487 + 1097		
Thai, Burma Internment camps Formalised November 1944	187	83 people released in early 1945	9
Borneo Internment camps Formalised January 1944	644 (Mar. 1945)	266 men 244 women 34 children	23
Hong Kong Internment camps First est. February 1942 Re-organised August 1943	2818		82
Formalised January 1944	2513		

Table 11.1 (cont.)

Name of camps	No. of internees	Comments	Internee deaths
Shanghai Internment camps Formalised November 1942	345		13
....			
Renamed **Fengtai** Internment camps and moved to Fengtai	317		
Canton Internment camps Est. November 1942	9	4 Americans 5 British	

Note: At the time of the occupation enemy citizens were interned by various regiments, and when Military Administrations were established in the various regions control of these internees was transferred to the command headquarters of the Military Administration. In 1944 when the 'Regulations for the Treatment of Military Internees' were put into effect, military internment centres were established on a formal basis and internees placed under their control.

In addition to the deaths listed here a further 5 internees died at Kanpili, 50 at Palembang, 98 at Menado and 1 at Taboi.

Source: Prisoners of War Internee Information Bureau, *Records of the Treatment (Furyo Toriatsuka no Kiroku)*, Tokyo, Prisoners of War Information Bureau, 1955.

(mentioned above), it was permissible for internees to supplement their food rations out of their own savings; however, not all had equal savings to begin with, and as the period of internment lengthened the struggle against starvation became increasingly intense. Young women suffered from deterioration of their teeth through a lack of calcium, eye ailments were caused by insufficient vitamin B, as well as dysentery and ulcers. Because of the poor quality of the rice, which often came into the mess riddled with mouse droppings, and the accumulated effects of a diet of consisting mainly of rice and gruel, on the few occasions when animal protein was provided to the internees many of them were unable to digest it.

Although the date is not clearly recorded, at some time during 1942 the essayist and scholar, Yoshikawa Eiji, prompted by a 'sudden stirring of curiosity', embarked on a trip to Saint Thomas University to examine the lifestyle of the internees:

Perhaps because it happens to be evening mealtime, the wide steps and countless corridors are crowded with people, so that there is not even room to stand. British, Australian, American, Dutch; all of them were men and women of hostile origin. Each one taking a large plate and soup bowl, they receive their food at the window, cheerfully making their way through the great human wave to their own group or table.

What a rich feast! To provide food such as this to 3,500 people must be a task indeed. Even those of us in the inner territories (Japan proper) don't eat as well as this vast assembly.[17]

Yoshikawa walks through the crowd taking detailed notice of the menu; finding fried chicken, vegetables and macaroni, potato, curry and soup, he reaches the conclusion that 'every night, food of this standard is provided equally to the citizens of our enemies; there can be no mistake about this', and he ends up suffused with emotion at 'the munificent benevolence of the Imperial Army and Japan'.

The Saint Thomas internment centre, as perceived through the eyes of Yoshikawa, was 'a pool of indolent humanity. In this now-turbulent world, there can be none others maintained in such a state of carefree yawning. Their situation is complete; food, clothing, even care for the young'. Reading his account, the internees are seen to be enjoying a life which is 'almost that of a summer holiday resort'. Was Yoshikawa unable to see the reality of the camps, or did he deliberately not try to perceive it?

Repeated and increasingly strident protests about the treatment of the internees, supposedly existing in luxury at a place comparable to a 'summer resort', were made by the US and other countries, along with requests to the 'Office for Affairs of Enemy Civilian Internees' within the Ministry for Foreign Affairs, for improvements in their conditions. America and other countries persistently prepared well-stocked parcels and endeavoured to have these distributed as relief goods, and requests for an exchange of ships to transport these materials were made to Japan. Because the Japanese side could not provide the ships necessary for this arrangement however, they were unable to respond adequately to these proposals.[18]

The judgment by the Japanese government, that further neglect of the treatment of the masses of internees could develop into a serious international problem, was accompanied by the serious problem of security measures in a rapidly worsening war situation. As a result, the army embarked on the establishment of internees centres, in order to 'constrict the activities of enemy citizens', as well as to ensure their 'protection'. On 7 November 1943 Togo, Minister for War, issued 'Asian Directive 7391', containing 'Regulations for the Treatment of Military Internees', which was sent to all army divisions.[19] According to this regulation, the management of enemy citizens was transferred from the surveillance department of the military government to the main army command. Military internment centres were subsequently established in the occupied territories of Java, Sumatra, Philippines, Malaya, Thailand, Burma and Borneo.

The Military Internment Camps on Java

Registration and Internment of Enemy Citizens

Enemy citizens on Java numbered about 66 000. Following the surrender of the Dutch-Indies army on 7 March Commander Imamura Hitoshi of the 16th battalion declared the establishment of military administration, with the aim of making 'effective practical use of all remaining local structures and personnel'. However, Military Chief-of-Staff Yamamoto, and Head of Military Affairs Sugiyama, who arrived from Tokyo for a tour of inspection, complained that 'the handling of citizens of hostile countries by the 16th battalion is far too lax and magnanimous'. Although Imamura replied that he was running the administration along the guidelines of the 'Principles for Rule of Occupied Territories in Accordance with the Strategy for Southern Advancement', issued by Imperial Headquarters, this was not taken into account by the visitors.[20] Because of this, by April of the same year it was decided that about 2000 Dutch officials would be interned, and that citizens of enemy states, citizens of hostile states and those from third-party states should be forced to register with the authorities. With the exception of native Indonesians, all 'foreign' men and women over the age of seventeen years were obliged to register their residence, as well as swear a 'pledge of sincerity'. The compulsory submission of information concerning the name, age, current address, nationality, occupation, period of residence and near relations of each individual was followed by the issue of a 'Certificate of Registration of Alien Residence and Pledge'. A photo and the imprint of the individual's thumb were affixed to this certificate, and it was required that the certificate be 'carried at all times'.[21]

People who carried out this registration as required were divided into the three categories of 'persons of ardent hostility', 'persons of restricted residence', and 'persons of designated residence', and their treatment was regulated according to these categories. Those designated 'persons of ardent hostility' consisted of those Dutch administrative officials and workers already interned, executives and managers of essential industries, general individuals who had shown particular hostility, and 'hostile' overseas Chinese. These people were separated according to sex and nationality and interned in nineteen different places across Java; according to a 1942 census they numbered 4492 people. Those interned were permitted a certain level of self-government after appointing representatives, group leaders and dormitory heads from among themselves. Food was provided corresponding to the 'Rules for Provisions to Captives', but contact with the outside world was forbidden, and visits were restricted to family members and close friends. All items of mail were censored. However, even among 'persons of ardent hostility', those deemed useful in the restoration of facilities that had been damaged in battle were not interned but 'put to practical use'.

Persons categorised under the 'restricted residence' heading were males aged between sixteen and sixty years, and deemed 'capable of reasonably vigorous activity'. To prevent such people from engaging in anti-Japanese activities, they were made to live in designated areas, mostly confined in schools, gaols and private residences. Naturally, families were ordered to separate. Married couples under sixty years of age were confined separately from each other, while boys of sixteen years or over, sometimes including those as young as nine to eleven years of age, were separated from their mothers. There were no schools for the children; instead they were put to work aiding the self-sufficiency of the internees by raising domestic animals and participating in other agricultural activities. Those in the 'restricted residence' category numbered 15 252 people.

Persons of 'designated residence' consisted of males below the age of seventeen and above the age of sixty years, women and children. At the beginning of the military administration, those who complied with the 'Pledge of sincerity towards the Imperial Japanese Army' and who carried the compulsory 'Certificate of Alien Resident Registration and Pledge' were allowed to move freely. Despite the restrictions imposed on the recording of radio broadcasts and the use of particular wavelengths, in 1943, amid a worsening war situation, the free movement of such a large number of hostile citizens had become a grave security problem.[22] The army command section of the military administration subsequently constructed designated areas of residence by surrounding six relatively concentrated Dutch settlements with barbed wire fences. Women and children who counted as 'hostile citizens' from all areas of Java were then forcibly moved to these areas, taking with them only what few household implements and daily necessities they could carry.

Several thousand people now began a life crowded into a single, confined area. People who, for the most part, during the period of Dutch settlement had only known the marble floors and high ceilings of the spacious colonial houses, were now forced into small areas, surrounded by woven bamboo fences and barbed wire. Toilets, showers and kitchen areas were all shared, with restrictions on water and electricity. Although the Imperial Army claimed to aid the self-sufficiency of the internees by setting up a supply depot for daily necessities and a market to trade in, it is recorded in the diaries of some internees how items such as soap were in desperately short supply, and the people struggled constantly against starvation. By October 1943 it was recorded that 66 784 people had been moved to the 'designated areas of residence'.

Establishing the Military Internment Centres

For reasons of security, and also because of the lengthening duration of internment, new 'Regulations for the Treatment of Military Internees' were issued in November 1943. The management of citizens of enemy states was transferred from the military administration command headquarters to the army command. Under the army command, military internment camps were set up. However, by late 1943 the question of how to manage military internment camps containing such a large number of internees had surfaced. Obtaining extra personnel was difficult, and there were places where military internment camps had been merged with POW camps.

On Java, the Java military internment camp was established together with a POW camp (organised in August 1942). The post of camp head was undertaken concurrently by Major-General Saitō Shōei, and additional officers and civilian army employees were transferred to work in the POW camp. Headquarters and the main camp were established at Jakarta, while second and third camp divisions were built at Bandung and Semarang respectively. All internees were herded into these three sites and numbered 69 779 people.

The military internment centres were established, but there were not enough personnel to manage and guard the internees. After the 'Treatment Regulations' were communicated, the army's vice-commander issued Asian Directive 7852, in which 'the requisition of POW camp personnel to assume additional duties as military internment camp workers' was ordered. Under this directive army personnel and civilian employees who had previously been in charge of managing detainees under the military administration were transferred to work in army detention camps. In August 1942, at the Java military administration surveillance division, a survey of disbanded military auxiliaries and volunteer auxiliaries was undertaken, and thirty-two people were gazetted on 13 September and subsequently despatched to the camps.[23] The next to be mobilised to work in the camps were Korean auxiliaries. Under the name of 'working troops', they were ordered to the military internment camps. These employees were on a two-year contract, and had been drafted from the Korean peninsula in June 1942, so their period of work should have expired. Despite this, they were not released from their contracts, but despatched afresh to new positions in the camps. Their position as army employees did not change for two years. Among the Japanese officers in charge of the Korean civilian employees were some who had previously been stationed in the Japanese colony of Korea; among them, a contemptuous attitude toward the ethnic Koreans was quite common.

Of those Koreans who had been recruited before conscription on the Korean peninsula started, a large proportion were comparatively well-educated, most having completed middle and high school and graduated from university. The pride of being well educated, along with a fierce sense of national honour, was the cause of much friction between these Koreans and their Japanese commanders. Among the Koreans, feelings of dissatisfaction and oppression were accumulating. Friction between the Koreans and other Japanese officers and senior officers was also on the rise. Prior to their transferral to the POW camps, Korean POW supervisors with whom there were 'problems' were taken to Sumorwarno, close to Semarang in central Java, for intensive combat retraining.[24]

Even after mobilisation of the Korean civilian employees, it was still impossible to secure the personnel necessary to oversee the internees, who now numbered around 70 000; because of this, about 3000 Indonesian youths were also collected. In this way, native youths of the Dutch colony became responsible for guarding their previous colonisers. The Indonesians' status was described as 'troop supplements', and they were given about two months' training by Japanese senior officers before being installed as guards at the military internment centres. However, because of insufficient personnel at the military internment camps, Korean civilian employees of the army worked as assistants, and occasionally acted as trainers to the Indonesians. In an interview conducted on 25 August 1994 at a remote village in the district of the town of Salatiga, in the south of Semarang, a Mr Sutarto, who was one of the Indonesians originally recruited as 'troop supplements' to work at the military internment centre at Ambarawa, related that his immediate superior, or group leader, was a Korean civilian army employee. He also said that the Indonesian 'troop supplements' were forbidden any direct dealings with the internees, and also forbidden to speak with them. On Java, three military internment camps guarded by Indonesians were established.

Internment Centres in Jakarta

The First Headquarters in Jakarta began the internment of women and children under sixteen years at six sites from April 1944. Following this, five more of these camps were established. At the time of the Japanese defeat, 21 875 people were interned in camps at eleven different places. Among these, the treatment of internees at the Tjideng Camp was said to be so cruel that the very mention of its name still induces a chill in the spines of the survivors. According to Lieutenant-Colonel Collins of the English Division of the Legal Office of the Supreme Allied Forces Command, who was present at the evacuation of the internees from the camp at the end of the war, the women were in such a state of starvation that they were controlled almost solely by the desire to satisfy their hunger, and failed to respond to anything else around them. They also displayed an abnormal attachment towards material belongings. Among the camps which Collins was to witness, apparently Tjideng camp was the worst.[25]

The Tjideng camp was located on a site sandwiched between the Tjideng River, which runs from north to south slightly west of the central town area, and the railway line. Nowadays, there remains no trace of the shadow of the camp in this site, which forms part of the rapidly developing district of central Java. Extensive work has since been done on improving the river, which was often prone to flooding. The records written by the women survivors of the Tjideng camp reveal that internees were controlled mainly through fear. Internees were made to submit absolutely to camp authority, and were treated like horses or cattle. Every morning and night internees were made to gather in the camp grounds and line up for a roll call. After the morning call they had to line up again to receive the morning meal. Meals consisted mainly of a meagre amount of tapioca gruel, while the midday and evening meals included rice and a vegetable called *kankun*, with tempe made from fermented soybeans added once every two weeks. Sugar was practically unavailable. Some of the starving internees hoarded salt and pepper in old tobacco tins; licking this mixture helped to stave off hunger pangs. The menstrual periods of many of the women ceased during internment. Infectious diseases spread quickly among the weakened bodies of the internees. Many of the older women and young children, their bodies unable to stand up to the harsh changes of environment, became the victims of whooping cough, amoebic dysentery, malaria, hepatitis and mental illnesses.

Compulsory labour was also enforced. The sanitary conditions of the camps, which housed 10 200 people, were appalling; latrines filled quickly. Included in the internees' daily work was the digging of gutters, into which the excrement was dumped using ladles and buckets. Although this job came around about once a week, no extra water or soap was provided for washing hands after its completion. Around the time of the Japanese defeat, the daily water ration for internees was about one cup, which was all that was provided for drinking, laundry and personal washing. If one internee caused any problems, all were punished, usually by the reduction of food rations.[26]

The Bandung Military Internment Camp

At the Second Out-Station in Bandung, camps were established at seven sites in the south of the city and 34 160 people interned there. At one of those, the Arubaros camp at Cimahi, the food allowance was extremely poor, with only about 1000 calories per day being provided to the internees. Because of this, internees were forced to sell their jewels and other valuables, and somehow survive by buying extra food with the income they received. Rats and dogs were cooked to provide meat to those internees who were ill. Although some medical goods were supplied, these were insufficient in amount and poor in quality.

A Japanese non-commissioned officer who was a paymaster in the military internment camps has also acknowledged the poorness of the food supplies. Even through negotiations with the warfare supplies freight depot, the paymasters were unable to obtain extra food. The view of the depot was that no extra food would be provided to enemies, when even Japanese soldiers were unable to eat enough. With food supplies in such difficulty, it was extremely doubtful whether the Japanese were able to feed their captives, let alone treat them in accordance with the Geneva Convention. He subsequently claimed in his defence that even though he sympathised with the internees and wanted to give them food, he was unable to do so. He also said that he felt sorry for the internees, herded into confinement at the orders of the Japanese army, and indeed it seems to have been the case that many of those responsible for the camps actually felt great anxiety about the way the internees were treated. According to the testimony of the paymaster, he tried his best to obtain extra supplies for the internees, but to no avail. Even though he knew that the supplies were insufficient, he was unable to obtain more; his hands were tied. Because of this situation, after 1945 the death rate of the internees who were exhausted after their long imprisonment greatly increased.

Differences of custom between the Japanese guards and their internees were also responsible for the aggravation of friction between them. To those in charge, the behaviour of the internees came across as insubordinate; they (the internees) were arrogant and rude, and insulting to the Japanese army. Affidavits submitted to the Tokyo Court relate how punishment was occasionally inflicted for these reasons.[27]

The Semarang Military Internment Camp

Camps One to Five were located at Semarang, in central Java. At the town of Ambarawa, in south Semarang, camps were established at seven sites. Women and children were interned at two camps located in a former Dutch army barracks and a Catholic school, and there was one men's camp. Camps were also established at Solo and Muntilan respectively, and transferral of internees to these camps was completed by March 1944.

The personnel at these multiple camps numbered no more than one junior Japanese officer and a few Koreans, the rest being left to Indonesian 'supplements'. Because of the impossibility of *de facto* management of the camps by official personnel, a certain amount of self-government by the internees was carried out. However, it was still up to a minority of warders to maintain their rule over a large number of internees. Those who attempted to make contact with the outside and those who infringed other rules were therefore punished and tortured as an example to the rest of the internees. According to evidence submitted to the Tokyo War Crimes trial, at the Karapanas internment centre in the old Catholic school (from the period of Dutch rule) within the Fifth Semarang camp, striking of the internees by personnel was habitual. Children above nine years of age were separated far from their parents. Women were forced to assume a heavy burden of labour, shared between groups of only a few, and food shortages were extreme.

The school mentioned above still remains, and is still used as a private Catholic school. The school building and grounds are surrounded by green, and it is easy to imagine that, as a place of internment, this must have been far more pleasant than Jakarta; the heat is also less intense, compared to Jakarta. However, the constant lack of food and the hard work in the fields must have been very difficult for the internees. The Indonesian teachers and caretakers at this school kindly showed me round this monument to the troubled history of relations between the Dutch and Japanese.

The Ranpesari internment centre of the Fourth camp was established in the middle of a residential area for Indonesians. Today this area is once again a residential one, with no trace of the camp remaining. Women were forced to do outdoors labour, and small girls were made to carry heavy rice bags. Group punishment was also inflicted; torture was often carried out, with one instance lasting seven days. At the

Banubil internment centre at Anbarawa, the meal allowance consisted of 90 grams of rice per day. Cruel punishment was inflicted through particularly brutal methods.[28]

At the internment centres, chances for Japanese and Koreans to deal directly with the internees were few. However, those in charge of the crowded internment centres were also in charge of the overcrowded POW camps. In addition to overcrowding of the camps, the insufficient supply of food and medicines to the camps toward the end of the Occupation period meant that many of the internees were severely weakened. Those that managed somehow to survive and ward off starvation, did so mainly because they were able to exchange their jewels and valuables for food. It is likely that this was assisted by the Indonesian guards. Korean auxiliaries were sometimes asked to exchange jewels at Chinese *toko mas* (pawn shops). With this money the internees were able to supplement their food supply. Korean employees of the army have told how after nightfall, the underground sewer pipes within the camp perimeters would light up with the lamps of Indonesian shops and small food stalls.[29] The superior engineering of the Dutch settlers meant that these pipes, large enough to drive a small cart down, ran under the whole of the Jakarta settlement. The trade of the Indonesian dealers who used these pipes provided some small relief to the starvation of the internees.

Two years prior to being transferred to the internment centres the internees had been forcibly crowded into residential areas so small they could be traversed on foot in no more than twenty minutes. It has been described how the internees, with both their mental and physical resistance at low ebb, were subject to emotional upheaval at the slightest instance, and were constantly shaking from fear and discomfort. There were no schools for the children inside the internment camps, and no picture theatres or other sources of entertainment. Mr H. L. B. Mahieu, interned in the Gudojati children's camp, established beneath the Ninth Banubil camp at Jakarta, gives the following description:

The camp for citizens of Japanese descent in America – that was nothing like an internment centre. They were contained within fences, but within those fences they were free. They had a picture theatre. They did not suffer from starvation. We struggled continuously against starvation. In the morning we had one cup of starch mixed with water, and our midday meal was one small bowl of rice, the same at night, with two spoons of sugar every week; that was all. We were forced to work. Every day we were taken from the camp to the fields, where we were forced to till them in all weather. I now suffer from skin cancer, brought on by those years when I was forced to work outside without covering for my back. At the camp we were crowded into two and three-tiered bunks, with only eight toilets for 1400 people. The toilets were always crowded and unsanitary.

This man, who spent the impressionable years between twelve and fifteen in the camp, remembers those days with great clarity. The statue of the starving boy in Kalibanten Cemetery is, indeed, a statue of him as he was at that time.[30]

The Case of the Semarang 'Comfort Station' and the 'Comfort Women'

About October 1943 it was suggested by the military police that military brothels should be established, using Caucasian women internees as 'comfort women'. The bottom section of a piece of thin rice paper, with the words 'Details regarding the establishment of the Semarang 'White' Comfort Station' written on it in black brush-calligraphy, is now preserved in an official documents repository in Holland. According to these details Colonel Ikeda Shoichi and Major Okada Keiji were the chief proponents of the 'comfort facility' plan; after conferring with the head of the military police, Captain Katsumura, they began rounding up internees for this purpose in the following February.[31]

This brothel was opened on 1 March 1944, following the collection of various 'volunteers' from the internment centres, and also a number of Indonesian women. According to the testimony of Colonel Ikeda, the establishment of the 'comfort facility' was 'conforming to regulations, permission being obtained from the existing military command, and a signature and letter of acceptance obtained from each "comfort woman"; all was carried out in reasonable fashion'. Following consultations among the head of the Semarang executive cadet troops, Lieutenant-General Nozaki Seiji, the head of the subordinate troops, Colonel Okubo, Lieutenant Nozaki's deputy, Major Takahashi, the second deputy Major Kawamura, etc., the 'comfort facility' was opened after obtaining permission from the military command. At this time, the military internment centres were still under the jurisdiction of the command headquarters of the military government, so Major Okada ordered a 'list of volunteers' from the Semarang state office. Okada, who undertook the logistics of managing the brothel, was given the status of 'Provisional Communications Officer', investing him with the authority to remove women from the internment centres.

In this way, the Semarang brothel was opened and Dutch women assembled there, through the planning and direction of the upper levels of the army and the military police, and the cooperation of the command headquarters of the military government. Major Ikeda went to Bandung specifically to inspect 'white' female internees prior to the opening of the brothel. 'White' military brothels had already been established in Bandung and Batavia (Jakarta).[32] Thirty-five young Dutch women were taken from the internment centres of Sombok, Halmahera and Gudagan within the town of Semarang, and forced into prostitution at four 'military recreation centres' at Futabaso, Hinomaru, the Semarang Club and the Officers' Club. However, under a directive from the 16th Army Headquarters, the brothels were closed down by the end of April. This was because the permission of the Southern Command Division was valid only if the women had left the internment centres of their own free will, but at least twenty-five of the women who were taken to the 'comfort facilities' had been moved there by force. Of these women, some attempted suicide and others fell prey to severe mental disturbance. After creating these victims, the Semarang 'comfort facilities' were forced to close down, but no responsibility was subsequently attributed to any of the military personnel who had established the brothels.[33]

According to a report put together in January 1994 by the Dutch government, in the Dutch East Indies region between 200 and 300 women of European origin were made to work in brothels run by the Japanese army, and it is clear from the document that among those at least sixty-five were forced into prostitution.[34]

Judgment by the Batavia Military Tribunals

The enemy citizens incarcerated in the military internment centres, without proper food and medical supplies, under the management of a Japanese army which paid no positive attention to their well-being, were made to walk a long, slow road towards starvation. After two years of living in the restricted residential areas had already weakened their resistance, a year and a half of internment in the centres finished off the lives of many of the internees. Death certificates were recorded in the 'Documents Pertaining to Internee Deaths', and the death rate climbs after April in the year of the Japanese defeat. It has been said that the repairs sections of the Jakarta internment centres were unable to keep up with demands for coffins; at the end, because boards to make coffins were unavailable, bodies were merely wrapped in bamboo matting.[35] Even compared to other internment camps, the death rate at the Java internment centres was particularly high, with figures reaching 6353 (about 9.1 per cent of the internee population).

In Article 11 of the Potsdam Declaration accepted by Japan upon its defeat, it was clearly stipulated that Japanese war criminals, including those found responsible for the mistreatment of captives, were to be severely judged. The concept of war crimes clearly outlined under the name of the Vice-Regent of the Dutch East Indies, H. J. van Mook, records thirty-nine sections, outlining details such as '5: Deliberately allowing civilians to fall into a state of starvation', '7: The inducement and/or selling of girls and women for the purpose of forced prostitution', '9: Internment of civilians under inhuman conditions', '18: Infliction of group punishment', '31: Forcing civilians to work under methods disallowed', '35: Mistreatment of civilians or prisoners', and '38: Deliberately failing to provide needed medical supplies to civilians'. Regulations such as 9, 18, 35 and 38 were interpreted as applying to all who had worked in the internment centres. The term 'deliberately' in section 5 involves subjective judgments. Furthermore, in the criminal code for war crimes established by the Dutch East Indies authorities, articles are included which cover 'war crimes where responsibility must be attributed to the whole group, in the case of actions committed within the field of the work for which that group is responsible', making it possible for 'all members of the group to be subjected to public prosecution, and found guilty'. Because of this, all personnel who had worked in the internment centres were imprisoned and investigated, without any separation of rank among them. In addition, these crimes are described as being 'acts committed against the regulations and custom of law by subjects of countries that were enemies during the war, and foreigners employed by the enemy'. Included among the 'foreigners employed by the enemy' were the Korean civilian employees who had been transferred to work as POW supervisors by the Japanese army. It was agreed between the chief investigator of the Dutch East Indies authorities and his British counterpart that as far as the war crimes trials were concerned, Korean nationals would be treated as 'Japanese'.[36]

The trial of those connected with the military internment camps began at the provisional military tribunal opened by the Dutch East Indies government at Batavia. The head of the Tjideng camp, (First section, First Division, Java Military Internment Centre), Sone Ken'ichi, who was most feared by the internees, was the first to be tried. The second was Pak Jo Gong, the head of the Bankon camp of Semarang (the name of which is now engraved on the statue of the boy in the Kalibanten Cemetery). The third was the military doctor of the Semarang internment centre, the fourth a Korean civilian army employee supervisor from the Bankon camp, and the fifth, a civilian manager at the military brothel located at the Sakura Club; the list continues. Among the fourteen people indicted in 1946, all of them were Korean and Japanese personnel employed at the civilian internment centres (there were five Koreans), with the exception of the manager at the Sakura Club brothel. This is an indication of the concern paid to the internee problem by the Dutch East Indies government.

In 1947 indictments were issued in sixty-five cases relating to war crimes. Among these, twenty-seven cases involving thirty-six people were connected with the civilian internment centres, and fifteen cases involving forty-seven people were connected with the POW concentration camps.[37] Indictments in 1948 concerning cases connected with the internment centres numbered seven, involving seven people (see table 11.2). Among the 109 cases (118 cases in all) tried at the Batavia tribunal, forty-seven were connected with the internment centres, involving fifty-six Japanese and Korean nationals who had been employed at the centres. If the twenty-two cases connected with the POW camps (involving fifty-four people) are added to this number, a total of sixty-nine cases involving 110 people (constituting 58 per cent of the cases tried and 30 per cent of all defendants in the trials) were connected with the POW and military internment centres in the Dutch East Indies. The central issue at the Batavia trials were the POW camps and civilian internment centres, as well as the trial of the Japanese military police (*kempeitai*).

Although the Dutch East Indies government opened courts in twelve

Table 11.2 Cases tried before the Batavia Tribunal, by occupation of defendant

Year	Employed in civilian camps	Employed in POW camps	Military/ special police	Other	Total
1946	13 cases 13 defendants	0	0	1 case 1 defendant	14 cases 14 defendants
1947	27 cases 36 defendants	15 cases 47 defendants	16 cases 125 defendants	7 cases 30 defendants	65 cases 238 defendants
1948	7 cases 7 defendants	7 cases 7 defendants	12 cases 72 defendants	12 cases 22 defendants	38 cases 108 defendants
1949	0	0	0	1 case 2 defendants	1 case 2 defendants
Total	47 cases 56 defendants (21 Korean)	22 cases 54 defendants (25 Korean)	28 cases 197 defendants	21 cases 55 defendants	118 cases 362 defendants

Note: Because some individuals were charged more than once, figures in the text have been adjusted to remove double counting

Source: Algemeen Secretarie 5286, Algemeen Rijksarchief, Holland.

places across the territory, all Korean defendants were tried at the two courts of Batavia and Medan; sixty-eight of them were found guilty. Of them, four were executed. All Koreans committed for trial for war crimes were civilian employees of the Japanese army who had been commandeered to work as supervisors in the POW camps; among them were some who had been sent to work in the internment centres even after their contracts with the army had already expired.[38]

The Second Semarang camp and the Halmahera camp may be taken as examples in examining the relationship between the military internment centres and the war crimes trials. Sixty Indonesian citizens in their capacity as 'troop supplements', worked as guards at the camps, which held 3400 internees. In June 1944 there were also two junior Japanese officers and one Korean civilian employee of the army. Among these, two had been shifted to that location within the past three months. The transfer of Japanese and Korean personnel was frequent; sometimes they were transferred after only one month. At the internment centres there would usually be no more than one or two junior Japanese officers, and one or two Korean employees. At the time of the Japanese defeat one Japanese officer and one Korean civilian worked at the camp office. During the period between the establishment of the internment centres and their closing, six junior Japanese officers had had experience of working there, and a similar number of Korean civilians (seven) had worked there, and of these four people were imprisoned in the Cipinang gaol about February 1947. All of these had worked for a comparatively long period at the Halmahera internment centre.

Those tried for war crimes in relation to the Java internment centres included high-ranking officers responsible for the camps, such as the first region commander, Saitō Shōei and the second, Colonel Nakata Masayuki, as well as lower-ranking officers, and also section chiefs, the military doctor, office workers, and even junior officers. 'Only one' of the doctors who had worked at the internment centres was not put on trial. The Indonesian 'troop supplements' who had been working as guards at the camp were not tried as war criminals. According to the Dutch East Indies War Crimes Penal Code, the Indonesians did not fall into the category of 'foreigners employed by the enemy'. Perhaps, to the Dutch East Indies government, the Indonesians were thought of as their own colonial subjects. Perhaps too, the murder and mistreatment of Indonesian 'troop supplements' by the Japanese in western New Guinea (now Irian Jaya), the Maluku Islands and the East Indonesian Ocean region, was also taken into account by the government.[39]

Among the trials connected with the military internment centres there were some cases concerning the forced prostitution of female internees at the military brothels: thirty-four people, including the above manager of the Sakura Club, and thirteen people from the Semarang case were judged for crimes committed in connection with the 'comfort facilities'. The Dutch East Indies tribunal, which placed heavy emphasis on the atrocities committed by Japanese personnel at the internment centres, brought military and police personnel connected with the forced prostitution of Dutch women to trial. On 22 November 1947 twelve people, including six junior officers and other military personnel, and six senior officers, including Colonel Ikeda Shōichi of the Japanese army, were prosecuted; ten were found guilty (among them, Lieutenant Okada was sentenced to death), and the remaining two were found not guilty. Colonel Nozaki, who held main responsibility for the planning and establishment of the 'comfort stations', was tried and sentenced separately from the other defendants on 14 December 1948. The indictment referred, not only to the charges relating to the internment centre mentioned above, but also an additional charge detailing the 'forced accommodation, prostitution and rape of a group of women (who had been interned at the Muntilan centre) at the 'Maguran' comfort facility'.[40]

The Dutch East Indies tribunal did not take into account the injuries inflicted on Asian women who were also forced into prostitution at the military brothels. In all areas of the Dutch East Indies occupied by the Japanese, military brothels containing women of Japanese, Indonesian, Korean, Chinese and mixed Dutch–Indonesian origin had been established.[41] Many of the women forced into being 'comfort women' for the Japanese military had been of Indonesian origin. It seems as though the forcing of Dutch (that is, Caucasian) women into prostitution was regarded as a 'war crime', while similar actions inflicted on Asian women were not. At the war crimes trials the Asian victims of the brothels were not seen as an issue, and those responsible for the injury inflicted on them were not prosecuted. It is possible that these women were never given the chance to state their cases. It may also be that they remained silent. The official inspectors from the Dutch East Indies government may not even have considered the harm done to the Asian women.

The Intricate Relationship between 'Aggressor' and 'Victim'

How do we treat our 'enemies'? The treatment of foreigners in wartime is often seen as a meter that indicates the maturity of a particular country's awareness of human rights has been developed. Japan, which since the establishment of the Meiji government had been involved in a number of foreign conflicts, had developed various policies

concerning the treatment of captives. For example, in 1904 after its
declaration of war against Russia, Japan stipulated 'Rules Concerning
the Treatment of Prisoners'. In addition, Japan both ratified and
promulgated the Hague Convention concerning 'Laws and Customs of
Land Warfare' on 13 January 1910. The Meiji government, as part of
its concern with the pending problem of the amendment of 'unequal'
treaties, accepted international law and endeavoured to ensure the
'humane' treatment of captives through international law. Although
the discrepancy in the treatment of Asians and Europeans was a
problem, both government and army were conscious of international
law. It is probably correct to say that the clear change in the position
of the Japanese army towards this matter dates from the period of the
Japanese invasion of China.

Japan had participated in the signing ceremony on 27 July 1929 of
the Geneva Convention Concerning the Treatment of Prisoners of War,
but it did not ratify the Convention. At the time of signing, agreement
concerning the treaty had not even been reached among the Japanese
Privy Council, and the Japanese army had opposed it for the reason
that:

> while members of the Imperial Army are not expected ever to become
> prisoners of war, the same cannot necessarily be said of members of foreign
> forces; accordingly, despite the seemingly mutual nature of the convention
> in form, the duty of adherence it imposes upon us is entirely one-sided.[42]

Also, the study of international law concerning war was excluded from
the curriculum of Japanese military academies. A customary phrase
concerning 'respect for international law' was erased from the Imperial
proclamation concerning the opening of hostilities. This disregard of
the international rules of war by the government and the military was
a significant factor in the subsequent mistreatment of internees and
captives during the war.[43]

The existence of a 'battlefield code' of not allowing oneself to be
taken captive was also significant. Soldiers were not taught of the
existence of the Geneva Convention, but they were forced to memorise
the 'battlefield code'. Such a mentality encouraged an attitude of
contempt among soldiers towards prisoners of war. The difficulties of
the paymaster in obtaining food for internees perhaps reflected this
deep-seated military antagonism towards their captives. We must also
recognise that the social atmosphere in which the enemy was referred
to as *Kichiku Beiei* ('American and British devils') promoted a
degeneration in the treatment of internees.

In addition to these problems of attitude within the military, there was also a significant discrepancy between Japan and the Allied States from the very beginning of the establishment of the POW camps and military internment centres, concerning interpretation of the 'application' of the Geneva Convention. The problem of the treatment of captives was not considered to form part of the main work of the Ministry for Foreign Affairs; instead it was passed on to diplomats and bureaucrats who had evacuated back to Japan after the war broke out, and who therefore had no firm position in the bureaucracy.[44]

There is also an evident discrepancy between Japanese and Anglo-American attitudes towards the concept of 'mistreatment'. In the lower ranks of the Japanese army it can be safely said that there were no 'human rights'. In the army, where harsh physical punishment was inflicted on recruits as a matter of course, anything other than complete obedience towards orders was not tolerated from non-commissioned officers and soldiers, let alone from the Korean civilian employees. Beating and striking of recruits and soldiers was a daily occurrence. Among the soldiers of the Japanese army, to whom cramped transportation, inferior living conditions and poor food and medicine were routine, such 'mistreatment' of internees may not have come across as such. Lacking awareness of their own human rights, their understanding of the concept of 'mistreatment' must have been hazy at best.

Differences in the perception of laws and rules should also be considered. Within the Japanese military, on-the-spot punishment of transgressors of camp rules and orders without taking matters further (*binta*), was seen as being too warm-hearted. Many Japanese soldiers were unfamiliar with the processes of a thorough investigation of the transgression, followed by debate over the justification of the action through militry law. Korean recruits and the Indonesian 'troop supplements' were also beaten in the normal course of their 'training'. In this way, junior officers with little or no knowledge of international law, and the Indonesian and Korean employees who had been trained under them, were placed in positions of authority at the military internment centres. Added to this situation was a shared mentality dominated by feelings of Japanese inferiority towards Anglo-American culture and fear regarding the superior physical strength of Caucasians, that had been prevalent in Japan since the beginning of the Meiji era. Racist attitudes among the internees themselves also cannot be overlooked. For example, there was apparently no attempt at solidarity between Dutch citizens born in Holland and those born in the colonies, because of a perceived difference in status between them. As has been noted by Pramoedya Ananta Toer, even among the Dutch who had been born in the colonies, those with mixed Dutch and Indonesian blood were looked down upon.[45]

In addition to racial prejudice among the internees, their own social discrimination further complicated their treatment. Among those children born of high-class officials from the colonisation period, there were those who would show their contempt for the Korean employees by calling them 'yellow monkeys'. There is some evidence that the Korean employee Pak Jo Gong (mentioned previously) was sentenced to death for hitting children in his anger at these insults. It seems possible that the sentences imposed on the guards varied according to the social status of the internees they assaulted.[46] However, among the internees, Pak was known as 'Orang Pukul' or 'the one who hits', so there was probably a side to him that was not visible to his Korean compatriots and was only witnessed by the internees.

Differences in gender relations between the Japanese and the Dutch should also be taken into consideration as a likely cause of friction. It can probably be assumed that the attitude of Dutch women came across as bold and arrogant to Japanese soldiers, used to compliant women who did not assert their rights, and acquiesced unquestioningly to the demands of men. These points were also touched on in affidavits later presented to the Tokyo court.

The gap in living standards between wartime Japan and the Dutch colonies was also apparent. There were flush toilets at the churches designated as military internment centres. Suddenly, those who had never eaten chocolate or cheese, or seen Parker pens and Omega watches, found themselves in a position of control. The Dutch East Indies was a former diamond-producing region. Among the internees who had previously lived as colony settlers were people who possessed large amounts of jewels, some of which were taken away by those in authority.

Differences existed in attitudes to war crimes and the attribution of responsibility. In the Japanese military there was little recognition of individual responsibility for war crimes. It was hard to persuade people to see themselves as responsible for actions taken when they had been obeying orders. The difference in cognition regarding personal responsibility was surely a factor in the inability of the Batavia trials – and also the courts later established by the Allied States – to produce (from an Anglo-American viewpoint), genuine 'repentance' among the Japanese. The 'Peace Group' that evolved at Sugamo prison in the post-war period can be said to be an exception to this tendency.[47]

The way in which the war crimes trials conducted by the Allied States utterly failed to address the problem of the former colonies of the Japanese empire is a highly significant issue. The existence of 'war crimes' committed by Korean and Taiwanese citizens, which was itself an outcome of the approach taken by the Allied trials, can perhaps be seen as a factor in the post-war Japanese tendency to see the war in terms of a dichotomy between Japanese, on the one side, and Americans and British on the other, thereby failing to recognise Japan's aggression in Asia. It goes without saying that the most important reason for this failing was the Japanese inability to pursue successful prosecutions of those in positions of responsibility.

The POW camps and internment centres were basically places where prisoners and internees who embodied Anglo-American customs, perspectives and values, were brought into daily contact with the Japanese and Koreans. Furthermore, Dutch citizens were guarded by Indonesians. In this way the power relationship of over 300 years was overturned in the internment centres. There were even instances of Indonesian 'troop supplements' striking their Dutch charges, something that would have been unthinkable in the time of Dutch rule. Thus, personal and social relations between Japanese and Korean, Dutch and Indonesian were developed and intricately complicated in the environment of the internment centres.

The treatment of enemy citizens during the war and the protection of Japanese people form opposite sides of the same coin. Nowadays, Japanese industries move across national borders, and the number of Japanese travellers abroad has reached over 10 million. 'Protection of Japanese citizens' has begun to assume a new significance. The overseas deployment of the Self-Defence Forces has also encouraged debate on this issue. However, on the other side of the coin, the concern of Japanese people about the treatment of prisoners and civilian captives during the war remains muted. If the treatment of such prisoners and internees is indeed an indication of a country's awareness of human rights, then our present awareness of these rights must be said to be gravely lacking. Can we really claim that the statue of the starving boy at Kalibanten Cemetery represents no more than a 'past' Japan?

This chapter is the English translation of the paper 'Kagai to Higai' ('Aggressor and victim'), from *Koza sekaishi vol. 8: Senso to minshu–Dainiji sekai taisen* (*A New World History*), Tokyo, Tokyo Daigaku Shuppankai (forthcoming).

Notes

1 Few Japanese publications concerning the internees are available apart from the translations of such works as Cyrius Lucas's *I was Interned by the Japanese Army*, Kan Shōhei (trans.), Tokyo, Futabasha, 1975, G. F. Jacob's *Prelude to a Monsoon; Diary of the Release of Allied Captives from the Sumatra Internment Centres*, Hara Motoko (trans.), Tokyo, Keisō Shobō, 1987. In Holland, apart

from many published notes, records and diaries, a wealth of unpublished material is available at the Royal Dutch Institute of War Documentation (Rijksinstituut voor Oorlogsdocumentatie, Amsterdam). Although many research texts are available, the best example is probably Dr D. van Velden's *The Japanese Civilian Camps* (*De Japanese Burger-Kampen*), Amsterdam, Uitgeverij T. Wever B. V. Franeker, 1977.

2 The collection of writings edited by the Sugamo Legal Committee, *Actual Facts of the War Crimes Trials* (*Senpan Saiban no Jissō*), mimeographed copy, 1952; reprinted by Maki Shuppan and Fuji Shuppan, is one representative example of this mentality.

3 *Kyokumitsugō*, ('confidential directive'), no. 227, 11 January 1945, 'Cases relating to the exchange of Japanese–American and Japanese–British citizens'. Japanese 'enemy states' numbered twenty-seven; among these, 260 000 Japanese were living in America (70 per cent of whom had American citizenship), and in the British Commonwealth there was a total of 208 000, 203 000 of whom lived in Canada. These numbers are for 1945. Until this time, exchange of interned citizens by boat had occurred twice between Japan and America, and once between Britain and Japan. One round trip involved the exchange of over 1000 internees, see 'Cases related to the Great East Asia War: problems relating to the handling and treatment of enemy citizens from adversarial states' (*Daitōa Sensō Kankei Ikken: Kōsen Kokukan Tekikokujin oyobi Furyō Toriatsukai Buri Kankei ippan, Oyobi Shomondai*) (hereafter referred to as 'Cases related to the Great East Asia War', 2nd vol., Tokyo, Diplomatic History Archive.

4 Internment of all people of Japanese descent was carried out, regardless of whether they had American citizenship or not. This included people who were less than one-half, or one-third, Japanese, and those who could not prove that they had not had dealings with the immigrant Japanese society. The total of Japanese interned was 120 303: Bernstein Committee Report, 'Individuals denied justice' (*Kyohi Sareta Kojin no Seigi*), trans. into Japanese and ed. by the Foreign Affairs Section of the daily newspaper, *Yomiuri Shimbun*, p. 140.

5 Amano Yōichi, *Descendants of Davao* (*Dabaokoku no Matsueitachi*), Tokyo, Fubaisha, 1990, p. 102; Shinosaki Mamoru, *Secret Records of the Singapore Occupation* (*Shingaporu Senryō Hiroku*), Tokyo, Hara Shobō, 1967, p. 20; Group for Japanese Evacuees from the Dutch East Indies, *Records of Japanese Evacuees from the Dutch East Indies*, (*Ran-in Zairyū Hōjin Hikiage Kiroku*), Tokyo, Nihon Yūsen KK, 1943, p. 3. A comprehensive account of the internment of Japanese in Australia is given by Yuriko Nagata in her unpublished PhD thesis, 'Japanese internment in Australia during World War II', University of Queensland, 1994.

6 Ministry of Home Affairs Military Protection Bureau (ed.), *General Conditions of External Police Affairs* (*Gaiji Keisatsu Gaikyō*), vol. 7, Showa 16, 1941, reprinted in Tokyo by Fuji Shuppan, 1987, p. 510.

7 'Cases relating to the exchange of Japanese–British and Japanese–American citizens', from 'Cases related to the Great East Asia War'.

8 Suzuki Kuman, former Consul to Egypt, was appointed to head this office. About forty former consulate envoys and deputy envoys who had been evacuated from overseas were also employed. This office was responsible for dealing with matters concerning the 101 065 enemy citizens interned in Japan's 'inner territories' and 'outer territories', as well as the 168 666

prisoners of war captured by the Japanese. Furthermore, according to an oral affidavit by Matsumoto Shunichi, on pp. 94–9 of the Research Association of Domestic Administrative History (ed.), *Recorded Exchanges with Mr Suzuki Kuman*, mimeograph, 1974, until November 1942 the Treaties Bureau was in charge of these affairs. See also, *Shorthand Notes, International Military Tribunals for the Far East* (*Kyokutō Kokusai Gunji Saiban Sokkiroku*), no. 6, Tokyo, Yushōdō, 1968, p. 406.

9 'Summary of Administrative Practices of the Southern Occupied Territories' (*Nampō Senryōchi Gyōsei Jisshi Yōryō*), decided 20 November 1941 by the Coordinating Committee of the Imperial General Headquarters. Furthermore, on 25 November, Article 9 of the 'Guide for the Administrations of Territories Occupied in relation to the Southern Advance Strategy' (*Nampō Sakusen ni tomonau Senryōchi Tōji Yōryō*) was published, its contents being almost identical to the above directives; see Defence Agency, Defence Research Institute, War History Division (eds), *Military Government in Southeast Asia* (*Nampō no Gunsei*), Tokyo, Asagumo Shimbunsha, 1985, pp. 90–3. The position of the Japanese army concerning the problem of captives caused major problems during the invasion of China, but there are no traces of any further particular concern being paid to this issue upon the start of the war. Concerning 'The Constitution of the Japanese Army and its Captives', see Yoshida Hiroshi, *The Emperor's Army and the Nanjing Event* (*Tennō no Guntai to Nankin Jiken*), Tokyo, Aoki Shoten, 1985, pp. 43–51; on the reaction of the Ministry of Foreign Affairs, see 'The final lecture of Professor Nakayama Yoshihiro', in *Aoyama International Political Economy Collection* (*Aoyama Kokusai Seikei Ronshū*), no. 13, 1989. An interview was conducted with Nakayama on 23 March 1994.

10 Concerning the International Red Cross Committee, see the Captives Information Bureau's *Collection of Rules and Laws Pertaining to Prisoners of War*, 1943, pp. 181–2; regarding the Geneva Treaty and its appendix, pp. 134–67 of the Treaty; regarding the American request for application of the Treaty, see 'Showa 16 (1941) December 27, Letter Addressed to Foreign Minister Tōgō from the Head of Diplomatic Mission in Switzerland', *Collection of Rules and Laws Pertaining to Prisoners of War*, post-war re-edited version, p. 135.

11 Tōgō Shigenori Memorial Association (eds), *Foreign Minister Tōgō Shigenori: One Face of the Times* (*Jidai no Ichimen*), vol. 1, Tokyo, Hara Shobō, 1985, p. 295.

12 An answer from Army Vice-Secretary Kimura Heitarō to Vice-Foreign Minister Nishi Haruhiko, 'Asian Directive, no. 189: Answers to British, American and other inquiries pertaining to the treatment of prisoners of war, dated January 23, Showa 17 (1942)'. In an answering document relayed to the Allied states, dated 29 January, a written note was included stating 'application following the necessary amendments'. Contained in *Cases concerning the Great East Asia War, Treaty Relations pertaining to the Treatment of Captives and Treatment of Citizens of Enemy State during Wartime* (*Daitōa Sensō Kankei Ikken Kōsen Kokukan Tekikokujin oyobi Furyo Toriatsukai Buri Kankei. Furyo no Taigū ni Kansuru Jōyaku Kankei*), Tokyo, Foreign Ministry Archives.

13 Research Committee of the Tokyo Court, *The Pal Judgements Documents* (*Paru Hanketsusho*), Tokyo, Kōdansha Gakujutsu Bunko, 1984, p. 632.

14 Communication of this intent was made to all countries with an interest in

the matter on 13 February 1942. See 'February 1942: Telegram from Foreign Minister Tōgō to Pro-Consul Nishikuni Mitsuya', in *Rules and Laws*, p. 144.

15 According to the 'Final lecture of Professor Nakayama' and a personal interview conducted with Professor Nakayama, the seriousness of the internee and prisoner problem began to be recognised by the Ministry for Foreign Affairs after the beginning of the atrocity campaign by then British Foreign Minister Eden.

16 Military Protection Bureau of the Ministry for Home Affairs (eds), *General Conditions of External Police Affairs (Gaiji Keisatsu Gaikyō)*, vol. 8, Shōwa 17, Fuji Shuppan, [1942] reprinted 1987, pp. 78–80. Following the outbreak of war the Ministry of Home Affairs stipulated the 'Guidelines for the treatment of interned enemy citizens' (*Yokuryū Tekikokujin Toriatsukai Yōkō*). *While 'emergency security measures' (hijō bōshō sochi)* form the main point of this directive, it is also advised in the guidelines through some twenty-nine articles, that the dignity and humanity of the internees be respected, that freedom of belief be allowed them, and that care should be taken to maintain their physical condition.

17 In Lucas, *I was Interned by the Japanese Army*, comprehensive details of the internment centres in the Philippines are given. In Yoshikawa Eiji's *Southern Journey (Nampō Kikō)*, Tokyo, Zenkoku Shobō, 1943, pp. 67–78, in February 1942, an account is given which claims that the Vice-Secretary of the army issued 'Communications concerning the maintenance and treatment of destitute enemy citizens' (*Tekikokujin Seikatsu Konkyūsha Shori ni Kansuru Ken*) to all relevant army divisions. See Prisoners of War Information Bureau, *Records of Treatment (Furyo Toriatsukai no Kiroku)*, Tokyo, Prisoners of War Information Bureau, 1955, pp. 78–9.

18 See Research Association of Domestic Administrative History (ed.), *Recorded Exchanges*, pp. 97–8, and Utsumi Aiko (ed.), *Collection of Protests from Various States Regarding the Treatment of Wartime Captives (Furyo ni Kansuru Shogaikoku kara no Kōgi Shū)*, Tokyo, Fuji Shuppan, reprinted 1989.

19 See 'Cases related to the Great East Asia War'.

20 War History Dvision, Research Centre, National Defence Agency, *Army Strategy for the South-west (Nansei Hōmen, Rikugun Sakusen)*, Tokyo, Asagumo Shimbunsha, 1967, p. 415.

21 Seventh Declaration of the Java Military Government Surveillance Division, Shōwa 17, 1942, 11 April: 'Items Concerning Alien Residence Registration' (*Gaikokujin Kyojū Tōroku ni Kansuru Ken*), 'With the exception of the citizens of Imperial Japan, and the original Residents of the East Indies, all males and females of 17 years of age or above are required to register their residence with the Imperial Japanese Army, and swear a Pledge of Sincerity'; a further order was issued under 'Items pertaining to the registration of Aliens who have failed to register' in relation to those who had failed to register by 11 April, regarding the payment by monthly instalments of and temporary postponement of the registration fee. According to accounts given in *Government Report*, vol. 1 (collected) (issued December 1942, and held in the Rijksinstituut voor Oorlogsdocumentat, Amsterdam), and Nell van de Graaff, *We Survived* (St Lucia, University of Queensland Press, 1989), all residents excepting the aged, children and pregnant women were ordered to present themselves for registration at designated areas. As the banks were already closed, the residents were only questioned as to the amount of money they were carrying with them at the time.

22 Declaration 33, 9 September, Showa 17, 1942, 'Items concerning designated residence of Dutch Citizens' (*Waran Hongokujin Tō Kazoku Kyojūchi Shitei ni Kansuru Ken*), 'Dutch residents of Batavia, British, American and Australian females (excepting those of mixed blood), those living separately from spouses and dependants, also all males between the ages of 17 and 60 years' were all moved to designated areas of residence. The recording of radio broadcasts was dealt with by Declaration 21, 16 June, Showa 17, 1942, 'Items concerning 'radio' broadcasts' (*'Rajio' Torishimari ni Kansuru Ken*); in order to enforce a ban on listening to foreign radio broadcasts, the compulsory registration of all radio receiver machines, and a restriction on wave-length were imposed by means of a permit system in major cities by 30 June and in other areas by 31 July.

23 This 'Asian Directive' is on p. 78 of Captives Information Bureau, *Collections*, and is mentioned in 6 June 1943: 'Meeting Report' (*Kaihō*) of the Military Surveillance Unit, also 20 October 1943: 'Order 248, Various orders of the Military Surveillance Division' (*Gunsei Kanbu Hibi Meirei*), Archives, Algemene Secretarie 5179, Algemeen Rijksarchief Den Haag, and in an interview conducted on 20 December 1993 with Mr Ishii Seikichi.

24 Among those Korean civilian army employees gathered at Sumorwarno, the anti-Japanese resistance group 'Youth Group for Independent Kōrai (Korea)' was formed. For a detailed account see Utsumi Aiko and Murai Yoshinori, *The Korean Rebellion Beneath the Equator* (*Sekidōsenka no Chosen hanran*), Tokyo, Keisō shobō, 1980. For numbers of Indonesian 'troop supplements', see Jafu Association (ed.), *Name List, Jafu Association Members*, Tokyo, Jafu Association, n.d.

25 See *Shorthand Notes*, no. 137, pp. 650–1.

26 In van de Graaff, *We Survived*, the author gives an account of her experiences, from her forced removal to the designated residence areas, life in Tjideng camp, her eventual release from the camp and evacuation to Australia, to her journey back to Indonesia.

27 See testimony of the Jafu Association, a group of people who worked in the Java military internment camps, dated 10 April 1944, in *Shorthand Notes*, no. 139, pp. 674–5; for figures see table 16 in *Record of Treatment*.

28 See *Shorthand Notes*, no. 139, p.675.

29 There were some Korean civilian employees who were thanked by Dutch ex-internees after the war ended, because of the services they provided to the internees. Regarding one of these, see Kim Man Su, *Korean Rebellion*, and interview conducted by the present author with Park Yong Won, a former civilian employee at the Bandung internment centre, at Seoul, on 5 August 1992.

30 From an interview with Mr H. L. B. Mahieu, 28 February 1994, in Goes, Holland; the statue of the boy at Kalibanten Cemetery is modelled on his actual appearance.

31 Archives, Algemene Secretarie 5200, Algemeen Rijksarchief Den Haag.

32 Testimony from Ikeda Shōichi, Nakajima Shirō, from the Sugamo Legal Association (eds), *Actualities of the War Crimes Trials*, pp. 79–80, published in *Asahi Shimbun*, 30 August 1992.

33 'Judgment by the Batavia Provisional Military Tribunal pertaining to the instances of forced prostitution of Dutch women', *War Responsibility Research Quarterly* (*Kikan Sensō Sekinin Kenkyū*), no. 3, Spring, 1994, pp. 44–57.

34 Report of a study of Dutch Government, 'The forced prostitution of Dutch

women in the Dutch East Indies during the Japanese occupation', translated 24 January 1994.

35 These certificates are in the Algemene Secretarie 5247. Archives of the Algemeen Rijksarchief Den Haag, testimony of Ishii Masakichi from the former buildings and repairs division, and a member of the above-mentioned Jafu Association.

36 The concept of 'war crimes' was included in the 1946 'Official Report of Laws and Ordinances of the Dutch East Indies' (Ranryō Indo Hōrei Kōhō), *War Crimes Trials Data* (*Sensō Hanzai Saiban Shiryō*), no. 2, *Laws and Ordinances Pertaining to the Judgment of War Crimes* (*Sensō Hanzai Saiban Kankei Hōrei Shū*), vol. II, (Judicial and Legislative Survey Division, Secretariat of the Minister for Justice, 1965), p. 216. The prosecution of all members of a group is dealt with in no. 45, 1946, 'Judicial matters pertaining to the War Crimes Criminal Code', ibid., item 10, p. 12. Regarding the treatment of Korean nationals, see 'Proposed Legislative Interpretation Pertaining to War Criminals', ibid., item f, p. 212.

37 There were cases of people being prosecuted simultaneously in their capacities both at the military internment centres and the POW camps; this double counting has been removed in calculating the number of people prosecuted. There are sixteen separate cases concerning the military police (including the Special Police Force), but because the number of defendants in each case was large, altogether 125 people were prosecuted. Those working as prison officers, legal officers, etc., numbered thirty people.

38 Concerning the war crimes of the Korean personnel, see Utsumi Aiko, *Record of Level B and C Korean War Criminals* (*Chōsenjin B,C Kyū Senpan no Kiroku*), Tokyo, Keizō Shobō, 1982. For the trial records of Pak Jong Gong's prosecution and execution, see Utsumi and Murai, *Korean Rebellion.*

39 Among the Dutch East Indies trials, the courts at Medan, Morotai, Ambon and Hollandia handed down judgments on the murder and mistreatment of the Indonesian 'troop supplements', and Japanese officers were found guilty and sentenced to death. For further information on the Indonesian 'troop supplements', see the Indonesian Troop Supplement Association (eds), *Claims of the Indonesian Troop Supplements*(*Indoneshia Heiho no Uttae*), Tokyo, Nashinoki Sha, 1993.

40 'Document of judgment, submitted to the Provisional Military Tribunal' (*Ruiji Gunpō Kaigi Futaku Kettei Sho*), for Nōzaki Seiji, Algemene Secretarie 5286, archives, Algemeen Rijksarchief Den Haag.

41 Investigation of information about the 'comfort women' is still being continued by researchers and by the Japanese government. Yoshimi Yoshiaki (ed.), *Data on 'Comfort Women' under the Military* (*Jūgun Ianfu Shiryōshū*), Tokyo, Ōtsuki Shoten, 1992; Centre for Data on Japanese War Responsibility periodical, *War Responsibility Research Quarterly*, Autumn 1993, Spring 1994, etc. Regarding the Indonesian 'comfort women', see Kurashige Yoshio, *Diary of My Stay in the Dutch East Indies* (*Ranin Taizaiki*), Tokyo, Kiyomizu Kōbundo, 1988, pp. 59–60; Nogi Harumichi, *The Special Navy Police Forces* (*Kaigun Tokubetsu Keisatsutai*), Tokyo, Taihei Shuppan, 1975, pp. 109–21; etc.

42 See 'Cases related to the Great East Asia War'.

43 Ichimata Masao, 'A theory on the war crimes trials' (*Senpan Saiban Kenkyū Yōron*), *Journal of International Law and Diplomacy* (*Kokusaihō Gaikō Zasshi*), vol. 66, no. 1, 1967.

44 See *Research Association of Domestic History*, also interview by the present author with Mr Nakayamo Gayō, 23 March 1993.
45 Pramoedya Ananta Toer, *Bumi Manusia*, Jakarta, P. T. HastaMitra, 1980, translated into Japanese by Oshikawa Noriaki, gives an account of inter-racial complications.
46 From an interview with Kanemitsu Seikichi, at his residence in Osaka, 8 March 1978.
47 The 'Peace Group' (*Heiwa Gurupu*), born at Sugamo prison, is involved in activities aimed at pursuing Japanese responsibility for the war. For further details, see Utsumi Aiko, 'Sugamo prison and the Korean War' (*Chōsen Sensō to Sugamo Purizun*), *Shisō*, August 1985.

PART FOUR

The Japanese Family

CHAPTER TWELVE

Modern Patriarchy and the Formation of the Japanese Nation State

UENO CHIZUKO

The Invention of the *Ie*

Although the *ie* institution of an exclusively patrilineal extended family system has been widely thought to be an historical survival from the feudal age, recent studies on family history prove that it was, in fact, the invention of the Meiji government, accomplished through the Meiji civil code. The *ie*, though modelled on the household of the Edo-period samurai class, which comprised about 10 per cent of the population in that period, was unknown among the commoners who constituted the vast majority. It was a case of 'the invention of tradition', as Eric Hobsbawm puts it.[1]

The twenty years of debate which led to the making of the Meiji civil code showed that more than a few alternatives were considered. It was 1870 when the government first started to consider the code· in 1873 the tentative law was made; based on an investigation of civi' practices at a local level, the draft was then made in 1878. Among ne models considered was the matrilineal succession rule practised by commoners. Outside the samurai class, a peasant or merchant family daughter could inherit the family property or business. In fact, it was considered a clever family strategy to maximise the chances for a future successor to be a son-in-law. However, in the process of making the civil code, this practice was rejected as a barbarian custom.

The first civil code was not announced until 1890, ten years after the draft. The law was supposed to come into effect in three years, but it caused a great controversy, known as the 'civil code debate'. As the first law was modelled on the individualistic French civil code, conservative ideologues such as Hozumi Yatsuka criticised it for being destructive of the Japanese family tradition. It became such a big political issue that

213

the government had to abolish and remake the law. It was not until 1898 that the Meiji civil code came into effect. The process of making the law itself shows how the institution of *ie* was created as a political artefact.

The *ie* institution was made to fit the model of the modern nation state, which itself was modelled on the family structure. Itō Mikiharu carefully investigates the process of invention of the concept of *ie* by officials.[2] Prior to the Meiji civil code, the Imperial Rescript on Education was announced in 1890. In the following year, Inoue Tetsujirō, the Meiji government's authorised political ideologue, published his *Commentaries on the Imperial Rescript*, which included the following passage: 'The emperor is to his subjects, as a parent to his children. In other words, a state is an expansion of a family. The emperor rules commoners as parents guide their children with mercy'.[3]

In his *Guidelines for Education* which he published in 1879, Motoda Eifu, a Confucian ideologue for the Meiji government, stressed the Confucian ethic of loyalty to emperor and filial piety to parents. He also published *Guidelines for Early Education* in 1882. His ideas formed the basis for an ethics textbook, published in 1883, which called on people to 'respect our emperor as you obey your parents'.

Inoue Tetsujirō later wrote *Rinri to kyōiku* (*Ethics and Education*), in which he argued:

> If you extend your filial piety to the nation, it is identical with loyalty to emperor. Because our emperor stands in the position of patriarch of the Japanese nation as a whole, you serve his majesty as you obey your parents. Therefore, loyalty to the emperor is identical with filial piety to parents.[4]

Ito points out that this identification of loyalty to emperor with filial piety to one's parents was necessary to establish the nation state modelled on a family.[5] It was a deliberate creation by government ideologues relying on their interpretation of Confucian ethics.

Satō Tadao, an independent film critic, goes further. In his *Katei no yomigaeri no tameni: Hōmu dorama ron* (*Towards a Revival of the Family: on the Home Drama*), he deals with the Imperial Rescript for Public Education in search for the origin of the *ie* institution, and examines the original text of Motoda Eifu.[6] While Ito points out that loyalty is made identical with filial piety, Satō notes that the hierarchical relationship between filial piety and loyalty is reversed in the process of making the Imperial Rescript. In Motoda's *Guidelines*, filial piety comes first as the Confucian ethic is developed from within, but the order is reversed in the Imperial Rescript.

There is always a potential conflict between family ethic and national ethic, and their integration calls for a deft and highly tactical trick. For example, the state conscription system was in conflict with the interests of the family, and Yosano Akiko's protest song against the Sino–Japanese War stressed the priority of the family and opposed the loss of life for the state; but if filial piety was to be given priority, the national interest might be put at risk. Therefore, the Imperial Instructions put the highest priority on loyalty, in the guise of harmonious relationship between filial piety and loyalty. Satō reached this finding by contrasting the Japanese family ideology with the family values which he saw represented in European films. In Italian films, a patriarch would reject state interference in order to preserve the autonomy of his household; if his son commits a crime, he would punish the child himself. A Japanese patriarch, on the other hand, acts as an agent of the state; if his son is a social drop-out, he will refuse to be a parent and commit the child to some public institution. Therefore, Satō concludes, there is nothing natural about the *ie* institution, and the Japanese family was constructed as a basic unit of the imperial system.[7]

Aoki Yayohi argues the same point from a woman's point of view.[8] She discusses the way in which the Confucian ethic was applied to construct femininity in the process of modernisation. The circulation of a Confucian text such as *Onna daigaku* (*The Great Learning for Women*) was limited to the dominant literate class. Among commoners, on the other hand, chastity and virginity were of little importance in matchmaking. Contrary to the commonplace view, 'Japanese femininity' is a modern construct, and not at all traditional.

Ie and Modern Patriarchy

There is a strong inter-relationship between the public and the private sphere, in other words, between the nation state and the family unit, both of which (as we learn from family history) were created at the same time. It was the modern social system that divided the autonomous, subsistent community life into separate but inter-dependent realms. In this respect, the *ie* institution is by no means 'traditional' or 'feudal', but to be interpreted as a Japanese version of the modern family. Two major reasons, one ideological and the other theoretical, have prevented us from understanding.

Historians have long seen the *ie* as a feudal survival, without questioning its historical construction. They are themselves victims of the *ie* ideology, which works to prohibit questioning its own origin. They failed to see through the ideology of the times that they themselves were living in, and instead contributed to reinforcing the ideology of their own times by taking it as 'tradition'. Calling this a tradition was not entirely false, since it was a tradition that belonged to the dominant class. Historical positivism based on written documents led them to focus only on literate people. Until recently, historians generally shared the biased hierarchical view according to which political events in the dominant class were valued more highly than the everyday life among commoners, and it was not until the rise of the new field of people's history that historians realised the diversity of mores and customs in the everyday life of a class society such as Edo.

Above all, there is the matter of gender bias: when the private sphere was made the indispensable but invisible other half of the public sphere – its 'shadow' so to speak – it became a shelter or a retreat, a sanctuary of affection and consort which compensated for the hardship of life in the public arena. The private sphere was constructed as something that existed across time and space, and that left no room for doubt about its reason to exist. When feminists started to debate the historical and ideological construction of the family, transgressing the boundary of this sanctuary, historians, as well as family sociologists (most of whom were male), were embarrassed. They shared a common interest in the attempt to preserve the status quo of the male-dominant family system.

The second reason for the failure to understand the *ie* is theoretical. Modelled on the European modern family, it appears that the concept of modern family is consistent only with the nuclear household, which does not seem to fit the institution of *ie*. The social historian, Ochiai Emiko, points out eight characteristics of the 'modern family'.[9] These are: separation of public and private spheres; strong affection among family members; centring on the child; differentiation of male and female gender roles in public and private spheres respectively; household autonomy; decline of neighbourhood association links; exclusion of those who are non-kin; and the nuclear household. Nishikawa Yūko has some reservations about the eighth point and argues that a 'nuclear household' is not a necessary qualification for the *ie* to be considered representative of the modern family. Nishikawa adds two more points: 'The leadership belongs to the husband; and each family serves as a basic unit of the nation state'.[10] The first of these additions stresses the power of a husband, which is often neglected in the name of 'patriarchy', instead of that of a father.

Ochiai bases her own work on the controversial book by Edward Shorter, *The Making of the Modern Family*,[11] in which Shorter shows the modern family to be characterised by the romantic revolution, the affectionate tie between mother and child, and household autonomy. He does not specifically mention the nuclear household, but the 'romantic relationship' between a husband and a wife seems to result in a nuclear household setting.

So far as statistics are concerned, the first, reliable, nationwide population research was the national census data of 1920, which showed that 54 per cent of all Japanese households were nuclear households.[12] Half a century later, the 1970 census data show that 64 per cent of households were nuclear, an increase of only 10 per cent over 1920. There is not much of a change in terms of figures. According to Yuzawa's average-family-cycle model of pre-war families, both parents-in-law usually died within ten years of the marriage, the father-in-law in the sixth year and the mother-in-law in the tenth year.[13] Sixteen years out of the twenty-six years of an average family cycle would be lived in a nuclear household. At any given time, the probability of nuclear household was 16 out of 26, approximately two-thirds if it is assumed that all the people followed the patrilineal succession rule. This probability rate coincides with the actual statistics.[14] In view of the high birth rate, and assuming all first-born sons were living in extended households, the percentage of nuclear households might have been even higher. Accordingly, the nuclear household was not uncommon even in the pre-war period.

There is another argument by the British school of family history that insists on the universality of the nuclear household regardless of time and space.[15] Should that be right, it would be impossible to claim that the nuclear household was the necessary condition of the modern family.

Apart from statistics, social historians have argued not about family structures but about mentality. In sociological terms, they are concerned more about a normative than a descriptive model, as people live more 'family norms' than 'realities'. This is why they prefer the term 'nuclear family' rather than 'nuclear household', assuming that a 'nuclear family' should require a certain mentality which is epitomised in a 'romantic relationship'. If family members do not share the 'nuclear family ideology' and just happen to live in a nuclear household due to the family cycle, they live the family norms of extended family system. This is often the case with a household initiated by a second or third son. Though living in a nuclear household, parents want their first-born son to live with them as the future successor of the household, and they consider themselves to be founders of a new family stem. This attitude resulted in boosting the construction of family tombs in the post-war period because each family, although lacking ancestors, wanted to found its own tomb for future offspring. This is what the folklorist, Takatori Masao, calls 'the cult of offspring'.[16]

Therefore, we see a nuclear household which maintains the norms of an extended family. However, the attitude of household members to the building up of the new family line is itself a modern product, as industrialisation offered them new opportunities to be independent from their parents other than by succeeding to the family property.

Demystification of Romance

There is a stereotypical view that the Japanese family has not yet been 'modernised' because it lacks this 'romantic relationship' between husband and wife. But what is a 'romance'? Shorter himself seems to romanticise the concept. Among the criteria of romance, he points out the non-utilitarian choice of spouse. If a daughter of a wealthy family marries an ambitious, poor, young man against her father's will, she opts for future prosperity rather than today's security. It could be the choice of leaving a declining class so as to join a new rising social class, as marriage gives a daughter the chance to be recruited into classes other than her own. Modernisation, accompanied by high social mobility, has given boys the possibility to climb the social ladder by education, and girls to marry a promising young man.

The definition of 'romance' as non-utilitarian choice of a spouse is denied by Pierre Bourdieu on the basis of his research into matchmaking in contemporary France.[17] According to Bourdieu, marriage is still practised as a highly utilitarian family strategy to 'maximize the social resources'. The current statistics of matchmaking in Japan also show the same tendency that Bourdieu demonstrates among modern French. In the 1960s the number of marriages based on the notion of 'romantic love', or what is called 'love marriage', exceeded those of arranged marriages, but the macro data on marriage show only a slight difference as the result of matchmaking. There is an 'iron rule' of class endogamy, or marriage between people alike in terms of education and family background, regardless of the type of marriage. The endogamous tendency, or tendency to find a spouse in a close community, is stronger in love marriages than in arranged marriages in which the third party works as a go-between for a distant matchmaking. Reversed hypergamy is rarely the case with a love marriage as well. If the outcome of the matchmaking does not make much of a difference between 'love marriage' and arranged marriage, we could conclude that the same criteria are internalised by individuals in the name of love.[18] When the choice is imposed by parents it might be called 'oppression', but when it is chosen by the exercise of free will it is called 'individualistic'. The family strategy is taken into account by individuals, and realised through their voluntary will with few exceptions.[19] This is what Foucault called 'subjectification', that is to say, complete subjugation of the individual to a norm by means of internalisation. No doubt this constitutes a more efficient way of distribution of brides and bridegrooms in the seemingly 'free market' of marriage.

Terry Eagleton, author of *The Rape of Clarissa*, argues that 'romantic love' serves as a 'springboard' for a girl to shift from the dominance of father to that of husband.[20] A daughter's choice of a spouse appears as an act of rebellion against a father, who might never forgive her for this betrayal. She makes an irreversible shift from her own family to that of a husband, losing any place to go back to. By so doing, she voluntarily places herself in the position of victim of her husband's dictatorship. 'Romantic love' ideology on the part of women is the condition for the establishment of modern patriarchy. Thus, a woman becomes the 'subject' of an individual choice she makes herself.

Having demystified the concept of 'romance', we come to the point of what Shorter really wanted to say: the priority of the conjugal bond in modern family. If we set aside all the ideological frame made up of the sentiments and affections of alliance, this priority of the conjugal bond can also be observed in the institution of the *ie*. For the first time in Japanese history the Meiji civil code forbade polygamy. As well, the *ie* institution, from its origin in samurai households, gave great power to a wife (the first wife), as the mediaeval historian, Wakita Haruko, argues.[21] The wife of a patriarch sometimes worked as a house-head in household management. She often became a successor of the family business after the death of her husband. Even today, a considerable number of women representatives can be found among small-scale family businesses, which might appear unusual in such a male-dominant society. The fact that a wife, the outsider of a patrilineal family line, is qualified to represent the household in public is difficult for people from other East Asian countries to understand. In fact, the *ie* institution is not so much patrilineal as oriented to the autonomy of a household under the control of a conjugal couple. So far as the survival of this autonomous household or *ie* is concerned, blood relationship has no particular importance, and the patrilineal succession rule was readily broken to allow adoption of non-kin.

Autonomy of the Household

The most important intention of the Meiji civil code was to establish the *ie* as an autonomous household unit, free from community control. Apparent autonomy was, in turn, subjugated to public control. The outcome, in fact, was rather the isolation and exclusiveness of households from each other, whether extended household or nuclear household does not matter in this respect. It is often misunderstood that what industrialisation had to set free from community control was not the individual, but the household. As Shorter argues, the modern family is characterised by its independence and exclusiveness, qualities also shared by pre-war Japanese families.[22] If there is a higher probability of the existence of an extended household in the Japanese case, it is more likely to be in the process of proto-industrialisation based on cottage industry. Unlike European societies, the employment rate in Japan has never been over 90 per cent. Industrialisation has been supported largely by small-scale businesses based on family management.

The norm was made while the reality of the family system was in decline. Kano Masanao writes in *Senzen ie no shisō* (*The Idea of the Ie in Pre-war Japan*) about 'disintegrated reality and reinforced ideas'.[23] Industrialisation undermines the basis of an autonomous household. By and large, samurai households were in decline at the time of the establishment of the idea of the *ie* institution which was modelled on them. The primitive accumulation of capital, together with repeated depressions, also accelerated the disintegration of poor households. From the beginning when the *ie* institution was conceived, there was a serious gap between the cultural ideal and reality. Because of that, the ideal had to be reinforced.

Murakami, Kumon and Satō develop a similar argument which supports Kano's view in their book, *Bunmei to shite no ie shakai* (*Ie Society as Civilization*).[24] They agree that the modern nation state was invented as an extended *ie* in connection with family units made into small *ie*. The *ie* in this context is not an entity but rather an organisational principle. However:

> as modernization proceeds, there is a tendency for pseudo *ie*, or small house-holds, to be disorganized. High social mobility gave a heightened possibility for a household successor to take up other job opportunities than the family business in the name of freedom of choice. Especially among urban employed workers' families, the *ie* had lost its character as a productive unit, and trans-formed itself to a mere 'home' as a unit of consumption and retreat.[25]

They argue that *ie*, as an organisation principle, survives in corporations more successfully than in the nation state and family, as it is most of all suitable to the business unit; first because the *ie* is originally a management unit, and secondly because the other two agents lack the material basis to constitute *ie*. That explains why the family ideology is taken over by corporations.

Conclusion

If the *ie* is neither based on 'tradition' nor on historical survival, talk about Japanese identity based on the family system is dubious. As we have seen, the family system as well as its ideology has been transformed through history. And if the *ie* is the Japanese version of the modern family, the hypothesis of a culturally specific Japanese family system also becomes dubious. Such a system may be specific, but is neither peculiar nor ahistorical. Then too, we can question the process of making the model. Nakane Chie's well-known argument in *Japanese Society* makes the family system the basic unit of the society, and explains all levels of social structure as an application or expansion of the family model.[26] Thus Nakane makes it ahistorical. But we may suspect that it is possible only when the family system was made as such, that is to say, as an autonomous unit separated from all other levels of social organisation. The irony is that this separation and isolation of the family unit resulted in its being opened and made permeable to the public sphere despite its seeming 'autonomy'.

It is now clear that the family, as such, is a modern historical construct. Most theories of the family, not only Nakane's, follow this modern construction of the family system, and fail to see how it was constructed. The theorists reproduce the social construction of the family in their model-making, and become tautological. Accordingly, these theories themselves become a part of the family model and contribute to reinforcing the ideology of the family.

Because the family ideology is so overwhelming, we might suspect that the modern age is the age of family. Social scientists are also trapped in this family ideology and serve as its ideologues. They reverse the logical structure of explanation and make the family a determinant. What needs to be explained, in fact, is the social construction of the family. It is quite understandable that Freudian theory is rampant in the twentieth century, because it accounts for the modern family. In other words, Freudianism itself is a modern product and by no means universal. It is also reasonable for the state to be described in modern discourse in terms of a family model. Because the family itself has been constructed as such, it is tautological to explain the cause by the result.

Finally, all the efforts of modern family ideology are devoted to one aim: to make the family unquestionable. The secret of the making of the modern family is the separation of the public and the private sphere. The state, or the public sphere, needed to conceal its dependency on the private sphere, or to be more exact, its exploitation of the family. It was a patriarchal conspiracy to make the family a sanctuary that no one was to be allowed to transgress. The Japanese modern family was no exception. Later feminist studies have made it clear that this sanctuary is one small unit in the tyranny of patriarchy.

Notes

1 E. Hobsbawm and T. Ranger (eds), *The Invention of Tradition*, Cambridge University Press, 1983.

2 Itō Mikiharu, *Kazoku kokkakan no jinruigaku (Anthropology of the Idea of the Family-State)*, Kyoto, Minerva Shobo, 1982.

3 Inoue Tetsujirō, *Chokugo engi (Commentaries on the Imperial Rescript)*, 1981, vol. 1, pp. 10–11.

4 Inoue Tetsujirō, *Rinri to kyoiku (Ethics and Education)*, Tokyo, Kōdōkan, 1908, pp. 474–5.

5 Itō, *Kazoku kokkakan no jinruigaku*, pp. 8–9.

6 Satō Tadao, *Katei no yomigaeri no tameni: Hōmu dorama ron (Towards a Revival of the Family: on the Home Drama)*, Tokyo, Chikuma Shobō, 1978.

7 Satō argues that individualism grows only within the context of a family which is valued against public interference. In contrast to Italian familism, the Japanese family institution was organised after the state had disintegrated the traditional household into fragments. Modern Japanese familism is discontinuous with the premodern one.

8 Aoki Yayohi, 'Seisabetsu no konkyō wo saguru' (In search of the basis of sexual discrimination), in T. Yamamoto (ed.), *Keizai sekkusu to jendā (Economics, Sex and Gender)*, series: *Puragu o Nuku (Unplugging)*, vol. 1, Tokyo, Shinhyōron, 1983.

9 Ochiai Emiko, *Kindai kazoku to feminizumu (The Modern Family and Feminism)*, Tokyo, Keisō Shobō, 1987.

10 Nishikawa Yūko, 'Kindai kokka to kazoku moderu' (The modern state and the family model), in Kawakami (ed.), *Justitia 2*, special issue, 'Kazoku, shakai to kokka' (Family, society and the state), Kyoto, Minerva Shobō, 1991.

11 Edward Shorter, *The Making of the Modern Family*, London, Collins, 1976.

12 The conduct of this census actually reflected the gap between the supposedly comprehensive household registration system and the reality of high social mobility.

13 Yuzawa Yasuhiko, *Zusetsu kazoku mondai (Family Problems in Contemporary Japan)*, Tokyo, NHK Books, 1987, p. 19.

14 Seiyama Kazuo, "'Kaku kazokuka' no Nihonteki imi' (The specific meaning of 'nuclear family' in Japan), in Naoi Michiko (ed.), *Nihon Shakai no Shin Chōryū (New Trends in the Japanese Society)*, Tokyo University Press, 1993.

15 Peter Laslett and Richard Wall (eds), *Household and Family in Past Time*, Cambridge University Press, 1972.

16 Takatori Masao and Hashimoto Mineo, *Shūkyō izen (Before Religion)*, Tokyo, NHK Books, 1968, p. 33. The cult of offspring can also serve as a basis of the trans-individual duration of the household, instead of the worship of ancestors. The current practice, the pre-paid rite for the dead before the death, represents the cult of offspring, in which they make the tomb not for the individuals but for the family line, with expectation of the future participation of their children.

17 Pierre Bourdieu, *La Distinction: Critique Social du Jugement*, Paris, Editions de Minuit, 1979.
18 The ninth statistical survey on fertility by the National Institute of Population Problems in 1987 showed a strong tendency towards class endogamy based on educational career even among love marriages.
19 Ueno Chizuko, 'Ren'ai no shakaishi' (A social history of love), in Ueno Chizuko (ed.), *New Feminism Review*, vol. 1, 'Ren'ai Tekunorogii' (The technology of love), Tokyo, Gakuyō Shobō, 1990.
20 Terry Eagleton, *The Rape of Clarissa*, London, Basil Blackwell, 1982.
21 Wakita Haruko, 'Nihon ni okeru ie no seiritsu to josei' (Women and the creation of the *ie* in Japan: an overview from the medieval period to the present), in *U.S.–Japan Women's Journal*, no. 13, US–Japan Women's Center, 1993.
22 The family suicide, which is often seen as a uniquely Japanese sign of collective mentality, has become common only since the Meiji period. It was a result of the isolation of families from the community. Despairing parents, no longer able to rely on communal support for taking care of their children after their death, decide to take them together in death.
23 Kano Masanao, *Senzen ie no shisō (The Idea of the Ie in Pre-War Japan)*, Tokyo, Sōbunsha, 1983.
24 Murakami Yasusuke, Kumon Shumpei and Satō Seizaburō, *Bunmei to shite no ie shakai (Ie Society as Civilization)*, Tokyo, Chūō Kōronsha, 1979.
25 Ibid., p. 464.
26 Nakane Chie, *Tate shakai no ningen kankei (Human Relationships in the Vertical Society)*, Tokyo and New York, Kodansha, 1967 and *Japanese Society*, London, Weidenfeld & Nicolson, 1970. Nakane's argument is based on the model by F. L. K. Hsu in *Clan, Caste and Club*, Princeton, NJ, Van Nostrand, 1963. Hsu takes the family as the minimum unit of a social structure and applies this family model to all other levels of social structures. But the universality of his model is doubtful, first, because there are cases in which the structure of the upper level of the social system can contradict or counteract with that of the lower level, and secondly, because a family structure can change through history. Influenced by Freudian theory, we may suspect that Hsu's family model is itself a modern product.

CHAPTER THIRTEEN

The Modern Japanese Family System: Unique or Universal?

NISHIKAWA YŪKO

(translated by Sakai Minako and Gavan McCormack)

Introduction

Before the Second World War Japan declared itself a family state and most Japanese people believed that the family state was unique to Japan. This chapter, however, takes the view that all nation states are family states, with the modern family as their basic unit. It is for this reason that modern Japan was forced to invent its own traditions of family state, centred around the imperial family.

It is important to compare the various forms of the modern family in all nations. The model of the modern family has been influenced more by the nation state than by the developmental level of capitalism. As power relations among nation states altered the internal state structure, modern family models changed. This chapter traces historical change in models of the family and of the physical structures that contained it. The Japanese family has been based on a dual structure made up of the *ie* (household) and *katei* (family) institutions. Through historical analysis of family models, Japanese society deserves cross-cultural comparison. The concept of *ie* and its identity within the Japanese version of the modern family has been discussed by Ueno Chizuko in the previous chapter.

Ie/katei Institutions

The *ie* institution has been regarded as that family system which is distinctive to Japan. The word itself means literally 'house'. After the Second World War the *ie* was regarded as a relic of the feudal patriarchal family system headed by a father and succeeded by his eldest son, and was therefore abolished by the post-war Japanese

Constitution. The *katei*, on the other hand, was regarded as a Japanese equivalent to the English word 'home', based on the marital relationship. Thus, the term *ie* was assumed to refer to a feudalistic kind of family, while *katei* meant a modern family. *Katei* became popular and was widely in use in the process of constructing a modern state in Japan.

Both were either neologisms or at least commonly used words after the Meiji Revolution and they were used either in opposition or as complementary terms. The Meiji civil code (1898) established the core of the *ie* institution, granting the head of the household (the patriarch) the right to control family members and the duty to worship ancestors, and establishing the principle of succession by the eldest son.

The *ie* was the basic unit of the nation state and the state was regarded as a higher organisation above the *ie*. The fact that Japan was a late participant in the nation-state system forced the government to form an absolute state system headed by the emperor. The Imperial Rescript on Education (1890) represented the nation as an enlarged form of family. The concept of *ie* referred not only to a contemporary household but incorporated all the members on a family registration in the *koseki* (household register).

The word *katei* (literally 'house-garden') was known in ancient Japan, and has Chinese roots. It became widely used in periodicals and novels in the 1880s, and entered into mass usage as a term contrasting with *ie* from the 1920s. *Katei* referred to the nuclear family, while the emphasis in *ie* was on ancestor worship and parent-children relations. The two words did not stand in a simple relationship of contradiction but comprised a dual structure, constituting in sum the abstract framework for the Japanese version of the modern family.

Magazines which included the word *katei* in their title came into circulation from the late nineteenth century. These journals emphasised the construction of *katei* based on the marital relationship, and therefore sharply different from the *ie*. The expected readers of these enlightening journals were urban male intellectuals and their wives, who were high school graduates. Yet, the number of housewives reading these journals who actually did housekeeping was very small. The term *katei* became truly popular after women's commercial magazines had attracted a mass readership. *Shufunotomo* (The Housewife's Friend) defined *katei* as a consumption unit separated from production, and recommended household book-keeping and practical child-rearing. The purpose was to provide housewives with an opportunity to reflect on their daily life in order to facilitate practical house management. As these magazines became popular, the opposition between *katei* and *ie* gradually became less clear. One of the most heated issues discussed in these magazines was the conflict between a wife and her in-laws, especially her mother-in-law, which came into being precisely because of the dual family structure under which wives were forced to give service not only to the *katei* but also to the *ie*.

The Industrial Revolution brought a flow of youth into the cities as labourers. The majority of those from farming areas were not eldest sons, but second or third sons who belonged to the *ie* merely by family registration. They frequently married in cities and remained there. This fact indicated that a dual family system operated: those who were still on the same family registration but who, in practice, formed separate nuclear families – *katei* – in the cities. The foundation of these urban new families was so fragile that when they encountered recession and war they went back to their home town, seeking assistance from their *ie*. Soldiers returning from wars were also accepted by the *ie*.

The dual structure of the modern family was the strategy of the Meiji government for forcing entry into the modern world-system of nation states as a latecomer and of catching up in the world-wide capitalist competition: the rule of eldest-son-inheritance prevented the dispersal of capital; second and third sons could become factory or white-collar workers between or within a dual family system in which they remained on the *ie* register but actually ran urban *katei*; daughters of poor families were sold by their families as cheap labour to the factories; when urban *katei* were crushed by depression or war, members could return to their village *ie*, minimising state welfare provisions.

From *Iroribata* Home to *Chanoma* Home

Ie and *katei* signify abstract containers of the modern Japanese family. But houses as the concrete containers of the modern family have also changed greatly. After the Meiji Revolution there were two types of house in farming areas. A few people lived in large and comfortable houses with *iroribata* (traditional open fire-place) hearths. In such houses the patriarch held sovereign power and was entrusted with the worship of the ancestors. (To have been born in such a house a person would today need to be about eighty years old.) The majority, however, lived in shanties called *koya*, which originally meant a space designed exclusively for sleeping. The poor who lived in *koya* went to cities to work and settled in urban *koya*, equivalent to communal lodging (or doss) houses and known as *kishukusha*, *naya* or *nagaya*. A survey in 1899 showed that membership of these lodging houses was very fluid; regular marriages were few and commonly did not last long; rooms were tiny, with two or three families to a four- or six-tatami mat space, with only one window (or none) and a communal bathroom.[1]

Surveys conducted up to the time of the great Kantō earthquake of 1923 showed little change in these conditions; the beginnings of indoor kitchens and toilets were noted, but families had grown in size, space was commonly restricted to one person to a tatami mat, and there were few windows. Rent was being paid monthly rather than daily.[2] The housing type changed greatly after the 1923 earthquake, when many houses were destroyed. The number of housing units (*heya*) in the communal lodging houses decreased from twenty to eight, or even two. A number of separate shanties became available for rent.

During the Taisho period (1912–1926), a new-style urban house with a *chanoma* (Japanese-style dining room) was introduced. An ideal middle-class family, consisting of husband and wife, two children and a housemaid, lived in such a house. The layout was based on demarcation providing public space for maids and guests and private space for the family members. Guests were restricted to public space. The lifestyle where families used to kneel and sleep on the floor changed to one where they sat on chairs and slept in beds. This model represented the core of a housing plan for those who lived on monthly salaries and put emphasis on their family life as *katei*. The *chanoma* was the venue for materialising the ideal family of the *katei*.

The difference between *ie* and *katei* was clearly represented in their housing layout. At a house with *iroribata* (*ie*), seating order was hierarchical, with the father-patriarch at the head, and each member having his or her individual small meal place. By contrast, at a house with a *chanoma* a single round table provided the locus for meals for all the household, representing symbolic equality among the members. However, the seat for the father was clearly designated in front of the family altar with a photo of the emperor. A clock regulating universal time and a radio conveying world information were placed near his seat. These symbols associated a *chanoma* with ancestors and the state beyond this nuclear family.

The common feature linking a house with an open hearth *iroribata* (*ie*) and that with a *chanoma* (*katei*) was the patriarchal authority and power which controlled space in both.

From *Chanoma* House to Western-style House

The new Constitution and revised Civil Family Code (1947) abolished the *ie* institution, but the family registration and a family name remained in use. A married couple was required to register the surname either of the husband or wife. Where the couple took the wife's family name, the household was registered as headed by the wife. In this sense, family registration demarcated the family members and governed individuals as a corporate entity. The pre-war dual family structure which had consisted of *ie* and *katei* institutions was altered, but the end of the *ie* did not mean the complete disappearance of *ie* elements, some of which were transferred to the *katei*.

After the Second World War there was an immense housing shortage and people craved to have their own houses. They dreamed of realising an ideal *katei* by possessing their own house. The market for books on housing grew. The architect, Hamaguchi Miho, advocated a relocation and redesign of the kitchen, which had long been despised as a work place for housemaids and was traditionally located below the living room. She suggested that the kitchen should be put on the same level as the *chanoma* and be situated in the south, facing the sun. She foresaw that renovation of the kitchen would lead to the improvement in the status of women.[3]

On the day on which the Commander-in-Chief of the Occupation Forces, General MacArthur, departed from Japan, the American cartoon 'Blondie' which had introduced modern American family living to Japanese readers was replaced in the *Asahi* by '*Sazae-san*', whose heroine was a full-time housewife who lived with her husband, a son, and her siblings at her parents' place. The popularity of this comic revealed that the *chanoma*-type house was no longer governed by a patriarch, but rather was centred on a woman – the housewife.

The partition between the kitchen and the *chanoma* was also removed to make a Western-style living room for the family and guests. A studio for the father was also incorporated into this unique living room as the husband/father worked outside and spent little time at home. A house with this living room was obviously under the control of women. But, at that same time, as husbands began to feel a sense of alienation in these 'woman houses' (*onna no ie*), and male architects referred disparagingly to trend-chasing and over-decoration, housewives began to feel enclosed and isolated in their domestic space.

From Urban Development Corporation Flats (1950s) to One-Room Studios (1975–)

In the 1950s the Japanese government emphasised housing problems. It set up the Housing Loan Corporation in 1951 and provided financial assistance for building houses for the middle class. It also built a lot of public apartments (*kōdan jūtaku*) to cope with the housing shortage. By constructing standardised housing, it eventually regulated the size of the family and instituted a unique lifestyle.

The history of these public apartments may be divided into three periods. The first (1955–1964) was one of probation. All public apartments were made of concrete, with a dining–kitchen facing south, and an inside bathroom. These modern public apartments were regarded as progressive compared with wooden houses without a bathroom. Residents were eager to purchase newly introduced electric appliances, for example, washing machines, vacuum cleaners and fridges.[4] The public apartment units abolished the feudalistic features of the *ie*, yet at the same time they confined the size of the family to a nuclear family due to the absence of a guest room for grandparents. Shortage of space also restricted the number of children.

In the second phase (1965–1974), the emphasis was on the quality of the apartments and this was supported by rapid economic growth. A living room was introduced and the popular size of each unit became '3LDK' – a housing unit with three bedrooms and one space used for living, dining and cooking (kitchen).

In the third phase (1975 onwards), people lost interest in standardised public apartment units because they did not meet with the diversity of their needs. The apartment became more luxurious and several types of units, including even 5 or 6 LDK, suitable for extended families or the disabled, became available.

Looking at the history of public apartments, 1975 appears to be a milestone in terms of Japanese families and their housing. From this year onward, *katei* and its housing model started to go hand-in-hand. The most popular size, 3LDK, was suitable for a nuclear family with one or two children. Eligibility was restricted to those with a certain amount of income. Temporary foreigners, single families and bachelors, who did not fit the image of *katei*, were all excluded from these public flats. 3LDK became an appropriate residence for only a good *katei*.

Due to the restricted space in public apartment units, wedding ceremonies, births and funerals were undertaken outside the residence. This lifestyle also penetrated into Japanese society through the private real estate industry.

However, immediately after the 3LDK units became prevalent, a new type of residence, the *wan rūmu manshon* or one-room studio, came into existence. These rooms were initially meant for university students who had been brought up in a house with a Western-style living room and had come to the city for higher education. Financed by their parents, they took up residence in these single studios. After graduation they frequently started living in an apartment provided by the company that employed them. Husbands who commuted long distances also found it convenient to take up temporary residence in such a unit. The wealthy, and those who had given up buying a house in a city because of rising land prices, also started to buy second homes (*bessō*) in rural areas.

In the 1970s housewives started to work part-time to compensate for their tight house budget. The burden of education costs for their children and high housing rent brought them into the labour market.

The 3LDK and the house with a Western-style living room marked the completion of the modern Japanese family, and has been followed by a further change in the form of the modern family. Thereafter, not only the husband but also the wife spent little time at home. In a house with a Western-style living room, each member started living in his or her own room as if they were living in one-room studios in a city. Therefore, the government started introducing a new family policy to strengthen the bonds of the *katei*. The introduction of the government family policy has had a long history, but what was new this time was that it was the first time the government had followed the people in presenting an ideal model for their family and housing.

Conclusions

Heya, meaning 'a room', was long used as a pejorative word.[5] The maid's room, for example, was clearly demarcated to show her lower status within the family. The *ie*, where a patriarch controlled the whole space, was a container for all the family members, and there was no single space reserved for any individual member except the head of the household. Yet the meaning of *heya* has been transformed recently. 'One-room studio' has a neutral connotation in terms of function, compared with the masculine *iroribata*-type or *chanoma*-type house, or with the feminine house with its Western-style living room. Magazines began to appear with articles headed by titles such as 'My Room' or 'Beautiful Room'. Changes in the model of the modern Japanese family have been profound, and these changes were characterised by the rapidity and thoroughness with which they spread through the society as the people were mobilised through school education, print, radio and electronic media.

Now we can foresee a new dual family structure comprising a house with a Western-style living room and one-room studio. University students who reside in one-room studios refer to their parents' houses as *jikka*, a term traditionally used by a woman after marriage to refer to her parents' house. These students regard their parents' house as a 'real house', while their studio is a temporary residence. If this is correct, it reveals the dual family structure continuing in this modern era. Furthermore, the term *katei* recently seems to have been given a new meaning as representing an ideal family life, although the reality no longer correlates with the ideal. The word *katei* is essentially a bureaucratic tool, but one with a powerful normative value.

At the same time that Joan Scott was stressing the political content of the concepts of gender, and Lynn Hunt was revealing the workings of 'family romance' in the images and rituals of the world's first modern revolution,[6] we in Japan were attempting to rewrite the history of everyday life, and discovering that the pre-war imperial house had subtly modulated within a dual system of *ie* and *katei*, functioning not only through rituals of ancestor worship and the creation of a myth of an eternal blood line, but through images of imperial domestic life displayed in the pages of glossy, new, women's magazines. When put in comparative perspective, the standard schema of pre-war Japanese society based on a unique 'emperor-system family state' has to be reversed. The Japanese system was not in the least peculiar; all modern states have been 'family states'. That is precisely why modern Japan was pressed to invent its own traditions of family state centred on its imperial house.

A further new trend is foreshadowed. Individuals who reside in a *heya* seek new forms of co-habitation. The *shiruba* housing plan (housing plan for seniors) illustrates one new style of co-habitation. Female writers and cartoonists, such as Tomioka Taeko, began to write about a form of living where co-habitation would not be limited to conjugal or blood ties, but where an individual could pursue the maximum achievement of life's objectives.[7] The male household and the female household were both receptacles for families *for* society, where the family was the basic unit of the nation state, but in experimental or futuristic novels we can see a groping towards a family of the future (and the housing in which it will live). The neutral *heya* rooms which once had been scattered would be gathered into places which would serve as supports for the fulfilment of the individual, including a relevance not only for how to live but also how to die, rather than as receptacles of the family *for* society.

Notes

1 Yokoyama Gennosuke, *Nihon no kasō shakai* (*Japan's Low Society*), 1899, Tokyo, Iwanami bunko edn, 1949, p. 57.

2 Shakai fukushi chōsa kenkyūkai (ed.), *Senzen Nihon shakai jigyōchōsa shiryō shūsei* (*Collected Materials of Investigation into Pre-war Japanese Social Enterprises*), 3 vols, Tokyo, Keisō Shobō, 1989.

3 Hamaguchi Miho, *Nihon jūtaku no hōkensei* (*The Feudal Quality of Japanese Housing*), Tokyo, Sogami Shobō, 1949.

4 *Nihon jūtaku kōdanshi* (*History of the Japan Housing Corporation*), Tokyo, Nihon Jutaku Kodan, 1981.

5 See, for example, Yanagida Kunio's *Meiji Taishōshi sesōhen* (*Meiji and Taisho History from the Perspective of Social Change*), Tokyo, Nihon Jutaku Kodan, 1931.

6 See Joan W. Scott amd Judith Butler (eds), *Feminists Theorize the Political*, New York, Routledge, 1992, and Lynn Avery Hunt (ed.), *The Invention of Pornography: Obscenity and the origins of the modern*, New York, Zone Books, 1993, and by the same author, *Eroticism and the Body Politic*, Baltimore, Johns Hopkins University Press, 1991.

7 See Nishikawa Yūko, 'Three kinds of *ie* houses in modern Japanese literature', *Intercultural Communication Studies*, vol. 1, no. 2, Fall 1991.

PART FIVE

Culture and Ideology

CHAPTER FOURTEEN

Emperor, Rice, and Commoners

AMINO YOSHIHIKO

(translated by Gavan McCormack)

Translator's Introduction

Among present-day Japanese historians, Amino Yoshihiko is unusual: a Tokyo University graduate (1950), he chooses to work in a provincial women's college; from a core specialisation in mediaeval history he explores backwards to ancient Japan and forward to the contemporary; he is deeply iconoclastic, raising fundamental questions about Japanese identity; and he is enormously popular, such that his books sell up to 100 000 copies.

Amino sees the history of Japan through fresh eyes, focusing not so much on the imperial and elite-controlled, rice-field based, Kyoto-centred, male-dominated warrior and scholarly traditions, as on the regional kingdoms and countries, especially the patterns of pre-fourteenth century, pre-patriarchal diversity, and the mountains and villages and coastal settlements where different dreams stirred local communities throughout the archipelago and beyond, before the homogeneous myths of 'Japan' and the pretences of 'emperor' and sun goddess were imposed over the land.

The world Amino explores excites many in Japan, not least because, like the best historians, he is also partly a prophet. While shedding light on the forgotten or concealed past, he also suggests a new future which, by being imagined, becomes a possible agenda for social and political action.

An overwhelming majority of Japanese people believe even now that from the Yayoi to the Edo periods Japanese society was an agricultural society based on paddy fields, and if asked about 'the ethnic identity of the Japanese' the first thing they think of is paddy fields and rice. Whether they thought of it as a good thing or not, they would often see the emperor (sometimes referred to as the 'Rice King'), who performed the rituals and ceremonies based on the paddy fields, and who has in one way or another been connected to the apex of the 'Japanese state' for about 1300 years, as one of the unique features of Japanese society. From the viewpoint of Europe and America, this may seem strange for a highly developed capitalist country. On the other hand, to the people of Asia upon whom paddy fields and Shinto shrine faith were forcibly imposed in the name of the emperor, emperor and rice are symbols of the hated Japanese.

However, this is a 'false consciousness' or ideology, which has taken deep roots in the Japanese themselves and sharply constrained their behaviour. The proposition that the society has been agricultural from ancient times until now has always been dubious. Consequently, the notion that the emperor, as one of the kings born into this society, might be described as exclusively connected with paddy fields is completely wrong.

In that case, why are contemporary Japanese held captive by such 'false consciousness', and when did such an understanding of Japanese society take root? I am not yet able to respond completely to this query, but I should like to point in a provisional way to some important problems.

The overwhelming majority of contemporary Japanese, including scholars in all fields beginning with history, have come to believe that *hyakushō* (commoner) means farmer. Since 80 to 90 per cent of the population of Edo-period Japan were farmers (= *hyakushō*), there was no ground for doubt that Japanese society was agricultural, and academic debate was conducted on this basis. Therefore, the scientific vocabulary of history and economics was all weighted towards agriculture, with terms such as *handen* (farmer), serf (*nōdo*), peasant (*reinō*), tenant farmer (*kosakunō*), rich, middle and poor peasant, and so on. The common assumptions of the people took shape as the society and economics of ancient to modern times were discussed on the basis of such understanding.

Hyakushō is a word from the Chinese continent. It was first used by the *Ritsuryō* (or law-code) state that was formed at the end of the seventh century as the first mature state in the Japanese archipelago. It was used from then until the Edo period as part of official terminology. In the modern period, too, it was commonly used in everyday speech. Now, however, the mass media avoids this term since it has acquired a pejorative meaning. One circumstance that gave rise to this was the influence of social movements such as the farmers' unions which disliked the discriminatory nuance of the word and demanded that the *hyakushō* be called *nōmin* (farmers). This clearly showed how deeply Japanese thinking had been affected by the understanding of *hyakushō* as equivalent to *nōmin*.

However, *hyakushō* does not mean 'farmers' at all but 'people of many different family names' – ordinary people. It is still used in this original sense in China and South Korea, and it is only Japan where it is interpreted as meaning 'farmers'. When one reconsiders the reality of *hyakushō* as it appears in the historical materials, it becomes clear that *hyakushō* was used in its original sense in Japan too, including people who made their livelihood in various ways that could not be considered agricultural, while words such as *nōmin* or *nōfu* were used to denote farmer.

Among the *hyakushō* of ancient times were included many maritime people (who engaged in fishing, salt-making or shipping), and many mountain people (who engaged in hunting, trapping, mining, or wood crafts), while to these were added in post-mediaeval times various artisans, merchants, people engaged in shipping and maritime transport, warehousing, banking, and the arts. The modern *hyakushō* included many town people. It is difficult now to estimate the proportion of people who were engaged in such non-agricultural pursuits, but it may have reached 40 to 50 per cent, in which case Japanese society from ancient times had a definite non-agricultural colouring, with a strongly urban flavour from after the fourteenth century when the circulation of money came to permeate the society, and it becomes impossible to call it an agricultural society. As far as agriculture is concerned, it included not just paddy cultivation, but growing dry field crops such as wheat, millet and pulse, and trees such as mulberry, lacquer, chestnuts and persimmons; in the everyday culinary lives of the people, rice had no particular significance. Therefore, the common view that Japan was an agricultural society based on paddy fields and rice must be seen as a fabrication, completely at odds with reality, and based on the mistaken idea that *hyakushō* is the equivalent of farmer.

It is precisely this belief which lies at the origin of the state which first formalised 'Japan' as a country name and the appellation *tennō* (emperor), indeed, that gave rise to the very 'Japanese state' (*Nihonkoku*). This state, based on Yamato and its surrounding territories and therefore also known as 'Yamato', recorded all the people of Honshu, Shikoku and Kyushu, which it had more or less subjected to its control by the beginning of the ninth century, and conferred paddy fields in accordance with standards fixed for everyone over six years of age, male and female, from good folk (*ryōmin*) to servants, and exacted taxes on that basis. In other words, this state had a strong tendency to treat all *hyakushō* as paddy field farmers. It clung firmly to an 'agricultural fundamentalism' grounded in the Confucian idea that 'agriculture is the basis of all things'.

However, this 'farmland allocation' (*handen shūju*) system of remaking the family registers and redistributing paddy fields every sixth year, actually lasted only about a hundred years, with the family registers becoming meaningless as a result of lack of paddy fields, or people fleeing the countryside. From the tenth century the state system underwent great change, but the exaction of taxes based on paddy fields and the agricultural fundamentalism continued to exert a great influence on the state system. Even in the manorial-domain (*shōen kōryō*) system which took shape in the eleventh and twelfth centuries, the taxes and levies known as *nengū* (land tax) or *kōji* (public duties) were based on paddy field assessments. Until the thirteenth century the political line of agricultural fundamentalism retained its strength, both in the dynasty in Kyoto and in the bakufu newly set up at Kamakura in *Tōgoku* (eastern country).

Although the reality of the taxes in kind or in labour (*chō* and *yō*) levied in the capital based on the *handen* fields bore a strong agricultural fundamentalist orientation, being either in textile products such as silk or cloth, or in gold, iron or paper, or the rich marine produce such as salt, seaweed and marine products, the *Ritsuryō* state had a strong marine flavour. Furthermore, although the annual levies on the manorial domains were also levied on paddy fields, non-agricultural products such as silk, cloth, gold, iron and paper constituted an overwhelmingly great proportion, and rice payments as a proportion of the land tax (*nengū*) were a minority. In this detail, the non-agricultural quality of the society is clearly etched.

This tax system was already the basis of the trade between the regions from the *Ritsuryō* period, but from the tenth century tax burdens became systematised and were directed at the person who carried the obligation, while trade, commerce and banking also developed with primitive kinds of credit notes. This distribution was sustained by burgeoning river and marine communications.

Originally the communications system within and beyond the archipelago was mostly by boat on river or sea, but the *Ritsuryō* state with its ancient imperial orientation looked on the seas as boundaries and based its transport system on straight land highways of military significance. This communications system, which largely ignored the natural circumstances of the archipelago, collapsed in less than 100 years and the communications system again reverted to river or marine transport. After the tenth century this extended throughout the whole archipelago, became stabilised and supported the communication of peoples and the transport and distribution of goods. In this sense, from the tenth century at the latest, the society of the archipelago entered upon a 'river and sea period' in which the sense of national boundaries was very weak.

Rice and silk were widely used as a medium of payment and exchange in communications and served the function of currency until the eleventh or twelfth centuries, but with the spread of bronze coins from China and their diffusion from the twelfth or thirteenth centuries, a commodity and currency economy developed even more rapidly from the late thirteenth century. The activity of merchants, bankers, and shippers, based on river and sea communications, became more pronounced and through their networks exchange instruments also began to circulate on a stable basis. Many monks appeared who accumulated capital as temple funds and mobilised handicraft workers, or engaged in large-scale engineering or construction. Many towns emerged at river fords or anchorages which constituted nodes of river or maritime communications. In this way, the society deepened its non-agricultural colouration.

From the second half of the thirteenth century through the first half of the fourteenth, a fierce struggle ensued between the political line of giving positive organisation and promotion to this trend on the one hand, and maintaining the agricultural fundamentalist stance on the other. The emperor Godaigo (1288–1339), who took the former position, was dominant for a short period, but against the backdrop of social upheaval that followed his collapse, sixty years of disturbances followed. The Muromachi bakufu (1392–1573) eventually brought this under control at the end of the fourteenth century, but no sign was to be seen of agricultural fundamentalism in its laws and edicts.

On the one hand, commerce, mining and manufacturing, banking, and marine transport developed further and self-governing towns were established in various places. On the other hand, self-governing villages were also set up against a backdrop of multi-faceted agriculture, including paddy fields, and the development of the fishing industry. The burdens of meeting the land tax (*nengū*) were imposed on these villages and towns. Literacy and numeracy, which certainly spread at least through the upper levels of such towns and villages, facilitated this.

With the weakening of the Muromachi bakufu from the latter half of the fifteenth century, the whole country entered a period of disturbance. Fierce confrontation and war broke out between the *daimyō* rulers of the petty 'warring states' that set up in the regions. These *daimyō* seized control over commerce and mining and manufacturing, including trade, and strove to enhance their military and political power through control over the towns and villages. In this context the agricultural fundamentalist orientation made a comeback. However, while these *daimyō* avoided a decisive confrontation with the religious forces of *Ikkō* (a sect of militant believers in salvation through faith in the goddess Amitabha, who rebelled against the system of *daimyō* rule during the sixteenth century), Nichiren Buddhism, or

Christianity which were supported by the merchants and craftspeople of the towns, Oda Nobunaga, Toyotomi Hideyoshi and the Edo bakufu who unified the 'petty states' in the late sixteenth to early seventeenth centuries and began to move towards unification, did battle with these religious forces and crushed them decisively.

While the bakufu-*daimyō* state set up in this way got rid of the castle towns and the townspeople and samurai who had congregated there, calling the large and small towns which had sprung up prior to the sixteenth century 'villages' and the townspeople *hyakushō*, it also put commerce under control by forbidding sea travel, and instituted the *kokudaka* (crop yield) taxation system, whereby profits from dry fields and paddies, residences, fishing places or salt farms were all converted into rice which became the standard of taxation. The people who bore the tax burden were all *hyakushō*, even if they were in commerce or industry, banking or shipping. Those who had no *kokudaka* and were only liable to corvée labour, even though they may have been rich merchants, were treated as poor peasants (*mizunomi*). The reason why this state ceaselessly advocated an agricultural fundamentalism grounded in Confucian ideology despite the fact that it was completely dependent on commercial, financial and shipping networks, was precisely because it depended on taxes levied on the yield from the land – the land tax or *nengū* – for its basic taxes. Nothing was more important than for the *hyakushō*, who bore the tax burden, to be 'healthy farmers'. The social status of those engaged in non-agricultural pursuits, which naturally included commerce and industry, had to be low. In this way, the understanding that *hyakushō* means 'farmer', which had been making inroads into the society in the late sixteenth century, spread even more deeply along with the diffusion of literacy, and through the state education which, to a greater or lesser degree, inherited the agricultural fundamentalist ideology, the idea that *hyakushō* = farmer took root decisively in Japanese thinking.

Why did the Edo bakufu (1600–1868), which established itself in a society where commerce, banking and shipping were so developed, choose a system which indicated rice as its standard of taxation and adopt the principle of collecting the annual tax, the *nengū*, in rice? The complete elucidation will have to wait on a future occasion, but there is no doubt that the long history of rice in the Japanese archipelago and in 'Japan' (*Nihonkoku*) was a factor.

When paddy rice culture was brought to the archipelago before the third century BC it seems already to have possessed the maturity that might be described as a rice culture system. As part of that system, rice, with *sake* (rice wine), was treated as a sacred grain for offering to the gods. It was kept in a sacred granary and it served as the earliest model of a primitive currency for lending to people. Needless to say, the rituals connected with the paddy were the core of the festivals of the collective that chose rice cultivation – the community.

This rice cultivating culture spread quickly through the western archipelago, accompanying the movement of peoples from North Kyushu through the Seto Inland Sea, to San'in, Hokuriku, Kinki, and then to the east and north-east of the archipelago. The distinctiveness of the various regions took shape during this process of confrontation, friction, reconciliation and assimilation: the society of the east of the archipelago, where there was a long tradition of gathering, fishing, and hunting; the society of the marine people along the coasts; and the society of the mountain people, based on charcoal burning and hunting in the mountains.

From the third to the fifth centuries there was a vigorous movement towards the formation of a state based on the political forces generated in North Kyushu, the Seto Inland Sea, San'in, Hokuriku and Kinki. Influenced by the political system of Sui and Tang China from the sixth to seventh centuries, a proper state with the name *Nihon*, based mainly in Yamato and its environs, was established at the end of the seventh century. As noted above, it vigorously expanded the state system and the festival/ritual system based on paddy cultivation through the regions under its control, and as it did so in the realms of *Nihonkoku* (Japan) the superiority of the rice cultivation system was more or less determined.

Not only did this state adopt paddy fields as the basis of tax, it also incorporated the primitive financial system into its state organisation as the *suiko* system and used *rito* (interest-bearing rice loans) as the source of funds for all the domains. Although this state minted coins, they circulated only in Kinai and its vicinity. The payment and exchange of rice was a necessary medium for running the economy. The fact that rice functioned as money from very early times was no doubt based on its special character as the sacred grain. Amid the development of commerce and banking accompanying the changes in the state system after the tenth century, these functions of rice became even more pronounced. At the same time, the first ears of rice that were offered to the gods as best rice (*jōbugome*) became loan and finance capital, and already by the twelfth century rice instruments, known as exchange rice (*teigome*), had begun to circulate.

As the commodity and currency economy reached full-scale development after the late thirteenth century, coins soon began to circulate in the east of the archipelago, but in the western regions rice retained its role as a medium of payment and exchange, circulating in parallel with coins. Therefore, rice often accumulated, together with coins, in the cities and urban markets along the coast.

In the fourteenth and fifteenth centuries it became common for the *kandaka* system of denomination of the income of the lord (*ryōshu*) from his domains in monetary terms to be the basis for assessing military and other labour service requirements, but in the 'petty states' of the sixteenth-century 'warring-states' *daimyō*, especially in the west of the archipelago, we begin to see the alternative system of denoting it in rice which came to be known as the *kokudaka* system. In the circumstances of the destabilisation of the flow of copper coin from China, and insufficient good coin among the large volume circulated, and against the backdrop of the long tradition in western Japan of the use of rice for payment, circulation and exchange, this system of denoting *kokudaka* (yield) was born. At the end of the sixteenth century, Toyotomi Hideyoshi, who unified the 'petty states' from a western Japan base, inherited this system and extended it to the whole country.

The *kokudaka* system was maintained throughout the Edo period as the basis of the tax system, possibly because the *kandaka* (or *eidaka*) denomination survived for a long time in the *Tōgoku* region where there was a long history of coinage and the particularity of each region stubbornly survived. Although this was, in principle, a 'reversion from a currency economy age to a produce age', it was by no means a 'reversion from a currency economy to a produce economy'. The long-established function of rice as currency was, in this way, made to constitute the tax system, but in the commercial, banking and shipping networks which had matured by the sixteenth century it was not possible to maintain it. The fact that fiduciary instruments such as rice stamps (*kitte*) and rice instruments (*tegata*) circulated, and that a futures trade was conducted in the rice market in response to rice speculation (*sōba*), should be sufficient evidence of this.

Because of this, rice remained the staple of urban people in the Edo period, while for the *hyakushō* who were actually engaged in agriculture in the villages it was the food for special occasions, and had only a subsidiary meaning among everyday foods. But by the same token, due attention must be paid to the fact that rice had played an important role as the staple of the urban people from the fifteenth century, and that society had a strongly urban flavour through the Edo period. This is precisely why rice shortages led to famine throughout the modern period, from the Edo period and until the end of the Second World War.

Rice, therefore, had great significance as a sacred grain from ancient times, and then also became tax, currency, and capital, and naturally a grain with a strong urban flavour. Be that as it may, rice has a long history of being under strong Japanese state control as tax and currency, and the ideology of 'Japan is rice-ear land' (*Mizuhonokuni*) or 'Rice is the symbol of Japan' (which stemmed from the same root as the notion that *hyakushō* means farmer), penetrated deeply through state education in the modern period. The reason why the post-Meiji 'empire of Japan' destroyed the livelihood of the Ainu by forcing agriculture on them, promoted the development of agriculture in various parts of Asia which became colonies, and enforced the Shinto faith to go with it, was because many Japanese people were deeply captivated by such ideology. This force also turned Hokkaido, where rice cultivation was said to be impossible, into a rice belt.

One major task in considering the rice problem will be to clarify the relationship between image and reality, and to grasp the role that rice has played in the social life of the Japanese.

The ideology of paddy fields and rice is undoubtedly connected with the emperor. The ruling strata from ancient times deliberately placed the emperor at the centre of the sacred rites of the rice harvest through the ritual festive days beginning with his accession ceremony, and saturated the people with this imperial image. In essence, this was to stress one aspect of the character of the ancient emperor. There is a sense in which the emperor, who was actually chieftain of *Nihonkoku* (the legal-code state based on the paddy fields), was a 'rice king'. However, the rites which he conducted were certainly not confined to rice cultivation. The emperor was the *kami* to whom the people of sea and mountain areas offered fish and shellfish and game as 'first fruits offerings', and at such times he wore a different countenance appropriate to the occasion. After the tenth century, when the character of this state changed, the rituals conducted by the emperor gained a strongly Buddhist colouration; this was even the case with the rituals of accession.

It is true that the emperor at this time, as ruler of the manorial domains (*shōen/kōryō*), maintained the role of issuing laws and edicts in conformity with 'agricultural fundamentalism', but he also had the role of divine king, subordinating directly to himself as servants (*kugo*) those engaged in commerce, finance, shipping and so on. These *kugonin* had precisely the same character as the priest and *yoriudo* (merchants, financiers and shippers) who were attached as 'slaves' (*dohi*) to the gods (*kami*) and Buddhas. The sense in which the nature of the emperor was equivalent to that of the gods and Buddhas is nicely illustrated by this.

In response to the post-fourteenth-century social transformation, the rulers began to move in the direction of positive control of the commercial, financial and shipping networks, but remained locked in struggle with the *Hōjō* clan, backed by the Tōgoku authority, which was vigorously promoting their interests in particular. When the emperor Godaigo defeated the *Hōjō*, as noted above, he looked to base his authority on those commercial, financial and shipping interests.

Godaigo took Kyoto, the centre of communications, under his direct control, and also seized control of roads and of the setting-up and dismantling of barriers (*sekishō*), and began minting coins and using paper currency. It has commonly been thought that the use of paper currency until this time was just copying Yuan China, but it is possible to see it as quite a realistic measure which rested on the existing circulation of exchange instruments. Furthermore, Godaigo's administration inclined towards reliance on commerce and finance, taxing Kyoto wine shops, denominating the income of domainal lords from their estates in coin and fixing the tax at one-twentieth of that, entrusting the financial administration to seven banking groups, and moving to bring all the merchants and financiers controlled by the shrines and temples as priests and *yoriudo* under his direct control as *kugonin*. Godaigo is surely to be seen as heading towards absolute monarchy, controlling circulation, communications and trade, rather than being a 'rice king'.

However, in less than three years his administration collapsed, and the divided imperial house virtually lost real power in the ensuing disturbances. The military government of the Muromachi bakufu inherited Godaigo's policies and brought the disturbances under control, ushering in a brief period of stability from the early fifteenth century. Thereafter, the emperors could do no more than hold their power as centre of the traditional court culture, with limited powers of investiture of office or rank or occasionally as mediator in war, against the Muromachi *Shoguns*, who were granted the title 'king of Japan' and paid tribute to the Ming dynasty of China, and thereafter against the 'warring-states' *daimyō*, the Toyotomi administration, and then the Edo bakufu.

In this sense, it was the modern state's 'reactionary' ideology which relinked rice and emperor. Though in reality it was just a fabrication remote from the reality and history of Japanese society, nevertheless this ideology continued to hold the minds of the people firmly in its grip, so that many came to believe in this fabrication as 'the special quality of Japanese culture' or 'the ethnic identity of the Japanese'. And, since even scholars are not free of this, it may be anticipated that it will take a long time before the people grasp the reality of their history and come to perceive themselves correctly. As a matter of fact, I am a kind of 'oddball' among historians. The views that I am expressing in this chapter are confined to a tiny minority and should be understood in that light.

CHAPTER FIFTEEN

Two Interpretations of Japanese Culture

NISHIKAWA NAGAO

(translated by Mikiko Murata and Gavan McCormack)

Introduction

In writing about *Nihon bunka ron* the first difficulty is how to translate the term. Commonly in English it is rendered as 'Japanese culture theory' or 'theory of Japanese culture', but the term 'discourse' may be more appropriate than 'theory'.

The fact that there is such a thing as 'Japanese culture theory', or 'Japaneseness' (*Nihonjinron*) theory, has been seen as indicating a certain oddness about modern Japanese society. There are, I think, many elements of 'Japanese culture theory' which reveal either an inferiority complex in regard to Europe and the United States, or its opposite – narcissistic conceit and a sense of superiority. In this chapter, I stress the need to recognise this phenomenon, and to see it not just as a peculiarity but from a more universal point of view. It should be possible to cast light from a fresh angle on the nature of Japanese 'distinctiveness'.

There is a 'culture theory' not only in Japan but in every country. In France, for example, discussions regarding the 'French spirit' (*l'esprit français*) have recurred since the eighteenth century. Against the background of a distinction between civilisation and culture, in Germany the notion of *geist* is set against the French concept of *l'esprit*. As for an 'Australian culture theory', a recent newspaper article discussed the need for 'national awareness' as a necessary part of the transition to a republican system of government.[1]

To the extent that the nation state exists, a national culture will be necessary as an ideology to integrate it. Without fail, it will emphasise the originality and the superiority of its own culture and its difference from others. This becomes clear when one analyses discussions in

245

various countries about their own culture. It is also evident in the evolution of the concept of culture. Although 'culture theory' varies somewhat according to the circumstances of different countries, its essential nature is constant as an ideology used to maintain the nation state. If the primary, direct ideology of the state is what is known as 'state consciousness' or nationalism, the secondary, even more deceptive, national ideology is culture (and civilisation). My principal proposition is that 'Japanese culture theory' ranks as one such state ideology.

The role of culture as an ideology for national integration may be confirmed by considering the relationship between the key concepts of culture and nation (*Volk* or *minzoku*). Culture and nation are, needless to say, recent (late eighteenth century) concepts of Western origin. In so far as the establishment of French- and German-type nation states may be distinguished in the history of establishing the modern nation state, the lineage of the 'culture-nation' (*Kultur-Volk*) idea is to be found in the German-type nation state, while the key concept of the French-type nation state is 'civilisation-nation'. In Japan, both *bunmei* (civilisation) and *bunka* (culture) are modern translations. Until the decade beginning around 1885 the term 'civilisation' was predominant (as in *bunmei kaika* or 'civilisation and enlightenment'), but thereafter, along with the introduction of German thought, the term 'culture' gradually supplanted it. I cannot say exactly when the translated term *minzoku* (nation or *Volk*) came into general use, but it was certainly part of the diffusion of the concept of culture. Incidentally, the term, *minzoku* (nation) was reimported into China at the end of the Meiji era (along with 'civilisation' and 'culture') and seems to have played an important role in China's 'national revolution'.

The anthropological concept of culture has a great influence on our concept of culture today. Anthropology has generated hundreds of definitions of culture since Tylor's: 'Culture, or civilization, . . . is that complex whole which includes knowledge, belief, art, law, morals, custom, and habits acquired by man as a member of society'.[2] This may be seen as part of the attempt to emancipate the concept of culture from national ideology. Yet I doubt if such an attempt was successful. Let us consider one of the fruits of anthropology: the theory of cultural relativism, which acted as the conscience of anthropologists and intellectuals by affirming the original and absolute value implicit in every culture (and every nation) in opposition to the ethnocentrism which regarded its own culture as supreme. It functioned as the conscience of anthropologists and intellectuals in the period of colonialism and Nazism. Nevertheless, even cultural relativism was based on a static cultural model which was exclusive and self-contained, and as a result served to produce cultural frontiers. Cultural relativism which insists on the independence and distinctive value of every culture, corresponds in the cultural domain to the ideology of the sovereign state (which equates self-determination of peoples with nationality).

If this argument is too abstract, consider as an example the great anthropologist, Ruth Benedict. Benedict conducted research on American Indians from the stand-point of cultural relativism. There are traces of her activism against racial discrimination in her 1940 work, *Race: Science and Politics.* However, a later book, written at the request of the US intelligence services during the Second World War, *The Chrysanthemum and the Sword: Patterns of Japanese culture* (1946), reveals Benedict as a kind of 'racist'.[3] Local diversity and historical transition are disregarded and, as a result, Japan is depicted as a country in which a homogeneous race and a changeless culture have long existed. Moreover the myth of 'nationality', supposedly abolished by anthropology, is revived as the 'mould of Japanese culture'. It can be described as a return to the German concept of culture in anthropology. Benedict's *The Chrysanthemum and the Sword* might be considered as the post-war version of Taut's *Nihon bunka shikan* (*A Personal View of Japanese Culture*).[4]

Returning to culture and nation (*minzoku*), by what criterion is a nation defined? It is by race, physical similarity, religion, language, cultural tradition, etc. – in short, by cultural characteristics. It may be possible to define culture as 'the actual state of the nation', while the definition of nation would be 'the upholders of culture'. These definitions may appear too simple, but to a surprising degree they capture the essential quality of culture and nation. However, in reality no nation fulfils all objective indexes, such as the cultural characteristics mentioned above. It is gradually becoming clear, through observing ethnic problems in almost every region on the earth, that 'nation' is a fiction of the nation-state era. As the concept of nation begins to unravel, the concept of culture in the sense of national culture should also be questioned, yet it is not. Proof of this is the fact that 'Japanese culture theory' is going from strength to strength.

There seem to be three stages in the process of emancipation from the ideology of the nation state. First is emancipation from the 'state'. In post-war Japan this has proceeded quite far. The second is emancipation from the concept of the 'nation'. In post-war Japan the term *hikokumin* (literally 'non-nation person', used for someone thought to be unpatriotic) seems to have disappeared. However, 'nation', in the context of the independence of the countries of the

Third World and the establishment of new nation states, has become a sacred word. I remember being attracted by the words 'national independence', and sympathising with Takeuchi Yoshimi's 'national literature theory' and his critical viewpoint towards a modernism which 'had no idea of nation in the process of thinking'. According to Takeuchi, there was bad nationalism (such as in Europe or Japan) and good nationalism (such as in China, Asia, or the Third World). However, the half century since the Second World War shows that the distinction between good and bad nationalism is just as meaningless as the distinction between a good and a bad atomic bomb. Whatever the circumstances, a state is a state, nation a nation, and nationalism nothing but nationalism, without exception.

While the concept of 'nation' has been thrown into doubt, 'culture', which is its obverse, is positively thriving. 'Culture' means essentially 'national culture'. Post-war Japan rebuilt its 'nation' in the name of 'culture'. Japanese intellectuals, right and left wing, cooperated in rebuilding the 'nation' by means of discussing 'culture'. It seems that only rogues like the novelist, Sakaguchi Ango, who stood for the destruction of culture, were aware of the implicit deception. Sakaguchi was right to target Taut's *A Personal View of Japanese Culture* for his criticism, since Taut's book is a perfect model of Japanese culture theory. Sakaguchi's proposition – that culture is interactive and transformative – fundamentally overturns the old nationalistic culture theory which insisted on its purity and originality. His proposition also looked towards the fundamental principle of the global age: that one has to change oneself so as to accept and understand the other (foreign culture).

Let me relate an experiment I conducted in order to demonstrate the ideological power of the term 'culture'. While the death of the Showa emperor in January 1989 and the new (Heisei) emperor's accession were being widely discussed, I conducted a survey about the emperor system among the 500 students who were attending my comparative culture seminar. Almost 80 per cent said that they were against the emperor system. Two weeks later, I asked them to write a report on 'Japanese culture and the emperor system'. Most were earnest supporters of Japanese culture and recognised the important role played in it by the emperor. In other words, once they started to argue about the emperor from the viewpoint of Japanese culture, they turned into supporters of the emperor system. The term 'culture' clouds our eyes and blinds us to reality. Accordingly, in discussing Japanese culture, we have to be alert to discern the ideological character attached to the term in the nation-state era.

The following discussion is predicated on a certain understanding of nation state. I cannot here elaborate on my thinking about the nation state, but table 15.1 may be used for reference and to illustrate my understanding of similarities and differences between the French Revolution and the Meiji Revolution.

Two 'Personal Views of Japanese Culture': Bruno Taut and Sakaguchi Ango[5]

Some readers might wonder why there should be two 'Personal views on Japanese culture' and why Bruno Taut and Ango Sakaguchi? Bruno Taut (1880–1938) was a world-famous German architect renowned for his design of the 'Glass house' and the 'Housing complex' (*Siedlung*), who died in Ankara in 1938. In 1980, on the centenary of his birth, a commemorative exhibition was held in West Berlin, indicating a growing tendency to reevaluate his work.[6] Sakaguchi Ango (1906–1955) was a literary outsider, known for his novels such as *Darakuron* (*Degeneracy*) and *Hakuchi* (*The Idiot*) and for his critical writing.[7] Had Taut not fled to Japan from Berlin after the rise of the Nazis, had he not published his *A Personal View of Japanese Culture* during his stay of

Table 15.1 Prerequisites and factors for national integration

1	Economic integration:	Traffic (communication) network land system taxation standardisation of currency and weights and measures, markets, including colonial
2	State integration:	Constitution, national assembly, (centralised) government, local (prefectural) government, courts, police–prison, army (national army, conscription system)
3	National integration:	Census and family registration, school–church (temples and shrines), museums, theatres, political parties, newspapers (journalism)
4	Cultural integration:	Various national symbols, mottos, pledges, national flag, calendar, national language, literature, the arts, architecture, compilation of history, compilation of local studies
5	Citizen (state):	Religion and festivals (what Michelet refers to as the creation of new religion and Hobsbawm as the invention of tradition)[a]

Note: [a] See the writings of Jules Michelet (1798–1874), the renowned historian of the French Revolution, including *Histoire de France*, Paris, Gallimard, 1952, and of Eric Hobsbawm in Eric Hobsbawm and Terence Ranger (eds), *The Invention of Tradition*, Cambridge University Press, 1983.

nearly three-and-a-half years, and had Sakaguchi not been stirred by that book to write a book by the same title, these lives would have remained completely unrelated. Although Sakaguchi criticised Taut's view of Japanese culture severely in his own *Personal View of Japanese Culture*, hardly anyone regarded Sakaguchi's views as significant enough to topple the established theory on Japanese culture, or tried seriously to re-examine those two different views or compare them closely. It is probably the radical phraseology observed here and there in Sakaguchi's book – such as: 'It would not matter in the slightest if Hōryūji temple or Byōdōin temple burnt down. If necessary, it would be fine to tear down Hōryūji to build a station' – which certainly drew the readers' attention to his rhetorical skill but made it difficult for them to see the revolutionary novelty of Sakaguchi's concept of culture. Furthermore, Taut was a world-famous architect and Sakaguchi an unknown and youthful writer.

Re-reading Bruno Taut's *A Personal View of Japanese Culture* today, I am struck by the fact that not only is it a remarkable model of the Japanese culture theories written by foreigners, but it is also the most typical example of the so-called 'Japanese culture theory' and indeed of 'culture theory' in general. Most of the theories on Japanese culture since then could be considered variations on Taut's *A Personal View of Japanese Culture*. On the other hand, Sakaguchi's *Personal View of Japanese Culture*, which has been regarded as wildly fanciful and having nothing to do with established 'Japanese culture theory', is not only the most fundamental critique of established theories on Japanese culture but also provides useful suggestions towards the innovative theory on culture which is required in the present age – which may be called the global age, or the age of post-nation or post-nationalism.

This is why I study the texts of *Personal View of Japanese Culture* by Taut and Sakaguchi. My primary aim is not to comment on the literary style of Sakaguchi Ango, or the architectural style of Bruno Taut, or his aesthetics in general, but to focus on them as the moulds for two different views of culture. I am aware of the risk of inviting reproach, especially by admirers of Sakaguchi and Taut, for distorting the image of the authors through partial references to their writings. As someone who loves Taut and respects Sakaguchi, however, I am confident that it may be seen as a high tribute to those two thinkers to treat them in this way.

Bruno Taut's View

On 3 May 1933 Taut arrived from Berlin at Tsuruga from Vladivostok by way of France, Greece and Turkey, after departing from his first refuge in Switzerland. He had been invited to Japan by the members of the 'Japan International Architectural Society' which had been established by a group of architects living in the Kansai area. After Taut and his wife were met by Ueno Isaburō and other architects, they headed directly for Kyoto where they were guests of Shimomura Shōtarō, the president of Daimaru department store. On the day after his arrival, Taut visited Katsura imperial villa for the first time; it was his fifty-third birthday.

Until the autumn of 1936, when he was invited to Turkey as the head of the Architecture Department at the National University of Arts, Taut had considerable influence on Japanese architects and intellectuals through his direct association with architects and his writings and lectures on architecture and Japanese culture, although he had few opportunities to work as an architect. Above all, his high evaluation and enthusiastic references to Katsura gave birth to a myth of Taut as its discoverer. There are several publications on Japan: *Nippon* (*Japan*), (Tokyo, Meiji shobō, 1934), *Nihon bunka shikan* (*Personal View of Japanese Culture*), (Tokyo, Meiji shobō, 1936), *Nihon no kaoku to seikatsu* (*Houses and People of Japan*), (Tokyo, Sanseido, 1936, Japanese edition published in Tokyo, Iwanami shoten, 1966), *Nihon – Tauto no nikki* (*Japan – Taut's Journal*), (1933, 1934, 1935–36, Tokyo, Iwanami shoten, 1959, 1975), *Gajō-Katsura rikyū* (*Sketchbook – Katsura Villa*), (Tokyo, Iwanami shoten, 1981), etc. For the purposes of this chapter I am going to dealt principally with *Nippon* and *Personal View of Japanese Culture*, which may be considered its sequel. Both books have the sub-title 'From a European point of view'.

Surveying Taut's publications on Japanese culture, what is astonishing first is how quickly he grasped the notion of 'Japaneseness' (*Nihon-teki naru mono*). His experience of visiting Katsura on the day after his arrival may have been decisive in etching on his mind an archetypal image of Japanese culture. It is probable, however, that he was able to grasp Japanese culture because he had a preconceived image of Japan. Also, the Japanese around him must have affected him a great deal. The explanations of his Japanese friends must have played an important role since Taut could not understand Japanese, and in particular, the work of publishing his books must have been done in collaboration with his translators.

Accordingly, Taut's discourse, although certainly an image of Japan reflected in European's eyes, is also greatly influenced by ideas about Japanese culture widely shared by Japanese intellectuals in the 1930s, with the result that sometimes an image can be detected in his work that is more Japanese than the Japanese themselves. It is enough to glance at the contents list of his first publication, *Nippon*, to get this impression: Introduction – Why do I write this Book?; Tsuruga; Ise; Katsura Villa; Emperor and Shogun; Living Traditions; Direct to New York?; No. via Katsura Villa.

His first chapter expresses his expectations for Japan where the mould of 'artistic culture', which had declined in Europe because of 'modern mechanical civilisation', still remained just as in ancient times. For him, Japan was 'the country which renewed one's courage because it had been able to preserve pure and untrammeled form for thousands of years'(p. 15).[8] His expectations had been half satisfied and half betrayed on the day he arrived at Tsuruga. In Taut's opinion, Ise shrine was 'the source of all that Japan has offered the world, the key to its completely distinctive culture, and the cradle of Japan, absolutely perfect in its form, at which the whole world stares in admiration' (p. 29). Katsura Villa was the perfect example of Japanese traditional form. He writes: 'I was so happy to hear it repeatedly affirmed among intelligent people that Katsura Villa in its classical grandeur was the archetype of all Japanese traditional form' (p. 35). What Ise shrine and Katsura Villa represented was purely Japanese, the good tradition of Shintoism and the emperor. In opposition to this was the Shogun, whose impact had been destructive, nicely demonstrated by the vulgar taste of Tōshōgū shrine at Nikko. Thus 'emperor and Shogun' demonstrated the good tradition and the bad tradition, or the true path and the heretical path. 'Living tradition', needless to say, was the expression of the good tradition which was manifest in the contemporary arts, architecture, and lifestyle. He observed that another factor accelerating the destruction of the good tradition was the westernisation or Americanisation of Japan, represented, above all, by the words 'New York'. Taut's advice to the Japanese was that they should not go 'directly to New York' but 'via Katsura Villa', that is, they should return to their good tradition.

In *A Personal View of Japanese Culture* (the original title of which was *Japanese Art – As Seen by a European*), published two years after *Nippon*, his enquiry ranged broadly through all the arts – painting, sculpture, craft, architecture, and so on – yet Taut's perspective on Japanese culture hardly changes. Let me cite just one sentence which illustrates this quality. In criticising the work of Emil Lederer (1882–1939), who regarded European culture as a 'dynamic culture' which was active and open to other influences, whereas Japanese culture was a 'static culture' which was fixed and immovable, Taut wrote as follows:

Japanese culture is not merely one of the various cultures of the earth, but it is a harmony filled with vitality. Therefore, the use of terms such as stiffness and other qualities of the dead to refer to a phenomenon which is vitally alive will lead to mistaken conclusions. It would seem rather more necessary to point out the falsity of European culture and to emphasize that the characteristic of culture is to integrate the diverse aspects of human life into a harmonious whole. If Japanese culture has a constant preference for simplicity in art and life, this is precisely what properly educated people call 'modern' in the good sense of the word. Therefore, the concept of a vital culture, such as is held by perceptive people in the West (although there are not very many such people), is in perfect accord with the principle that may be observed in the good Japanese tradition.

In order to elucidate this, it is necessary to retrace one's steps back to the origin and core of Japanese culture. Shinto is the origin and core of Japanese culture, because the origins of Shintoism go back to ancient times, nearly two thousand years ago, and it is a pure Japanese heritage with no foreign influences. The basic idea of Shintoism is extremely simple: it is the idea of ancestor worship, which has fostered the unity of the Japanese people and relationship of the people to their national territory, and which crystallizes around the emperor. Lederer, however, sees this simple principle as the cause of what he describes as a state of rigidity. (pp. 73–5)

Ultimately Taut's quest for pure Japanese culture rooted in the distinctive tradition of Japan led him to Shinto and to the emperor system. The key concepts in Taut's work on Japanese culture were manifest in words such as: purity, tradition, national characteristics, national qualities, Japanese spirit, imperial spirit (or Shogunal spirit). The characteristics of Japanese culture were shown in words such as: simplicity, plainness, purity, clarity, chasteness, classicality, and other such terms. The things that he praised highly were all seen as part of the good Japanese tradition: Katsura Villa, Ise shrine, Japanese artists from Sesshu to Tessai, *noh* theatre, *bunraku* (puppet theatre), tea ceremony, Japanese cuisine, *sumo* (wrestling), *jūdō*, *kendō*, *kyūdō* (archery), *kemari* (Japanese football), and so on.

The perspective of comparison with Europe is always present in Taut's Japanese culture theory. Katsura Villa, for example, is compared to the Acropolis or the Parthenon in Athens (*Nippon*, p. 33), Sesshu to Grünewald, Kano Eitoku to Rubens, Chikuden to Friedrich, Gyokudō to van Gogh, Tessai to Cezanne, etc. (*A Personal View of Japanese Culture*, 'Paintings'). Furthermore, he insists that Ogata Kōrin is the originator of the Jugend school (*Jugend stil*) and 'expressionism has also its ancestry in Japan' (p. 122), while Gyokudō is, in a sense, 'the pioneer of European impressionism' (p. 132). He even employs expressions like 'Grünewald, a German Sesshu' (p. 102) and 'Cézanne is a French Tessai' (p. 156), rather than saying 'Tessai is a Japanese Cézanne'. It is easy to imagine how such remarks appealed to the national pride of the Japanese who had been suffering from an inferiority complex towards the great powers of Europe and the United States. Before long, the Japanese began to talk about their own culture in the same manner as Taut. Such a phenomenon is not confined to the Japanese but may be observed, to greater or lesser degree, in all countries preoccupied with the idea of 'national pride' or 'national glory'.

But what are the grounds of this sort of comparative view? Cultural interaction or 'influence', perhaps, is one possible such ground, and it is true, as Taut indicates, that from the latter half of the nineteenth century to the beginning of the twentieth century the influence of Japanese arts in Europe was remarkable. It can be conceded that Japonisme was an important mediating element accelerating the artistic revolution in Europe. Nevertheless, as is evident in the above explanation, the gist of Taut's views on Japanese culture was to reject or exclude the influence of foreign culture, and to seek out and preserve the inherent cultural tradition.

Taut also uses the concept of universal 'world sentiment' (*Weltgefühl*). 'Just as the pattern of every wave, the softness of every breeze, and the serenity of every calm spell, reveal to us the totality of the nature of the ocean, so the totality of artistic creation gives us the sense of what is called the universal world sentiment' (p. 106). In other words, whatever the country or style, a superior work of art can be endowed with universality. If this is true, what is the significance of national character or distinctiveness on which Taut had been insisting so passionately? What is the specific role of Japanese culture?

He seems to be trying to answer this question in the final chapter of his *Personal View of Japanese Culture* (entitled 'The third Nippon'). 'The first Nippon', according to Taut's explanation, was the 'Yamato' era, when Japan assimilated prehistoric culture in a unique way that even today is recognisable in Ise shrine. 'The second Nippon' was the Japan which absorbed Korean and Chinese culture. At this time, Kobori Enshu, as well as other great poets and painters in the seventeenth century, accomplished the restoration of Japanese culture exemplified in Katsura Villa. What is 'The third Nippon' then? Taut writes: 'It is the state of chaos that is to emerge after Japan has assimilated the culture of the European world, the world which is located on the other side of the earth' (p. 320). According to Taut, however, there was no sign yet of the dawn of such a culture in Japan. (Here, as elsewhere, Taut treats Japanese culture as something 'purer' than European culture.)

Taut's discourse on culture is based on an explicit distinction between East and West. The two are open to each other, but are in nature different and complementary. In Taut's opinion, the essential difference between East and West is that for the European the former is a 'stillness carried to the nth degree', or 'silence and cosmic meditation carried to the nth degree', while Europe for someone from

East Asia is 'motion carried to the nth degree' or 'systematic analysis and synthesis, methodical thought and activity, and individual activity, carried to the nth degree'.

It is the greatest achievement of the universal Logos to have created in humanity both elements of difference and elements of mutual complementarity. Nevertheless, since both constitute merely parts within the single *Logos*, it would be the utmost stupidity to think of one as superior to the other, or to consider that one is unnecessary and may be suppressed or overthrown by the other. (p. 324)

Here, the basis of Taut's internationalism and cultural relativism is conceptually expounded. It could be described as a sort of pacifistic pre-ordained harmony (*harmonie préétablie*) theory. Taut employs the term *logos* at this point in order to signify both that the domain of culture is different from that of politics or economics (that it is to say, it is a question of spirit), and that it cannot be destroyed by force or money. *Logos*, however, means 'Word of God' and it seems to me indicative of the bankruptcy of Taut's theory of culture that he was forced, in the end, to refer to divine providence.

Sakaguchi's Counterview

Sakaguchi's *Personal View of Japanese Culture* was published in a special issue of *Gendai Bungaku* in March 1942, nearly six years after the publication of Taut's work of the same title. The experiences that Sakaguchi describes in his *Personal View of Japanese Culture* had occurred in 1938 while he was in Kyoto. This had been a painful time of constant vacillation and confusion, so it is not surprising that it took six years for him to be able to publish his text. Furthermore, Japan's political circumstances, both domestic and foreign, changed greatly during these years. What Taut had referred to as Japanese spirit and Japanese tradition had become ideology for a militaristic nation, while the Ise shrine and Katsura Villa that Taut had admired had become symbols of the divine country of Japan, endowed with greater nationalistic significance than they had had during Taut's time in Japan. It may be that this was why Sakaguchi had to criticise Taut's *Personal View of Japanese Culture*. However, Sakaguchi was not merely engaging in ideological disputation, but raising problems which were to prove fundamental to his later views on life and literature.

Sakaguchi's *Personal View of Japanese Culture* comprises four chapters: On 'Japaneseness'; On vulgarity (Humanity as human); On the home; and On beauty. The book begins with the following passage:

I know almost nothing of ancient Japanese culture. I have never seen the Katsura Villa which Bruno Taut so much admired, and I know nothing about Gyokusen, or Taigado or Chikuden or Tessai. Even less do I know about names such as Hata Zoroku or Chikugen Saishi, and, since I seldom go anywhere, I don't even know the names of the towns and villages, or the customs, or the mountains and rivers of my own country. I was born in Niigata city, which according to Taut is the most vulgar town in Japan, and I love the downtown area from Ueno to Ginza and its neon signs which Taut despised and detested. Although I don't know anything about how to conduct the tea ceremony I know how to get blind rotten drunk. Living in my solitary abode, I could not give two hoots for a *tokonoma* [alcove].

But, just because I have lost sight of the tradition of Japan's glorious and ancient culture I do not see my life as impoverished – although I do indeed suffer from a different kind of poverty.[9]

The painters that Sakaguchi mentions here are all named in Taut's book. Sakaguchi somewhat exaggerates his own cultural ignorance. This may be regarded as a rhetorical device in order to criticise Taut from the point of view of someone located squarely within what Taut called the bad Japanese tradition. Sakaguchi was indeed from Niigata, which Taut abhorred as the most vulgar city in Japan. The reason that Sakaguchi refers to *tokonoma* is because that was the title for the first chapter of Taut's *Personal View of Japanese Culture*. However, instead of examining the various interpretations and discoveries about Japanese culture that Taut presented, Sakaguchi suddenly switches attention to fundamental questions: 'What is tradition? What does it mean to talk of national characteristics? Was there some inevitable quality about the Japanese people that made them have to invent Japanese-style clothes, some decisive factor that made them have to wear such clothes?'

Taut employs key concepts such as 'tradition' and 'national characteristics', not to enter into elaborate discussions about them, but more or less without pre-condition. The references here to 'Japanese-style clothing' are because of Taut's allusions to *wafuku* (Japanese-style clothing or *kimono*) as one expression of the Japanese sense of beauty. Sakaguchi also recalls that when Jean Cocteau, the French poet, came to Japan he deplored the eagerness of the Japanese to Europeanise themselves and abandon their own tradition, wondering why they did not wear *kimono* any more. Edward Saïd would cite this episode as unmistakable evidence of orientalism, but Sakaguchi leads us to the more basic questions of what is 'tradition' and what are 'Japanese characteristics'. And his answers take us all by surprise. In Japanese historical novels or tales, for example, there are a great number of tales of vengeance. Do these tales show a Japanese national characteristic of propensity to revenge? Sakaguchi thinks probably not, and attributes it rather to a tradition and a national characteristic *imposed* upon people.

> Such deception is often hidden even in what are referred to as tradition or as national characteristics. We are made to shoulder customs and traditions which run counter to our own nature as if they were our innate wishes. It does not follow that things that used to be done in Japan in ancient times must be inherently Japanese just because they used to be so practised. It may be that customs which were not practised in Japan, but were practised in foreign countries, might actually be more suitable to the Japanese, or, to the contrary, it is also possible that customs which were practised in Japan but not in foreign countries may prove to be suitable for foreigners. It is a matter of finding out, not imitating. (p. 355)

Here is an approach which completely reverses the established idea of 'tradition' or 'national characteristics', that the further one traces back into the past, the purer and the more original they become. Culture moves and changes shape. May not the same be said of Japanese dress?

> What is *kimono*? It is just that we were a thousand or so years late in adopting European clothes, and that we were not given any technique that might have suggested new invention but left only with limited techniques. It is not that the frail Japanese body somehow invented the *kimono*, or that anything but the *kimono* is unbecoming on the Japanese. Foreign men of stout build would certainly look much better in *kimono* than we. (pp. 355–6)

While I would rather reserve my opinion on this last phrase, in any case this is a view which absolutely disposes of the concept of 'Japaneseness'.

One more thing that we should not forget is Sakaguchi's view on imitation. In the passage above where he writes 'It is a matter of finding out, not imitating', Sakaguchi then went on: 'Just as Goethe accomplished his masterpieces inspired by the works of Shakespeare, even in the arts, where individuality is paramount, it commonly happens that imitation leads to discovery. Inspiration begins in the spirit of imitation and bears fruit in discovery' (p. 355). The reason why Sakaguchi places such particular emphasis on the significance of 'imitation' is because Taut's *Personal View of Japanese Culture* contains the epigraph: 'Beauty disappears when imitation appears'. Without here entering into a discussion on the theory on imitation from Aristotle to Auerbach,[10] I would just like to mention that 'originality' is a preoccupation in the era of the modern nation state, and to reiterate that 'imitation' also plays an important role when culture is discussed from an interactive perspective.

The choice of the theme 'The vulgar' for Sakaguchi's second chapter is because it opposes what Taut labelled the 'vulgar', 'impure', 'baroque', 'dandy', 'kitsch', 'imitation', etc. to Taut's good Japanese tradition. In the first half of his second chapter, Sakaguchi relates what he himself had seen and heard during his sojourn in Kyoto (from the beginning of 1937 to the early summer of 1938): Higashiyama dance hall to which he had accompanied the *geisha* girls of Gion in the middle of the night; Kurumazaki shrine in Sagano where countless stones were inscribed with people's names and the amounts of money they hoped to get; the small playhouse at the back of the shrine; the travelling actors and the seats stinking of urine at Higashiyama theatre; the demolished buildings of the headquarters of Ōmoto-kyō in the ruins of Akechi Mitsuhide's castle at Kameoka; a tea shop along the street nearby and the packhorse driver whom he had got to know there; and so on. These were scenes etched deeply on his mind in the painful period of his life when he was living a vagabond existence. It is a world that Taut did not see, or that, if he saw it, he rejected as 'vulgar'. Sakaguchi contrasted these scenes in his mind with the famous temples and historic places of Kyoto, and points to the 'vulgarity' of the temple buildings and Japanese gardens. It may seem contradictory for someone who upholds 'vulgarity' to reproach anything as 'vulgar'; nevertheless, the 'vulgarity' to which Sakaguchi refers here originates from the gap between the profound idea which those temples and gardens are supposed to seek and its actual embodiment. In other words, Sakaguchi chooses the journeying of the seventeenth-century poet, Basho, to the constrictions of the stone garden at Ryōanji temple or the *Hōjōki*'s transitory outlook on the world, where one sticks to a simple hermitage. In other words, Sakaguchi chooses the spirit of 'best is to have nothing' which resulted not from poverty or abstinence but from extravagant indulgence in desire.

Does Sakaguchi eventually deny all expressive behaviour? His logic shifts at this point. The spirit of 'best is to have nothing' can exist as a criticism but not as a work of art. What sort of artistic work would be recognised by the spirit of 'best is to have nothing'? Here, Sakaguchi brings up 'vulgarity' (*zokuaku*) again: 'If both the simple and the extravagant are vulgar, it is better to opt for the vulgarity which is vital, free and extravagant, and to dare to be deliberately vulgar, rather than the misery of being vulgar in spite of having every intention not to be'. Sakaguchi thus emerges diametrically opposed to the sort of Japanese beauty so highly valued by Taut. As the most thorough-going and large-scale example of a vulgarly vital and free spirit, Sakaguchi cites the case of Hideyoshi. (Toyotami Hideyoshi, 1536–1598, was a commoner who rose to become the most powerful military figure in the country.) Sakaguchi devotes quite a few pages to discussion of Hideyoshi's 'world ruling' spirit. But this seems to be by way of a riposte to Taut, who had referred to Nishi Honganji temple and Momoyama Palace as examples of bad Kyoto culture, in contrast to Katsura Villa; and Sakaguchi's real intention in the argument seems to be contained in the passage, 'a vulgar person in his vulgar way, a petty person in a petty way, everyone living out their sincere wishes to the full, one as vulgar as the other'. Why did Sakaguchi add the enigmatic phrase 'Humanity as human' to the title for this chapter? The answer is found in the passage at the end of this chapter:

> The temples of Kyoto and Nara are all more or less the same, and do not remain in my memory, but the coldness of touch from the stones of Kurumazaki shrine remains in my hand, and the tunnel formed by the vast, crimson red and unspeakably vulgar *torii* at Fushimi-Inari shrine is unforgettable. Despite its ugliness, there is something about it which, when it connects with one's earnest wishes, can be deeply moving. It is not so much a case of 'the best is to have nothing' in this case, as the sense of something that had to be, however crude and vulgar it might seem. Although I never feel any desire to rest in the stone garden of Ryōanji temple, I do sometimes feel like losing myself in reverie while watching some farce at Arashiyama theatre. Human beings love only other humans. There is no point in art in which people are absent. No-one would want to rest in a grove which evoked no nostalgia.

In this we can see Sakaguchi's 'humanism' or what might be called his 'vulgar life-ism', in opposition to Taut's 'culturism'.

The third chapter, entitled 'On houses', might bewilder the reader who was expecting some direct criticism of the housing expert Taut, for there is no description either of Japanese houses or of the family system. Instead, what Sakaguchi writes is that, even though there is no mother or wife to reproach him, he feels guilty and senses a peculiar sadness and guilt when he comes back to his empty room after being out drinking and amusing himself with girls, or on a trip somewhere: 'Though there is no mother to reproach me, or wife to get angry at me, still I am scolded when I come home. Even when alone and living a carefree life one is never free. In such places, I believe, literature is born'.

Why was it necessary for him to insert such a passage in *Personal View of Japanese Culture*? His essay, 'Bungaku no furusato' ('Literature's Native Village') in *Gendai Bungaku*, published a year before *Personal View of Japanese Culture*, hints at the answer to this question. Sakaguchi begins this essay by expounding on the cruel beauty and absence of a moral lesson in 'Little Red Riding Hood', and goes on to discuss 'the absolute isolation inherent in human existence itself'. For Sakaguchi, 'home' is that place where an individual has to face the human condition, in other words, 'the absolute isolation inherent in human existence itself'. And it is precisely this view which was lacking in the established theory of culture. In this essay, Sakaguchi penetrates deception and equivocation embedded in a theory of culture which habitually talks about the customs and character of particular groups of people rather than the choices or decisions to be made by individuals. Is not culture fundamentally a matter, not of tradition or national character, but of the problem for each individual, faced with 'absolute isolation', of how to live? Established theories of culture have no response to this question of Sakaguchi's.

The final chapter, 'On beauty', requires virtually no explanation. Sakaguchi describes three structures observed out of the carriage window: Kosuge prison, a dry-ice factory, and a destroyer anchored offshore.

> Why is it that each one of these is so beautiful? Nothing has been added to them to make them beautiful. Not a single pillar or piece of steel has been added for aesthetic reasons, nor has any pillar or piece of steel been taken away for disfiguring the object. Only that which was necessary has been put in its necessary place. Yet, in so doing, the unnecessary is removed, and a unique form is created exactly as was needed. It is a shape which resembles nothing but itself.

This is the definition of beauty which flows from Sakaguchi's 'life-ism'. He seems to be unaware that here he approaches closely the functionalism which made Taut admire Katsura Villa. Yet, even if it is the same functionalism, the goals of these two men were exactly opposite. Sakaguchi ends his *Personal View of Japanese Culture* with the following passage:

> It would not matter in the slightest if Hōryiji temple or Byōdōin temple burnt down. If necessary, it would be fine to tear down Horyuji to build a station. The glorious culture and tradition of our people would never be destroyed by that. Although the quiet Musashino sunset is no more, the sun still sets over many layers of barrack roofs, cloudy with dust even on a clear sunny day, and instead of scenes of moonlight the neon lights are shining. Still, if the spirit of our life takes root in such things, how can they not be beautiful? ... If necessary, dig up the park and make it a vegetable garden. If it is really necessary, a true beauty will be born there too, since real life is lived there. And so long as the life lived is genuine, there is no need to be ashamed of imitation. So long as the life lived is genuine, there will be the same superiority about the imitation as in the original.

Two Cultural Models – Towards a New Theory on Culture

Rereading these two *Personal Views of Japanese Culture* written half a century ago, one cannot help feeling conscious of their historical limitations. As may be seen in Taut's remarks on 'crafts', for example, what he was thinking of when he mentioned imitation was the 'cheap and shoddy' Japanese exports of the time. Taut seems to have been of the view that non-European countries could never attain the level of European civilisation. I also wonder whether, in the face of today's terrible environmental destruction, Sakaguchi would have dared to say: 'If necessary it would be fine to tear down Hōryūji to build a station'. Besides, while insisting on his position as a supporter of individuality, Sakaguchi occasionally lets slip a commnent about 'the glorious culture and tradition of our nation'. Still, while conceding such restrictions and contradictions, these two *Personal Views of Japanese Culture* still raise many problems of contemporary relevance.

In the Introduction to this chapter, I mentioned that Taut's *Personal View of Japanese Culture* was a typical example of the 'Japanese culture theory'. Having now completed my analysis, I hope that that point is established. If any doubts are left after my analysis, I might draw attention to the fact that Taut's *Personal View of Japanese Culture* fulfils all twelve characteristics of Harumi Befu's 'theory on Japanese culture'. However, my argument proceeds from a slightly different perspective from that of Befu, the Stanford University sociologist. Befu's book is entitled *Ideorogii to shite no Nihon bunkaron* (*Japanese Culture Theory as Ideology*).[11] I agree with the argument of the book, but taking it a step further, I would like to insist that not only Japanese culture theory but American culture theory, French culture theory, German culture theory, Korean culture theory – in short, all culture theories, regardless of whether a country's name attaches to them or not – are ideological, and are ideologies of states.[12]

Let me put it in more concrete terms. Despite their variety, there is a common mould of perception in all the various theories of culture, past and present. While I find it hard to decide on an appropriate name, I call it a 'classical static cultural model'. Most culture theories, for instance, specify particular qualities of specific groups (commonly the nation or an ethnic group constitutes a basic unit) to emphasise the differences of one from another. Further, in most cases, the character picked out in this way is traditional, and there is an implicit premise that the further one traces back to its origins, the purer and more original it becomes. Also, it is presumed that those who constitute the group can acquire a stable sense of happiness and life purpose only to the extent that they assimilate this ancient tradition.

In this way, contemporary theories on culture, despite different patterns and manifold ideologies, are characterised by a very limited common vocabulary, which includes terms such as 'purity' (or its opposite, 'hybrid'), 'tradition' (that is to say, 'oldness'), 'deep structure' or 'fundamental structure' (meaning 'past'), 'uniqueness' (usually 'national character'), 'originality' (indicating contempt for 'imitation'), 'harmony', 'unity', 'identity', and so on. With the exception of 'identity', a term which was adopted in the 1960s, these terms are all to be found in Taut's *Personal View of Japanese Culture*, but they are also common to almost all culture theories. (Outstanding examples of Japanese culture theory may be found in the work of Katō Shūichi, Kinsohita Junji, Maruyama Masao and Takeda Kiyoko, or in the edited volume entitled *Nihon bunka no kakureta katachi* (*Invisible Forms of Japanese Culture.*)[13] Although all the authors in this volume are contemporary Japanese thinkers whom I respect, unfortunately they employ a common model of culture.

No matter whether right or left, democrat or fascist, socialist or liberal, once they enter into a discussion on culture they all use the same terminology and are pulled in the same direction. This is horrifying but true. It seems to be basically due to the concept of 'culture'. Although there are hundreds of definitions, the most inclusive and basic would probably be 'the actual state of the nation' (*minzoku*), while the definition of 'nation' would be 'the supporters of culture'. This can be confirmed by tracing the history of the term and the concept of culture in the time of the German Romantics. The concept of culture developed in the period of the establishment of the nation state in Europe as a nationalistic assertion on the part of the newly developing countries, in opposition to the concept of civilisation which was equated with the progress and universality of the advanced countries (such as France or England). It is evident from any consideration of nationalism in the contemporary Third World that nation and culture go together. Those who use the term 'culture', whether or not they refer to Japanese culture, are, to a greater or lesser extent, nationalist. Culture is an ideology which constructs internal frontiers.

Sakaguchi saw through the nationalistic ideology intrinsic not only in Japanese culture theory but in culture theory itself. Post-war Japan repudiated nationalism, and was rebuilt in the name of culture. Now that the basis of the nation state is threatened on a world-wide scale, the true value of Sakaguchi's *Personal View of Japanese Culture* may be understood. In Sakaguchi's *Personal View of Japanese Culture* I think we can see a cultural model suitable for the world of today and of the future. The essential points are:

1 Cultures are mobile and interchangeable. Therefore, what is called Japanese culture, or so-and-so culture, divided by some frontier, does not exist. The myth of nationality has to be demolished.
2 Cultures are constantly interacting and transformatting. It therefore makes no sense to seek pure culture or cultural identity. Ideological distinctions such as those between East and West should also be abolished.
3 The meaning of imitation should be re-examined and the myth of originality demolished.
4 Culture concerns the life of each individual; in the last resort it is a matter of individual choices and decisions.

A radical culture theory of this kind might eventually lead to the repudiation of the term 'culture'. Now that the deception implicit in the term 'nation' has become problematic, 'culture' has become, perhaps, the last glorious ideology of the nation-state era.[14]

Notes

1 Malcolm Turnbull, chairman of the (Australian) Republican Advisory Committee, quoted in *Asahi shimbun*, 12 August 1993.
2 Edward Burnett Tylor, *Primitive Culture: Researches into the development of mythology, philosophy, religion, language, art and custom* (1871), 5th edn, 2 vols, London, John Murray, 1929.
3 Ruth Benedict, *Race: Science and Politics*, New York, Modern Age Books, 1940 and *The Chrysanthemum and the Sword: Patterns of Japanese culture*, Boston, Houghton Mifflin, 1946. 'Racist' is Douglas Lummis's term; see his *Uchi naru gaikoku – Kiku to katana saikō, 1946* (*The Foreign Country Within: Reconsideration of* The Chrysanthemum and the Sword, 1946), Tokyo, Jiji tsūshinsha, 1981.
4 Bruno Taut, *Nihon bunka shikan* (*A Personal View of Japanese Culture*), Tokyo, Meiji Shobō, 1936.
5 This is exactly the same as the title for chapter 9 of my 1992 book: Nishikawa Nagao, *Kokkyō no koekata – hikaku bunkaron josetsu* (*Ways to Cross Frontiers – An introduction to the comparative study of culture*), Tokyo, Chikuma Shobō, 1992. I chose the same title because I wish to take this opportunity to reorganise the ideas I had at the time of writing that book, this time examining them more closely as problems in culture theory.
6 See Dohi Yoshio, J. Posener, F. Bollerey, K. Hartmann (eds), *Burūno Tauto to gendai – 'Arupusu kenchiku' kara 'Katsura rikyū'* (*Bruno Taut and the Present Time: from 'Alpine Construction' to 'Katsura-rikyū'*), trans. by Ikimatsu Keizō and Dohi Yoshio, Tokyo, Iwanami shoten, 1981. The following essays are also collected in this book: Dohi Yoshio, 'Bruno Taut to Nihon'; Julius Posener,

'Tauto no nokoshita mono' ('Bruno Taut, Vortrage zur Eröffnung der Ausstellung' in der Berliner Akademie der Kunste am 29 Juni, 1980 (Bauwelt, 71, annual set 18. 7. 1980); Franziaka Bollerey and Kristiana Hartmann, 'Gensō-teki bigakusha kara biteki shakai (risō) shugisha e' ('Bruno Taut, Vom phantastischen Astheten zum asthetischen Sozial (ideal) isten').

7 Sakaguchi Ango, *Sakaguchi Ango Zenshū* (*Complete Works of Sakagushi Ango*), 14 vols, Tokyo, Chikuma Bunko, 1974.

8 Subsequent references are to the Japanese translations by Mori Toshio – Bruno Taut, *Nippon* (*Japan*), and *Nihon bunka shikan* (*A Personal View of Japanese Culture*), Tokyo, Kōdansha, 1991 and 1992.

9 *Sakaguchi Ango Zenshū* (*The Complete Works of Sakaguchi Ango*), Tokyo, Chikuma Bunko, 1990, vol. 14. (All subsequent references are to this edn.)

10 Eric Auerbach, *Mimeshisu – Yoroppa bungaku ni okeru genjitsu byōsha* (*Mimesis: Description of reality in European literature*), Japanese trans. by Shinoda Kazushi and Kawamura Jirō of *Mimesis: Dargestelle Wirklichkeit in der abendländischen Literatur*, 1946, Tokyo, Chikuma Shobō, 1967.

11 Befu Harumi, *Zōho – ideorogii to shite no Nihon bunkaron* (*Enlarged Edition: Japanese Culture Theory as Ideology*), Kyoto, Shisō no Kagakusha, 1987.

12 For further observations on this subject, see Nishikawa Nagao, 'Kokka ideorogii to shite no bunmei to bunka' (Civilisation and culture as national ideology), *Shisō*, May 1993.

13 Takeda Kiyoko (ed.), *Nihon bunka no kakureta katachi* (*The Hidden Form of Japanese Culture*), Tokyo, Iwanami.

14 For some works illustrating the present state of nation (*minzoku* or *ethnos*) theory, see Uchibori Motomitsu, 'Minzokuron memorandamu', in Tanabe Hanji (ed.), *Jinruigaku-teki ninshiki no bōken – ideorogii to purakutisu* (*Adventures in Anthropological Cognition: Ideology and practice*), Tokyo, Dōbunkan, 1989; and Nawa Katsuo, 'Minzokuron no hatten no tame ni – minzoku no kijutsu to bunseki ni kansuru riron-teki kōsatsu' (Towards a theory of *ethnos* – on description and analysis of nations and ethnic groups), *Minzokugaku kenkyū*, vol. 56, no. 3, December 1992. These papers emphasise that there can be no objective definition of 'nation' and that the ideological role of 'nation' is to give substance to something which has no substance.

CHAPTER SIXTEEN

Kokusaika: Impediments in Japan's Deep Structure[1]

GAVAN McCORMACK

The collapse of the Cold War removed the mask of assumed Communist (and anti-Communist) entities from states and societies around the world. As the bipolar hegemonic system broke down, component countries could turn sideways to face their neighbours. The quest for identity flared with renewed force, and attention turned to who people were and how they differed from their neighbours. It precipitated a search for identity.

Since all identity is imagined construct, the quest for 'true' identity was vain from the start, and often led into layers of atavistic fantasy about the nature of racial, ethnic or cultural orders, in which the simple, pure and holistic was preferred to the complex or the real. The politics of identity became a common theme across much of Europe, Latin America and the Middle East. Walls may have fallen in 1989 but others quickly replaced them, setting new tracers of division and sub-division along ethnic, linguistic and religious lines across continents and countries, even as the voracious market threatens to swallow all in its undiscriminating maw.

The process is at work in Japan with peculiar force because Japan is the favoured child and beneficiary of the Cold War, and also because deep-rooted historical questions have never been resolved, and because the long-term goals of the modern Japanese state – wealth, power, and equality of status with the West – having been achieved, the achievement was experienced as hollow. Where was Japan to go from there?

The contest between rival conceptions of Japanese identity is fed by Japan's rise as economic superpower in an increasingly borderless world. Its deepening engagement with the world raises questions about orthodox formulations of 'Japaneseness' stemming from antiquity, and how/whether 'Japaneseness' and modernity in the political sense of a civil society can be combined. The intellectual failure to perceive the outside world (save, ironically, in a classically 'orientalist' fashion) preceded and prepared the way for the moral failures of the mid-twentieth century, and permitted a widening gap between Japan and the rest of the world in the 1980s and 1990s – and underscores the importance of this historical work.

Japan's modern triumph was achieved at the cost of a series of negations and fabrications about its origins and essence which are now increasingly visible. Rendered visible, the compulsion of the mode which operated behind screens, by use of mirrors, myths and magic, is lost. Once revealed, the subject of the negations of the past regains voice and enters into the discourse about the construction of the future; the fabrications become capable of transcendence. The myth of 'Japaneseness' as the quality of a monocultural, blood-united, pre-ordained people confronts the historical reality of the emergence of the earliest Japanese states out of a complex of more or less equal communities which traded, contended and communicated across the islands and peninsulas of the adjacent continent. The fantasies which were imposed over the people of the archipelago created a gulf between them and their neighbours and, internally, a hierarchical structure in which dissidence and difference were negated. But the fantasies, rather than being negated, were entrenched.

Official myths only lose their power through the historian's labour of deconstruction and exposure. The study of history is thus deeply political, through its capacity to illuminate the contested nature of the identity of tribal, ethnic and national communities over time, to reveal the power constructs and the violence which underpin the mask of consensus.

The re-imagining of the Japanese past offers hope for a re-creation of tradition through which Japan might present a vision for the future which would satisfy world pressures and expectations. History in the 1990s is therefore political and contested, in a sense as profound as during the 1930s; the Japanese question 'Who are we?', takes centre stage in historical and political debate, as did the debates of the 1930s over mode of production, or in the 1950s and 1960s over the peace constitution, or in the 1970s and 1980s over aid, international responsibility and the environment.

Many commentators point to the current Japanese problem of isolation in the region and the world. German observers, whose experience in many respects parallels the Japanese, are especially sensitive to it.[2] The hypothesis of this chapter is that, for Japan, the quest for a sense of ease with itself, its region and the world is blocked by the set of values and ideas associated with its own rise: the notion of Japan as a special land, directly founded by the gods, superior to its neighbours. The deep conviction of uniqueness is reflected in a whole vocabulary, from the simple *Nihon-teki*, (literally 'Japanese' but with a distinctly ineffable quality to it), through *tennōsei-teki*, by which radical scholars themselves conceded that Japanese institutions could not be compared with other social formations but were special, and the simple 'island people complex' (*shimaguni konjō*). In contemporary terms, the debates over 'difference' (*ishitsu*) and the US–Japan negotiations over 'structural impediments' concern just this problem.

The core to the whole system of such values, once known as *kokutai*, more recently as *Nihonjinron*, is the emperor himself, the greatest blockage to Japan's engagement with the world, the only structural impediment not yet named by Washington, the taboo of taboos, the repository of the ultimate magic. This is another reason why the historical debate is profoundly political.

The sword of primordial 'Japaneseness' is, however, double-edged.[3] It was just such 'Japaneseness' which, by creating a sense of membership and solidarity and fostering it through the following centuries, facilitated Japan's remarkable, if sometimes terrifying progress, especially in the twentieth century. But it was also the tragic blemish which increasingly bedevilled the Japanese enterprise.

'Japan', according to Amino Yoshihiko, began in the late seventh century in the *Ritsuryō* or legal code state of western Japan around the chieftain who was now called *tennō*. The process was probably stimulated by events in Korea where, by AD 668, Silla had assimilated its Paekche and Koguryo rivals and achieved unified rule over the peninsula, creating a need for the dwellers of the 'Japanese' islands to conceive of a common identity for themselves, and perhaps to prepare for a unified response to any invasion. Essential elements of a superior, monolithic and racist ideology were concocted by the ideologists of the ancient Kinai courts as they appropriated the name 'Nippon',[4] perhaps linked to the pretensions of the early emperors as sun princes (*hi no miko*).

The state built around the Kinai region gradually extended its domain. The intellectuals of the time served it by formulating out of folk memory and legend a dominant text of unique, divine, imperial identity. To compensate for, or to conceal, the realities of diversity and (probable) foreign origins of the imperial family among the tribes of Korea, direct descent from the sun goddess was claimed;[5] although the notion of superiority writ large in the texts actually declared, in its contrapuntal sub-text, insecurity and fear. And the ideology of a chosen race united around a divine emperor was incompatible with harmonious relations with neighbour states. Their domains, whether known as Yamato, Kinai or Nihon, long remained relatively insignificant, co-existing even on the Japanese archipelago with other social organisations, other states.[6] But their power as 'Japan' encroached gradually upon the rival centres in the archipelago: the Ainu society to the far north, the domain of the 'king of Ezo-Chishima', the principality known apparently as Hinomoto (an alternative pronunciation of the characters for Nihon) that rose and fell in the north-east, or the societies centring on the south-west, sometimes referred to contemptuously as the realm of the *wakō* or pirates, who freely communicated across the Yellow Sea between Kyushu and Korea, or, finally, the independent kingdom of the Ryūkyūs on Okinawa. By about the twelfth century, however, a pattern of culture and authority had emerged which was sufficiently homogeneous for the consciousness of living in 'Japan' to become widespread.[7] Thus, as Amino notes, neither the culture and people of Jōmon (*ca.* 10 000 BC to *ca.* 300 BC) or Yayoi (period of origins of agriculture, *ca.* 400 BC to AD 300), nor the Yamatai kingdom of the Wa people, nor even Prince Shōtoku (574–622), were, strictly speaking, 'Japanese'; all were *pre*-'Japanese' dwellers and civilisations of the archipelago.

Out of these ancient constructions, however, the myth of 'Japaneseness' as the quality of a monocultural, blood-united, pre-ordained people was concocted and evolved till, in the state-building processes of the late nineteenth century, it penetrated 'into the very souls of the people'.[8] It was never negated, although the historical reality was very different from the myth.

The notion of the Japanese people as homogeneous, pure, rice-growing and rice-eating, distinct from antiquity, whose essence was most purely distilled in the person of the emperors, became central to the ideology of 'Japaneseness'.[9] The elements of this ideology and polity – which originated in Kinai and which, for convenience, may be called 'Yamatoist' – having filtered through the archipelago were woven into a fabric of exceptional coherence and suasive force during the seventeenth and eighteenth centuries by the scribes of the 'National Learning' (*Kokugaku*) school, who codified the original legitimating myths of the Yamato founding fathers, projected back upon that age the notion of a lost, 'golden age' utopia, when the gods communicated directly with humans, and saw the link with this pristine age as preserved through the sacerdotal family of the *tennō*, who maintained and embodied the *kōdō* (imperial way). All that impinged upon Japan from outside over later millennia was inferior and defiling, including the very notion of Chinese learning. Motoori Norinaga (1730–1801) expressed the point beautifully:

Magokoro o tsutsumi kakushite kazaraite
Itsuwari suru wa Kara no narawashi[10]

For which a rough translation might be:

Enveloping, concealing, embellishing
the true heart,
and deceiving it:
Chinese customs.

If Chinese learning represented the fall from pristine grace, how much more so the later foreign influences? The notion of a unique, pre-foreign, superior polity, preserved in essence in the *tennō* institution but shared in some measure by all 'Japanese', became an integral part of the national polity or *kokutai*, codified in the early twentieth century and still powerful today. *Tennōsei* subsumed much of the popular folk ethic and aesthetic of 'simplicity' (*soboku*), 'sincerity' (*magokoro*), harmony with the forests and *kami*, but subverted it fatally by subordinating it to the imperial cult – for long turning the shrines, those focal points of popular animist religion and festival, into centres of imperial cult. Here was *itsuwari* (or trickery) far more damaging to the *magokoro* (or pure heart) of Japan than Chinese learning.

Utopian political movements in Japan have commonly thought of themselves as 'restorers' who would return to an earlier, uncorrupted order (often one ruled directly by the *tennō*), rather than creators of a new one. The changes would be referred to as *kigen* (return to the origins) and were commonly experienced as a fundamentalist 'rebirth'; but the price was the revival of 'xenophobic chauvinism' and the notion of Japan as 'superior global progenetrix'.[11] These structures of myth came to hold powerful sway over the popular sub-conscious.

Though this version of identity gained official sanction, it was by no means the only one generated in the country. Apart from the political contention that was reflected in the co-existence of separate states, there was ideological contest too. One influential current of utopian thinking was quite opposite in its stress on the universal human moral qualities of brotherhood and equality rather than particular (non-moral or non-ethical) qualities of 'Japaneseness'. As shown in the sixteenth-century *Ikkō Ikki* movements (militant believers who rebelled against the system of *daimyō* rule), this could be a powerful force for social change. Its weakness, however, was that it became structured and mythologised in terms of the non-Japanese, imported doctrines of Buddhism and, in different ways, Christianity.

Historians such as Irokawa Daikichi (of the *minshūshi* or people's history school) focus on the regional, anti-mainstream, popular counter-traditions which in the modern period contested ideological hegemony.[12] As Irokawa demonstrated, it was commoners who continually insisted on the universalist principles of the social order.[13] Thus, in the 1880s the democratic and rational elements of modernism were affirmed as a fulfilment of tradition in the constitutional drafts prepared by the farmers of Itsukaichi: the court and political elites felt threatened, since they seemed to face a challenge to official notions of 'Japaneseness' built around the imperial family. The universalist principles affirmed by commoners were therefore rejected as heterodox, foreign and subversive, which meant that they were incompatible with the unspoken taboos surrounding the imperial institution. Intervention was necessary to preserve 'Japan' against those who would dissolve its unique and special imperial subjectivity.

The idealism and energy with which the Japanese people built the nation into a modern, industrial state is unquestioned. However, the channeling of that energy and idealism through the myths defined by the National Learning scribes meant that ideological 'closedness' (*sakoku*, literally 'closed country') continued though in other senses the country was 'opened' after Meiji (1868), and in some respects this 'closedness' continues to the present. While the dominant strain of eighteenth-century *kokugaku*-thinking proved a powerful instrument for the ruling establishment to use to mobilise the Japanese people under the emperor as divine centre of the race, and project Japan as a dynamic nation in the 1890s and again in the 1930s, the same mythology, because of its stress on the unique and superior qualities of 'Japaneseness', made it difficult for Japan to be accepted in the world view. It is no coincidence that the pre-war structures of family state (*kazoku kokka*) and imperial army (*kōgun*), and the post-war structure of the Japanese business enterprise (*kigyō*), are similarly hierarchical, authoritarian and absolutist, or that 'internationalisation' presented such enormous problems then and now.

Faced with the question of how to relate to its nearest neighbours before the war, Japan chose alternately the apparently opposite policies of 'sloughing off' Asia, and embracing it. But the idealism of both policies (*datsu-A* and *Ajiashugi*) was predicated on the inherent difference and superiority of Japan. In the former case, Japan was to set itself off as non-Asian and therefore superior; in the latter, it assumed that the only way for Japan to 'return' to Asia was as leader (*meishū*), in an hierarchical alliance of nations, in which any *other* leader was unthinkable. All the world was to be brought under the benevolent family roof of Japan (*hakkō ichiu*).

This chapter argues that, to present a credible, universalist message to the world, Japan has to slough off not its 'Asianness' but its

'Japaneseness', to negate the core of its officially-defined identity. Yet this capacity for self-negation (*jiko hitei*) has been conspicuously lacking at official levels in modern Japan, and the identification of the deep 'self' with the *tennō* as Japan's true and singular 'subject' makes it particularly difficult ever to do so.

The point perhaps emerges clearly if, alongside Japan's contemporary difficulties in relating to the world, its earlier attempts are considered. The most 'successful' Japanese attempt at expansion is commonly thought in Japan to be the Manchukuo episode.[14] After 1931 when the Manchurian incident occurred, it was not possible for Japan to proceed by directly colonial means, that is to say, neither a 'Taiwan' model nor a 'Korean' model was possible because Chinese nationalism had powerful forms of political, diplomatic, and military expression. In Manchukuo, therefore, Japan faced a fresh problem: to develop an ideology and practice of 'internationalisation' (*kokusaika*). It needed to be able to justify the continuance of a set of special Japanese rights and interests without claiming simple hegemony. Clearly there should be lessons to learn from this experiment in 'multi-culturalism and co-existence'.

Those most threatened by Chinese nationalism and rights recovery, the Japanese settlers and employees of the South Manchuria Railway Company who had developed some attachment to Manchuria, gradually generated the vocabulary of appropriate terms: 'autonomy' (*jichi*), 'inter-racial harmony' or 'harmony of the five races' (*minzoku kyōwa, gozoku kyōdō*, etc.), and the appropriate institutional structures and symbols (flag, anthem, and mass organisation) and cultural expression in film, song and literature. This state would be post-imperialist, anti-communist and multicultural. 'Manchukuo' combined elaborate utopian aspiration with other Japanese longings for a non-capitalist, non-exploitative, just, rational economic and social order.

The faith in such a future was actually the inverse image of the reality of the crisis of agriculture and the failures of the Depression in Japan itself. Such failures were to be avoided in Manchukuo through economic planning. The beginnings of Japanese planning were here, in the desire to match the performance of the First Soviet Five-Year Plan (1928–1932), and it was a returned Moscow student, Miyazaki Masayoshi, who drafted the first Manchukuo plans. This approach later extended into attempted comprehensive economic planning for the whole region. In short, the formula of Manchukuo combined radical utopianism with radical rationalism.

The reality beneath this glossy representation was one of comprehensive direction from Tokyo: the entire apparatus of state was a charade to conceal 'control by hidden manipulation' (*naimen shidō*) by

the Japanese military, with Pu Yi (the 'last emperor') a puppet; instead
of peace and equality there was constant violence and mobilisation; in
place of 'inter-racial harmony' there was entrenched Japanese privilege
and discrimination. Unit 731 at Harbin (sometimes known as the Ishii
unit), in which Chinese and Koreans were reduced to 'logs' (*maruta*)
to dehumanise them prior to torture and experimentation in the name
of medicine, constitutes a central and powerful symbol of the reality of
Japan's 'multiculturalism' of the 1930s.

In a sense, the victims of this disastrous experiment were victims of
the National Learning school's success in formulating myths that
dominated the deep structures of the minds of the Shōwa planners.
This becomes most evident when the process of constructing myth is
considered. Take the case of determining the nature of the authority
of the Manchukuo emperor. While the mass-mobilising Concordia
Society (*Kyōwakai*) promulgated (and many of its members believed
passionately in) inter-racial harmony, equality of the five races, etc., the
Kwantung army insisted that a state cult which clarified the 'special
relationship' between Manchukuo and Japan was necessary, and in the
end a state cult based on Amaterasu, the mythical sun goddess who was
supposed to have founded Japan, was chosen. In June 1940 Pu Yi visited
Japan for the 2600th anniversary of the founding of Japan and agreed
that Japan would not be just ally, but mother country (*shinpō*), and that
he would undergo the ceremony of incarnating Amaterasu (by which
he would become a 'Living Amaterasu' or 'Iki-Amaterasu'). In July 1940
ceremonies modelled on Japan's *Daijōsai* were conducted by court
officials from Tokyo. The three treasures of mirror, sword and jewel
were solemnly adopted and a gaggle of *gagaku* court musicians
performed appropriate music; the imperial portrait became an object
of reverence and the morning ceremony of bowing to the palaces in
Tokyo and Hsinking was inaugurated. The National Foundation Shrine
(*Kenkoku shinbyō*) was established as a surrogate Ise, and in August the
shrine was dedicated to those who gave their lives in founding the
country. An entire tradition was created, as it had been, of course, a
millennium earlier in Japan itself. But the crudity and deception of the
enterprise was transparent. The attempt to create something new
ended in reproduction of the deep 'DNA' structure of superiority,
uniqueness, and 'Japaneseness' (*kokutai*) that had been constructed by
the National Learning scholars. This most important pre-1945 attempt
at 'internationalisation' ended in mockery of that goal.

The fatally flawed enterprise of Manchukuo is commonly acclaimed
in Japan, however, as a model, a key foundation for China's post-1949
industrialisation and a pattern which Japan might strive to emulate in
its relations with South-east Asia.[15] Criticism of the venture in terms of

its revealing the internal contradictions of 'Japaneseness' is rare. In the discourse of identity, the deep structure of 'Japaneseness' hewn by the National Learning ideologues out of ancient Yamato myths remains privileged, and any challenge to the *tennō*-centred notion of 'Japaneseness' fiercely resisted. The modern ideological creations – flag, anthem, ceremony (of imperial burial and accession especially) – and the struggle to define national 'heroes' or 'martyrs', also consistently privilege the most deeply embedded definition of identity. The special, unique and sacred 'Japanese national polity' (*kokutai*) of the 1930s remains fundamentally unchallenged in its dominance of the 'Japanese' symbolic world. Reference to the post-war imperial institution as *merely* symbolic has a nice irony, since of all forms of power it is the symbolic which is most profound and unchallengeable (because it is unrecognised).

Japan's economic 'modernity' and power contrasts sharply with its encumbrance of pre-modern ideological survivals: the intense *étatisme* of the modernising state's bequest resulted in a strong sense of *kokumin kokka* (nation state) but a weak sense of *shimin shakai* (civil society); the notion that the superiority of civil society over state is the desirable orientation of mature societies remains weak and narrowly based. Where, for example, political value discourse in the most deeply rooted modern state, France, stresses universal values of citizenship, equality, fraternity, solidarity and enlightenment,[16] Japan's dominant discourse has been to see these as 'Western' values, to be transcended.

Japanese ideologists have had difficulty in finding in the repertory of approved values (other than those relating to business organisation) any of universal appeal. Instead, the organic, essentially mystical, formula slogans, imposed from above to pre-empt popular aspiration and mobilise and co-opt, have been preferred: from 'inter-racial harmony' and 'co-prosperity' in the 1930s and 1940s to the most contemporary 'symbiosis' (*kyōsei*).[17]

The circumstances of Japan's shift from defeat to occupation to the regaining of sovereignty as a dependent unit and a crucial front-line state in the Cold War meant that the settlement of accounts with its militarist past was checked, domestic responsibility was not debated and determined – Japanese courts did not accept suits concerning war responsibility till the late 1980s – and the same conservative elites (minus only the military) who had guided Japan a generation earlier were assigned to guide it into high-growth, anti-communist renewal. In short, while the Cold War brought great benefits, it also distorted the evolution of institutions, blocking the process of coping with its past and accommodation with its neighbours. External reconciliation (and expiation) between Japan and its neighbour countries was forestalled by the Cold War walls that imperceptibly but almost totally cut Japan off from its region, accomplishing its second 'removal from Asia' (*datsu-A*).[18]

As the first removal of Japan from Asia was followed by 'return', which reached a high point in the intense ideological campaigns to justify and legitimise superiority that crystallised in Manchukuo, so the second removal was followed by a 'return' after 'normalisation' of relations with South Korea in 1965 and China in 1972. While the economic sinews of the new relationship have become clear, the ideology has been muted. There is little talk of Japan as 'mother country' to Asia, or suggestion that the sun goddess be worshipped in Beijing or Bangkok. The force of expansion by economic means is rational and secular; Japanese spokesmen are loath to interpret or attach any name to the emerging new order.

Japan's reluctance to face the past, in a region where memories are long and bitter, does not augur well for accommodation. The Korean relationship is fraught with particular tension for this reason. On the eve of 'normalisation' in 1965, the Japanese delegate, Takasugi Shin'ichi, declared:

> Japanese rule over Korea was a good thing for Koreans. Certainly, we outlawed their language and imposed Japanese-style names. But these actions only stemmed from our good intentions. We wanted to give them the status of true Japanese. Unfortunately, the war frustrated our efforts, but Korea today would be a more civilized country if Japan had ruled it for another twenty years.[19]

Only in December 1991 was the Japanese government driven, by outside pressures, to climb down from forty-six years of official denial of involvement in the slave trade in women throughout Asia. Even then, contradictory statements from high levels of government and the bureaucracy continued to affirm the priority of Japanese purpose in the 1930s and to declare the war of 1931–1945 a war for the liberation of Asia.[20]

From the early 1980s prosperity fed the desire to go beyond 'economism' and elucidate the significance of the Japanese accomplishment.[21] 'Internationalisation' (*kokusaika*) became the watchword. It signified the greatly increased weight of the Japanese in the world economy, the structure of inter-dependence of a tri-polar world centred on Japan, North America and the European Community, and the high levels of finance, technical matters, humans and goods that flowed between them. 'Internationalisation', however, did not necessarily imply the internal transformation of Japanese society; rather, it was accompanied by a continued, perhaps growing Japanese insistence that economic success demonstrated the unique qualities of the Japanese way – a superior, non-Western way. Other advanced countries adopted the paradoxical attitude of trying to borrow aspects of the Japanese formula while insisting that Japan change to conform to their pattern. Yet the contradictions between Japanese hubris and Western resentment and importunity led to growing international friction. The politics of Japanese identity was transformed into a global issue, with the 'Structural Impediment Initiative' talks (1989 and continuing) as its most prominent manifestation.

Economic success did, however, have a growing impact on Japanese society, as its wealth and economic scale drew large numbers of migrants (many illegal), and its ageing demographic profile made it increasingly unable to satisfy demand without importing labour. The Japanese Labor Ministry estimates a labour shortage of 2.6 million by the year 2000, and 5.6 million by 2005 if economic growth were to continue at about 3 to 4 per cent annually during the 1990s.[22] However, *kokusaika* has not yet been accompanied by any significant social opening and diversity; instead the established pattern of treatment of minorities – assimilation, discrimination – is reproduced. The very 'success' that creates this *kokusaika* continues to stimulate a Japanese desire to assert its identity more forcefully, which in turn, sharpens tensions internationally and domestically, in an intensifying vicious circle.

From the 1980s a new wave of foreigners, attracted by the prospect of sharing in Japan's prosperity, began to pour into Japan's cities, while the villages (where 'pure' 'Japaneseness' was supposed to be concentrated), suffering depopulation as a result of the urban-oriented growth strategy and desperate to find brides for young farmers, began to turn to the rest of Asia and to import brides from countries such as China, Korea, the Philippines, Thailand and Sri Lanka. At the same time, the number of Japanese citizens living abroad, many of them married to foreigners, also increased dramatically, as did the number of Japanese-born people who returned after being wholly or substantially educated abroad. A new stage of hybridisation of culture was underway, carrying with it a positive potential for opening, globalising and achieving *kokusaika* even if it were not of the kind desired or foreseen by cultural mandarins.

In the process, the repertory of imperial and *kokutai* myths of uniqueness, exclusiveness and superiority regained respectability and were articulated at the highest levels. The legal principle that the years should be known by the name of the reigning emperor was established (by the Gengōhō in 1979); Japan was declared a 'monoracial society' and 'a natural community' (*shizen kyōdōtai*), not 'a nation formed by contract',[23] in contrast to polyglot America, whose problems were put down to its large coloured population; the 'heroes' of Japan's past were gradually reinstated in school texts, including figures such as Admiral Tōgō Heihachiro (hero of the Russo–Japanese war of 1904–1905, embodiment of the stubborn and irrational belief in superiority of Japanese spirit, and a famous opponent of reconciliation with the West in the 1930s) who was revived as role model in primary school texts from 1989.[24] The purity and virtue of Japan's wartime mission in Korea and Manchukuo was reiterated; and the idea of restoring the shrine built to honour all who had 'fallen while punishing the country's enemies' (Yasukuni shrine) as a national shrine was promoted by political leaders, especially Prime Minister Nakasone who in 1985 declared: 'Without such monuments of gratitude, who would be willing to lay down their life for their country?'[25] Nakasone also commended the former Kamikaze pilots as role models,[26] and urged the restoration to central place in education of the Imperial Rescript on Education – a fundamental text used to indoctrinate *tennō* myths before the war.[27] Nakasone was far from unique, but he was the most powerful and articulate advocate of clarifying the national identity, liquidating 'the post-war', and reasserting internationally the unique virtues of 'Japaneseness'.

From 1989 the Ministry of Education ordered all schools to adopt the 'Hinomaru' and the 'Kimigayo' as obligatory elements in school ceremonies,[28] and in the funeral and succession rituals following the death of emperor Hirohito in January 1989, the state was drawn deeply into collusion in tennoist and state Shinto ceremonies (despite the clear provisions of the Constitution's Article 20 forbidding state involvement in any religious activity). Norma Field observes of this moment: 'Both funeral and ascension exemplify that fraught moment when the central elements of modern statehood – the dreary requirements of rationality and the dangerous allure of myth – threaten to erupt and produce a chasm in the insouciant surface of routine'.[29] As Carol Gluck recently observed, what is at work here is the incorporation of the emperor at the centre of a newly evolving 'cultural nationalism'. She adds: 'As before in Japanese history, fundamental national issues are being played out on the contested public terrain of the emperor system, which ground is no less slippery for its being now symbolic'.[30]

Despite evidence that the progressive role of the nation state is exhausted and needs to be replaced by what Sakamoto Yoshikazu calls a 'planetary democracy',[31] a strong nationalist under-current continues to flow through official Japanese thinking, contrapuntal to the commitment to *kokusaika*. The persistence of classic pretensions of *tennōsei* in the garb of contemporary 'symbolic *tennōsei*' is noted by critical anthropologists. If *tennōsei* could be identified with the cultural and spiritual essence of 'Japaneseness' as the soul of the Japanese technological civilisation, the respect and admiration of international society might be focused on it, while Japanese society could maintain its coherence and avoid the fissiparousness of other modern societies. If the process was really successful, Sakai Naoki and Yamaguchi Jirō suggest: 'if Japanese civilization theory can be fused with Japanese *tennōsei*, an omnipotent and universal *tennōsei* could become the very axis of international society'.[32] They note, ironically, that such cultural nationalism reflects an internalisation of 'the Western stereotype of the Japanese based on a certain kind of racism that sees the Japanese as emotional, illogical, uncomprehending of freedom'.[33] It might be described as a 'reverse orientalism'. And, though clad in democratic garb, the basic function of the imperial institution of fusing an ontological unity out of disparate elements by co-option and rejection, reinforcing the capacity to engage successfully other (outside) bodies, remains unchanged. In the pursuit of monolithicity in which the 'hearts of one hundred million people beat as one' (*ichioku isshin*), dissenters and heretics are isolated and the reproduction of an identical mechanism of bullying, ostracism and discrimination throughout the society represses diversity and enforces standardisation. The imperial institution and family floats sublime and unchallenged over society, protected by superstition and terror, forces powerful enough to cow even the ruthless and voracious Japanese media into the cowardice that it calls *jishuku* or self-restraint. Although in earlier days the pretensions of *tennōsei* to symbolise the whole people were limited by the technology available, contemporary technology makes it possible to reach the minds and imaginations of all, so that there is no refuge from the 'symbol'.[34]

The quest for an acceptable identity to present to the world in the process of *kokusaika* reached a peak in the 1980s. Prime Minister Nakasone seized upon the sixtieth anniversary of the accession of the Showa emperor in 1985, which also happened to be the fortieth anniversary of the end of the Second World War, to articulate the aspiration to discover and proclaim a distinctive Japanese identity.[35] The group of Kyoto-based scholars who responded to his call looked back to the pre-agricultural, forest-dwelling, hunting and gathering Jōmon society, in which they found an harmonious, ecologically sound, animistic community which impressed a distinctive and apparently permanent mould on the deep or sub-conscious mind of the subsequent peoples of the archipelago. That pattern was unique and would seem to have been most purely transmitted through the imperial institution as it was crystallised in the time of Prince Shōtoku (574–622), although the deep consciousness of all 'Japanese' was shaped by it and concepts such as *wa* (harmony), *ie* (household, as distinct from individual), *aida* or *aidagara* ('space' or 'in-between-ness', as distinct from 'that-ness' or 'there-ness'), and concave-patterned (receptive) rather than convex-patterned (outward-thrusting) characterised it.[36] For much of this prescription there are precedents in the ideas of the pre-war 'Kyoto School' associated with Nishida Kitarō and Watsuji Tetsurō. The search for a clear vision of what it meant to be 'Japanese' in the 1980s bore striking resemblance to the 1930s' drive to clarify the national polity (*kokutai meichō*).[37]

Though the ideas of the 'New Kyoto School' were criticised and derided by scholars and independent thinkers in the mid-1980s, that soon changed. When a lavishly-funded International Research Center for Japanese Studies (*Kokusai Nihon Bunka Kenkyū Sentā* or *Nichibunken*, literally 'International Centre for Research on Japanese *Culture*') was established in Kyoto in 1988, it drew the active involvement of many scholars. The peculiar resonance, even in its name, with the pre-war *Kokumin Seishin Bunka Kenkyūjō* (National Institute for Spiritual Culture), and the highly political context of its birth, was noted, and its purpose – to identify the unique quality of Japanese culture and pass it on to the rest of humanity – drew widespread criticism from independent academic organisations, but in due course its academic programs (and its budgets) disarmed the criticisms of all but a few. The more bizarre claims – of a deep-structured Jōmon-rooted Japanese distinctiveness – were not pressed, but neither was there any such process of criticism, negation and transcendence as would inspire confidence that they had been rejected. It seems likely that similar assumptions still persist among Japanese elites and continue to bedevil the *kokusaika* agenda. The ghosts of the *Kokugaku* scholars, still hungry to find and neutralise the *itsuwari* of the 1990s and assert the uniqueness and pristine beauty of the Japanese essence, remain to be laid. Cultural *tennōsei* nationalism is *tennōsei* none the less.

Debate swelled briefly to a climax in exchanges between the designated head of Nichibunken, Umehara Takeshi, and the Western scholar, Ian Buruma, in the pages of *Chūō Kōron* in 1987. Various academic organisations in Japan also took critical positions, or expressed concern.[38] But that moment soon passed. Post-Nakasone, the work done in Kyoto seemed harmless enough, prominent scholars, foreign as well as Japanese, cooperated in Nichibunken programs, the budgets were generous, and the opportunities for research were welcome, especially by scholars of history, literature, anthropology, religion and philosophy for whom other sponsors were few. Late in

1994 some 650 scholars, including 250 from abroad, gathered in Kyoto in response to a Nichibunken invitation to participate in the most lavish conference most had ever attended.

Japan undoubtedly underwent a crisis of values following the collapse of the *kokutai* in 1945, but the process was quickly arrested. The crimes of the 1920s and 1930s were interpreted in such a way as to leave the central voodoo intact. When the US and Japanese conspirators of 1946 agreed to protect the *tennō* from prosecution and to shift blame to lower echelons around the throne in order to cover up for Hirohito, they agreed that the emperor, serving the US and Japan alike as the incarnate Japanese essence, must be sacrosanct.[39] He was, therefore, the absent centre around which the Tokyo trials evolved. (To represent the gods before the court there was only the hapless Pu Yi – but *his* relationship with the gods was forgotten on all sides.)

The process of critical transcendence that was interrupted early in the wake of the defeat of 1945 remains to be carried out by democratic and internationalist Japanese. As Tsurumi Shunsuke puts it, what is needed is not so much 'inter-national studies' (*kokusaigaku*, with its implicit centrality to the role of the state) as 'inter-people studies' (*minsaigaku*).[40] The universalist civil society prescriptions of human rights, democracy and equality and intercourse continue to be suspect as part of a hegemonic Western imposition. Rejected in 1942 in the name of 'transcending modernity' (*kindai no chōkoku*), they are rejected now in the name of affirming a 'robust' autonomous 'Japaneseness'. 'Inter-nationalisation', by a perverse logic, is defined as the equivalent of 'ultra-nationalism' (*kokusaishugi = kokusuishugi*).[41]

Absence and invisibility was, and has remained, the characteristic of the centre of the Japanese ontology, an absence noted but not named by observers from Maruyama Masao in the 1940s to Karel van Wolferen in the 1980s. Till today, the total absence from debate on political reform is the same empty imperial tabernacle, for who dare raise a republican standard in Japan's political reform debate? Knowing the force of unwritten tribal conventions and observing the waves of repressive force that swept over the society before the death of Hirohito in January 1989, considerable bravery would be required to challenge Japan's deepest and most invisible 'structural impediment'.

In the 1990s, as in the 1930s and 1940s, the ramifications of the challenges to the Japanese people to define who they are and what they wish to signify to the world, closely concern both their Korean neighbours (and residents) and the members of social and regional minorities, especially those who remember being victims of previous quests to realise the 'true' 'Japaneseness'. If Japan is to discover now the solution to the problem of co-existence and co-prosperity that evaded it in the 1930s, it is the Koreans and the other minorities who will know first. The large minority of Koreans, together with other minorities such as the Ainu and foreign workers from all over Asia, are at the forefront of the challenge to achieve a fully democratic civil society, open to diverse, equally relating, parallel but different communities. It is therefore ominous that deep distrust persists between South Korea and Japan, while North Korea is still an unrecognised limbo-land, and that Koreans resident in Japan continue to be the most vocal critics of the Japanese 'system'. It is scarcely surprising that attempts to define 'Japaneseness' in terms of racial purity or 'natural community' hold little appeal for them.

Okinawa represents a different kind of periphery, where pre-'Japanese' traditions have preserved vitality and the pretensions of Yamato and Tennō remain alien. The cosmopolitan, commercial culture of the Ryūkyūs in the fifteenth and sixteenth centuries had no place for fancies of uniqueness and superiority, and the popular memory of Tennō (and the flag and anthem associated with him) as symbol of discrimination and terror remains fresh.[42] The resurgence of interest in Japan in the culture of these islands, whose flavour and tempo is distinctly Pacific, where music, dance and quality of non-material life are cause of deep pride, such that the first priority in the wake of the devastation of the war was to turn various scrap materials into musical instruments (samisen), suggests that radically alternative, 'soft' models of what it means to be 'Japanese' survive and may yet prosper.[43]

As in the 1930s one test of Japan's *kokusaika* was Manchukuo, in the 1990s one could point to a number of test cases, including Australia. The importance of Manchukuo to pre-war Japan derived from its strategic location and its resources (including food). In the post-war world structure Japan has long been deprived of the right to an autonomous foreign policy because of the basic conditions of its existence within Ampo (the US–Japan Security Treaty) and the Cold War. After the Cold War, the problem of imagining a relationship with the region (and the world), not defined either by Japanese hegemony (as in the decades to 1945) or by US hegemony, vexes Japanese minds, and although there is no direct parallel in strategic terms, in terms of resources the importance of Manchukuo in the 1930s has been paralleled since the 1960s by that of Australia. Despite the importance of Australia to Japan, Australia is ignored in most discussions of Japanese foreign policy or economic relations. Again, with the major qualification that the prospects for a 'control by hidden manipulation' (*naimen shidō*) solution have never been considered seriously for

Australia, it is nevertheless interesting to note the utopian language that has marked Japanese overtures to Australia since the 1980s.

Japan's future city of the 1930s was the north-east China city of Changchun, then at the heart of Manchukuo and known as Hsinking, or new capital. In 1987 MITI proposed to build in Australia a future multi-function polis as a joint Japan–Australia project.[44] The utopian aspiration was marked by language appropriate to an age of structural economic transformation (hi-tech and information capitalism), ecological and planetary crisis, and rise of a 'leisure society': the city of the future would be hi-tech, green, and hi-touch. This utopianism, however, had as little relation to any actual need or desire on the Australian side as did the construction of Changchun in the 1930s (a project modelled, ironically, on the construction of Canberra, Australia's own future city project of that time).

Unlike Canberra or Changchun, it is far from clear that Australia's multi-function polis will ever be built, but much has been learned from the way the project was handled, and there are some indications that the Japan–Australia relationship might be occasion for pursuing a fundamentally different approach to the problems of *kokusaika* that Japan so signally failed to resolve in Manchukuo. In that sense, the relationship with Australia in the 1990s presents problems for Japan which are broader than the mere bilateral relationship.

In a very cold international climate the relationship between Australia and Japan is marked by an unusual affection. Top Japanese business leaders build their private retreats in Australia, and political leaders take their holidays there. To which other country can Japanese leaders go with light hearts? And it is not only leaders. Surveys commonly show Australia as the country most liked; 630 000 Japanese visited it as tourists in 1992, and the number is steadily rising. In 1992 Canberra's collective heart-rate leapt as a senior Japanese Foreign Ministry official suggested that Australia was the country with which Japan was most likely to achieve a 'partnership'.[45]

The forces driving this are not merely economic. In strategic terms, Australia is closely linked with most of the major countries or groups important to Japan: the US, European Community, China, ASEAN, the South Pacific, etc. It neither threatens nor competes with Japan, and it is therefore possible to work together on many issues (Cambodia is but one example). Even more important is the fact that Australia shows Japan a way out of its historic cultural dilemma. Both Australia and Japan were once proud of their identities as monoracial states (*tan-itsu minzoku kokka*); both saw themselves as superior, racially pure, better than their Asian neighbours; 'sloughing off Asia' (*datsu-A*) for Japan was paralleled by the Australian fiction of racial purity known as 'white Australia'.

However, over the past twenty years Australia has moved to abandon its monoracial pretensions and open itself to the creation of a new identity as a multicultural state. Already its population make-up is 5 per cent 'Asian', soon to be 10 per cent. Without actually becoming 'Asian', the country is fast becoming both post-Asian and post-European, transcending its own original European cultural and racial hegemony and the monolithic ethnic, cultural or religious structures of some parts of the region, while choosing to be open to people of all races and beliefs.

In the growing commitment to republicanism, too, as the mature form of civil society for an independent and democratic people, Australia is pushing against the frontiers of social and political development, as it has since it pioneered the eight-hour work day at the end of the nineteenth century and political rights for women in the twentieth. In doing so, it also presents an implicit challenge to Japan in terms of both state organisation and society, and in the possibilities of radical (and profoundly liberating) change in the deep structure of 'identity'.

Where Japan moves to restore (or create) the symbols of monoculturalist tribalism (flag, anthem, shrine, myth and cult) and the fundamentals of the 'national polity' remain as stern and bound by defences of terror and taboo,[46] Australia is engaged in uninhibited debate over what nation it is and what it would become; it recently changed its national anthem (after wide-ranging public discussion), and the question of what to do about a flag is widely canvassed. A recent suggestion (that Australia decide to have no flag at all) probably has little support but it forms part of the debate, and cartoonists help to focus the imagination on what is involved by engaging in uninhibited and irreverent speculation on the possibilities.

Conclusions

In the continuing discourse of identity, the deep structure of 'Japaneseness' hewn by the National Learning ideologues out of ancient Yamato myths remains privileged, and any challenge to the *tennō*-centred notion of 'Japaneseness' fiercely resisted. The modern ideological creations – flag, anthem, ceremony (of imperial burial and accession especially) and the struggle over the definition of national 'heroes' or 'martyrs' – also consistently privilege the most deeply embedded definition of identity. The special, unique and sacred 'Japanese national polity' (*kokutai*) of the 1930s remains fundamentally unchallenged in its dominance of the 'Japanese' symbolic world.

A country like Australia bears certain similarities with Japan in terms of its identity confusion in modern times. For Australia, coping with a transformed international environment now requires only renunciation of a sovereign who is already remote and (whose heirs in particular) more than faintly ridiculous, and acceptance of an internal diversity and external complexity which few would even want to challenge and many positively enjoy. Japan faces a greatly more complex challenge: to renounce the mask of 'Japaneseness' as a unique, imperial essence that it has worn for over a thousand years. Historically, the dawning of the realisation that much in the orthodox and historically established notion of 'Japaneseness' has been an external imposition, the earliest and most successful foreign takeover, makes the future sloughing-off process imaginable – for what can be understood to have had a beginning can be expected to also have an end. The process of *datsu-Nichi* or sloughing off of the false, imposed and unnecessary components of the Japanese identity could open the way to rediscovery of an archipelago which, like the pre-'Japanese' archipelago, was home to multiple different cultures and peoples, each engaged in exchange and cooperation with its neighbours both within the archipelago and beyond. The end of one particular identity of 'Japan' constructed around a single subjectivity could open the way to the fulfilment of multiple subjectivities, the flourishing of many 'countries' (in the sense of autonomous democratic communities), just as the end of the many countries (in the sense of feudal domains) of Edo Japan led to the flourishing of the modern state known as 'Japan'.

Notes

1 For slightly earlier versions of this chapter in Japanese and Korean, see 'Kokusaika o megutte: kōzō shinbu ni hisomu shōheki no teppai o', *Kokusai kyōroku ronsō*, Kobe University, vol. 2, no. 1, June 1994, pp. 71–90; and 'Ilbonsahoe-ui simeh'ung kujo-wa kukjehwa', *Changjak-kwa Pipyong*, Seoul University, vol. 22, no. 2, 1994, pp. 122–49.

2 Helmut Schmidt, 'Nihon koritsuka susumu osore', *Nihon keizai shinbun*, 17 February 1992.

3 Of Japan's three 'sacred treasures', the other two – the (bronze) mirror and the jewel – are almost certainly of Korean-peninsular origin.

4 Or 'Nihon', both equally possible pronunciations of the Sino–Japanese characters.

5 Genealogical tables drawn up early in the ninth century showed one-third to one-half of the aristocracy to be of Chinese or Korean ancestry. See Kato Norihiro, ' "Nihonjin" no seiritsu' (The establishment of 'the Japanese'), *Kokusaigaku kenkyū*, Meiji Gakuin Daigaku, no. 2, March 1988, pp. 1–32, at p. 26.

6 The following discussion relies on Amino Yoshihiko, *Nihonron no shiza: rettō no shakai to kokka* (*Perspectives in Japan Theory: Societies and states of the archipelago*), Tokyo, Shogakukan, 1990. See my translation of pp. 6–20 and

59–70 of this book in 'Deconstructing "Japan"', *East Asian History*, no. 3, 1992, pp. 121–41.

7 See also Kato, '"Nihonjin" no seiritsu', p. 17.

8 Tadashi Jujitani, 'Inventing, forgetting, remembering: toward a historical ethnography of the nation-state', in Harumi Befu (ed.), *Cultural Nationalism in East Asia: Representation and identity*, Berkeley, California, Research Papers and Policy Studies, Institute of East Asian Studies, University of California, Berkeley, 1993, pp. 77–106.

9 Amino Yoshihiko, 'Emperor, rice and commoners', *Japanese Studies* (Bulletin of the Japanese Studies Association of Australia), vol. 14, no. 2, September 1994, pp. 1–12.

10 Carmen Blacker, 'Two Shinto Myths: The golden age and the chosen people', in Sue Henny and J. P. Lehmann (eds), *Themes and Theories in Modern Japanese History: Essays in honour of Richard Storry*, London, Athlone, 1988, at p. 71. For a fuller discussion of Norinaga, see Maruyama Masao, *Studies in the Intellectual History of Modern Japan*, Mikiso Hane (trans.), Princeton and Tokyo University Presses, 1974, pp. 154–76; also H. D. Harootunian, *Things Seen and Unseen: Discourse and ideology in Tokugawa nativism*, London and Chicago, University of Chicago Press, 1988, *passim*.

11 Peter Nosco, *Remembering Paradise: Nativism and nostalgia in eighteenth-century Japan*, Cambridge and London, Harvard University Press, 1990, pp. 240, 243.

12 Carol Gluck, 'The people in history; recent trends in Japanese historiography', *Journal of Asian Studies*, vol. 38, no. 1, November 1978, pp. 25–50.

13 Irokawa Daikichi, 'Popular movements in modern Japanese history', in Gavan McCormack and Yoshio Sugimoto (eds), *Modernization and Beyond: the Japanese trajectory*, Cambridge University Press, 1988, pp. 69–86 (and works cited there).

14 For details on this, see Gavan McCormack, 'Manchukuo: constructing the past', *East Asian History*, no. 2, December 1991, pp. 105–24.

15 The latter sentiment was expressed by former Prime Minister Kishi Nobusuke. See *Manshūkokushi* (*A History of Manchukuo*), 2 vols, Tokyo, Manshūkokushi hensan iinkai, 1970 and 1971, *passim*.

16 See, for example, Paul Thibaut, 'Paradoxes du nationalisme francais', *Le Monde*, 5 February 1992.

17 For fuller discussion, see Gavan McCormack, *The Emptiness of Japanese Affluence*, New York, M. E. Sharpe, 1996.

18 For a perceptive discussion, see Rosemary Gray Trott, 'Japan and the modern system of states: constructing a national identity', MA (International Relations) thesis, Australian National University, 1993.

19 Quoted in Chung Kyung-Mo, 'Korea today, Korea tomorrow', in *Two Koreas, One Future*, J. Sullivan and Roberta Foss (eds), Lanham, MD, University Press of America, 1987, pp. 135–58, at p. 147.

20 See McCormack, *The Emptiness of Japanese Affluence*, ch. 6.

21 See Gavan McCormack, 'Beyond economism: Japan in a state of transition', in G. McCormack and Sugimoto Yoshio (eds), *Democracy in Contemporary Japan*, New York, M. E. Sharpe, 1986, pp. 39–64.

22 Yamamuro Shin'ichi, 'Seijiteki naru mono no dansō' ('Fault lines in the political'), in Uchiyama Hideo (ed.), *Seijiteki naru mono no ima* (*The Political Today*), Tokyo, Sanrei shobō, 1991, pp. 164–99, at p. 189.

23 Quoted in Yamamoto Haruyoshi, *Gendai shisō no shōten* (*Focus on Contemporary*

Thought), Tokyo, Keisō shobō, 1987, p. 100. Nakasone would have understood the nineteenth-century Russian poet, Tyutchev's protestation of his country that it 'is not to be grasped with the mind'. (Quoted in T. H. Rigby, 'Russian nationhood from its origins to Yeltsin', in R. J. May (ed.), *Ethnicity and the State*, forthcoming.)

24 Yamazumi Masumi, *Gakushū shidō yōryō no kyōkasho*, Iwanami bukkuretto, no. 140, 1989, p. 29.

25 Fukatsu Masumi, 'A state visit to Yasukuni', *Japan Quarterly*, vol. 33, no. 1, 1986, p. 19.

26 Yamazumi Masumi, 'Educational democracy versus state control', in McCormack and Sugimoto (eds), *Democracy in Contemporary Japan*, pp. 90–113, at p. 108.

27 Prime Ministers Kishi, Nakasone and Tanaka all supported this goal (Yamazumi, ibid.).

28 Ohe Shinobu, 'Yasukuni, Hinomaru, Kimigayo', in Hidaka Rokurō (ed.), *Gendai Nihon o kangaeru (Thinking about Contemporary Japan)*, Tokyo, Chikuma shobō, 1987, pp. 41–68, at p. 63. Amino notes that it is precisely such acts of imposition that *should* be seen as 'un-Japanese' (Amino, *Nihonron no shiza*, p. 139).

29 Norma Field, *In the Realm of a Dying Emperor: Japan at Century's End*, New York, Vintage, 1991, p. 269.

30 Carol Gluck, 'The idea of Showa', in Carol Gluck and Stephen R. Graubard (eds), *Showa: The Japan of Hirohito*, New York and London, W. W. Norton, 1992, pp. 1–26, at p. 18.

31 For a brief introduction to Sakamoto's thinking, see Philippe Pons, 'Un entretien avec Yoshikazu Sakamoto', *Le Monde*, 8 December 1992, p. 2.

32 Sakai Naoki and Yamaguchi Jirō, 'Jiko tōsui to shite no tennōsei' ('Tennosei as self-intoxication'), *Sekai*, March 1989, pp. 23–35.

33 Ibid., p. 35.

34 Ibid., pp. 32–3.

35 For succinct treatment of this question, see Yamamoto Haruyoshi, '"Nihongaku" saikō' ('Revival of "Japan Studies"'), in Yamamoto Haruyoshi (ed.), *Gendai shisō no shoten (Focus on Contemporary Thought)*, Tokyo, Keisō shobō, 1987, pp. 98–124; and Ajisaka Makoto, '"Shin Kyoto gakuha" no Nihon bunkaron' ('The Japan culture theory of the "New Kyoto School"'), *Bunka Hyōron*, May 1986, pp. 97–114.

36 If one was to single out one work of the considerable literature written in this spirit, it might be the work by Umehara Takeshi, *Mori no shisō ga jinrui o sukuu (Forest Thinking to the Aid of Humanity)*, Tokyo, Shōgakukan, 1991.

37 On which, see Iwai Tadakuma, 'Iwayuru "Nihongaku" o megutte' ('Concerning so-called "Japaneseness Studies"'), *Nihonshi kenkyū*, no. 285, May 1986, pp. 78–81.

38 See, for a few samples of the Japanese literature, Nihonshi kenkyūkai iinkai (Committee of the Japan History Research Society), '"Kokusai Nihon bunka kenkyū sentā" no setsuritsu kōsō ni tsuite – Nihonshi kenkyūkai no kenkai' ('On the matters leading to the establishment of Nichibunken – the position of the Japan History Research Society'), *Nihonshi kenkyū*, no. 284, April 1986, pp. 76–80; Iwai Tadakuma, 'Iwayuru "Nihongaku" o megutte' ('On so-called "Japanology"'), *Nihonshi kenkyū*, no. 285, May 1986, pp. 78–81; Yamamoto Haruyoshi, 'Nihongaku saikō' ('Reconsideration of Japanology'),

in Yamamoto Haruyoshi, *Gendai shisō no shoten*, Tokyo, Keiso shobō, 1987, pp. 98–124.

39 On this question, see especially the 1992 NHK television documentary, 'Tokyo saiban e no michi – naniga naze sabakarenakatta ka' ('The road to the Tokyo trials: what was not at issue, and why'), 15 August 1992.

40 Tsurumi Shunsuke (in discussion with Amino Yoshihiko), 'Nihon no kinshitsusei o hikikaesu bane' ('The spring to reverse Japan's conformism'), *Asahi jānaru*, 22 May 1992, pp. 78–85.

41 Yamamuro, 'Seijiteki naru mono no dansō', p. 185.

42 For a sensitive discussion, see Norma Field, *In the Realm of a Dying Emperor*, *passim*.

43 Tanaka Kazuo, 'Ryūkyūnesia – yawaraka no bunka' ('Ryūkyūnesia – a soft culture'), *Sekai*, February 1993, pp. 73—82.

44 Gavan McCormack (ed.), *Bonsai Australia Banzai: Multifunctionpolis and the Making of a Special Relationship with Japan*, Sydney, Allen and Unwin, 1991; 'Nichi-Gō no omowaku chigai de hyōryū suru MFP keikaku' ('MFP plan drifting amid differing Japanese and Australian conceptions'), (with Sasaki Masayuki), *Ekonomisuto*, 7 April 1992, pp. 44–8; and 'Mo hitotsu no nanboku kankei – Ōsutoraria kara mita Nihon' ('A different kind of North–South relationship – Japan as seen from Australia'), *Kokumin bunka*, no. 390, May 1992, pp. 2–10.

45 Ogura Kazuo, (Director-General of the Economic Affairs Bureau), 'Chiiki tōgō to Nihon no sentaku' ('Regional integration and Japan's options'), *Gaikō Forum*, December 1992, pp. 3–11.

46 I have in mind not only the recent assassination attempts on Mayor Motoshima of Nagasaki and the film director Itami Jūzō, but also the scholars who regularly receive death threats designed to silence their questions over the black-box questions of modern Japanese history, and the Teachers Union which is hard-put to find a place to hold its annual convention for the same reason.

Afterword: Diversity and Identity in the Twenty-First Century

Mark Hudson and Tessa Morris-Suzuki

In this Afterword, we briefly discuss new developments relating to the themes of this book and make some corrections to the first edition. Since the mid-1990s, cultural diversity and its relationship to national identity has become a topic of intense debate within Japanese society. The principal contributors to this debate include the authors of several chapters in the volume. Amino Yoshihiko has published a number of widely discussed works drawing attention to the fluidity of the historical boundaries of Japanese identity. His study '*Nihon' to wa nani ka* (What is 'Japan'?), the introductory volume to a 26 volume series surveying Japanese history, highlights both the regional and cultural diversity which has always characterised Japanese history and the long history of cross-border interactions between inhabitants of the Japanese archipelago and the surrounding Asian regions.[1] Nishikawa Nagao's works have continued to explore the political construction of the modern Japanese sense of national identity and to expose the ways in which images of 'the nation's people' (*kokumin*) were used to obscure the diversity and contradictions within Japanese society.[2]

Meanwhile, Ueno Chizuko's widely debated study *Nashionarizumu to jendā* (Nationalism and Gender) seeks to open a space for the expression of a complex personal identity that can transcend essentialised categories of ethnicity and nationality.[3] John Maher's work has also produced further contributions to the understanding of cultural and linguistic diversity in Japan which he helped to pioneer during the 1990s.[4]

Prominent in this rethinking of national identity is consideration of the legacy of Japanese colonialism. During the second half of the 1990s, debates over apologies for Japan's wartime aggression stimulated reassessments of Japan's colonial past. Defeat in the Pacific War brought the sudden loss of a colonial empire and, arguably, a collective amnesia about colonialism. Consequently, the Japanese public by and large ignored de-colonisation and the persistent legacies of empire within post-war Japanese society.[5]

In revisiting the history of Japan's colonial empire, scholars have reassessed the separation of 'Japanese people' and 'Japanese culture' from the rest of Asia. Oguma Eiji has emphasised that the politics of empire building made it expedient for many pre-war scholars and policy-makers to acknowledge the ethnic diversity of Japan and to draw attention to the historical intermingling of Japanese and other Asian populations. Efforts to impose assimilationist policies on Korean, Taiwanese and other colonial subjects (who were at that time 'Japanese nationals' under international law) were not readily compatible with notions of Japan as a racially pure and culturally unique nation. Given this, Oguma argues that the dominant image of Japan as a clearly bounded and ethnically homogeneous society is a recent ideology that became more strongly entrenched in the post-war years than it had been in the early part of the twentieth century.[6] The writings of literary scholar Kawamura Minato, too, have drawn attention to the colonial dimensions of Japanese culture, redirecting attention to the long neglected history of the literature written in the Japanese language within the pre-war colonial empire and of literature produced by Korean residents in Japan.[7]

Post-colonial approaches remind us that colonisation is not just a matter of Japan's pre-war past. It remains a living issue for the 'internal colonies': Okinawa and the Ainu people of northern Japan. Near the end of the twentieth century, the Japanese government seemed more willing to acknowledge some aspects of the distinctive identity of Okinawan and Ainu people. In 1997, the assimilationist Former Aborigines Protection Act (discussed by Hanazaki Kōhei in chapter 7 of this volume) was repealed and replaced by the Ainu Cultural Promotion Law (*Ainu Bunka Shinkō Hō*), offering a measure of government support for the preservation and transmission of Ainu language and traditional culture. In 2000, the Kyushu–Okinawa Summit showcased large-scale, officially sanctioned displays of distinctive Okinawan culture.

Acknowledgement of diversity has generally remained limited to a very narrowly defined sphere of 'traditional culture'. Many Ainu activists regarded the Ainu Cultural Promotion Law with disappointment, because it failed to address more far-reaching demands for access to land and resources and for a measure of economic autonomy. Similarly, public performances of Okinawan music and dance did little to resolve more fundamental concerns about the continuing use of Okinawa as the major site for US military bases in Japan or the exploitation of Okinawa's natural resources by large-scale corporations based in other parts of Japan.

Another crucial legacy of pre-war colonialism is the continued presence within Japan of more than 600 000 descendents of pre-war colonial subjects, mostly from the Korean peninsula. As a third generation of *Zainichi* Koreans (Korean residents in Japan) comes of age, issues concerning the identity and social position of the Korean community in Japan have become the focus of renewed debate.[8] This debate has also been stimulated by moves towards Korean reunification and the consequent weakening of the once-rigid dividing lines separating those *Zainichi* Koreans who identified themselves with South Korea from those who identified themselves with North Korea.

Meanwhile, the emergence of a substantial population of more recent immigrants ('newcomers', as they are usually called, to distinguish them from the *Zainichi* 'oldcomers') has added a new level of complexity to questions of cultural diversity in Japan. In 1985, there were around 850 000 registered foreign residents in Japan (0.7% of the population); by 1998, the figure was over 1 500 000 (1.2% of the population).[9] The presence of an expanding and increasingly diverse population of long-term foreign residents raises practical issues concerning citizenship, education and welfare policies. A major topic of debate from the late 1990s has been the possibility of extending local voting rights to foreign permanent residents.[10]

Continuing debate over the nature of the Jōmon–Yayoi transition has shown that these contemporary questions of immigration and ethnicity have a strong resonance with the late prehistory of the Japanese Islands. In his chapter here, Katayama Kazumichi supports Hanihara Kazuro's model of Yayoi immigration but in his more recent work, Katayama has started to argue for a more complex view of the biological interactions between natives and newcomers in the Yayoi period.[11] Maher's model of a Jōmon–Yayoi creole proposed in chapter 2 of this volume has yet to receive the attention it deserves in linguistic circles. While the model has been criticised by Hudson who finds little evidence from the Yayoi period of the intensive trading activities that a creole implies, Maher's concept of a North Kyushu creole nevertheless provides a useful way of modeling broader social relations between Jōmon and Yayoi and demonstrates the potential for collaboration between scholars working on recent and early periods.[12]

Against this background of wide-ranging debate on Japanese identity, a growing number of publications have debated the 'multicultural' character of Japanese society, and the possibility of creating meaningful forms of 'coexistence' or 'symbiosis' (*kyōsei*) within a socially and ethnically diverse society. For example, *Zainichi* Korean scholar Kim Teyong argues for the creation of a form of 'multiculturalism' that would allow members of the Korean community to develop their own sense of identity in diverse and flexible ways, rather than forcing them into a pre-determined mould of 'national/ethnic identity'.[13] From a somewhat different perspective, sociologist Kurihara Akira and others have sought to develop the notion of coexistence/symbiosis (*kyōsei*) into an effective tool for social criticism. In common media currency, the term *kyōsei* tends to convey rather bland images of social harmony. For Kurihara, however, *kyōsei* does not suggest a lack of social conflict, but rather represents hard-won points of intersection and communication created by 'the suffering' (*jukusha*) through constant struggle with structures of power.[14]

As lively debates have emerged around the possibilities for multi-culturalism within Japan, so has a nationalist backlash which seeks to re-assert notions of ethnic homogeneity and cultural uniqueness. Perhaps, the most visible symbol of this trend has been the rise of the Association for History Textbook Reform, founded in 1996 by Tokyo University academic Fujioka Nobukatsu and others. Fujioka and his associates aim to 'restore national pride' by producing books which emphasise the glories of the Japanese past and exclude what the Association terms 'masochistic' discussions of issues such as war responsibility.[15] In April 2001, a junior high school history text authored by the Association was approved by the Ministry of Education (with numerous revisions) for use in Japanese schools, sparking intense controversy within Japan and heated protests from the Chinese and South Korean governments. Ishihara Shintarō, populist Governor of Tokyo, has also played on fears of difference by derogating foreign residents and linking immigration to crime and social disorder.

A major correction of the first edition of *Multicultural Japan* relates to the discussion of the Palaeolithic period. Both Katayama and Kaner mention discoveries of stone tools in Miyagi prefecture which were thought to date back about half a million years. In November 2000, amateur archaeologist Fujimura Shinichi admitted to planting much later artifacts during excavations at the Kamitakamori site in that prefecture and at the Soshin Fudozaka site in Hokkaido. Fujimura is known to have worked at at least 33 other Palaeolithic sites in Japan, and his confession throws the whole existence of an Early and Middle Palaeolithic in Japan into question. Attempts are currently underway to re-evaluate these early sites.

Many of the issues surrounding the Fujimura scandal were anticipated in the first edition of this book. The chapter by Clare Fawcett shows that it is not easy for archaeologists to balance professional and scientific concerns with the demands of the mass media and local tourism.[16] Broader questions of the use of history in Japanese society are also relevant. More recently, Amakasu Ken, current President of the Japanese Archaeologists' Association, has written that Japanese trust, since the

Second World War, in the scientific objectivity of archaeology to critique the old, emperor-centered mythologies exacerbated the shock. Given such high political aspirations for post-war Japanese archaeology, it was perhaps natural that its objectivity would be compromised. It is not yet clear how Japanese archaeology will overcome its present crisis, but Hayashi Kensaku has already compared attempts to downplay the Fujimura scandal with continuing Japanese reluctance to accept responsibility for war crimes.[17]

Fujimura's reported desire to find the oldest human remains in Japan finds appropriate critique in Simon Kaner's argument that Japanese archaeology needs to go 'beyond ethnicity and emergence'. Since archaeology is poorly suited to the reconstruction of prehistoric ethnicity, Kaner is right that most of the variability visible in the archaeological record does not relate to past ethnic groups. At the same time, however, Hudson[18] has argued that to ignore ethnicity entirely leaves prehistory open to political interpretation by non-anthropologists (such as Nishio Kanji[19]).

In a complex world where communications media, cultural flows and human lives increasingly extend across national boundaries, debates over diversity and national identity show no signs of abating. The way in which these debates are played out in Japanese society over the next decade or so will have crucial implications for Japan's place in the Asian region and in the global order.

Notes

1 Amino Yoshihiko, '*Nihon' to wa nani ka*, Tokyo, Kodansha, 2000.
2 Nishikawa Nagao, *Kokumin kokka ron no shatei*, Tokyo, Kashiwa Shobō, 1998; Nishikawa Nagao, Kang Sangjung and Nishi Masahiko (eds), 2000, *20 seiki o ika ni koeru ka*. Tokyo: Heibonsha.
3 Ueno Chizuko, *Nashionarizumu to jendā*, Tokyo, Seidosha, 1998.
4 See, for example, John Maher and Gaynor Macdonald (eds), *Diversity in Japanese Culture and Language*, London, Kegan Paul, 1995.
5 Kang, Sangjung, 'Kokumin no shinshō chiri to datsu-kokuminteki katari', in Y. Komori and T. Takahashi (eds), *Nashionaru histor̄i o koete*, Tokyo, Tokyo Daigaku Shuppankai, 1998.
6 Oguma Eiji, *Tan'itsu minzoku shinwa no kigen*, Tokyo, Shinyōsha, 1995; Oguma Eiji, '*Nihonjin' no kyōkai*, Tokyo, Shinyōsha, 1998.
7 Kawamura Minato, *Umaretara soko ga furusato: Zainichi Chōsenjin bungakuron*, Toyko, Heibonsha, 1999; Kawamura Minato, *Sakubun no naka no Dai-Nippon Teikoku*, Tokyo, Iwanami Shoten, 2000.
8 See, for example, Kim Teyong, *Aidentiti poritikusu o kōete: Zainichi Chōsenjin no esunishiti*, Tokyo, Sekai Shisōsha, 1999; Sonia Ryang, *Koreans in Japan: Critical Voices from the Margin*, London, Routledge, 2000.
9 Hōmushō Shutsunyūkoku Kanrikyoku, *Shutsunyūkoku kanri kihon keikaku (dainiji)*, Tokyo, Hōmushō Shutsunyūkoku Kanrikyoku, 2000.

10 See Kondō Atsushi, *Gaikokujin sanseiken to kokuseki*, Tokyo, Akashi Shoten, 1996; Miyajima Takashi (ed.), *Gaikokujin shimin to seiji sanka*, Tokyo, Yūshindō, 2000; on both 'oldcomers and 'newcomers', see also John Lie, *Multiethnic Japan*, Cambridge Mass., Harvard University Press, 2001.

11 Katayama Kazumichi, *Jomonjin to 'Yayoijin': Kojinkotsu no Jikenbo*, Kyoto, Showado, 2000.

12 See Mark Hudson, *Ruins of Identity: Ethnogenesis in the Japanese Islands*. Honolulu, University of Hawaii Press, 1999, pp.89–90. For an interesting example of a creole model applied to immigration and social change, see S. Mintz and R. Price, *The Birth of African American Culture*, Boston, Beacon Press, 1992.

13 Kim, Aidentiti poritukusu o kōete.

14 Kurihara Akira, 'Kyōsei to iu koto', in A. Kurihara *et al.*, *Kyōsei no hō e*, Tokyo, Kōbundō, 1997.

15 See Fujioka Nobukatsu, *Kyōkasho ga oshienai rekishi*, Tokyo, Sankei Shinbunsha, 1996; Nishio Kanji *et al.*, *Kokumin no rekishi*, Tokyo, Sankei Shinbunsha, 1999; for a discussion of these trends, see Gavan McCormack, 'The Japanese movement to correct history', in L. Hein and M. Selden, *Censoring History: Citizenship and Memory in Japan, Germany and the United States*, New York, M. E. Sharpe, 2000.

16 For a more recent discussion of these issues, see Junko Habu and Clare Fawcett 1999, 'Jōmon archaeology and the representation of Japanese origins', *Antiquity*, vol. 73, pp. 587–93.

17 Hayashi Kensaku, 'Iwayuru "netsuzo jiken" o megutte', *Kikan Kokogaku*, vol. 74, 2000, pp. 74–9.

18 Hudson, 'Foragers as fetish in modern Japan', in S. Koyama and J. Habu (eds), *Hunter-Gatherers of the Pacific Rim*, Osaka: Senri Ethnological Studies (in press); see also Mark Hudson, 'Japan and the anthropology of origins', in M. Hudson (ed.), *Interdisciplinary Study on the Origins of Japanese Peoples and Cultures*, Kyoto, Omoto Project, 2000, pp. 6–7; Mark Hudson, 'Foragers as fetish in modern Japan', (in press).

19 See Nishio, *Kokumin no rekishi*.

Index